SOCIALIST WOMEN

This fascinating new study examines the experiences of women involved in the socialist movement during its formative years in Britain. By giving full attention to this much-neglected group, *Socialist Women* examines and challenges the orthodox views of labour and suffrage history.

The opening chapters examine the ideas and political journeys of individual socialist women. Torn between competing loyalties of gender, class and party, socialist women did not have a fixed identity but a number of contested identities. Believing above all that being a woman was vital to their politics, these individuals sought to develop a woman-focused theory of socialism and to put this new politics into practice. June Hannam and Karen Hunt go on to probe the issues that created divisions between these women, as well as those which gave them the opportunity to act together, in three fascinating case studies: women's suffrage; women and internationalism; the politics of consumption.

Socialist Women explores what it meant to be a socialist woman against the backdrop of the pioneering days of the socialist movement, the growth of the Edwardian women's suffrage campaign and the enormous political and social upheaval caused by the First World War. The viewpoint of these women brings a new perspective to both socialist and feminist politics, which will make this book absorbing reading for anyone interested in gender history or the politics of this period.

June Hannam is Reader in History at the University of the West of England in Bristol. Her publications include numerous articles on socialist and suffrage politics and a biography *Isabella Ford, 1855–1924* (1989).

Karen Hunt is Senior Lecturer in History at Manchester Metropolitan University. She has published widely on women's politics, particularly on aspects of the gendering of socialism, including *Equivocal Feminists: The Social Democratic Federation and the Woman Question, 1884–1911* (1996).

SOCIALIST WOMEN

Britain, 1880s to 1920s

June Hannam and Karen Hunt

London and New York

First published 2002
by Routledge
11 New Fetter Lane, London EC4P 4EE

Simultaneously published in the USA and Canada
by Routledge
29 West 35th Street, New York, NY 10001

Routledge is an imprint of the Taylor & Francis Group
© 2002 June Hannam and Karen Hunt

Typeset in Baskerville by Taylor & Francis Books Ltd
Printed and bound in Great Britain by The University Press, Cambridge,
United Kingdom

All rights reserved. No part of this book may be reprinted
or reproduced or utilised in any form or by any electronic,
mechanical, or other means, now known or hereafter
invented, including photocopying and recording, or in any
information storage or retrieval system, without permission in
writing from the publishers.

British Library Cataloguing in Publication Data
A catalogue record for this book is available from the British Library

Library of Congress Cataloging in Publication Data
Hannam, June, 1947–
Socialist women : Britain, 1880s to 1920s / June Hannam and Karen Hunt.
p. cm.
Includes bibliographical references and index.
1. Women socialists–Great Britain–History. 2. Women and socialism–Great
Britain–History. 3. Socialism–Great Britain–History. 4. Feminism–Great
Britain–History. 5. Women in politics–Great Britain–History. 6.
Women–Suffrage–Great Britain. I. Hunt, Karen. II. Title.
HX243 .H35 2001
320.53'1'0820941–dc21
2001031760
ISBN 0–415–14220–2 (hbk)
ISBN 0–415–26639–4 (pbk)

CONTENTS

Acknowledgements		vi
Abbreviations		viii
	Introduction	1
1	Socialist women: on the margins of history	16
2	Biographies and political journeys	31
3	Constructing the Woman Question	57
4	Mixed-sex politics	79
5	Socialist women and the suffrage	105
6	Socialist women and a politics of consumption	134
7	Socialist women and internationalism	166
	Conclusion	202
	Bibliography	207
	Index	221

ACKNOWLEDGEMENTS

This book began when we played hookey from a session at a social history conference. Curled up in arm chairs in a hotel in York, we discovered just how many connections there were between our individual research. The questions that we now wanted to explore fired each other's imaginations. We wanted to follow 'our' socialist women into the First World War and the 1920s and to pursue our hunches about continuities in their politics; we wanted to find a way to explore the differences between socialist women as well as what drew them to making a political life; we wanted to understand what made them persist in refusing to choose when both the socialist movement and the women's movement were pressurising them to do so; we wanted to make the case for a labour history and women's history in which socialist women were no longer marginalised.

We would like to thank all those who responded with enthusiasm to our ideas and who continued to ask after a project which took much longer to complete than our optimism had allowed for. Those who warned that a collaboration would take longer than a single-authored project were right but the benefits were enormous and are, we hope, apparent. We were also advised that academic collaborations can undermine friendships – we proved them wrong! But we would not have been able to do this without the support and encouragement of others.

June would like to thank: Angela John and Helen Meller for their encouragement; members of the History School at UWE for their interest and support, in particular Moira Martin and Kath Holden for their friendship; the Research Committee of the Humanities Department at UWE for granting research leave; Bath friends (Stella, Penny, Mike and Linda) for reminding her that there is a life beyond socialist women; her family and, most of all, Arthur Baxter for domestic and emotional support.

Karen would like to thank: David Howell, Ann Hughes, Stephen Bowd, Alan Kidd and Louise Willmot for listening at crucial moments and Pat Ayers for being not only a colleague but also a good friend; the Research Committee of the History Department at MMU for granting her research leave; all those she met in Australia on her Research Fellowship at UNSW in 1997, particularly

ACKNOWLEDGEMENTS

Lucy Taksa and Deb Oxley, and more formally the Australian Bicentennial Fellowship and British Academy for making that trip possible; friends and family for encouragement and welcome distractions; Mega and TC for all their feline charms; and, most of all, Colin Divall for doing more than his 'fair share' and for believing in me even when I wavered.

Chapter 6 draws on Karen Hunt, 'Negotiating the boundaries of the domestic: British socialist women and the politics of consumption', *Women's History Review*, 9, 2, 2000. This new and expanded version is published with the permission of Triangle Journals Ltd.

We would both like to thank our past and present editors (Heather McCallum and Vicky Peters); the Women's History Network; Jane Rendall (for reading the whole manuscript); and each other!

ABBREVIATIONS

ASS	Adult Suffrage Society
BSP	British Socialist Party
CP	Communist Party
CPGB	Communist Party of Great Britain
ELFS	East London Federation of Suffragettes
FWG	Fabian Women's Group
GWHA	Glasgow Women's Housing Association
ICW	International Council of Women
ILP	Independent Labour Party
IWSA	International Woman Suffrage Alliance
LCTOWLRC	Lancashire and Cheshire Textile and Other Workers' Labour Representation Committee
LRC	Labour Representation Committee
LSI	Labour and Socialist International
LWC	Labour Women's Conference
NAC	National Administrative Council of the ILP
NEC	National Executive Committee of the Labour Party
NUWSS	National Union of Women's Suffrage Societies
NWC	National Women's Council of the BSP
PSF	People's Suffrage Federation
SDF	Social Democratic Federation
SPD	German Social Democratic Party
WCG	Women's Co-operative Guild
WEB	Women's Enfranchisement Bill
WFL	Women's Freedom League
WIC	Women's Industrial Council
WILPF	Women's International League for Peace and Freedom
WLF	Women's Liberal Federation
WLL	Women's Labour League
WNHC	Workmen's National Housing Council
WPC	Women's Peace Crusade
WSF	Workers' Suffrage Federation/Workers' Socialist Federation
WSPU	Women's Social and Political Union

INTRODUCTION

[W]e shall endeavour to make it clear to socialist women that the obtaining of the vote is not an end in itself – the gaining of more privileges for women as a sex; but it is desirable only as a means to an end – and that end is the revolutionising of society for the benefit of all who are now exploited and oppressed.

(Dora Montefiore, 1909)[1]

The denial of the right of citizenship to women must assuredly delay the winning of a reality of freedom for men. Only public spirited mothers will rear sons capable of building the ideal city, as only public spirited wives and sweethearts will nerve their husbands and lovers to the brave work needed for the overthrow of oppression in the world today.

(Katharine Bruce Glasier, 1912)[2]

These statements were written by two leading female socialist propagandists in support of women's claim to exercise the parliamentary franchise. Along with many others after the mid-1880s they had been attracted to socialism because of the promise it held to transform the lives of working-class people and of women. And yet they had very different views about the basis on which women should demand their citizenship, the meaning of women's emancipation and the relationship between feminism and socialism. Such differences were expressed in practice as well as in theory. Katharine Bruce Glasier never wavered from her commitment to the Independent Labour Party (ILP) and, while supportive of the demand for women's enfranchisement on the same terms as men, increasingly thought that too much emphasis was being given to the vote. She did not take an active part in the suffrage movement but, instead, took a leading role in the Women's Labour League, which acted as an auxiliary of the Labour Party. Dora Montefiore, on the other hand, was a member of the Social Democratic Federation (SDF) but also joined the militant suffrage group, the Women's Social and Political Union (WSPU). In 1907 she left the Union to join the Adult Suffrage Society (ASS), becoming its honorary secretary in 1909, while retaining her involvement in SDF politics. These two political careers provide examples of the complex and very different ways in which socialist women developed a political identity as they negotiated between their feminism and their socialism. Women not only differed from each other in the political choices that they made, but they also changed their own views, allegiances and priorities in the course of a lifetime. This book explores the diverse ways in which socialist women struggled to translate the tension between socialism and feminism into a creative political practice in the period from the mid-1880s to the 1920s.

British socialism

As socialist politics developed in Britain in the 1880s, the new political organisations which were formed were unusual, compared with the Conservative and Liberal parties, in permitting women to be full members.[3] Socialist groups were all committed in their political programmes to the creation of a future society in which there would be sexual equality, although there was less certainty as to what exactly that would mean in everyday life and how such aspirations ought to influence the political practice of socialists in the meantime. The socialism of the 1880s and the early 1890s was characterised by an emphasis on the 'making of socialists': the conversion of individuals to socialism through propaganda made in street-corner meetings and public halls; in various socialist weekly newspapers and through cheap pamphlets and books; as well as through interventions in a range of political campaigns such as fights for free speech, organising the unemployed, trade union activity, particularly the new unionism of the late 1880s, and also electioneering. The assumption was that once the public was exposed to the socialist critique of capitalism and the vision of a new society built on justice, liberty and equality, the scales would fall from their eyes and they would become converts to what was called 'the Cause'. Making political propaganda and evangelising for the Cause, wherever the working class might be persuaded to listen, was central to the early years of British socialism and was to mark the politics of the early pioneers of the movement well beyond this period. Among the most effective of the first generation of socialist propagandists were a number of women whose example inspired others to 'cross the river of fire', as William Morris characterised the life-changing experience that becoming a socialist represented in the last decades of the nineteenth century.[4]

For many in the early years the Cause was more important than the particular organisation or organisations through which they might express their new politics. There were a number of socialist groups formed in the 1880s and the early 1890s. Among the most important were the Social Democratic Federation, formed in 1884, the Fabian Society, established in the same year, and the Independent Labour Party, which dates from 1893. These three groups had the longest and most continuous history, although in 1911 the SDF (which in 1908 had changed its name to the Social Democratic Party) joined with some dissident ILP members and unaligned socialists to form a new group, the British Socialist

Party. In order to limit the number of acronyms, we will generally refer to this strand of socialism as the SDF, except when discussing a particular event or when quoting from contemporaries. The SDF and the ILP were also the two largest parties – the ILP had a paying membership of approximately 30,000 in 1912, while at its most successful the SDF reached 4,500.[5] Although it is difficult to determine with any accuracy how many of these members were women, detailed studies of particular groups or local branches suggest that they formed approximately ten per cent of active members.[6] In contrast members of the Fabian Society were drawn largely from the educated middle classes and were never numerous, but women formed a higher proportion of the membership than in the ILP or the SDF.[7]

These three organisations represented the breadth of views that could be found in the socialist movement. The SDF was a Marxist party which recognised a class struggle in capitalist society which would eventually and necessarily resolve itself into a classless socialist society. The task of SDFers, as members of the party were called, was to expose the pernicious nature of capitalism and attempt to channel discontent into outright opposition to the system – as it said on the SDF membership card, 'Educate, Agitate, Organise'.[8] The language of the SDF was one of class, which was the dominant discourse of most socialist parties in the international socialist movement. In contrast, the ILP was much less likely to appeal to class antagonism, emphasising an evolutionary rather than revolutionary socialism. Many of its leaders repudiated class war and sought to appeal to all social groups on the grounds that the current system was unjust and impoverished the human spirit. For example, Keir Hardie claimed that: 'Socialism, like every other problem of life, is at bottom a question of ethics or morals. It has mainly to do with the relationships which should exist between a man[sic] and his fellows.'[9] Although the ILP soon established that its strategy as a political party was to seek independent labour representation in alliance with the trade union movement, it showed much less hostility than the SDF to the Liberal Party. Many ILPers had been formed by liberalism and Christian nonconformity and these influences, along with a pragmatism borne out of electoral politics, created a broader church with a less confrontational rhetoric than the SDF. Some have seen this as 'working with the grain of British politics' while others have condemned the ILP for 'its lack of theoretical sophistication, its obsession with parliamentary and electoral questions and its ready compromising with the prejudices of existing power-holders'.[10] Unlike the SDF and the ILP, the Fabian Society was not a political party as such. It was more of a 'think tank' which sought to influence others through a policy of permeation of the Liberal Party. This strategy makes its status as a socialist organisation debatable. As a Fabian admitted to another Society member in 1910, 'What on earth is the use of our talking about socialism and anything when we do nothing whatever to advocate socialism?'[11]

Alongside the main socialist organisations were other smaller parties. Some had resulted from divisions within the SDF over political tactics, such as the short-lived but influential Socialist League, established in 1884 by William Morris and Eleanor Marx with other SDF dissidents.[12] Within a few years the League had been taken over by anarchists and many of the ex-SDFers returned to their earlier affiliation. Later even smaller groups split away from the SDF such as the Socialist Labour Party (1903) and the Socialist Party of Great Britain (1904).[13] Local socialist groups also flourished for a time such as the Hammersmith Socialist Society and the Bristol Socialist Society, both of which were formed in the 1880s.[14] Individuals might belong to several of these organisations at once, although after the turn of the century it became harder to sustain multiple memberships as the politics of the main parties became more polarised. Nevertheless, these were not centralised parties and there was considerable autonomy at the level of the rank and file, so what happened locally could be considerably more cooperative and more diverse than the traditional focus on the leaderships of the ILP and the SDF would lead one to believe.[15] For there is a tenacious stereotype of Britain's leading socialist organisations in which the SDF is represented as a 'bitter, dogmatic and impractical sect inherently unsuitable to English politics' in contrast to the more congenial ethical socialism, and even labourism, of the ILP.[16] General works on the labour movement still tend to reiterate this view despite the fact that specialist studies have long identified this stereotype as 'tendentious, partial and misleading'. At a local level, for instance, individuals were drawn first and foremost to socialism rather than to particular parties. They moved between groups when their strategies and priorities, developed through day to day involvement in trade union struggles and municipal politics, appeared to be out of step with the outlook of the national leadership of particular organisations.[17] Moreover, although always much smaller than the ILP, the SDF provided a training ground for many socialist and labour militants who at one time or another were members. Indeed it has been claimed that the SDF 'influenced the thinking of an entire generation of working-class leaders'.[18]

Many socialists did not characterise their politics in sectarian terms but were moved by the desire to create a better world for the mass of the population. This was the politics of the 'new life', so eloquently described by Stephen Yeo and by Sheila Rowbotham and Jeffrey Weeks.[19] This version of socialism was particularly influential in the first half of the 1890s and prompted an expansion in formal political organisations: the membership of the SDF grew and a new party, the ILP, was formed. But new life socialism was just as likely to be expressed in cultural forms, particularly through the many activities associated with the *Clarion* newspaper, whether it be cycling clubs, choirs, rambling groups, potato-pie suppers or the Socialist Sunday School movement. For a brief moment conversion to the Cause was as likely to involve attempts to prefigure the new relationships of the future socialist society in the everyday lives of individual socialists as it was to take the form of acquiring a membership card, paying dues or attending branch meetings. There is ample evidence that, although this was not a politics which swept up huge numbers of people, women were as likely to respond to its initial appeal, if (and this was a large if) they came into contact with socialist propaganda. Yet women also suffered the frustrations of a politics which focused so much on the future and so little on the means to achieve it. In all forms of socialist politics, from its most economistic to its utopian elements, there remained the issue for women of the extent to which the new politics would recognise and seek to remedy the unequal position of women in capitalist society: what was known as the Woman Question.

Our earlier separate research on women who became active in the SDF and the ILP before 1914 suggests that the conventional wisdom that the ILP was sympathetic to women in contrast to the supposed misogyny of the SDF must be questioned.[20] We found that in both organisations hostile attitudes were at times expressed by individual leaders or branches towards the Woman Question and priority was rarely given to issues of interest to women, while female members, in the main, were confined to gender-specific roles. In an attempt, therefore, to examine in greater depth what it meant to be a socialist woman in the period from the 1880s to the 1920s we decided to look beyond the boundaries and perspectives of one particular socialist party and to explore the range of experiences, campaigns and issues which drew women together across organisational boundaries.

Indeed, a range of different views were expressed within socialist groups, as well as between them, about what socialism meant and how it should be achieved. Converts to the Cause all shared a belief that the capitalist system, based as it was on private ownership, profit making and competition, should be replaced by a society characterised by collective ownership and cooperation. British socialists were influenced in their views by the debates which took place on these questions in the Second International, an umbrella group which brought together representatives of national socialist parties and labour organisations from across the world, in particular from Europe and the United States. The Second International was dominated by the German Social Democratic Party (SPD), which provided leadership on theoretical issues, drawing heavily on an orthodox Marxist approach which emphasised economic change and class struggle at the point of production. However, in Britain, while there was an emphasis on the importance of economic change, for many, regardless of the group to which they belonged, the attraction of socialism was its promise of an end to injustice and exploitation and its vision of a society based on beauty, morality and new human relationships, in particular between men and women. This imparted a sense of belonging to a socialist movement which was broader than individual organisations.

There were considerable differences, however, between socialists about how the new society should be achieved, in particular about whether emphasis should be placed on the class struggle or whether socialists should seek to make more short-term practical changes to the lives of working people by getting elected to municipal bodies, the School Boards and the Boards of Guardians as well as to parliament. Within the main groups there were disagreements about strategy.

Thus in the 1890s, when there was strong support from the leadership of the ILP to strengthen ties with the trade union movement and to concentrate on building an effective electoral machinery, rank and file socialists inside and outside the ILP and the SDF pressed for an alternative: socialist unity. These socialists foresaw the increasing emphasis on the pragmatism of electoral politics as necessarily compromising the socialist vision. Although the ILP played an important part in the formation of the Labour Party (initially called the Labour Representation Committee) in 1900, and remained affiliated to it in the period under review, there was considerable discontent among the rank and file about the Labour Party's performance in parliament during the period of labour unrest before the First World War. This led to renewed calls for socialist unity and contributed to the formation of the BSP. Moreover, in the early 1920s, when the ILP was unsure of its role in relation to the Labour Party, which had at last made a formal commitment to socialist objectives, the relationship between ILP socialists and the Communist Party of Great Britain was far more fluid and less distinct than it was later to become.

From the 1880s to the 1920s socialists had a close relationship with the broader labour movement, largely the trade union movement and the cooperative movement. Socialists were often members of labour organisations and sought to make political propaganda within the broader movement. That does not mean that socialism and labour politics, or socialists and members of the labour movement, can be seen as synonymous. There may have been several varieties of socialists in Britain during this period, many of whom worked alongside non-socialist members of the labour movement in industrial and political campaigns; but socialists remained distinct from labourists, for whom the representation of working men[sic] in parliament was an end in itself rather than a means to fundamental social change. This is a book about socialist women, not labour movement women or women associated with the Labour Party (Labour women). Socialist women could and did organise in the labour movement and in the Labour Party and its auxiliaries but that did not make these organisations socialist.

As there was no united socialist party in Britain, socialist women had to deal with loyalties to rival political groups, which in turn affected their own tactics and strategies. On the other hand, regardless of their organisational affiliation, they faced comparable problems in their attempt to engage in a socialist politics which was male-defined and whose theory and practice concentrated on the male worker, his struggles at the workplace and class-based politics. Socialist women raised a common set of issues about how to attract women to socialism, the relationship between women's emancipation and socialism, and whether or not they should join together with members of the women's movement in specific campaigns. They talked extensively to one another about what it meant to be a socialist woman, particularly in the 1890s, and how far socialist men were sympathetic to their needs. This in turn meant that they influenced each others' ideas, regardless of the organisation to which they belonged, and helped to reconfigure the nature of left-wing politics.

Socialist women could be members of several groups at once or shift between groups at different times in their lives. Annie Besant, for example, was a member of the Fabian Society before joining the SDF in 1889, while Margaret Bondfield was an SDF member until 1908, when she changed her allegiance to the ILP and took an active part in the Women's Labour League (WLL). Local socialist groups could at times provide women with a congenial space to gain experience of socialist politics; both Katharine Bruce Glasier and Enid Stacy, for example, were members of the Bristol Socialist Society and lectured for the Fabian Society before becoming full-time propagandists for the ILP in the early 1890s. Since socialist women found little space in the ILP and SDF for the development of a woman-centred politics, they often made contact with women who were not socialists but who worked in groups such as the Women's Industrial Council (WIC), which sought to improve women's social, political and economic position.

In an attempt, therefore, to analyse in greater depth what it meant to be a socialist woman in the period from the 1880s to the 1920s this book will examine issues and themes which concerned socialist women, rather than focusing on the policies and developments of individual socialist organisations. It will consider socialist women's activities in Scotland and England, where the ILP and SDF had a strong presence, but our discussion does not extend to Ireland where the nationalist question raised a different set of concerns. Although there were a few short-lived Irish socialist groups which affiliated to the British ILP, most socialists saw the boundaries of their national parties as extending only to the shores of mainland Britain. They regarded the Irish Question as a separate matter, believing that the Irish people should decide on the appropriate forms of political organisation and affiliation for them.[21] Irish branches of the SDF and the ILP were almost non-existent. The British socialist women discussed in this book are therefore almost exclusively Scottish, English or Welsh.

This study also extends beyond the usual watershed of the First World War and into the 1920s. Most standard accounts of both the women's movement and the socialist movement adopt a chronology in which 1914 marks the end of one phase, the next coming in the inter-war years, when a new context was provided by the growing importance of the Labour Party, the formation of the Communist Party (CP) and women's achievement of partial enfranchisement.[22] We argue, however, that although the 1920s and 1930s did provide a new context for socialist women's political activities, at the same time a number of the debates remained the same. Many women who participated in labour and socialist politics in the inter-war years had also been involved in the pre-war movement which had helped to shape their ideas and their concerns. It is important, therefore, to examine continuities as well as discontinuities in terms of personnel, strategies and issues between the pre-war and immediate post-war periods. Thus the chapters in this book, wherever appropriate, discuss particular themes and questions across the whole period under review.

INTRODUCTION

Socialist woman – a definition

What are we presuming in the term 'socialist woman'? A socialist woman was someone who was a member of one of those groups which defined themselves explicitly as having socialist objectives.[23] She identified herself primarily as a socialist and this provided the framework within which she engaged in a range of political activities. It is recognised here, however, that individual women could change the focus of their politics over time and therefore in certain contexts might not be included in the definition of a socialist woman; Margaret Bondfield, for example, became distanced from the ILP after the First World War as she defined herself more clearly as a Labour woman. As we have said, socialist women could be found in a variety of labour organisations which were not explicitly socialist and which had many non-socialist members, including trade unions, the Women's Industrial Council, the Women's Labour League and the Women's Co-operative Guild (WCG). Nonetheless, although socialist and labour politics overlapped and interconnected in complex ways, they were not one and the same thing. This book will not, therefore, examine socialist women's activities in labour organisations in any detail but rather will focus on the ways in which they used the space, and the audience, of potential socialists to make socialist propaganda.

A detailed analysis of women's role within the Labour Party and the Communist Party also lies outside the scope of this study. The Labour Party did not make an explicit commitment to pursue socialist objectives until the adoption of Clause IV in 1918. The ILP, however, saw this commitment as so tenuous that it continued to act as a pressure group for socialism within the Labour Party during the 1920s and maintained a separate identity. Our interest, therefore, lies with those women who identified most closely with the ILP and who sought to develop a woman-centred socialism both within the ILP and in the Labour Party. The formation of the CP introduced a new dimension to the politics of the Left in the 1920s, but it functioned in a very different way to socialist groups; its membership of the Third International, attitude towards the Comintern and commitment to democratic centralism meant that its language and practice were distinct.[24] Moreover, from the mid-1920s the spaces within which communist women and socialist women might work together were prescribed. It is recognised here, however, that the differences between socialists and communists in the early 1920s were far less clear than they were later to become. The boundaries between them remained fluid in the immediate post-war period and a number of men and women were members of both the ILP and the CP. This book will concentrate, therefore, on women's involvement in the two largest socialist groups, the SDF and the ILP. Other socialist organisations will be considered at points where they had an impact on socialist women's political journeys, their theoretical perspective or their political practice.

We also argue that to be a socialist woman meant more than simply being a female member of a socialist group – we are taking it to imply that the woman concerned reflected upon, showed an awareness of and carried out some of her activities around the gendering of politics. Socialist women thought that being a woman was significant to their politics and this provided a lens through which they viewed their theory and practice. The term presumes that socialist women, to a greater or lesser extent, identified themselves with other women, recognised that they suffered from inequalities and oppression because of their sex, and attempted to do something to address this in their day-to-day politics. Our emphasis, therefore, is on those women who sought a variety of ways to balance their politics as socialists and as women and who attempted to create a space to challenge a male-defined socialist politics.

We also describe socialist women as being woman-focused in their political activities. They were engaged in a movement which was class-focused in its concerns, but socialist women drew attention to the ways in which issues and events, such as war, had a specific impact on women. They did not simply take up issues which were seen as relevant to women, or part of a woman's sphere, but rather explored the ways in which socialist practice was gendered and had an impact on women as a social group. We have chosen to use the term '*woman*-focused' rather than '*women*-focused' since the latter suggests that women could just be added in a general way into an existing framework of socialist politics.[25] Woman-focused, on the other hand, implies a recognition of women's subordinate position and the need to challenge it, which in turn would change the character and nature of socialist politics. The ILPer Lily Bell, the pseudonym of Isabella Bream Pearce, summed up this approach when explaining that, as a suffragette, she was fighting not for women but for woman:

> Women are individuals, but woman represents the feminine half of man which at present is denied its true place and power in society … this is a question of deciding once and for all that no sex disabilities shall remain.[26]

In contrast to most other studies of women involved in socialist or labour politics, the word feminist has not been used as a way to distinguish the female subjects of this book from other women who were active within the socialist movement. The word feminist is invested with meanings which can exclude women whose politics did not quite fit the definition put forward. It tends to be assumed, for example, that an essential component of the label feminist for those active in the early twentieth century is support for women's suffrage on the same terms as men, or a limited franchise. Those women who did not support this demand wholeheartedly, who included many socialist women, are then seen as lacking an interest in, or else as antagonistic to, gender issues. Thus the diverse ways in which socialist women themselves viewed the Woman Question and the extent to which they organised around gender issues are rarely explored.

We argue, however, that it is crucial to examine the language in which socialist women described their own activities if we are to gain an insight into how they understood women's emancipation and how they hoped to achieve it, rather than looking at them through the distorting lens of pre-existing categories. Socialist women did not use the term feminist to describe themselves, in particular before 1918. They invariably claimed to be socialists, but then added other terms such as democrat, suffragist or humanist. In 1905 Emmeline Pankhurst described herself as an 'adult suffragist, a socialist and a democrat', while Teresa Billington of the ILP and the WSPU began an article on women's suffrage with the phrase 'I write as a Democrat'.[27] Annot Robinson, a member of the National Union of Women's Suffrage Societies (NUWSS) and the ILP, claimed in 1912 that 'I am a suffragist and a socialist', while Dora Montefiore of the SDF wrote in the *Clarion* 'as a Socialist and an Adult Suffragist'.[28] Socialist women from different parties and with a variety of perspectives on women's suffrage used a common language of human rights. Teresa Billington expressed the need to win 'equal human rights for our sisters', while Dora Montefiore called for the enfranchisement of 'individual human beings' and Annot Robinson argued that the suffrage was a 'human cause'.[29] Some socialist women were prepared to describe themselves as feminist in the 1920s, but most were reluctant to use the term since it was equated with antagonism to men. Helen Gault of the ILP urged socialist women to try to understand feminism and to resist the common phrase 'I am not a feminist'. Using arguments which were remarkably similar to those of Lily Bell over thirty years before, she claimed that 'the feminist neither claims to be man's equal nor his superior. She simply desires freedom to be herself'.[30]

When socialist women are discussed in histories of the labour or the women's movement, they are usually given a label to distinguish their political outlook from that of other women involved in 'first-wave' feminism. The terms most commonly used are socialist feminists[31], feminist socialists[32], labour feminists[33], social feminists or maternalist feminists[34]. These labels reflect a tendency within earlier histories to emphasise distinct and often opposing strands within the women's movement.[35] Socialist and labour women have most often been described as maternalist or social feminists, either because of their interest in achieving social reforms to improve the economic and social position of working-class women, or because they believed that women had a distinct approach towards politics based on their experience and status as mothers. Ellen Mappen, for instance, claims that social feminists were 'those women who were interested in social questions affecting women's lives and who wanted to obtain economic rights for women'.[36] She acknowledges that they usually also wanted the vote, but suggests that they were not prepared to wait for it before demanding other rights. Although the ideas and activities of many socialist women could be described in this way, the complexities of individual women's engagement with 'feminist' politics and the changes in their position over time can be obscured by placing them in a neat category labelled 'social' or 'maternalist' feminism.

More recent studies of women's involvement in feminist politics, and indeed in political activity more generally, have been critical of earlier attempts to identify distinct strands of feminism and have suggested that the ideas and political strategies adopted by 'first-wave feminists' were far more complex and interrelated than such categories might imply. Instead, the emphasis has shifted to an exploration of how women developed and constructed a political identity or political identities, which Stuart Hall has defined as 'the process of representing symbolically the sense of belonging which draws people together into an "imagined community" and at the same time defines who does not belong or is excluded from it'.[37] The assumption that there is a unitary political category 'woman', based on a shared set of common interests as a sex, has been questioned and a greater stress has been placed on the conflict of interest among women, which can be based on identities other than gender, such as class and ethnicity.[38] It is the intention of this book to explore some of these perspectives in relation to socialist women in the late nineteenth and early twentieth centuries. Rather than asking how far socialist women were or were not feminists, and which strand of feminism they adhered to, we aim to explore the diverse ways in which they developed a political identity as women, the extent to which they emphasised a woman-focused politics and their different conceptions of citizenship and 'what is required to become a citizen'.[39]

Central to the approach used in this book is the attempt to examine how women sought to find new ways to balance their socialist and women's politics and how they tried to put their ideas into practice. Despite over thirty years of research which has revealed the extensive and complex ways in which middle-class and working-class women were active within the labour movement, labour historians have paid little attention to women's political work as socialists and have failed to explore gender issues in any systematic way within their studies of the British socialist movement. Thus questions are rarely asked about how far the different social positions of men and women might mean that they experienced or perceived events differently, or whether relations of power between the sexes helped to shape the nature of socialist politics.[40] At the same time, historians of the women's movement have been slow to examine the distinctive perspective of 'feminists' who were also socialists. Part of the purpose of the book, therefore, is to comment on the specific inadequacies of the historiography, to highlight new work which is less accessible to the general reader and to point out the most fruitful primary sources. Prompted by absences or caricatures in the historiographies of both the socialist movement and the women's movement, this book is an attempt to foreground women who were socialists and also woman-focused in their activities.

Rather than providing a detailed history of women's involvement in socialist organisations, we have adopted a thematic approach. This allows us to explore the complex ways in which socialist women developed a political identity and to examine their attempts to create a space and a political practice which challenged a male-defined socialist politics. The first part of the book provides a historiographical review and considers the relationship between the political journeys made by individual women and the specific contexts of the organisations of which they were a part. It also examines how women sought to create a socialist theory and practice in which they could develop a woman-focused politics. The second part of the book consists of three case studies of socialist women in relation to the suffrage, a politics of consumption, and to internationalism. All these areas exposed divisions between women as well as providing opportunities for them to act together. The case studies explore how socialist women put their ideas into practice over particular issues and consider the negotiations that they had to make between class, gender and party loyalties as they forged a political identity. They also enable us to interrogate terms such as adult suffrage, democracy and citizenship, which are used very loosely in secondary texts. In some cases the issues themselves are new, in others, such as women's suffrage, the arguments put forward attempt to provide a reappraisal of a more familiar story.

This book is not organised around the biographies of a few leading female propagandists, but the attitudes and activities of individual women are referred to throughout in order to explore the varied ways in which socialist women brought together their socialist and their woman-focused perspectives. We want neither to presume homogeneity between women nor to produce a patchwork of individual stories, but to reflect on what the key issues were for women who were socialists; what caused conflict between them and why; and how did this change over time? Is there a strand within women's political activism which should be labelled as that of 'socialist women' and how does this relate to something which has been called 'socialist feminism'?

An examination of the political perspectives of socialist women in relation to what they themselves saw as appropriate tactics and priorities should allow for a much more complex reading of women's engagement in socialist politics. It is an approach which takes account of shifting or overlapping boundaries in the positions taken[41] and which recognises that the term socialist women does not imply a fixed identity, but rather a series of contested identities. In focusing on the experiences of socialist women we seek to go beyond an act of reclamation and to develop a new approach to the study of British socialist politics, since we argue that both socialism and feminism can be mapped differently if seen through the eyes of socialist women. Such an approach not only poses a challenge to the orthodoxies of labour and suffrage historiography but also demonstrates the continuing relevance of untangling the problematic relationship between socialism and feminism in particular periods. Our aspiration is to contribute to a remaking of the history of women's politics in this period which recognises socialist women in all their complexity within the stories told. We also seek to contribute to a socialist/labour history which, instead of relegating gender to the margins, integrates this perspective into its mainstream conceptual frameworks.

INTRODUCTION

Notes

1 *Justice*, 20 March 1909.
2 *Labour Leader*, 23 January 1912.
3 L. Walker, 'Party political women: a comparative study of Liberal women and the Primrose League, 1890–1914', in J. Rendall (ed.), *Equal or Different. Women's Politics 1800–1914*, Oxford, Blackwell, 1987.
4 William Morris quoted in E.P. Thompson, *William Morris: Romantic to Revolutionary*, London, Merlin Press, 1977, p. 244.
5 K. Laybourn, *The Rise of Socialism in Britain*, Stroud, Sutton, 1997, pp. 44–5; K. Hunt, *Equivocal Feminists. The Social Democratic Federation and the Woman Question, 1884–1911*, Cambridge, Cambridge University Press, 1996, p. 204.
6 For example, Reid found that just under ten per cent of the 652 active ILP socialists in Manchester and Salford were women (C.A.N. Reid, 'The origins and development of the Independent Labour Party in Manchester and Salford, 1880–1914', PhD, University of Hull, 1981).
7 Brian Harrison estimates that the seventeen per cent of female Fabian Society members in 1893 had increased to forty-three per cent in 1912 (*Prudent Revolutionaries: Portraits of British Feminists between the Wars*, Oxford, Clarendon, 1987, p. 128), but the Society was never large. In 1908, the year of its formation, the Fabian Women's Group had a total of 175 members (P. Beals, 'Fabian feminism, gender, politics and culture in London, 1880–1930', PhD, Rutgers University, 1989, pp. 1, 13).
8 The card was originally designed by William Morris for the Democratic Federation, the SDF's predecessor (F. MacCarthy, *William Morris. A Life for Our Time*, London, Faber & Faber, 1994, p. 484).
9 K. Hardie, *From Serfdom to Socialism*, 1907, quoted in G. Foote, *The Labour Party's Political Thought: A History*, Basingstoke, Macmillan, 1997, p. 44.
10 These points are from David Howell's characterisation of the negative and positive stereotypes of the ILP, both of which he refutes in his influential study of the party (*British Workers and the Independent Labour Party 1888–1906*, Manchester, Manchester University Press, 1983, pp. 5–6).
11 H. Bland to G.B. Shaw, 13 October 1910, quoted in P. Thompson, *Socialists, Liberals and Labour. The Struggle for London 1885–1914*, London, Routledge & Kegan Paul, 1967, p. 237.
12 For the Socialist League see Thompson, *William Morris*; Y. Kapp, *Eleanor Marx: The Crowded Years, 1884–1898*, London, Lawrence & Wishart, 1976.
13 See W. Kendall, *The Revolutionary Movement in Britain, 1900–21: The Origins of British Communism*, London, Weidenfeld & Nicolson, 1969; R. Challinor, *The Origins of British Bolshevism*, London, Croom Helm, 1977; R. Barltrop, *Monument: The Story of the Socialist Party of Great Britain*, London, Pluto, 1975.
14 See Thompson, *William Morris*; S. Bryher, *An Account of the Labour and Socialist Movement in Bristol*, Bristol, Bristol Labour Weekly, 1929.
15 See L. Barrow and I. Bullock, *Democratic Ideas and the British Labour Movement, 1880–1914*, Cambridge, Cambridge University Press, 1996.
16 Thompson, *Socialists, Liberals and Labour*, p. 297. Thompson argues against this view of the SDF. For a discussion of the stereotype of the SDF, see Hunt, *Equivocal Feminists*, pp. 7–16.
17 E.P. Thompson, 'Homage to Tom Maguire', in A. Briggs and J. Saville (eds), *Essays in Labour History Vol. 1*, London, Macmillan, 1967, pp. 292–302, shows how a small group of Leeds socialists moved from the SDF to the Socialist League and then to the Fabian Society and local socialist clubs before joining the ILP.
18 K. Burgess, *The Challenge of Labour*, London, Croom Helm, 1980, p. 61.

INTRODUCTION

19 S. Yeo, 'A new life: the religion of socialism in Britain, 1883–1896', *History Workshop Journal*, 4, 1977; S. Rowbotham and J. Weeks, *Socialism and the New Life: The Personal and Sexual Politics of Edward Carpenter and Havelock Ellis*, London, Pluto, 1977.

20 Hunt, *Equivocal Feminists*; J. Hannam, 'Women and the ILP, 1890–1914', in D. James, T. Jowitt and K. Laybourn (eds), *The Centennial History of the Independent Labour Party*, Halifax, Ryburn, 1992.

21 G. Bell, *Troublesome Business. The Labour Party and the Irish Question*, London, Pluto, 1982, chaps 1 and 2, esp. p. 21.

22 The most recent example of this is H. Gruber and P. Graves (eds), *Women and Socialism. Socialism and Women. Europe between the Two World Wars*, Oxford, Berghahn, 1998.

23 For a recent overview of British socialist organisations and their development, see Laybourn, *The Rise of Socialism*.

24 S. Bruley, *Feminism, Stalinism and the Women's Movement in Britain, 1920–1939*, New York, Garland, 1986; N. Branson, *History of the Communist Party of Great Britain, 1927–1941*, London, Lawrence & Wishart, 1985; S. Macintyre, *A Proletarian Science: Marxism in Britain, 1917–37*, Cambridge, Cambridge University Press, 1980.

25 Graves claims that Labour Party women in the inter-war years attempted to create a 'women-centered' socialism. She does not give an explicit definition of this, but implies that women sought to address the needs of working-class women and their families through social reform measures (P. Graves, 'An experiment in women-centered socialism: labour women in Britain', in Gruber and Graves (eds), *Women and Socialism*, pp. 182–3). Krista Cowman, however, prefers to use the term feminist, even though it was not in use in the 1890s, 'rather than the more cumbersome "woman-friendly" or "woman centred" ' (K. Cowman, ' "Giving them something to do": how the early ILP appealed to women', in M. Walsh (ed.), *Working Out Gender: Perspectives from Labour History*, Aldershot, Ashgate, 1999, fn.7, p. 131).

26 *Forward*, 15 December 1906.

27 *Labour Leader*, 3 February 1905; *Forward*, 2 February 1907.

28 *Labour Leader*, 31 October 1912; *Clarion*, 26 May 1905.

29 *Clarion*, 14 September 1906; *The Vote*, 19 November 1915; *Labour Leader*, 9 January 1913.

30 *New Leader*, 5 September 1930.

31 C. Collette, *For Labour and for Women: The Women's Labour League, 1906–1918*, Manchester, Manchester University Press, 1989, pp. 4–5; P. Graves, *Labour Women: Women in British Working-Class Politics, 1918–1939*, Cambridge, Cambridge University Press, 1994, p. 85; Graves, 'An experiment in women-centered socialism', p. 180.

32 B.S. Anderson and J.P. Zinsser, *A History of Their Own: Women in Europe from Prehistory to the Present*, Vol. II, Harmondsworth, Penguin, 1990, ch. 4.

33 Linda Walker describes members of the Fabian Women's Group, the ILP and the SDF as socialist feminists and those of the WLL, Labour Party women's sections and the WCG as labour feminists, although she suggests that the position of individual women could be complex (L. Walker, 'The women's movement in England in the late nineteenth and early twentieth centuries', PhD, Manchester University, 1984, pp. 158–9).

34 J. Liddington, *The Long Road to Greenham: Feminism and Anti-Militarism in Britain since 1820*, London, Virago, 1989, pp. 89–94.

35 This approach is discussed in K. Offen, 'Defining feminism: a comparative historical approach', *Signs*, 14, 1, 1988.

36 E. Mappen, *Helping Women at Work: The Women's Industrial Council, 1889–1914*, London, Hutchinson, 1985, fn.1, p. 27. See also O. Banks, *Faces of Feminism*, Oxford, Martin Robertson, 1981, ch. 9; Graves, *Labour Women*, pp. 178–80, Conclusion; Graves, 'An experiment in women-centered socialism', pp. 187–91.

37 S. Hall quoted in C. Hall, *White, Male and Middle Class: Explorations in Feminism and History*, Cambridge, Polity, 1992, p. 21.
38 A.S. Orloff, 'Reply: citizenship, policy and the political construction of gender interests', *International Labor and Working Class History*, 52, 1997, pp. 36–7; D. Riley, *'Am I That Name?' Feminism and the Category of 'Women' in History*, London, Macmillan, 1988; J.W. Scott, *Gender and the Politics of History*, New York, Columbia University Press, 1988; Hall, *White, Male and Middle Class*, Introduction.
39 C. Saraceno, 'Reply: citizenship is context specific', *International Labor and Working-Class History*, 52, 1997, p. 27.
40 For a discussion of the implications of an approach which recognises the importance of gender, see N. Cott, 'On men's history and women's history', in H. Brod (ed.), *The Making of Masculinities. The New Men's Studies*, Boston, Allen & Unwin, 1987; 'Introduction', *Gender and History*, 1, 1, 1989.
41 Orloff, 'Reply: citizenship', p. 36.

1
SOCIALIST WOMEN
On the margins of history

Histories of both the socialist movement and the women's movement have tended to marginalise the role of socialist women and their concerns. Contemporaries themselves were aware that this might be the case. When the ILP began to look back after 1913 on its early history and encouraged members to write reminiscences of the pioneering days, female propagandists attempted to ensure that women were not forgotten. In an article written for the party's newspaper, *Labour Leader*, in 1914, entitled 'The part women played in founding the ILP', Katharine Bruce Glasier noted that, although there were only three women delegates at the founding conference of the ILP in Bradford in 1893, this was 'no sort of criticism of the amount of service women had been putting in all over the country for the new workers' movement'. She then went on to recall the names and varied activities of women who had helped to build up support for socialist politics in the early years. In Bradford, for instance, 'women would gather round me and prove over and over again that they were as keenly alive to the ideals of socialism and as ready to make sacrifices for the Cause as was any man'.[1]

Histories of socialism and the women's movement

Despite such attempts by contemporaries to ensure that women's involvement in the socialist movement would not be forgotten, socialist women have rarely been the subject of systematic historical enquiry in their own right, while their appearance in histories of the labour or feminist movements has been patchy or hard to identify. There are several key texts which provide a detailed account of the history of individual socialist organisations and of the development of the late nineteenth and early twentieth century socialist movement.[2] However, these fail to give attention in any systematic way either to the contribution made by women or to the importance of gender for an understanding of labour and socialist politics in the period.[3] This is the case even in texts which move beyond an institutional framework. Chris Waters' study of British socialists and popular culture, for instance, devotes only a few pages to women and is not concerned with gender.[4] Yeo's pioneering article on the 'religion of socialism' gives numerous examples of women's conversion to socialism and of their role in 'making socialists'. Nonetheless, he fails to discuss whether or not women's experiences were different from those of men and whether there was a gender dimension to 'new life' socialism or to the process of becoming a socialist.[5] His argument that the ILP shifted tactics after 1895 towards building up an electoral machinery and an alliance with the trade unions, and away from 'making socialists', is never explored in terms of the impact that it might have had on women socialists who contributed so much to propaganda.[6]

Women continue to be marginal to the story of late nineteenth/early twentieth century British socialism despite a growing body of work, usually by feminist historians, which has shown that women were extensively involved in labour politics and that there was an important and complex relationship between socialism and feminism in the period. Debates within the women's movement and the labour movement in the late 1960s and 1970s focused attention on the extent to which it was possible to integrate a feminist with a Marxist analysis and explored the tensions between an analysis based on sex and one based on class.[7] Although this debate was a theoretical one which was never entirely resolved, for many of those who participated it was also bound up with their own practical concerns about how to bring their socialism and their feminism together and where to put their political energies.[8] This in turn prompted research into how such issues had been approached in the context of the nineteenth and early twentieth centuries. The attitudes of socialists to the Woman Question were analysed with a particular focus on Engel's *Origin of the Family* (1884) and Bebel's *Woman under Socialism* (1879), key texts which influenced debates among members of the Second International. An emphasis was placed on the conflict between loyalty to sex or class, although there was also an acknowledgement of differences between women, in particular in terms of race and sexuality.[9]

The approach used in such studies implied a stark dichotomy between identification with sex and with class or between socialism and feminism, and it is usually argued that socialist women put their class or party first whenever conflicts arose between the different positions. Anderson and Zinsser, for instance, cite Clara Zetkin of the German Social Democratic Party (SPD) as an example of a feminist socialist who was determined to champion women's rights as well as socialism, but who would subordinate her feminism for the sake of party unity.[10] In a similar vein Quataert describes German women as 'reluctant feminists' who experienced tensions in their loyalties to sex and class, but who in the end put their feminism second to their socialism. She notes how Clara Zetkin was not unsympathetic to the aims of the 'bourgeois women's movement', but felt that these needed to be differentiated from those of proletarian women and the socialist women's movement.[11]

In Britain, the focus of labour historians on women's activities within the Labour Party, coupled with suffrage histories which highlight the splits between the WSPU and the labour movement, have also encouraged an approach which emphasises the conflict between loyalty to sex or to class.[12] In both instances socialist women are judged through the eyes and priorities of others and are usually found wanting. The arguments of historians tend to be reinforced by the views of contemporaries, which are often quoted without comment. Thus, socialist women were criticised by members of the labour movement for helping to foster a sex war and therefore diverting the attention of working-class women away from the wrongs of their class, whereas suffrage activists complained that socialist women did not give enough priority to the political demands of their sex.[13]

With some notable exceptions little attention has been paid to women's involvement in British socialist politics. Sheila Rowbotham's biography of Edward Carpenter and her broader studies of the interconnections between feminism and socialism explore the relationship between personal emancipation, sexual politics and social emancipation which was a feature of the 'new life' socialism of the 1880s and 1890s.[14] She raises important questions about the gulf between women's aspirations for a different life and the reality of everyday socialist politics in Britain in the late nineteenth century. Nonetheless, her concern has been to explore the relationship between women's liberation and revolutionary politics in several countries over a long period of time, rather than to develop an in-depth study of women's engagement in British socialism up to the 1920s.

Barbara Taylor's path-breaking study of the Owenite movement also explores the close connections between early socialism and feminist aspirations. She suggests that the Owenites called for 'a multi faceted offensive against all forms of social hierarchy, including sexual hierarchy' and that they sought 'the democratization of personal relations'.[15] Her study demonstrated how a political movement could be reinterpreted if viewed through the perspective of gender, but this was not followed up by a similar analysis of the late nineteenth century socialist movement.[16] Taylor's own conclusions may have contributed to this neglect. She argues that, in contrast to Owenite socialism, late nineteenth century socialist groups were dominated by an emphasis on the 'class based economic struggles of the industrial proletariat' and that, as the boundaries of the socialist project became narrowed, 'so women's independent aspirations became stranded outside them'. Although the new socialist groups did contain feminists, and at times gave them support, there was 'a significant shift away from the radical feminist commitment of the 1830s and 1840s'.[17]

Far more attention has been given to women's involvement in the Labour Party and to women's groups which were attached to the labour movement, such as the Women's Co-operative Guild and the Women's Labour League.[18] Such studies tend to focus on the ways in which women dealt with their often conflicting loyalties to class, sex and party and explore the extent to which notions of difference underpinned women's participation in Labour politics and enabled them to exercise an influence on policy. Emphasis has been placed on the inter-war years, when newly enfranchised women joined the Labour Party in large numbers and aimed to gain support for welfare measures which would improve the lives of working-class women. Debate has centred around the extent to which this meant that women's feminist aspirations became more narrowly focused and whether their involvement in mixed-sex politics put a strain on feminist solidarity in the 1920s. Johanna Alberti, for example, suggests that women gained a sense of collective identity from working together in the suffrage movement and that once they left this environment they found it difficult to retain their confidence.[19] Over a number of issues, such as protective legislation, Labour women's loyalties to their party and to their class drove a wedge between them and feminist groups, which, argues Harold Smith, was encouraged by a labour leadership which was hostile to feminism.[20]

Pat Thane, on the other hand, suggests that Labour women retained a broad commitment to 'feminist' objectives and were able to exert some influence on Labour politics. She claims that they put welfare on the Labour Party's agenda in the inter-war years, brought more women into public life and helped to improve health care, in particular at a local level. Nonetheless, Thane also concedes that women's gains were small compared to their overall aspirations and that they drew back from all out confrontation with the party leadership when their demands were so contentious that they might cause disunity.[21] These themes are explored further in a recent article by Pamela Graves, which suggests that women attempted to create a 'women-centered' socialism within the inter-war Labour Party by pressing for a reform programme based on the needs of working-class women. She argues that they had their greatest success at a local level, where they built strong grass roots organisations, represented women's interests in their local party branches and introduced reforms as elected members of local government bodies. She claims that traditional ideas about gender roles undermined their ability to influence the national policies of the Labour Party but worked in their favour at a local level, where they were seen as well suited for the 'care of mothers and infants, schoolchildren, the elderly, the sick and the insane'.[22] Graves also acknowledges change over time and argues that by the 1930s Labour women had abandoned their 'women-centered agendas' in favour of 'integration around the defense of their class against reactionary government and the threat of international fascism'.[23]

Women who were members of socialist groups, and whose politics were framed by those organisations, clearly played a key role in Labour Party politics, but the studies discussed above do not tend to single them out for any particular consideration or make a real attempt to identify whether they had a distinct perspective. If the reader looks hard enough then relevant material on socialist women can be found, but they are not the focus of the research. This is also the case in most studies of the suffrage movement. Nonetheless, some key texts have made an important contribution to the historiography of socialist politics. Liddington and Norris' pioneering study revealed the widespread support for women's suffrage amongst Lancashire working women and is one of the few suffrage texts to give sustained attention to the attitudes of male and female socialists to women's suffrage from the 1890s onwards. It was followed by Sandra Holton's important account of the alliance between the Labour Party and the National Union of Women's Suffrage Societies after 1912 and her later work tracing the radical currents within first-wave feminism.[24] Such studies have shown that, far from being separate movements, the socialist, labour and suffrage movements were closely intertwined in the period and affected each other's theory and practice at both a national and a local level. Nonetheless, all of these authors examine labour and suffrage politics through the perspective of those who supported a limited suffrage position, that is votes for women on the same terms as men, which then marginalises those socialist women who were adult suffragists or who did not prioritise suffrage in their politics.

Reclaiming a place for women in the stories of socialism and suffrage

In the last few years socialist women have begun to receive greater attention in suffrage and socialist histories,[25] although some of the more interesting research still lies hidden in unpublished doctoral theses.[26] Biographies of socialists such as Margaret McMillan, Isabella Ford, Selina Cooper and Sylvia Pankhurst have drawn attention to the complex relationship between women's engagement in socialist and suffrage politics and the way in which individual women negotiated a role for themselves within a male dominated mixed-sex politics.[27] Eleanor Gordon's study of women's involvement in the labour movement in Scotland provides a welcome reminder that British socialist politics are too often viewed through an English lens. She also draws attention to the importance of locality for understanding women's engagement in socialist and feminist politics. Gordon suggests, for example, that in Glasgow the focus of the ILP on community issues such as housing, rents and unemployment, rather than on workplace struggles, and the sympathetic coverage of women's suffrage in the Glasgow-based *Forward* meant that the ILP was relatively successful in attracting women as active members.[28] Recent studies of individual socialist organisations by the authors of this book have examined the ambivalence of socialist groups towards the Woman Question and the effects of such attitudes on women's willingness to become involved in socialist politics and the extent to which they were able to exert an influence on policy.[29]

Nonetheless, feminists who have explored women's complicated relationship with British socialism have, for the most part, had a very limited and particular impact on mainstream labour history. It is harder now to write a history of a socialist party without acknowledging its female membership – although Martin Crick's *The History of the Social Democratic Federation* comes very near this. Usually women are accorded either a separate chapter in a collection of essays, or are given a few pages in a much larger work.[30] Tom Woodhouse's study of labour politics in Leeds, for example, notes the importance of female labour in the city and refers briefly to the ILP socialist Isabella Ford, but there is no attempt to explore gender issues in relation to socialist politics in any systematic way.[31] There are, however, some exceptions to this. Michael Savage looks at working-class politics in Preston through the lens of gender as well as class and suggests that the hostility of trade unionists to female labour had a crucial influence on the nature of the policies put forward by the Labour Party. Even here, however, women remain undifferentiated and there is no attempt to discuss the various ways in which women positioned themselves within labour politics.[32] Martin Francis also explores the gendering of Labour politics in his article on the Labour Party in the twentieth century as a whole. He looks not just at welfare questions but also at consumption, sexuality and representations of masculinity and femininity, and suggests that gender had a 'complex and ambiguous status … within Labour discourse'.[33] He argues that the 'triumph of class over sex' model cannot do justice to Labour women's political attitudes, which were far more nuanced than this would imply, although he does not have the space to explore these in any depth.[34]

Stereotyping the ILP and the SDF

Women's continuing marginality to the story of British socialism has been commented on elsewhere.[35] What is not usually made clear, however, is that when women make their brief appearance, they, and their political parties, are frozen into an unforgiving and inaccurate stereotype. The conventional wisdom is that the ILP provided the most welcoming and congenial context for women to engage in socialist politics, which was related to its early commitment to sex equality and in particular its support for a limited franchise. This is contrasted with the SDF, which is seen as adopting a more rigid Marxist analysis of social change, based on the class struggle, which therefore had little room for gender-based issues.

Thus, as Olive Banks would have it, the ILP was 'feminist from its inception' while the SDF was 'anti-feminist'.[36] Jill Liddington and Jill Norris, while recognising the ambivalence towards women's suffrage at a national level, suggest that women were encouraged to take part in local politics by ILP branches. 'From the beginning the ILP accepted men and women as members on an equal basis, and unlike other political parties did not relegate women to support organisations'.[37] This argument is still being repeated, without comment, in the most recent textbooks on British feminism.[38] For James Hinton women played 'an exceptionally important role in the ILP', although he provides no real evidence for this judgement. Historians who do offer evidence do so selectively, in particular when reference is made to the SDF.[39] For Liddington and Norris the SDF's 'general attitude to feminism was unsympathetic' and to support this conclusion they cite the views of the SDF leaders Hyndman and Quelch.[40] Similarly, Jeffrey Weeks discusses Hyndman and the misogynist Belfort Bax's views on women as though they represented the SDF as a whole.[41] And yet there is a problem with representing any organisation in terms of its leadership. In both the ILP and the SDF there was a high level of autonomy at a local level combined with a healthy scepticism for leaders.[42]

The characterisation of the ILP and the SDF as feminist and anti-feminist respectively is part of a wider stereotype of the two organisations which has been remarkably tenacious; that the ILP/SDF represent a reasonable/unreasonable dichotomy in which the SDF is all that is alien to the British labourist tradition. Although some historians have recognised, as David Howell did in 1983, that the stereotype was 'tendentious, partial and misleading', few mainstream labour historians have acknowledged what this received view means for understanding the complexity of socialist and labour politics.[43] This has then discouraged retrieval of the richness of socialist women's politics in Britain.

When historians of the socialist movement do draw attention, however briefly, to the contribution made by women, they invariably focus on members of the ILP.[44] They usually spotlight a small group of ILP women propagandists in the 1890s; although there are some minor differences between historians on the membership of this group, the names of what could be called the 'Famous Four' (Enid Stacy, Caroline Martyn, Katharine St John Conway/Bruce Glasier, Margaret McMillan) crop up again and again in histories of the socialist movement and generally constitute the signifier of the feminism of the ILP.[45] These female propagandists *were* important for the development of socialism in Britain, but an emphasis on just a few individuals obscures the range of women who contributed to socialist politics, in particular those who were members of the SDF. It helps to perpetuate the view that the SDF had little interest in the Woman Question and reinforces the assumed positive relationship between the ILP and women. Moreover, a focus on a small number of leading women, who are rarely differentiated from each other, too often substitutes for a broader discussion of the way in which socialist politics were gendered.

Challenging conventional wisdoms

Recent studies which focus on women in individual socialist groups have begun to question these conventional wisdoms. June Hannam argues that although many women found local ILP branches were welcoming to their sex, in particular in Yorkshire, the ILP did not make gender issues a priority before the First World War.[46] The ILP's own claim that it was committed to women's equality tended to be based on its support for a limited suffrage which was only a small part of the broader vision of emancipation put forward by contemporary feminists.[47] Even the support for women's suffrage was lukewarm. Annual conferences passed resolutions in favour of a limited franchise for women, and individual MPs such as Keir Hardie were consistent in their support for women's suffrage in parliament, but the ILP as an organisation did not work very hard to promote the cause. Moreover, some of its leading members were wary of an issue which seemed to privilege sex over class.[48] This interpretation is supported by Laura Ugolini's research into the attitudes of ILP men towards women's suffrage. She found that until 1905 the party concentrated on economic questions and on winning the support of male trade unionists and showed little interest in franchise reform of any kind in its day-to-day politics.[49]

Karen Hunt's work on the SDF, on the other hand, suggests that women were more extensively involved in the organisation than is usually conceded. She compares the attendance of women at SDF and ILP conferences and the extent to which they held national and local office and found very little difference between the two organisations. In both cases around 10 per cent of conference delegates were women and very few were secretaries or treasurers of local branches.[50] The SDF made it clear that gender issues were of secondary importance to the class struggle but, at the same time, by making them a matter of individual conscience, enabled a widespread debate to take place on the Woman Question within the organisation. On the other hand, this meant that it was possible for an influential group of men to express misogynist views within the party and in its newspaper. These views have then been taken by historians to represent the position of the SDF as a whole.[51] Although Karen Hunt's analysis focuses on the SDF, it also makes clear that the party and its male and female members were very like other Second International socialists. It would seem that not only is the traditional dichotomous view of the SDF/ILP unhelpful but that, perhaps, loyalties other than party, such as sex, local political culture and position on suffrage, were more important to individual socialists and the framing of their political identities.

The SDF's stand on adult suffrage has also formed part of the stereotype of the two organisations, with polemical comments by contemporaries often being accepted uncritically by historians. So adult suffrage is seen as both the least progressive position available, and somehow anti-feminist, whilst at the same time being unrealistic and utopian.[52] The debate about women's suffrage – its centrality to the socialist project, the form that the demand should take and the strategies to be employed to achieve it – were contentious within both organisations, yet the received view remains that the ILP was unequivocally pro-women's suffrage and that the SDF was unequivocally opposed.

Despite our individual work and the overlapping work of revisionist suffrage historians, along with important new work in doctoral theses, the received view still persists. As already noted, the most recent mainstream histories of British labour and socialist politics do mention women's role and make reference to the findings of feminist historians. Nonetheless, questions relating to women's engagement in labour politics do not have a central place in the overall argument and the findings of feminist historians are used in very particular and partial ways. Keith Laybourn's *The Rise of Socialism in Britain* (1997), which is marketed as an account which is inclusive of women, quotes Joseph Clayton's judgement that in the early ILP women were quite literally the co-leaders and goes on to say that 'it is suggested that this meant that the ILP was more inclined to support the women's suffrage issue and the "women's question"'. He acknowledges that June Hannam throws doubt on some of these suggestions but, after giving her a sentence, concludes that 'nevertheless, the ILP was one of the most obvious sources of support for women'.[53]

Labour historians still seem reluctant in most cases to give women the same attention as they give to men in studies which claim to provide a general overview of labour or socialist politics. They also fail to deal with the gendering of socialism and its political practice.[54] For instance, new insights into the political process provided by recent studies of masculinity, in particular the gender dimension of working-class movements and the struggles around the extension of the franchise in 1867, have not been taken on board by historians of late nineteenth century socialism.[55] Perhaps including some women, even if this is only the 'Famous Four', is less challenging than exploring the extent to which the theory and practice of socialist organisations were gendered and the ways in which men and women negotiated around this across time, place and party. This would include consideration of the way in which the Woman Question was constructed by socialists and the extent to which this affected the priority given to women's issues on the socialist agenda. How socialists theorised women and represented them in socialist propaganda, as well as the extent to which socialist rhetoric was translated into practice, all affected women's participation in socialist political life.[56]

Towards a new perspective on socialist women

Over the last decade historians of feminism (or feminisms) have asked new questions and developed new approaches towards an understanding of the ways in which women created political identities in different times and places and how they constructed, or invented, a feminist history and tradition.[57] Rather than seeking to establish neat categories and definitions, or to explore dichotomies such as class and sex, or equality and difference, the emphasis has been on tracing the complexities and ambivalence in feminist theory and practice and on examining the 'role of imagination and fantasy in bringing about an enlargement of gender roles'.[58] In a study of Olympe de Gouges, for example, Joan Scott examines how women tried to exploit ambiguities in current political ideas in order to move beyond the restrictions they encountered because of their sex.[59] Catherine Hall also draws attention to the ambiguities inherent in the class relations between women and argues for an understanding of 'the interconnections between the hierarchies of power in any social formation' and in particular the way in which gender power stands 'in articulation with class/race/ethnicity'.[60]

These new perspectives have not, for the most part, been applied to a study of socialist women in the late nineteenth and early twentieth centuries. The main exception is Clare Collins' stimulating thesis on women in labour politics in the period 1880 to the 1930s. She avoids classifying labour women into different types of feminists and focuses instead on the way in which women involved in socialist, and then in Labour Party, politics constructed a political identity for themselves. She explores the way in which 'Labour Party women differed among themselves regarding their status as political women and regarding their reasons and methods for identifying specifically as women in politics'.[61] She suggests that too often differences between labour women, and the extent to which they were 'feminist', have been seen in terms of whether they decided to organise separately, to support a limited franchise for women or whether they used arguments based on equality or difference. Instead, Collins argues that Labour Party women had a broad agreement about what they saw as 'woman's place in society' and that most of them fitted a model of maternalist/domestic feminism. The key issue which divided them, Collins suggests, is the extent of autonomy which was appropriate to women organising separately in mixed-sex politics and the degree of political representation that they should have as women.

One of the ways in which Collins explores these differences is by comparing two women's groups, the WSPU and the WLL, which were both dominated by ILP women in their early years. She argues that if both are viewed as socialist organisations, then it is possible to see what divided women 'regarding their self identification and activities as political *women*' despite their shared party allegiance.[62] An approach which focuses on the complex ways in which women positioned themselves politically, and which questions the use of sex and class as unproblematic, unified and opposed categories, is a particularly useful one for an examination of women's involvement in mixed-sex politics and has influenced our own analysis of socialist women. Collins' thesis, however, concentrates on ILP women and then on gender politics within the Labour Party. Our own work focuses on a broader group of socialist women and the similarities and differences between them in the way in which they interpreted the meaning of a collective political identity for women. We seek to question both the identification of socialist women with 'domestic feminism' and also the extent to which the question of autonomy was *the* issue that they found to be most critical.

Our own project suggests that by focusing on socialist women and the importance of gender we can offer, in Gerda Lerner's phrase, a 'new angle of vision' to the story most commonly told in feminist and labour histories. Our aim is to explore what socialism meant to women, whether they identified as socialist women and, if so, how they viewed the meaning of this for their political practice. We would argue that the predominance of the suffrage movement in feminist historiography – and in particular the identification of the struggle for a limited franchise with the most acceptable feminist position – has distorted the view of groups and individuals who did not follow this path in a straightforward way and yet could claim to be woman-centred in their politics. Instead, we are interested in mapping the complex, and often different, ways in which women negotiated their socialist and their 'feminist' politics.[63]

One way to approach this is to explore the diverse political choices made by individual women. As the biographical work of both of us has shown, it is important to look at the ways in which there were shifts and re-negotiations which took place over a lifetime and to recognise that contextualising the politics of socialist women is complicated. There is a danger, however, that such shifts and changes might be lost or obscured in a book which is organised around themes rather than individual biographies. The next chapter, therefore, explores the complex relationship between the lives of individual women, the political choices that they made and the broader political and social context which provided a framework for those choices. The women spotlighted here have been selected to represent a variety of class backgrounds, generations, organisational affiliations and forms of activism. Most of them appear regularly throughout the rest of this book.

Notes

1 Katharine Bruce Glasier, 'The part women played in founding the ILP', *Labour Leader*, 9 April 1914.
2 For example, for the SDF see C. Tsuzuki, *H.M. Hyndman and British Socialism*, Oxford, Oxford University Press, 1961; M. Crick, *The History of the Social Democratic Federation*, Halifax, Ryburn, 1994. For the Socialist League, see E.P. Thompson, *William Morris: Romantic to Revolutionary*, London, Merlin, 1977; F. MacCarthy, *William Morris: A Life of Our Time*, London, Faber & Faber, 1994. For the ILP, see D. Howell, *British Workers and the Independent Labour Party, 1888–1906*, Manchester, Manchester University Press, 1983; D. James, T. Jowitt and K. Laybourn (eds), *The Centennial History of the Independent Labour Party*, Halifax, Ryburn, 1992; R.E. Dowse, *Left in the Centre: The Independent Labour Party, 1893–1940*, London, Longman, 1966. A useful guide to the literature can be found in K. Laybourn, *The Rise of Socialism in Britain*, Stroud, Sutton, 1997.
3 For a discussion of the omission both of women and of gender issues from labour history, including labour and socialist politics, see A. Davin, 'Feminism and labour history', in R. Samuel (ed.), *People's History and Socialist Theory*, London, Routledge & Kegan Paul, 1981; S.O. Rose, 'Gender and labor history: the nineteenth century legacy', *International Review of Social History*, 38, 1993; C. Steedman, *Childhood, Culture and Class in Britain: Margaret McMillan, 1860–1931*, London, Virago, 1990, p. 131. Steedman notes the partial picture of women's participation in British socialism which is found in much of the historiography.
4 C. Waters, *British Socialists and the Politics of Popular Culture, 1884–1914*, Manchester, Manchester University Press, 1990. And yet Waters does look at the fiction of socialist women in a separate publication (C. Waters, 'New women and socialist-feminist fiction: the novels of Isabella Ford and Katharine Bruce Glasier', in A. Ingram and D. Patai (eds), *Discovering Forgotten Radicals: British Women Writers, 1859–1939*, Chapel Hill, University of North Carolina Press, 1993).
5 S. Yeo, 'A new life: the religion of socialism in Britain, 1883–1896', *History Workshop Journal*, 4, 1977. A similar point could be made about C. Levy, 'Education and self-education: staffing the early ILP', in C. Levy (ed.), *Socialism and the Intelligentsia, 1880–1914*, London, Routledge & Kegan Paul, 1987.
6 This point is made by Clare Collins, 'Women and Labour politics in Britain, 1893–1932', PhD, London School of Economics, 1991.
7 For example, see Z.R. Eisenstein (ed.), *Capitalist Patriarchy and the Case for Socialist Feminism*, New York, Monthly Review Press, 1979; L. Sargent (ed.), *Women and Revolution: The Unhappy Marriage of Marxism and Feminism: A Debate on Class and Patriarchy*, London, Pluto, 1981.
8 See, for example, S. Rowbotham, L. Segal and H. Wainwright, *Beyond the Fragments: Feminism and the Making of Socialism*, London, Merlin, 1979.

9 J.L. Newton, M.P. Ryan and J.R. Walkowitz (eds), *Sex and Class in Women's History*, London, Routledge & Kegan Paul, 1983; A. Phillips, *Divided Loyalties: Dilemmas of Sex and Class*, London, Virago, 1987. For similar discussions in a European context, see M.J. Boxer and J.H. Quataert (eds), *Socialist Women: European Socialist Feminism in the Nineteenth and Early Twentieth Centuries*, New York, Elsevier, 1978; J.H. Quataert, *Reluctant Feminists in German Social Democracy, 1885–1917*, New Jersey, Princeton University Press, 1979.

10 B.S. Anderson and J.P. Zinsser, *A History of Their Own: Women in Europe from Prehistory to the Present*, Vol. II, Harmondsworth, Penguin, 1990, pp. 386–90.

11 J.H. Quataert, 'Unequal partners in an uneasy alliance: women and the working class in Imperial Germany', in Boxer and Quataert (eds), *Socialist Women*.

12 For example, see Phillips, *Divided Loyalties*. This point is discussed in C. Hall, *White, Male and Middle Class: Explorations in Feminism and History*, Cambridge, Polity, 1992, esp. pp. 10–11.

13 See letters to the *Labour Leader*, 18 November 1904, expressing different views on the latest women's suffrage bill. See also J. Hannam, *Isabella Ford, 1855–1924*, Oxford, Blackwell, 1989 and K. Hunt, *Equivocal Feminists. The Social Democratic Federation and the Woman Question, 1884–1911*, Cambridge, Cambridge University Press, 1996.

14 S. Rowbotham and J. Weeks, *Socialism and the New Life: The Personal and Sexual Politics of Edward Carpenter and Havelock Ellis*, London, Pluto, 1977; S. Rowbotham, *Women, Resistance and Revolution*, London, Allen Lane, 1972. For a later discussion of similar ideas, see S. Rowbotham, *Women in Movement: Feminism and Social Action*, London, Routledge, 1992.

15 B. Taylor, *Eve and the New Jerusalem: Socialism and Feminism in the Nineteenth Century*, London, Virago, 1983, pp. xv, 285.

16 Anna Clark's study of working-class politics in the nineteenth century explores how the claim for the vote was gendered and argues that citizenship was equated by artisans with men and the construction of a male identity. She also, however, concentrates on an earlier period through her focus on Chartists (A. Clark, *The Struggle for the Breeches: Gender and the Making of the British Working Class*, Berkeley, University of California Press, 1995).

17 Taylor, *Eve and the New Jerusalem*, pp. 285–6. For a discussion of 'new life' socialism, which showed some continuities with the aspirations of Owenites for a transformation of all areas of life, see Rowbotham and Weeks, *Socialism and the New Life*, pp. 63–75.

18 C. Collette, *For Labour and for Women: The Women's Labour League, 1906–1918*, Manchester, Manchester University Press, 1989; J. Gaffin and D. Thoms, *Caring and Sharing: The Centenary History of the Cooperative Women's Guild*, Manchester, Manchester Cooperative Union, 1983; G. Scott, *Feminism and the Politics of Working Women: The Women's Co-operative Guild, 1880s to the Second World War*, London, UCL Press, 1998; C. Rowan, 'Women in the Labour Party, 1906–1920', *Feminist Review*, 12, 1982; P. Graves, *Labour Women: Women in British Working-Class Politics, 1918–1939*, Cambridge, Cambridge University Press, 1994; C. Collette, 'Questions of gender: Labour and women', in B. Brivati and R. Heffernan (eds), *The Labour Party: A Centenary History*, Basingstoke, Macmillan, 2000.

19 J. Alberti, *Beyond Suffrage: Feminists in War and Peace, 1914–1928*, London, Macmillan, 1989.

20 H.L. Smith, 'Sex vs. class: British feminists and the Labour movement, 1919–29', *Historian*, 47, 1984.

21 P. Thane, 'Women in the British Labour Party and feminism, 1906–45', in H.L. Smith (ed.), *British Feminism in the Twentieth Century*, Aldershot, Edward Elgar, 1990.

22 P. Graves, 'An experiment in women-centered socialism: Labour women in Britain', in H. Gruber and P. Graves (eds), *Women and Socialism. Socialism and Women. Europe between the Two World Wars*, Oxford, Berghahn, 1998, p. 211.
23 Ibid., p. 212.
24 J. Liddington and J. Norris, *One Hand Tied Behind Us: The Rise of the Women's Suffrage Movement*, London, Virago, 1978; S.S. Holton, *Feminism and Democracy: Women's Suffrage and Reform Politics in Britain, 1900–1918*, Cambridge, Cambridge University Press, 1986; S.S. Holton, *Suffrage Days: Stories from the Women's Suffrage Movement*, London, Routledge, 1996 – in particular, the chapter on Mary Gawthorpe.
25 For example, see H. Kean, 'Suffrage autobiography: a study of Mary Richardson – suffragette, socialist and fascist' and K. Hunt, 'Journeying through suffrage: the politics of Dora Montefiore', in C. Eustance, J. Ryan and L. Ugolini (eds), *A Suffrage Reader: Charting Directions in British Suffrage History*, London, Leicester University Press, 2000; J. Hannam, '"I had not been to London": women's suffrage – a view from the regions' and J. Smart, 'Jennie Baines: suffrage and an Australian connection', in J. Purvis and S.S. Holton (eds), *Votes for Women*, London, Routledge, 2000.
26 See, for example, Collins, 'Women and Labour politics'. The first part of the thesis concentrates on women in the ILP. Laura Ugolini examines gender relations in the ILP in 'Independent Labour Party men and women's suffrage in Britain, 1893–1914', PhD, University of Greenwich, 1997. See also P. Beals, 'Fabian feminism, gender, politics and culture in London, 1880–1930', PhD, Rutgers University, 1989.
27 Steedman, *Childhood, Culture and Class*; Hannam, *Isabella Ford*; B. Winslow, *Sylvia Pankhurst: Sexual Politics and Political Activism*, London, UCL Press, 1996; J. Liddington, *The Life and Times of a Respectable Rebel: Selina Cooper, 1864–1946*, London, Virago, 1984.
28 E. Gordon, *Women and the Labour Movement in Scotland, 1850–1914*, Oxford, Clarendon Press, 1991.
29 Hunt, *Equivocal Feminists*; J. Hannam, 'Women and the ILP, 1890–1914', in James *et al.* (eds), *The Centennial History of the Independent Labour Party*. Women in the CP are examined in S. Bruley, *Feminism, Stalinism and the Women's Movement in Britain, 1920–1939*, New York, Garland, 1986. For the Fabian Women's Group, see S. Alexander, 'Introduction' to M. Pember Reeves, *Round About a Pound a Week*, London, Virago, 1979.
30 Crick, *History of the Social Democratic Federation*: See also James *et al.* (eds), *Centennial History of the Independent Labour Party*; Laybourn, *The Rise of Socialism in Britain*.
31 T. Woodhouse, *Nourishing the Liberty Tree: Liberals and Labour in Leeds, 1880–1914*, Keele, Keele University Press, 1996. Keith Laybourn devotes four pages to women in his recent history of socialism. He suggests that 'various cultural, social, economic and gender factors helped to shape the rapid development of the ILP', but gender is not fully explored in the text (Laybourn, *The Rise of Socialism*, p. 35).
32 M. Savage, *The Dynamics of Working-Class Politics: The Labour Movement in Preston, 1880–1914*, Cambridge, Cambridge University Press, 1987. The paragraph discussing this draws heavily on Collins, 'Women and Labour politics', p. 21. See also M. Savage and A. Miles, *The Re-making of the British Working Class, 1840–1940*, London, Routledge, 1994, for a stimulating discussion of the ways in which class and gender interact in mediating social and political change.
33 M. Francis, 'Labour and gender', in D. Tanner, P. Thane and N. Tiratsoo (eds), *Labour's First Century*, Cambridge, Cambridge University Press, 2000, p. 211.
34 Ibid., p. 201.
35 For example, see J. Hannam and K. Hunt, 'Gendering the stories of socialism: an essay in historical criticism', in M. Walsh (ed.), *Working Out Gender: Perspectives from Labour History*, Aldershot, Ashgate, 1999; Steedman, *Childhood, Culture and Class*, p. 131.
36 O. Banks, *Faces of Feminism*, Oxford, Martin Robertson, 1981, p. 123.

37 Liddington and Norris, *One Hand Tied Behind Us*, p. 127.
38 For example, see B. Caine, *English Feminism, 1780–1980*, Oxford, Oxford University Press, 1997, p. 153. Steedman also references Liddington and Norris when she suggests that the ILP 'offered a degree of participation to women that the blatantly misogynist SDF denied them' (*Childhood, Culture and Class*, p. 132).
39 J. Hinton, *Labour and Socialism. A History of the British Labour Movement, 1867–1974*, Brighton, Wheatsheaf, 1983, p. 78.
40 Liddington and Norris, *One Hand Tied Behind Us*, p. 44.
41 J. Weeks, *Sex, Politics and Society: The Regulation of Sexuality since 1800*, London, Longman, 1981, pp. 169–70.
42 For this point see L. Barrow and I. Bullock, *Democratic Ideas and the British Labour Movement, 1880–1914*, Cambridge, Cambridge University Press, 1996, especially chs 1, 2, 4.
43 Howell, *British Workers*, p. 389.
44 Laybourn, *The Rise of Socialism*, only discusses women in relation to the ILP.
45 For example, see G.A.N. Lowndes, *Margaret McMillan: The Children's Champion*, London, Museum Press, 1960; H. Pelling, *Origins of the Labour Party*, Oxford, Oxford University Press, 1965, p. 155; S. Pierson, *Marxism and the Origins of British Socialism*, Ithaca, Cornell University Press, 1973, pp. 161–9; Howell, *British Workers*, pp. 330–1. Joseph Clayton adds Isabella Ford and Emmeline Pankhurst to his list (*The Rise and Decline of Socialism in Great Britain*, London, Faber & Gwyer, 1926), while Keith Laybourn includes Isabella Ford and Isabella Bream Pearce (*The Rise of Socialism*, p. 34).
46 J. Hannam, '"In the comradeship of the sexes lies the hope of progress and social regeneration": women in the West Riding ILP, c.1890–1914', in J. Rendall (ed.), *Equal or Different. Women's Politics 1800–1914*, Oxford, Blackwell, 1987; Hannam, 'Women and the ILP', pp. 214–15. See also K. Cowman, '"Giving them something to do": how the early ILP appealed to women' in Walsh (ed.), *Working Out Gender*, pp. 121–3.
47 The way in which ILP members constructed their own history is discussed more fully in Hannam and Hunt, 'Gendering the stories of socialism', pp. 107–10.
48 Hannam, 'Women and the ILP', pp. 216–17.
49 L. Ugolini, '"It is only justice to grant women's suffrage": Independent Labour Party men and women's suffrage, 1893–1905', in Eustance, Ryan and Ugolini (eds), *A Suffrage Reader*, pp. 126–7.
50 Hunt, *Equivocal Feminists*, Appendix 2, p. 260.
51 Hunt, *Equivocal Feminists*, ch. 2.
52 For example, see J. Purvis, 'Christabel Pankhurst and the Women's Social and Political Union', in M. Joannou and J. Purvis (eds), *The Women's Suffrage Movement: New Feminist Perspectives*, Manchester, Manchester University Press, 1998, p. 164.
53 Laybourn, *The Rise of Socialism*, p. 35.
54 One of the most recent collections of articles on the history of the Labour Party, for instance, contains one article on the theme of gender, Collette's 'Questions of gender: Labour and women', which in fact concentrates on women. Issues relating to gender rarely make an appearance in the rest of the book, and nor do individual women, even in sections which deal with welfare questions (Brivati and Heffernan (eds), *The Labour Party*).
55 C. Hall, K. McClelland and J. Rendall, *Defining the Victorian Nation: Class, Race, Gender and the Reform Act of 1867*, Cambridge, Cambridge University Press, 2000. See also A.V. John and C. Eustance (eds), *The Men's Share? Masculinities, Male Support and Women's Suffrage in Britain, 1890–1920*, London, Routledge, 1992.
56 This can be compared with Australia, where there has been much more discussion of gender within mainstream labour history. See, for example, M. Lake, 'Socialism and manhood: the case of William Lane', *Labour History*, 50, 1986; B. Scates, 'Socialism,

feminism and the case of William Lane', *Labour History*, 59, 1990; M. Lake, 'Socialism and manhood: a reply to Bruce Scates', *Labour History*, 60, 1991.
57 For example, see K. Offen, 'Defining feminism: a comparative historical approach', *Signs*, 14, 1, 1988; Special issue on citizenship and politics, *International Labor and Working Class History*, 52, 1997; E.J. Yeo (ed.), *Mary Wollstonecraft and 200 Years of Feminisms*, London, Rivers Oram, 1997; T. Akkerman and S. Stuurman (eds), *Perspectives on Feminist Thought in European History: From the Middle Ages to the Present*, London, Routledge, 1998.
58 E.J. Yeo, 'Introduction', in Yeo (ed.), *Mary Wollstonecraft*, p. 2.
59 J.W. Scott, 'The imagination of Olympe de Gouges', in Yeo (ed.), *Mary Wollstonecraft*.
60 C. Hall quoted in Yeo (ed.), *Mary Wollstonecraft*, p. 7.
61 Collins, 'Women and Labour politics', abstract.
62 Ibid., p. 36.
63 For a discussion of the ways in which an integration of questions of gender into *labour* history would lead to more 'complex and multi-faceted explorations of historical contingency', see Rose, 'Gender and labor history', p. 162.

2
BIOGRAPHIES AND POLITICAL JOURNEYS

Writing in 1930, the ILP propagandist Helen Gault suggested that socialist women needed to know their own backgrounds, including the history of their sex, if they were to deal with the conflicts that would arise in the fight for economic equality. She suggested that when 'as we must profoundly hope, men and women comrades arrive at the same conclusions, we shall have arrived at agreement by different routes. For the journeying – no less than the end of the journey – is important'.[1] It is argued here that a consideration of individual life stories and the political journeys made by women over time provides one way to move beyond the stereotypes so often presented of socialist women and to interrogate the categories into which they are placed. Such an approach can reveal the diversity of women, both in terms of their backgrounds and also in the meaning that they gave to being a woman involved in socialist politics. It is not possible here to give a detailed biographical sketch of the many socialist women who appear in the pages of this book. Rather the intention of this chapter is to draw examples from the lives of individual women to explore the differences between them in the ways in which they identified as women in politics and to explain the changes which could occur over time in the choices that they made.

The focus is on those women who were socialists and who looked at their politics through the prism of gender. Women highlighted here are those who believed that being a woman was significant to their socialist politics and who chose to give some priority to issues relating to women's subordinate position. It is recognised that a number of women featured here can only be identified as socialist women at certain times in their lives; for example, during the immediate pre-war years Emmeline Pankhurst, Isabella Bream Pearce and Mary Gawthorpe, among others, moved away from socialist politics to concentrate on the suffrage campaign and did not return. In the new context of the 1920s socialist women could make different choices within the politics of the Left. Both Dora Montefiore of the SDF/BSP and Helen Crawfurd of the ILP became communists, while Margaret Bondfield and Florence Harrison Bell chose to develop their post-war political careers through the Labour Party rather than through a socialist organisation.

Approaches through biography

Using the lives of individual women to explore questions of political identity raises conceptual and methodological issues which have been debated extensively in recent years.[2] Not only has the process of biography writing been scrutinised, but the notion that individuals shape events through their own autonomous agency has even been rejected as 'the last gasp of "modernism" in a "post modern" age'.[3] Joan Scott, for example, while suggesting that the specific historical context of feminist action makes it valuable to focus on individuals, sees the latter as 'sites' on which 'political and cultural contests are enacted'.[4] Such criticisms have been important in questioning assumptions that there was a straightforward link between experience and political activity. We would argue here, however, that individuals were not simply passive 'carriers of cultural messages and discourses',[5] but also took an active part in helping to shape the society in which they lived. As Carolyn Steedman suggests in her biography of Margaret McMillan, the life story she presents

> is understood to illuminate ideas, ideologies, class and gender relations and the social practices of a particular period of British history. At the same time, a particular life is seen as being shaped by those ideas, relations and practices – a shaping that the biographical subject is cognisant of at some points in her life, quite unaware of at others.[6]

It is the creative interaction between the two which helps to produce complex political identities. Thus, as Susan Grogan argues in her biography of Flora Tristan, 'a focus on individuals engaging with the political and cultural contests being enacted on and around them at particular moments in time provides one way of exploring the past; one way of understanding the world they created and contested'.[7] Recent histories of 'first-wave' feminism have demonstrated how a biographical approach can provide a 're-configuration' of a familiar story.[8] For example, by exploring the suffrage movement through the lives of seven less well-known suffragists, Sandra Holton is able to bring different aspects of that movement to the fore, 'altering our view of the relationship between the parts'.[9]

New perspectives and debates about the writing of biography have been particularly helpful for our own attempt to understand the complex ways in which socialist women identified themselves politically. The assumption that biographers can present a coherent picture of the definitive personality and the 'real life' of their subjects has been questioned. Instead it has been suggested that historians can only hope to tell one among many possible versions of a life.[10] Individuals constructed multiple identities for themselves through diaries, letters, autobiographies and public documents which could shift in relation to different people and over time. Nonetheless, this self-definition was constrained by the historical context in which they operated, in particular by contemporary definitions of appropriate gender roles. This chapter, therefore, will be concerned not only to explore the different responses of individual socialist women to political events, strategies and ideas, but also to consider the ways in which they represented themselves, the process by which some women rather than others have been selected for biographical study and the implications of this for our interpretation of women's engagement in socialist politics.

As already noted in Chapter 1, when histories of the socialist movement mention women, the same few names appear again and again, in particular Caroline Martyn, Katharine St John Conway (Bruce Glasier), Margaret McMillan and Enid Stacy. These women, the 'Famous Four', were initially mythologised by the ILP when it began, after 1913, to construct its own version of the 'pioneering days' of the socialist movement. In a context in which an alliance had been formed between the Labour Party and the National Union of Women's Suffrage Societies, the ILP was keen to demonstrate its credentials as a consistent supporter of 'women's equality' and later in 1918 to persuade women to use their voting power on behalf of the socialist cause.[11] Within the historiography of British socialism, therefore, the image of the charismatic woman propagandist is identified closely with the ILP, while equally effective SDF propagandists such as Eleanor Marx, Amie Hicks, Rose Jarvis and Dora Montefiore tend to be neglected.[12] The SDF seems to have been less concerned to dwell on its own 'heroic' past and never sought to elevate its 'martyr' to the Cause, Eleanor Marx (who died in 1898), to the saint-like status that Caroline Martyn (who died in 1896) acquired in the ILP.[13]

An emphasis on the 'Famous Four' not only reinforces the stereotypes of the ILP and the SDF as friendly/unfriendly to women, but can also be a distorting lens through which to view the varied ways in which women attempted to link together a feminist and a socialist perspective. All four women were primarily identified as committed to the socialist cause and they were praised for their skills as speakers and their ability to 'make socialists'. Enid Stacy was the most closely associated with 'women's rights' issues, both by contemporaries and later by historians, but she died in 1903 just before the suffrage campaign highlighted existing tensions between issues of loyalty to sex or to class.

A different group of socialist women, notably Isabella Ford, Teresa Billington, Emmeline Pankhurst, Hannah Mitchell and Mary Gawthorpe, are highlighted in suffrage histories, but this can be equally misleading.[14] A focus on these women has reinforced the view that *their* political priorities and perspectives, in particular their support for a limited franchise, should be seen as *the* position which was adopted by socialist women, and the signifier of their feminism, rather than as representing one among a number of contested positions. Women who did not fit easily into the dominant narrative of pre-war suffragism have received little attention in the histories of the suffrage movement. Dora Montefiore, for example, who adopted an adult suffrage position on leaving the Women's Social and Political Union as well as retaining allegiance to the SDF, tends to be marginalised despite having written an autobiography.[15] The existence of an autobiography or a biography does not, therefore, guarantee that individual women will receive recognition, but those who did not write their life stories, or who have not been the subject of a recent biography, such as Ethel Snowden of the ILP or Mary Gray and Rose Jarvis of the SDF, tend to be overlooked in both socialist and suffrage histories.[16]

An emphasis on the activities of this small group of women raises questions about the extent to which their experiences were representative of the majority of women socialists or even of other women of the period. Sandra Holton has discussed this issue in relation to suffrage activists and concludes that, although it was not typical for women to engage in the campaign for the vote, this did not make the experience of suffragists atypical in every respect, since their political activity was not divorced from the rest of their lives. Rather it was informed by their everyday experiences. She concludes that suffragists were unusual because of their 'articulateness and public visibility but this did not render them absolutely different or completely separated from other women'.[17] Moreover, she argues that it is hard to find the 'average' woman, since 'aggregates necessarily encompass individuals whose experience corresponds only more or less to the average, and the differences are as important to understand as the conformities'.[18]

Not just national propagandists or local tea makers

It is argued here, therefore, that a biographical approach is crucial for understanding differences between socialist women and for taking us beyond the stereotypes so often found in histories of the socialist and of the women's movement. For the most part socialist women remain undifferentiated in such studies or else they are divided into broad categories with emphasis placed on the full-time propagandist. Thus David Howell asserts that ILP women were either propagandists from 'securely middle-class families' or else working-class wives and daughters of male activists who played a support role as tea makers and the organisers of social events.[19]

And yet this ignores the wide variety of ways in which women engaged with socialist politics, in particular at a local level. Here they might give a great deal of time to political activity over most of their adult lives, or else make what contribution they could, perhaps for just a short period. Invariably, however, they fitted their politics around domestic chores, childcare or making a living. Lena Wilson was a member of the SDF who represented her party on the Poplar Board of Guardians from 1895. She later became secretary of the Bow and Bromley Socialist Women's Circle and was a member of the SDF Women's Committee.[20] Similarly, Harriet Beanland, a tailoress from Nelson, was a member of the local ILP, a Poor Law Guardian and a suffrage supporter.[21] Many others, in particular from the ILP, were involved in both socialist and suffrage politics. Ethel Derbyshire (1879–1976), a mill worker before her marriage, was connected with the Blackburn ILP and was an open air speaker for women's suffrage.[22] Jennie Baines (1866–1951), who lived in Stockport, joined her husband, a boot and shoe worker and staunch trade unionist, in the local ILP. She had to work as a sewing machinist to add to the family's low income as well as look after five children. During that time she did not get involved in public work but afterwards stood unsuccessfully for the Stockport Board of Guardians and sat on the Unemployed Committee and the Feeding of Schoolchildren Committee. She carried out suffrage propaganda for the WSPU and was arrested on numerous occasions.[23]

Although many women found it easier to engage only in local politics, there were others who moved between local and national activities. Isabella Bream Pearce, for example, the wife of a wine importer and ILP parliamentary candidate, was the president of the Glasgow Woman's Labour Party, attended annual conferences of the ILP in the early 1890s and, under the pseudonym of Lily Bell, wrote a women's column between 1894 and 1898 in the *Labour Leader*, edited by her friend Keir Hardie. She later became honorary treasurer of the Scottish Council of the WSPU and wrote a suffrage column in 1906 and 1907, again using the name Lily Bell, in the ILP newspaper *Forward*.[24] Clara Hendin, who was married with at least one daughter, was secretary of the Kensal Town branch of the SDF, was a delegate to the London Congress of the Second International in 1896 and was a member of the SDF executive from 1902 to 1905. She was involved in the SDF Women's Circles from their inception and was honorary secretary of the Socialist Women's Bureau, the British women's section of the Second International. She took part in a wide range of activities, from the provision of refreshments and bazaar work to participation in the Women's Education Committee and providing training for public speaking.[25] The experiences of such women, although perhaps more typical than those of the better known full-time national propagandists, tend to be ignored. And yet their shifting positions in relation to gender politics need to be explored if we are to understand the range of perspectives adopted by socialist women.

If it is inadequate to describe socialist women simply as either national propagandists or local tea makers, it is equally misleading to differentiate them on the basis of their class position by using the broad categories of middle class and working class. In most texts the term middle class is used very loosely; it could refer to a woman's family background or to her own position within the workforce. Occupational status alone could cover a diverse set of social and economic circumstances. Schoolteachers, for instance, who made up the largest single occupational group amongst ILP women socialists,[26] are usually described as middle class and yet there were considerable differences in their circumstances. Thus Ethel Annakin, who was the daughter of a businessman and later married Philip Snowden MP, was able to attend a training college before becoming a teacher, whereas Mary Gawthorpe, from a Leeds working-class background, had to train through the pupil teacher system and then had to support her mother and brother on her earnings.[27]

Socialist women born into working-class families, such as Selina Cooper, Hannah Mitchell and Ada Neild Chew, tended to marry men from their own social class, but there were many other women from a lower middle-class or even middle-class background who married working-class male labour activists. For instance Annot Wilkie (1874–1923), a teacher, university graduate and secretary of the Dundee WSPU, married Sam Robinson, the son of a Salford mill worker, and both were active in ILP politics in Manchester.[28] Other women had more ambivalent class positions. Florence Harrison Bell (b. 1865), for instance, secretary of the Newcastle Women's Association of the ILP in the early 1890s and a member of the party's National Administrative Council (NAC) in 1897, was the wife of a trade union leader and had worked both as a cook and as a teacher.[29] Mary Gray, one of the most prominent SDF women in the 1890s and early 1900s, had a lower middle-class background but from the age of 15 had been in service. In 1876 she married a stonemason who was often unemployed because of his trade union activities, and they lived in considerable hardship until he took up another trade.[30] Some socialist women suffered when their husbands were victimised, whereas others faced victimisation in their own right, regardless of their class background. Both Katharine St John Conway (Bruce Glasier) and Enid Stacy, for instance, had to leave their jobs as schoolteachers in Bristol in the early 1890s after marching with women who were on strike, while Amie Hicks' daughter Frances had to give up the private school that she ran because of the family's political activities.[31]

Although some middle-class socialist women propagandists such as Isabella Ford, Mrs Cobden Sanderson and Charlotte Despard were able to live on income provided by their families, others, including Annie Besant, Eleanor Marx, Enid Stacy, Katharine Bruce Glasier and Caroline Martyn, had to earn their living from lectures and from journalism. The diversity of socialist women's economic and social backgrounds, therefore, meant that their own class positions, and the way in which they approached questions of class in their political theory and practice, were contingent and complex. Margaret McMillan, for example, identified herself as a working woman despite her middle-class, well-educated background because she had to engage in paid employment to support herself.[32]

Socialist pioneers

It was not just their class and social backgrounds which differentiated socialist women. Their generation and the time at which they entered the socialist movement also affected the way in which they negotiated between class, gender and party. The focus of their activities could then shift over time in response to a changing political context. Although women entered socialist politics in very different decades, their political activities and allegiances have been read through their involvement in the suffrage campaign which gained such a high profile in the pre-war years. As early as 1932 Labour Party officials claimed that Labour women had until then been dominated by 'the generation of women who pioneered the movement, who fought vigorously for the suffrage, and who have found in the Women's Sections ample scope for the sex consciousness thereby developed'.[33] Echoing these views, Pamela Graves suggests that women active in socialist politics before 1914 can be described as the 'suffrage generation' since their identity as women active in politics was influenced, and in some cases shaped, by the struggle for women's suffrage.[34] For socialist women, however, this angle of vision can be a misleading one. In the immediate pre-war period socialist women did have to engage with the question of suffrage. Nonetheless, many did not see it as the most important issue for women or argued for an adult suffrage measure. Until that point, however, they did not necessarily view their socialism, or their commitment to women's emancipation, primarily through the lens of suffrage.

Women who joined the newly formed socialist groups in the pioneering days of the 1880s and 1890s came from two generations. The first group were born in the 1840s and 1850s at a time when the ideology of separate spheres was at its height and when involvement in political life was thought unwomanly. Some were from working-class backgrounds, including Amie Hicks (1839/40–1917), who married a pianoforte maker, William Hicks, and moved to Australia in the 1860s, where she worked as a ropemaker and had six children. On the family's return to London in the early 1880s, Amie, William and their daughter Margaretta joined the SDF. Amie was elected on to the executive committee in 1884 and 1885, became a well known open air speaker and stood unsuccessfully for the London School Board in 1885 and 1889, when she gave her occupation as midwife. After becoming involved in the labour unrest of the late 1880s, she shifted the focus of her activities towards trade union organisation, although she continued to attend SDF meetings.[35] Her daughter Margaretta, on the other hand, remained active in SDF politics throughout her lifetime.

Many others were from middle-class backgrounds, although their financial circumstances and the date at which they became involved in socialist politics could vary considerably. Annie Besant (1847–1933) was an early convert to socialism, joining the Fabian Society and then the SDF in the mid-1880s. After the failure of her marriage to a clergyman, which led to the loss of her children, she took up radical causes such as the dissemination of birth control information and the legal inequalities faced by women before becoming a socialist propagandist.[36] Emmeline Pankhurst (1858–1928), on the other hand, who was also involved in radical and feminist politics, only joined the socialist movement in 1894, when she returned from London to Manchester with her husband, the radical lawyer Richard Pankhurst.[37] Charlotte Despard (1844–1939), a wealthy heiress, did not engage in public life until she was widowed in 1890, when she worked among the poor and then joined the SDF in 1895. She worked with that organisation and spent several years as a Poor Law Guardian, until she became a leading member of the Women's Freedom League (WFL) in 1907, when she was also more associated with the ILP.[38]

Annie Besant and Emmeline Pankhurst both faced financial difficulties; after the early death of her husband in 1896, Emmeline Pankhurst ran a small shop and also worked as a registrar of births, marriages and deaths, while Annie

Besant had to make a living as a speaker and a journalist once she had left her husband. On the whole, however, the earlier generation of middle-class women socialists had a very varied and patchy education and were not expected to take up paid employment. Isabella Ford (1855–1924) from Leeds, the daughter of a wealthy Quaker solicitor, enjoyed a very extensive education but after the death of her parents received an income which meant that she did not have to earn a living. Those middle-class women who were born in the 1860s and 1870s, however, were able to take advantage of higher education for women and expected to take up professional work. Enid Stacy (1868–1903) and Katharine St John Conway (1869–1950) were both educated at Newnham College, Cambridge, and became teachers in Bristol. Enid Stacy's father, an artist who had married the daughter of a Midlands hardware merchant, had moved to Bristol in 1881, where he set up a studio. Katharine Bruce Glasier, on the other hand, was one of seven children of a Congregationalist minister in Walthamstow and received a Clothworkers' scholarship to study in Cambridge.[39]

Margaret McMillan (1860–1939) also came from a middle-class family of limited means, although her mother was determined to ensure her daughters had a good education. After the death of her father, McMillan was brought up in Scotland by her mother and grandparents (her grandfather had been a landlord's factor) and she was educated at the Inverness Academy. She was employed for a short time as a governess, but then committed herself to working full time for socialism from a base in Bradford. She used her talents as a journalist and a speaker to earn a living and also received financial support from her sister Rachel, who worked as a schoolteacher and then as a sanitary inspector.[40] Caroline Martyn (d.1896), the daughter of a Lincoln clergyman, also supported herself through journalism and was the editor of *Christian World*.[41] Journalism provided a key source of extra income for women socialist propagandists as well as being a means to spread their ideas.[42] During the 1890s it was an expanding area of employment for women, and socialists were able to place their articles in newspapers and journals beyond those of the socialist movement.[43]

What these middle-class women had in common, whether living on a private income or their own earnings, was a consciousness of their own independence and an interest in the politics of gender.[44] This stemmed partly from economic security and the possibility of employment, but was also fuelled by debates around the Woman Question in radical and socialist circles. These encouraged men and women to attempt 'to understand themselves and the part they were to play in the society they inhabited'.[45] Working-class women socialists, however, still had to struggle from day to day to make ends meet, whether as the wives of working men or in their own low-paid female jobs. On the other hand, in the 1890s and early 1900s some working-class women were also able to gain a degree of independence by training as teachers through the pupil teacher system or by winning a scholarship, and it was many of these women, as already noted, who were attracted to socialism.

An increase in the number of paid positions within the women's movement and the labour movement opened up another route to economic independence for women from both middle- and working-class backgrounds, enabling them to give a full-time commitment to political work. Margaret Bondfield (1873–1953), a shop assistant, and Ada Neild Chew (1870–1945), who had worked as a tailoress, became trade union organisers, while Lisbeth Simm and Bertha Ayles, members of the Newcastle and Bristol branches of the ILP respectively, were organisers for the Women's Labour League. Selina Cooper (1864–1946) from Lancashire and Ada Neild Chew were employed before the First World War as organisers for the National Union of Women's Suffrage Societies, while Jennie Baines was paid as an organiser for the WSPU. After the turn of the century some women gained full-time positions within the socialist movement itself – the Manchester schoolteacher Teresa Billington became the first female organiser of the ILP in 1905. Minnie Pallister, the daughter of a Wesleyan minister from South Wales, held a similar post in the 1920s, while Margaretta Hicks, who worked as a tailoress, became the first woman organiser of the British Socialist Party in 1914. This work could then affect the amount of time women could give to socialist politics and their attitude towards particular issues and events.

During the early years of the socialist movement converts to the cause aimed to make socialists and there was less emphasis on allegiance to a specific party. Many women moved from one organisation to another until they found the most congenial space in which to pursue their interests – Enid Stacy and Katharine St John Conway, for instance, were members of the Bristol Socialist Society in the late 1880s and then became lecturers for the Fabian Society, before joining the ILP. Others, including the textile worker Selina Cooper, were members of both the SDF and the ILP.[46] Women could inspire each other irrespective of organisational affiliation – Amie Hicks of the SDF influenced the politics of both Margaret MacDonald (1870–1911) and Margaret Bondfield, although they joined the ILP and the SDF respectively, while Katharine Bruce Glasier remembered sharing her room in Bristol one night with Eleanor Marx, who for half the night 'held us spellbound' with her memories of the International.[47]

Men and women were also inspired by the writings of William Morris and Edward Carpenter to equate their politics with personal change and different forms of relationships, and to attempt to live out these new ideals in the shell of the old society. 'New life socialism' was not confined to any one party but drew men and women together across organisational boundaries.[48] But differences between the SDF and the ILP became more firmly drawn after 1895, when the ILP became more concerned to build an electoral machinery and to form an alliance with the trade unions. This differentiation was reinforced by the withdrawal of the SDF from the Labour Representation Committee (LRC) in 1901. It therefore became increasingly difficult for individuals to support both organisations, although the relationship between them remained more fluid at a local level.

Regardless of which group they belonged to, socialist women in the 1880s and 1890s faced a common problem of carving a place for themselves within a politics defined in masculinist and class terms and sought to raise issues related to gender inequalities, as well as pursuing socialist propaganda. Most of these early recruits had already been woman-focused in their activities before they became socialists; they engaged in social and educational work among working-class women and girls or took part in trade union organisation. Many remained involved in organisations which sought to improve women's work conditions. The working-class women Amie Hicks and Agnes Close were secretaries of the London Ropemakers' Union and the Leeds Tailoresses' Union respectively.[49] Isabella Ford was president of the Leeds Tailoresses' Union, while Margaret MacDonald was secretary of the Women's Industrial Council and secretary of the legislation committee of the National Union of Women Workers. She had been a visitor for the Charity Organisation Society before joining the ILP in 1895.[50]

Some socialist women also continued to be involved in the women's movement. Isabella Ford and Emmeline Pankhurst, for example, belonged to their local women's suffrage societies. Nonetheless, in a period in which the new socialist movement was struggling to attract members, it was more common for socialist women to be keen to differentiate themselves from the 'bourgeois women's movement', a perspective which was common to women in socialist organisations throughout Europe.[51] Mary Foster, an ILP member from Leeds, wrote a section on women for the report of the International Socialist Congress held in London in 1896 which claimed that:

> The bourgeois movement makes a great deal of noise, but its leaders demand mere palliatives ... while the bourgeois women's movement in all lands has tended to open up the minds of women generally to an examination of the questions which especially affect their sex, it cannot be compared in importance and significance with the organisations for working women ... and with the efforts of individual women working with men in the ranks of socialism to advance the cause of labour and political freedom.[52]

Enid Stacy also differentiated the collectivist approach of socialist women from the individualist standpoint of the women's movement and described the campaign for women's rights as a 'middle-class fad'.[53] Thus, although she attended suffrage conferences to argue her case from a socialist perspective, she did not give her time to the women's movement as such.

Socialists and suffrage campaigners

In a context in which the women's movement was weak and the socialist movement was in its infancy, socialist women were able to argue for an integrated approach to feminism and socialism even though it was difficult to persuade socialist groups to take gender issues seriously. This became much more difficult in the decade before the First World War with the growth in importance of the campaign for the vote. Women's suffrage now provided the context in which socialist women had to negotiate between their party, their class and their sex. Attitudes towards the Woman Question were no longer just part of a theoretical debate, even if that had in the past been directed towards specific issues, but began to involve women in the need to make political choices and to develop strategies which could be distinct from those of the socialist groups of which they were members.

It was not simply a question of whether socialist women supported a particular suffrage position, but a broader issue of how they should organise around their gender identity. Moreover, the development of separate women's organisations posed a new set of dilemmas and choices for socialist women. The WSPU, established by members of the Manchester ILP to fight for suffrage, the Women's Labour League, formed largely by ILP women to support the Labour Party, and the Women's Circles in the SDF not only made it explicit that women could be identified politically as women but also tended to be set up as rivals to each other. This in turn could sharpen women's awareness about their own political perspective since, as Clare Collins suggests, women's collective political identity was 'frequently created through opposition to that of other political women'.[54]

These developments affected the 'pioneering' generation as well as those who entered socialist politics after the mid-1890s, with many women feeling that they had to choose between their 'own cause' and socialist politics, although the choices that they made were diverse. Some of the new recruits to socialism, including Dora Montefiore (1851–1933), were part of the older generation born in the 1840s and 1850s. Montefiore was born into a large prosperous family in Surrey and was privately educated. She married in Australia and after her husband's death in 1889 became a campaigner for women's suffrage, an activity she continued when she returned to England. It was not until 1898 that she carried out propaganda for socialism with the Clarion Van and then joined the SDF, becoming a member of the executive in 1903. At the same time she was an active member of the WSPU, but in 1907 she left and became involved in the Adult Suffrage Society.[55]

A younger group of women, born in the 1880s and 1890s, also had to face this new context. The schoolteachers Mary Gawthorpe (1881–1973), Ethel Annakin (Snowden) (1880–1951) and Teresa Billington (Greig) (1877–1964), for example, joined the socialist movement just before women's suffrage became a key political issue; all three were to leave their socialist politics in favour of a full-time commitment to the fight for women's suffrage and only Ethel Snowden was later to re-join the ILP. Others took a similar position to some of the older generation such as Isabella Ford, Selina Cooper and Ada Neild Chew in trying to pursue both socialist and suffrage propaganda.[56] Ellen Wilkinson (1891–1947) joined the ILP when still a schoolgirl and was an organiser for the NUWSS between 1913 and 1915, while Dorothy Jewson (1884–1964), the daughter of a coal and timber merchant, became involved in socialist politics in 1907, when as a student at Cambridge she joined the ILP and then the WSPU. Both women became prominent in socialist and labour politics in the 1920s, when they were elected as Labour MPs.[57] Yet others took an interest in the extension of the franchise but rejected a limited suffrage position. They included Mary Macarthur (1880–1921), leader of the National Federation of Women Workers and a member of the National Administrative Council of the ILP between 1909 and 1912, and Kathleen Kough, who was active in the women's organisation of the SDF after 1905 and was a member of the Women's Committee and a speaker for the party. Both women took an active part in the Adult Suffrage Society.[58]

War and post-war

During the war and post-war period all of these women faced a new context in which to pursue their claims as socialists and as women. In many respects the onset of war provided a contrast to a period in which 'women's own issue' had been a key area of political debate. Socialist groups were concerned to work out their own stand on the war and, for those who sought a speedy end to the conflict, peace campaigning and involvement in industrial unrest came to predominate. The war enabled some women who had taken very different positions in the Edwardian period on suffrage, on protective legislation and on the focus of their activities, and who were members of different socialist organisations, to come together to work for peace and to improve the social and economic position of working-class women.[59]

A few women found space to pursue their socialist and woman-focused activities through smaller groups which were independent of the main political parties, notably the East London Federation of Suffragettes (ELFS), established by Sylvia Pankhurst (1882–1960) just before the war, which became the Workers' Suffrage Federation (WSF) (1916–18) and then the Workers' Socialist Federation (1918–21). The ELFS/WSF became involved in welfare questions affecting women and in agitation for peace as well as carrying out a vigorous campaign for full human suffrage. Sylvia Pankhurst, the second of Emmeline Pankhurst's five children, had joined the ILP as a young woman and was then active in the WSPU, before setting up her own group. During the war she became increasingly attracted to methods of direct action at the workplace and in the community and developed a more revolutionary politics.[60]

The ELFS/WSF attracted women such as Jessie Stephen, aged 20 at the outbreak of war, who was one of eleven children of a skilled tailor from Clydeside and Emma Boyce (1867–1929), who had had twelve children, four of whom survived. Jessie Stephen trained as a pupil teacher, but when her father was unemployed she had to take up work as a domestic servant.[61] She became involved in organising domestic workers in Scotland and was active in the ILP and the WSPU. After meeting Sylvia Pankhurst in London, she agreed to become a full-time organiser for the ELFS/WSF. Emma Boyce, on the other hand, had been involved from 1907 in the SDF as a speaker and an activist in the Women's Circles. She was appointed as organiser of the Women's Education Committee but resigned in 1910, although she continued her activism in the British Socialist Party. During the war she became an organiser for the ELFS/WSF, concentrating on Glasgow and Newcastle but also speaking several times a week all over the country. In 1918 she was elected a Labour councillor for Hackney and during the 1920s often spoke at ILP meetings.[62]

There was little space, however, in the midst of the upheavals and losses of wartime for a consideration of gender issues, and this continued after the end of hostilities when depression, mass unemployment, class conflict and eventual threats to world peace again took centre stage. Socialist groups whose revolutionary politics had been consolidated during the war, including the BSP, the Socialist Labour Party and the Workers' Socialist Federation, came together after the war to form the Communist Party of Great Britain (CPGB).[63] For the first time the Labour Party committed itself to socialism in its 1918 constitution and also allowed men and women to become individual members. Women joined in large numbers, comprising just over 50 per cent of individual members in the inter-war years, although they tended to work through women's sections and women's annual conferences, which were 'marginalised from the party's real centres of power'.[64]

In the new context of the war and immediate post-war period socialist women continued to press the claims of women but, as before, chose a variety of strategies with which to do this. It is difficult to find any clear patterns in their choices or indeed to suggest whether involvement in suffragette militancy or in particular types of peace campaigning and anti-war agitation had affected their political journeys. The different choices made by individuals can be illustrated by two women, Agnes Dollan and Helen Crawfurd. They were both active in socialist, suffrage and peace politics in Glasgow, where there were very close links between the ILP, the WSPU, neighbourhood campaigns and then women's anti-war protests.[65]

Agnes Dollan (b.1887), one of eleven children of a blacksmith, had worked in a factory and also as a telephone operator. She joined the ILP at the age of 18 and then the WSPU before, in 1912, marrying Patrick Dollan, an ILP journalist working for *Forward* who was later to become Scottish organiser for the party.[66] Helen Crawfurd (1877–1954), the daughter of a prosperous Tory baker, had married a clergyman in 1897 when she was 20. She later joined the WSPU, taking part in militant actions and going on hunger strike. In contrast to many other suffragettes, she subsequently became a socialist and joined the ILP in 1914. During the war Agnes Dollan and Helen Crawfurd worked together in the Glasgow Women's Housing Association, taking a leading role in the rent strikes, established the Glasgow branch of the Women's International League and spearheaded the local Women's Peace Crusade.[67] It was after this that their politics diverged. Dollan remained active in the ILP and the Labour Party both at a local and at a national level, whereas Crawfurd, always the more militant one, became increasingly critical of ILP reformism. She attended the second Congress of the Third International in Moscow in 1920 and then joined the C.P.[68] Jill Liddington suggests that Dollan and Crawfurd in Glasgow and Stephen and Boyce in London 'operated at the very edge of the law' in their anti-war agitation and challenged the state whether as suffragettes or as peace campaigners.[69] Nonetheless, after the war Dollan and Stephen were active in the ILP, Boyce became a JP and spoke regularly at ILP meetings, while only Crawfurd became a communist.

In the early 1920s women did waver between the ILP and the CPGB, and the situation was fluid enough to enable them to be members of both for a short time. Selina Cooper, for example, one of the pioneering socialist generation, was one among several ILP members who were sympathetic to the Communist Party, although Liddington argues that she did not become a member.[70] Ellen Wilkinson did join the CPGB, but when it became impossible to retain dual membership she chose to remain a member of the ILP and the Labour Party, which had adopted her as a parliamentary candidate in the 1923 election.[71]

In the inter-war period, it was more possible for women to pursue a career in politics and this in itself could affect the way in which they identified politically. Dorothy Jewson, elected as an ILP MP in 1924, sought to increase women's influence within both the ILP and the Labour Party and campaigned consistently for equal rights legislation, for access to birth control and for family allowances. When she was defeated in the 1924 election she became a member of the National Administrative Council of the ILP and was later elected as a local councillor; she used these positions as a base to continue to pressurise the Labour Party to be more responsive to women's interests and to gender inequalities which remained despite the vote.[72] At the same time she managed to make connections with the women's movement through her activities in the Workers' Birth Control Group. Ellen Wilkinson, on the other hand, had a long career in parliament as a Labour MP. She increasingly compromised her 'feminist' views, for example over birth control, if they threatened her party's chance of electoral success, while emphasising class rather than gender divisions and loyalties.[73] This shift in perspective must be seen in the broader context of the 1930s, when Graves suggests that 'women's issues faded into insignificance as the party became absorbed in the struggle against fascists and reactionary government to the right of them and communists to the left. Party leaders demanded unity and conformity in response to the crisis and, with few exceptions, Labour women were willing to comply'.[74]

Politicisation

It has been suggested here that socialist women's own background, and the context in which they entered socialist politics, could affect the choices that they were faced with and therefore the ways in which they worked out their individual and collective political identity as women. Equally important for understanding the specific ways in which socialist women approached their gender politics is a consideration of why they were attracted to socialism. As Jean Quataert suggests, 'by supplementing the writings of the movement's leaders with biographical materials, one can obtain insights into their hopes for the female sex that are more penetrating than an analysis of the written word alone'.[75]

An explanation of why individuals were drawn to socialism can partly be inferred from the timing of the journeys that they made from one activity to another, but many women also left direct testimonies about their attraction to socialism. They were interviewed in the socialist and labour press at various stages in their lives, were the subject of 'pen portraits' and also wrote their own reminiscences and autobiographies.[76] A disproportionate number of such accounts were, however, written by, or related to, middle-class rather than working-class women and historians need to ensure that these are not taken as representative of the process of politicisation of all women. Moreover, in recounting their lives women constructed a narrative of why they became socialists which was affected by their awareness that they were challenging conventional views of what it meant to be a woman, while at the same time using 'traditional' definitions of femininity as a justification for their actions.[77]

It is difficult to discern a common pattern in women's politicisation.[78] Middle-class women had usually been involved in radical liberal causes, including women's rights campaigns, or had taken an interest in the social, industrial or educational conditions of working people, in particular women and girls. For example, Rose Jarvis (Scott), the daughter of a Baptist minister, worked in the temperance movement and undertook educational work. She became used to speaking in public and was convinced women could make a contribution to the public sphere. Her conversion to socialism arose from her concern about the insanitary houses which she visited. After writing an exposé for the local paper, she came to the attention of the Social Democrats and was given a copy of *Justice* to read, after which she joined the SDF.[79]

The catalyst which confirmed many women's more active engagement with socialist politics was their involvement in the widespread strikes, in particular among female workers, which took place between 1888 and 1890. Isabella Ford, Margaret McMillan, Katharine Bruce Glasier and Enid Stacy all claimed that the strikes were a turning point. Enid Stacy's family were already influenced by Christian socialism, but Katherine Bruce Glasier later recalled that 'for Enid as for me, I think it was the strikes among female workers which brought things to a crisis', while Isabella Ford left the Women's Liberal Federation and finally committed herself to socialism after helping textile workers and tailoresses on strike in Leeds, where she found that 'it was quite impossible to obtain any help politically from either of the two political parties'.[80]

It has been suggested by Jill Liddington and Jill Norris that as far as working-class women were concerned 'politicisation began in the workplace and in the experience of organising around it'.[81] To some extent this reflects the experience of Ada Neild Chew and Agnes Close, who were both tailoresses. Ada Neild

Chew's letters to the local press in 1894 about conditions of employment for women in the tailoring trade in Crewe brought her to the attention of the local secretary of the ILP. Ada was not willing to join the ILP immediately, but agreed that if her identity became known she would work with the party 'in the effort to improve the conditions not only of the factory girls, but of all other workers'.[82] Once it had been revealed that she was the author of the letters, she duly became a member of the ILP. Agnes Close, on the other hand, came into contact with Isabella Ford and local socialists through her involvement in the Leeds tailoresses' strike of 1889. She became paid secretary of the small Leeds Tailoresses' Union and then worked as a caretaker for the Women's Union Club, which was financed by Isabella and her sister. Close also became an active member of the Leeds ILP but left for Canada at the turn of the century when her union merged with the mixed-sex Amalgamated Union of Clothing Operatives. Isabella Ford later recalled that Agnes Close, along with other committee members, feared that women's interests would be neglected if they were not thought to be the same as those of the men.[83] Other working-class women, however, could be influenced by a tradition of political radicalism in their families or among their friends. Amie Hicks and Julia Varley were the daughter and great granddaughter respectively of Chartists. Julia Varley (1871–1952), a mill worker, was active in the Bradford Trades Council and the local ILP, having been influenced by her mother, who had a lifelong interest in politics and social welfare questions, and by her grandfather.[84] At different times in her life Julia Varley repeated a story about her grandfather in which he explained the meaning of the term democracy by telling her that when she grew up she must 'work for the people, think for the people, and live for the people until they can do it for themselves'.[85] Varley was elected onto the Bradford Board of Guardians in 1901 and was for a brief period a member of the WSPU, suffering imprisonment in 1907, before concentrating on trade union work.

Most women who joined the socialist movement in its early years did have a vision, which they expressed in their writings or in interviews, that socialism would bring greater equality for women, and would provide them with personal fulfilment, as well as end the poverty, injustice and suffering which was faced by all working people. Nonetheless, the balance between these reasons could vary, as did the extent to which women thought that socialists should prioritise the Woman Question. Isabella Bream Pearce claimed that she had left the Women's Liberal Federation because of Gladstone's stand on women's suffrage: 'I find it difficult to understand how any woman can work for and with a party which declines to give official proof of its acceptance of her assistance on a basis of equality.'[86] She believed that the ILP was the only party which offered such a political role to women. Isabella Ford, on the other hand, severed her links with liberalism because of the way in which Liberal employers treated women workers during the labour unrest.[87]

Other women did not take an interest in the Woman Question until after they had joined the socialist movement. The SDF member Mary Gray helped to establish Socialist Sunday Schools at first and was elected to Battersea Board of Guardians. She later campaigned for universal suffrage and joined the Battersea Women's Socialist Circle. The schoolteachers Ethel Annakin and Mary Gawthorpe joined the ILP at the turn of the century. When she was studying at Edge Hill Training College, Ethel was influenced by the Reverend C.F. Aked, who converted her to socialism, and she preached teetotalism in the Liverpool slums. In her autobiography Mary Gawthorpe claimed that she was introduced to socialist politics by her fiancé, and they both became active in the Leeds Labour Church before Mary was elected as vice-president of the Leeds ILP.[88] Although they did not express an interest in the Woman Question at the time, both women had sought independence in their personal lives by qualifying as teachers. They subsequently became active in the women's suffrage movement, since, as Sandra Holton notes, 'it was impossible to be active in socialist and Labour movement politics in these years and remain unaware of the revival of interest in women's suffrage'.[89] Holton also argues that the testimonies of suffrage activists such as Mary Gawthorpe and Hannah Mitchell show how discontent in their personal lives predisposed them towards feminist politics.[90]

A later generation of women who joined the socialist movement just before or during the First World War, including Ellen Wilkinson, Dorothy Jewson and Minnie Pallister, showed a similar mixture of concern for the need to improve the lives of working-class people and an interest in the specific inequalities faced by women. Minnie Pallister described herself as a Christian woman and during the war was involved in helping conscientious objectors. In the 1920s, while working as an organiser for the ILP, she wrote pamphlets and articles attempting to persuade women to take politics seriously and supported the establishment of separate women's groups. She wrote that 'my politics are me … it seems almost impossible that there should still be people who believe that politics do not matter'.[91] In reflecting on why she was drawn to the socialist movement, she claimed that:

> it is the only movement in the whole world which bases its policy and programme upon the right of every person to equal opportunities, equal standards, equal responsibilities … But the glory of the ILP is that it was founded by people who felt other people's sufferings as they felt their own.[92]

Minnie Pallister's religious language, and the way in which she expressed her hopes for the end of human suffering in a future socialist society, sounds remarkably similar to Katharine Bruce Glasier's socialist writing. It reflected a particular millenarian, religious and sentimental rhetoric which was common in the ILP from its inception. Ellen Wilkinson later claimed that it was the power of Glasier's speech at the Manchester Free Trade Hall, and her encouraging words afterwards, which led her to work for socialism. On the other hand, her biographer, Betty Vernon, suggests that this says more about Ellen Wilkinson's view of her own achievements in the 1930s, when she had a well-established reputation as a 'moving orator', than it does about her feelings as a teenager.[93]

A similar point could be made about other reminiscences and autobiographies. Produced many years after the events described, these accounts were affected by a woman's interests at the time in which they were written.[94] Margaret Bondfield's autobiography, for example, published in 1948, downplays her involvement in the SDF and gives little space to 'feminist issues', although she does discuss her position on adult suffrage.[95] It was written after a period in which she had attained a leading position in the Labour Party, becoming a cabinet minister in the 1929 Labour government, and was identified with the right wing of the party. Her views on women had also become more conservative; she emphasised women's importance as homemakers and nurturers of children and saw their political role as one of demanding social reforms relating to housing and family life. Historians have tended to read Margaret Bondfield's politics through the lens of her later career, and yet, as Olive Banks points out, as a young woman Margaret Bondfield was an 'enthusiastic supporter of a woman's right to independence' and her views on feminist politics were far more complex than her later career might imply.[96] Not only was she woman-centred in her day-to-day activities – as a women's trade union organiser and as a leader of the Women's Labour League – but she also wrote articles arguing that women should play a full part in political life as well as proselytising for adult suffrage. When an account like Bondfield's autobiography is taken at face value by historians, it reinforces the tendency to categorise socialist women as feminist or non-feminist. In this way women such as Margaret Bondfield, and to some extent Margaret McMillan and Katharine Bruce Glasier, are defined as non-feminist or anti-feminist. Thus they appear in histories of the labour movement and socialism but are less likely to appear in histories of socialist women or of feminism.[97]

Some women were consistent in the way in which they told the story of what attracted them to socialism. In 1889, in the middle of the tailoresses' strike, Isabella Ford was interviewed by Ben Turner for the *Yorkshire Factory Times*. She began with a question put to her by her father in the middle of the Cotton Famine. 'What is an operative, Baby?' Her reply was, 'A starving creature'.[98] She then went on to claim that she had been brought up by her parents to take an interest in the education and working conditions of women workers and had been encouraged by them to help to organise women into trade unions. The labour unrest of 1888–90 in Leeds had brought her closer to local socialists and she had joined the ILP because it stood for 'equality and opportunity for the whole race ... women had never had such equality before'.[99] She gave virtually the same account, including the story about the 'starving creature', in a later article in 1913 and in an interview in 1914.[100]

This consistency may have been because throughout her life Isabella Ford never wavered from the attempt to integrate her woman-focused and her socialist politics. Margaret McMillan, on the other hand, changed the emphasis of her interests and of her views about the relationship between socialism and women's emancipation at different times in her life. In 1912, in an article about 'How I became a socialist', she mentions nothing about women's emancipation.[101] Instead she claimed that she had first become interested in socialism after discussions with an American friend about the history of land tenure in Scotland and through the influence of her sister, who had started going to socialist lectures in Edinburgh. Her interest was then confirmed by the London Dock Strike of 1889 and her meeting with Paul Campbell, the editor of the *Christian Socialist*, who encouraged her to speak in Hyde Park. In a later piece of writing, looking back over thirty years, she felt that the question of women's emancipation was only ever implicit in the early ILP and that 'it was not formed to champion women. It took that battle in its stride, and might drop it in its ardour. It was born to make war on capitalism and competition.'[102] And yet, as Steedman points out, in 1895 she had argued differently when she claimed:

> the Reveille of the proletariat is the Reveille of women. Their emancipation must be simultaneous. Each in freeing themselves must free the other. At the bottom all their efforts have the same aim; self realisation, a full and conscious life of social and personal activity. [103]

We must be careful, therefore, not to read women's involvement in socialist politics simply through reminiscences written much later or through the lens of suffrage alone. Certainly before the turn of the century women's attraction to socialism was based on a varied set of concerns which involved to some degree a recognition of the gendering of politics, but also involved a desire to see a social and economic transformation which would improve the lives of the working class more generally. The way in which individuals approached their politics as women, and sought to interpret the category of women in politics, could then be very different.

Varied journeys

If attention is paid to the lives of individual women, then what emerges is a complex narrative in which it is difficult, if not impossible, to categorise women neatly in terms of whether or not they had a 'feminist' approach or were woman-centred in their politics. Instead, it is more helpful to consider the varied choices that individual women made in the course of a lifetime about how to balance their different interests and perspectives. Thus at some moments they might identify with their party, whereas at others with their class or their sex.

Katharine Bruce Glasier provides an interesting example of someone who is rarely identified as a feminist and indeed in her later reminiscences was anxious to identify herself with the cause of the working class rather than with that of women. Looking back from the perspective of 1914, she acknowledged that, like her friend Enid Stacy, she had been interested in women's rights while a student at Cambridge, but the Bristol Socialist Society trained her 'to feel from the start that the vital cleavage of interests all the world over lay between the workers and the idle rich'. It was the influence of Eleanor Marx which then proved decisive:

> Sternly she bade us renounce, if we were to be worthy of the comradeship of the workers of the world, all the older feminist demand for equal political rights with men, until the franchise should be granted to human beings and not to property. It was the price of the workers' trust in us. Middle-class men had hardly used the workers in their battle for freedom. Let middle-class women, at any rate the Socialists among them, strive to make atonement.[104]

Glasier's emphasis on the importance of middle-class women prioritising the needs of the working class was a consistent one – she often urged young, educated women, or BAs as she called them, to understand and value the domestic labour performed by working-class women and also to be sensitive to the underprivileged background of working-class men. In an article urging a code of chivalry for women, she recalled how, at a demonstration, she noted a university trained woman

> using all her powers of wit and social charm ... to bewilder and destroy the power to speak of a Labour MP who, for all his sincere devotion to his cause, was a bit halting in his utterance and unready in his argument. And I, an old woman, felt shame for my younger sister. It was an Unknightly thing to do.[105]

And yet, in many respects, Katharine Bruce Glasier did look at her politics through the lens of gender and also contributed to the identification of women as a particular political group. Around the time of her marriage to John Bruce Glasier she was deeply concerned about the extent to which a woman like herself could continue to play an active propaganda role once she married and had children, and required assurances about this before agreeing to the marriage.[106] After 1906 she wrote a women's column for the *Labour Leader* under the pen name of Iona which raised a wide range of issues concerning women's emancipation and the basis on which they should engage in socialist politics. Her views on women's suffrage were ambivalent. She believed that women should be able to vote and welcomed the ILP's positive reaction to the revival of the women's suffrage campaign in 1905. Recalling how she, along with others, had long ago 'merged our enthusiasm for the emancipation of women in the general work of the Socialist movement', she felt 'the present splendid stand made by the ILP on the broad principle of women's *right* as citizens to the vote, is the highest possible justification of our past faith and action'.[107] Nonetheless, while she continued to express excitement at women's willingness to take independent action for the suffrage, Glasier increasingly began to feel that too much time was being spent on the vote and to question whether it was the key to social change for women.

Katharine Bruce Glasier also took a leading part in the Women's Labour League and increasingly argued that women should take part in politics because of their role as wives and mothers, since this could bring a unique dimension to socialism, rather than because socialism would challenge their unequal position. Nonetheless, she also objected to any restrictions on women's political activity, in particular on the basis of their biology. In 1913, for instance, she wrote to Ramsay MacDonald to complain about his use of the term 'man hungry' to describe militant suffragettes:

> a suggestion for which even I feel ready to strike to defend my sex's honour ... for that reason I grieved a little over your "suffragette" diagnosis, "physiological" ... (you wouldn't like me to define *your* duties in certain education in terms that would apply to mere malehood).[108]

The example of Katharine Bruce Glasier should remind us that socialist women were constantly seeking for ways to move forward on a broad political front; socialism for them meant a transformation in the lives of working-class people, and in particular of working-class women who were the focus of their attention, as well as emancipation for all women and the chance for their own personal self-fulfilment. If both the socialist and the women's movement are looked at through the eyes of socialist women, then a far more complex and many layered view of the relationship between class and gender emerges than the one most often found in mainstream histories.

It has been suggested throughout this chapter that the political journeys of individual socialist women do not fit neatly into the historiography of either the socialist or the women's movement. It has also been argued that more attention should be paid to the ways in which both socialist women themselves and historians have chosen to present their stories. The insights provided by a more complex reading of biography should enable us to move beyond an approach which seeks to classify women into distinct political groups, or to label them as feminist and non-feminist. In particular contexts it can be helpful to look at the similarities between women in their approach to specific issues, but this does not mean that they continued to agree with each other when different issues presented themselves. By taking a broad and flexible view of how to define socialist women, or indeed feminists, it should be possible to gain a more nuanced view of the varied ways in which they engaged in mixed-sex socialist politics. It is the intention of the rest of this book to explore the multi-layered ways in which socialist women tried to develop a political practice which was woman-focused and to gain an understanding of the meanings that they gave to the political category 'women'.

Notes

1. *New Leader*, 5 September 1930.
2. For example, see special issue on auto/biography, *Gender and History*, 2, 1, 1990; L. Stanley, *The Auto/Biographical I. The Theory and Practice of Feminist Auto/Biography*, Manchester, Manchester University Press, 1992; C. Steedman, *Childhood, Culture and Class in Britain: Margaret McMillan, 1860–1939*, London, Virago, 1990; B. Caine, 'Feminist biography and feminist history', *Women's History Review*, 3, 2, 1994.
3. S. Grogan, *Flora Tristan: Life Stories*, London, Routledge, 1998, p. 10.
4. J.W. Scott quoted in ibid., p. 11.
5. J. Belchem and N. Kirk, 'Introduction', in J. Belchem and N. Kirk (eds), *Languages of Labour*, Aldershot, Ashgate, 1997, p. 2.
6. Steedman, *Childhood, Culture and Class*, p. 245.
7. Grogan, *Flora Tristan*, p. 11. The introduction provides a stimulating discussion about approaches to biography writing.
8. S.S. Holton, *Suffrage Days: Stories from the Women's Suffrage Movement*, London, Routledge, 1996, p. 1; B. Caine, *Victorian Feminists*, Oxford, Oxford University Press, 1992.
9. Holton, *Suffrage Days*, p. 1.
10. See the introductions to the following: B. Crick, *George Orwell: A Life*, Harmondsworth, Penguin, 1982; J. Hannam, *Isabella Ford, 1855–1924*, Oxford, Blackwell, 1989; L. Stanley with A. Morley, *The Life and Death of Emily Wilding Davison*, London, Women's Press, 1988; A.V. John, *Elizabeth Robins: Staging a Life, 1862–1952*, London, Routledge, 1995. Also K. Israel, 'Writing inside the kaleidoscope: re-presenting Victorian women public figures', *Gender and History*, 2, 1, 1990.
11. For example, see reports of the Coming of Age Conference, *Labour Leader*, 9 April 1914; J.B. Glasier, *Keir Hardie: The Man and His Message*, London, ILP, 1919; Mrs P. Snowden, *The Real Women's Party*, Glasgow, Reformers' Bookstall, 1920; J. Clayton, *The Rise and Decline of Socialism in Great Britain, 1884–1924*, London, Faber & Gwyer, 1926.
12. In her reminiscences of the early days, however, Katharine Bruce Glasier did include women well beyond and different from the Famous Four. Some were SDF women, although she does not name their organisation (*Labour Leader*, 9 April 1914).
13. See, for example, John Bruce Glasier's speech at Stacy's funeral (*Labour Leader*, 19 September 1903) and Florence Harrison Bell's speech when chairman of the Labour Women's Conference (*New Leader*, 16 May 1924).
14. For example, see Holton, *Suffrage Days*; C. McPhee and A. Fitzgerald (eds), *The Non-Violent Militant: Selected Writings of Teresa Billington-Greig*, London, Routledge & Kegan Paul, 1987; Hannam, *Isabella Ford*; O. Banks, *The Biographical Dictionary of British Feminists, Vol. 1: 1800–1930*, Brighton, Wheatsheaf, 1985.
15. D.B. Montefiore, *From a Victorian to a Modern*, London, Edward Archer, 1927. See also, M. Bondfield, *A Life's Work*, London, Hutchinson, 1948.
16. For examples of autobiographies, see H. Mitchell, *The Hard Way Up. The Autobiography of Hannah Mitchell, Suffragette and Rebel*, London, Virago, 1977; M. Gawthorpe, *Up Hill to Holloway*, Penobscot, Maine, Traversity Press, 1962.
17. S.S. Holton, 'The suffragist and the "average" woman', *Women's History Review*, 1, 1, 1992, p. 20.
18. Ibid., p. 11.
19. D. Howell, *British Workers and the Independent Labour Party, 1888–1906*, Manchester, Manchester University Press, 1983, pp. 330–1.
20. K. Hunt, *Equivocal Feminists. The Social Democratic Federation and the Woman Question, 1884–1911*, Cambridge, Cambridge University Press, 1996, Appendix 5.
21. J. Liddington and J. Norris, *One Hand Tied Behind Us: The Rise of the Women's Suffrage Movement*, London, Virago, 1978, pp. 288–9.

22 Ibid., pp. 289–90.
23 J. Smart, 'Jennie Baines: suffrage and an Australian connection', in J. Purvis and S.S. Holton (eds), *Votes for Women*, London, Routledge, 2000, pp. 247–50. For references to other local studies which identify women who were active in socialist and suffrage politics, see J. Hannam, '"I had not been to London": women's suffrage – a view from the regions', in Purvis and Holton (eds), *Votes for Women*.
24 *Labour Leader*, 27 April 1895; H. Lintell, 'Lily Bell: socialist and feminist, 1894–1898', MA, Bristol Polytechnic, 1990, ch. 6.
25 Hunt, *Equivocal Feminists*, Appendix 5.
26 In a study of 66 female socialists in Manchester Reid found that the largest group, comprising 16 per cent, were schoolteachers (C.A.N. Reid, 'The origins and development of the Independent Labour Party in Manchester and Salford, 1880–1914', PhD, University of Hull, 1981, Appendix 11). See also C. Collins, 'Women and Labour politics in Britain, 1893–1932', PhD, London School of Economics, 1991, ch. 2.
27 For details of Snowden and Gawthorpe, see Banks, *Biographical Dictionary of British Feminists*.
28 J.M. Balshaw, 'Suffrage, solidarity and strife: political partnerships and the women's movement, 1880–1930', PhD, University of Greenwich, 1999, ch. 5.
29 *Labour Leader*, 2 June 1894; D. Neville, *To Make Their Mark: The Women's Suffrage Movement in the North East of England, 1900–1914*, History Workshop Trust/North East Labour History Society, Newcastle upon Tyne, 1997, pp. 15, 78; C. Collette, *For Labour and for Women: The Women's Labour League, 1906–18*, Manchester, Manchester University Press, 1989, Appendix 1.
30 Hunt, *Equivocal Feminists*, Appendix 5.
31 K.B. Glasier, *Enid Stacy*, London, ILP, 1924; J. Bellamy and J.A. Schmeichen, 'Hicks, Amelia (Amie) Jane, 1839/40–1917', in J. Bellamy and J. Saville (eds), *Dictionary of Labour Biography*, Vol. 4, London, Macmillan, 1977.
32 Steedman, *Childhood, Culture and Class*, ch. 6.
33 NEC minutes quoted in Collins, 'Women and Labour politics', p. 50.
34 P. Graves, *Labour Women: Women in British Working-Class Politics, 1918–1939*, Cambridge, Cambridge University Press, 1994, pp. 14, 126.
35 Bellamy and Schmeichen, 'Hicks, Amelia (Amie) Jane'; Banks, *Biographical Dictionary of British Feminists*.
36 A. Taylor, *Annie Besant*, Oxford, Oxford University Press, 1992.
37 Banks, *Biographical Dictionary of British Feminists*.
38 A. Linklater, *An Unhusbanded Life*, London, Hutchinson, 1980; M. Mulvihill, *Charlotte Despard: A Biography*, London, Pandora Press, 1989.
39 L. Thompson, *The Enthusiasts: A Biography of John and Katharine Bruce Glasier*, London, Victor Gollancz, 1971; Glasier, *Enid Stacy*; Balshaw, 'Suffrage, solidarity and strife', pp. 146–8.
40 Steedman, *Childhood, Culture and Class*, pp. 20–2, 27–9; D'Arcy Cresswell, *Margaret McMillan: A Memoir*, London, Hutchinson, 1948, pp. 13–31.
41 *Labour Leader*, 1 August 1896; *Forward*, 8 July 1922.
42 For example, see Thompson, *The Enthusiasts*, pp. 71–2; Y. Kapp, *Eleanor Marx: The Crowded Years, 1884–1898*, London, Lawrence & Wishart, 1976, pp. 33–5; Steedman, *Childhood, Culture and Class*, ch. 7.
43 D. Rubinstein, *Before the Suffragettes: Women's Emancipation in the 1890s*, Brighton, Harvester, 1986, pp. 85–7; M. Beetham, *A Magazine of Her Own: Domesticity and Desire in the Women's Magazine, 1800–1914*, London, Routledge, 1996, pp. 128–31.
44 M. Vicinus, *Independent Women: Work and Community for Single Women, 1850–1920*, London, Virago, 1985, Introduction; Rubinstein, *Before the Suffragettes*.
45 Steedman, *Childhood, Culture and Class*, p. 122.

46 J. Liddington, *The Life and Times of a Respectable Rebel. Selina Cooper, 1864–1946*, London, Virago, 1984, chs 5, 7. Socialist groups also supported each other's candidates for elections. The Limehouse ILP, for example, supported Annie Thompson of the SDF when she stood for the Limehouse School Board, while Rose Jarvis of the SDF was supported by the ILP when she stood for the Hackney School Board (*Labour Leader*, 14 July, 15 September 1894).
47 J.R. MacDonald, *Margaret Ethel MacDonald*, London, Hodder & Stoughton, 4th edn, 1913, pp. 112–13, 137–8; Bondfield, *A Life's Work*, pp. 32–3; K.B. Glasier, 'The Part Women Played in Founding the ILP', *Labour Leader*, 9 April, 1914.
48 S. Yeo, 'A new life: the religion of socialism in Britain, 1883–1896', *History Workshop Journal*, 4, 1977, pp. 35–6.
49 For Agnes Close, see Hannam, *Isabella Ford*, pp. 62–3, 80.
50 J. Saville and J.A. Schmeichen, 'MacDonald, Margaret Ethel Gladstone (1870–1911)', in J. Bellamy and J. Saville (eds), *Dictionary of Labour Biography*, Vol. 6, London, Macmillan, 1982; G. Holloway, 'A common cause? Class dynamics in the industrial women's movement, 1888–1918', PhD, University of Sussex, 1995.
51 E.C. DuBois, 'Woman suffrage and the Left: an international socialist-feminist perspective', *New Left Review*, 186, 1991, pp. 29–34; L.J. Rupp, *Worlds of Women: The Making of an International Women's Movement*, Princeton, NJ, Princeton University Press, 1997, pp. 34–6.
52 *Illustrated Report of the Proceedings of the Workers' Congress held in London July 1896*, 1896, p. 84.
53 *Justice*, 13 October 1894.
54 Collins, 'Women and Labour politics', Abstract.
55 K. Hunt, 'Journeying through suffrage: the politics of Dora Montefiore', in C. Eustance, J. Ryan and L. Ugolini (eds), *A Suffrage Reader: Charting Directions in British Suffrage History*, London, Leicester University Press, 2000.
56 D.N. Chew, *Ada Neild Chew: The Life and Writings of a Working Woman*, London, Virago, 1982.
57 Banks, *Biographical Dictionary of British Feminists*; B.D. Vernon, *Ellen Wilkinson*, London, Croom Helm, 1982.
58 Hunt, *Equivocal Feminists*, Appendix 5; D.E. Martin, 'Macarthur, Mary (1880–1921)', in J. Bellamy and J. Saville (eds), *Dictionary of Labour Biography*, Vol. 2, London, Macmillan, 1974.
59 A. Wiltsher, *Most Dangerous Women. Feminist Peace Campaigners of the Great War*, London, Pandora Press, 1985.
60 B. Winslow, *Sylvia Pankhurst. Sexual Politics and Political Activism*, London, UCL Press, 1996, ch. 4.
61 S. Fleming and G. Dallas, 'Jessie', *Spare Rib*, 32, February 1975; J. Liddington, *The Long Road to Greenham: Feminism and Anti-Militarism in Britain since 1820*, London, Virago, 1989, pp. 111–13; L. Leneman, *A Guid Cause: The Women's Suffrage Movement in Scotland*, Edinburgh, Mercat Press, 1995, Appendix 2.
62 Hunt, *Equivocal Feminists*, Appendix 5; K. Weller, *'Don't Be a Soldier!' The Radical Anti-War Movement in North London, 1914–18*, London, Journeyman, 1985.
63 W. Kendall, *The Revolutionary Movement in Britain, 1900–1929*, London, Weidenfeld & Nicolson, 1969; R. Challinor, *The Origins of British Bolshevism*, London, Croom Helm, 1977; Winslow, *Sylvia Pankhurst*.
64 M. Francis, 'Labour and gender', in D. Tanner, P. Thane and N. Tiratsoo (eds), *Labour's First Century*, Cambridge, Cambridge University Press, 2000, p. 196.
65 Liddington, *Long Road to Greenham*, p. 113.
66 Liddington, *Long Road to Greenham*, pp. 111, 113–16, 123–4; ILP Annual Conference Reports.

67 Liddington, *Long Road to Greenham*, pp. 112–13, 122–4; H. Crawfurd, 'Autobiography', unpublished typescript, National Museum of Labour History, CP/IND/MISC/10.
68 Liddington, *Long Road to Greenham*, p. 130.
69 Ibid., p. 122.
70 Liddington, *The Life and Times of a Respectable Rebel*, pp. 306–7; p. 498, fn. 20.
71 Vernon, *Ellen Wilkinson*, pp. 63–4.
72 Banks, *Biographical Dictionary of British Feminists*; W.F. Stella Browne, 'One of our liberators: Dorothy Jewson', *Critic and Guide*, August 1925. We are grateful to Lesley Hall for this reference.
73 P. Hollis, *Jennie Lee: A Life*, Oxford, Oxford University Press, 1997, pp. 38–9.
74 P. Graves, 'An experiment in women-centered socialism: labour women in Britain', in H. Gruber and P. Graves (eds), *Women and Socialism. Socialism and Women. Europe between the Two World Wars*, Oxford, Berghahn, 1998, p. 203.
75 J.H. Quataert, 'Unequal partners in an uneasy alliance: women and the working class in Imperial Germany', in M.J. Boxer and J.H. Quataert (eds), *Socialist Women: European Socialist Feminism in the Nineteenth and Early Twentieth Centuries*, New York, Elsevier, 1978, p. 117.
76 As argued in Chapter 1, men and women were often encouraged, in particular by the ILP, to explain why they became socialists. For example, see J. Clayton (ed.), *Why I Joined the Independent Labour Party*, Leeds, Leeds ILP, c.1896; series on 'How I became a Socialist' in *Forward*, July 1907 and *Labour Leader*, July 1912.
77 Steedman, for example, notes how theories of femininity in the nineteenth century could enable women to 'operate politically across a wide arena' (*Childhood, Culture and Class*, p. 249). See also M. Cross, 'Flora Tristan's socialist propaganda in provincial France, 1843–1844', in B. Taithe and T. Thornton (eds), *Propaganda: Political Rhetoric and Identity, 1300–2000*, Stroud, Sutton, 1999. Cross notes how Tristan made 'use of her identity as a sister or mother figure to preach union and fraternity', p. 159.
78 K. Hunt, 'Making socialist woman: politicisation, gender and the SDF, 1884–1911', paper to Ninth Berkshire Conference on the History of Women, Vassar College, 1993; Hunt, *Equivocal Feminists*, pp. 197–203.
79 Hunt, *Equivocal Feminists*, Appendix 5.
80 *New Leader*, 18 July 1924; *Labour Leader*, 1 May 1913.
81 Liddington and Norris, *One Hand Tied Behind Us*, p. 125.
82 Chew, *Ada Neild Chew*, p. 14.
83 *Leeds Weekly Citizen*, 16 January 1914; Hannam, *Isabella Ford*, p. 80.
84 J. Woollcombe, 'Julia Varley: A lifelong campaigner', *The Gateway*, 3, 14, 1930; J. Varley, 'Yesterday and Today', *The Record*, March 1931; Hunt, *Equivocal Feminists*, Appendix 5.
85 Julia Varley, 'Yesterday and Today', *The Record*, quoted in J.B. Thurlow, 'Julia Varley, 1871–1952', unpublished manuscript, University of Sussex, 2000, p. 8.
86 *Labour Leader*, 19 May 1894.
87 *Labour Leader*, 1 May 1913.
88 Banks, *Biographical Dictionary of British Feminists*; Gawthorpe, *Uphill to Holloway*.
89 Holton, *Suffrage Days*, p. 119.
90 Holton, 'The suffragist and the "average" woman', p. 13. Other accounts also emphasise the importance of women's experience of family life, in particular when children and adolescents, in explaining their later interest in socialism and feminism. For example, see the chapters by Ellen Wilkinson and Sylvia Pankhurst in M. Oxford (ed.), *Myself When Young*, London, Muller, 1938.
91 *New Leader*, 4 March 1927.
92 *New Leader*, 23 September 1927.
93 Vernon, *Ellen Wilkinson*, pp. 20–1.

94 For a discussion of the way in which suffrage autobiographies were influenced by the context of the 1920s and 1930s, see H. Kean, 'Searching for the past in present defeat: the construction of historical and political identity in British feminism in the 1920s and 1930s', *Women's History Review*, 3, 1, 1994; L. Mayhall, 'Creating the "suffragette spirit": British feminism and the historical imagination', *Women's History Review*, 4, 3, 1995.
95 Bondfield, *A Life's Work*, pp. 81–7.
96 Banks, *Biographical Dictionary of British Feminists*, p. 32.
97 There is little consistency to the way in which socialist women are labelled in secondary texts. Thus Margaret Bondfield and Mary Macarthur are both included in Banks, *Biographical Dictionary of British Feminists*, whereas Katharine Bruce Glasier and Margaret McMillan are not. Brian Harrison, on the other hand, considers the very different Labour women MPs Margaret Bondfield, Ellen Wilkinson and Susan Lawrence to be feminists because they 'did much to advance women's interests' (B. Harrison, *Prudent Revolutionaries: Portraits of British Feminists between the Wars*, Oxford, Clarendon, 1987, p. 125).
98 *Yorkshire Factory Times*, 1 November 1889.
99 Clayton (ed.), *Why I Joined the Independent Labour Party*, p. 5.
100 *Labour Leader*, 1 May 1913; *Leeds Weekly Citizen*, 12 June 1914.
101 *Labour Leader*, 11 July 1912.
102 Margaret McMillan, *Life of Rachel McMillan*, Dent, 1927, p. 85, quoted in Steedman, *Childhood, Culture and Class*, p. 133.
103 Steedman, *Childhood, Culture and Class*, p. 133.
104 *Labour Leader*, 9 April 1914.
105 *Labour Leader*, 2 October 1913.
106 Thompson, *The Enthusiasts*, pp. 79–80; letter from Katharine St John Conway to John Bruce Glasier, 18 May 1893, Glasier Papers, Sidney Jones Library, Liverpool University, 1.1. 1893/30.
107 *Labour Leader*, 20 January 1905.
108 Letter from Katharine Bruce Glasier to Ramsay MacDonald quoted in Collette, *For Labour and for Women*, pp. 148–9.

3

CONSTRUCTING THE WOMAN QUESTION

The rhetoric of socialism emphasised that it was a 'universal and emancipatory ideology' which included women and men on an equal basis. In the late nineteenth and early twentieth centuries, however, the politics of socialist organisations were gendered in theory and in practice, which served to marginalise women and their concerns.[1] Nonetheless, many of those women who became socialists in this period were determined to ensure that socialist claims of universality should not remain empty rhetoric and contested women's marginality in the movement. Although influenced by the arguments put forward by the contemporary women's movement about the oppression of women as a sex, they sought to approach the issues raised from a socialist perspective and to ensure that it was the socialist movement which gained the allegiance of working-class women. From the late 1880s onwards, therefore, the Woman Question was debated extensively within socialist groups, both in Britain and in the rest of Europe. The challenge they faced was to develop a theoretical framework for understanding women's distinct social, economic and political position within the capitalist system which could be integrated with an analysis based on class.

The key socialist texts which provided a framework for this debate were produced by Engels and Bebel, and these have been the subject of extensive discussion by historians and social scientists.[2] Far less attention has been paid to the writings of socialist women and yet they, too, sought to develop a theory which could make sense of gender, as well as class, inequalities and oppression. In so doing, they contested prevailing definitions of the nature and meaning of socialism. Although socialist women all drew attention to the importance of gender and sought to challenge masculine definitions of socialism, they disagreed with each other as well as with male socialists about what a woman-focused socialism would look like and over the meaning of women's emancipation. The aim of this chapter is to examine the arguments put forward by socialist women and to identify differences between them. It will be suggested that these differences, as well as changes in the perspective of individual women over time, need to be understood within their specific historical context and also in the context of the personal experience of the woman putting them forward.[3]

Engels and Bebel

Marxists were particularly influenced by Bebel's *Woman under Socialism* (1879) and Engels' *The Origin of the Family, Private Property and the State* (1884), which 'attempted to fill the obvious gaps in Marx's thinking about women's subordination and the means by which it would be overcome'.[4] Engels' interest was in the family, rather than in women's subordination, but his argument that class society and women's oppression had the same origin in the growth of private property, which belonged to the male, provided the cornerstone of the Second International's understanding of the Woman Question.[5] Engels made a distinct contribution to feminist theory with his view that women's oppression had an economic cause and that the family changed over time, taking a different form in various societies. He then added to his economic analysis by using the concept of the sex/class analogy. He suggested that 'the first class oppression coincides with that of the female sex by the male', since within the family 'he is the bourgeois, and the wife represents the proletariat'.[6] This analogy was never explored systematically – for instance, Engels simply assumed that both forms of oppression were at base economic and would cease with the end of class society – but his arguments were accepted by Bebel and incorporated into subsequent editions of his book.

Bebel in particular recognised that women suffered from sex as well as class oppression. He sympathised with the aims of the women's movement and argued that women should take an active part in struggling for their own emancipation rather than waiting until after the revolution. He also believed that women had a right to work and that domestic labour should be socialised so that they could exercise more choice. In that context he made an important contribution to debates about 'women's nature' by arguing against the idea that women had a 'natural calling' to raise families. Instead he explored the social construction of gender and claimed that 'the domination of women by men was rooted not in biology but in history and was thus capable of resolution in *history*'.[7] Nonetheless, in practice neither he nor Engels mounted a serious challenge to the sexual division of labour.

The arguments of Engels and Bebel provided the framework within which the Second International debated the Woman Question. Bebel's book, for instance, went into many German editions before 1914, was translated into English and widely reviewed in the socialist press, including the *Clarion*, *Justice* and the *Labour Leader*.[8] And yet there was an ambivalence at the centre of Bebel's construction of the Woman Question. By raising the subject, he ensured that sex oppression would become an issue for socialists. On the other hand, by also asserting the primacy of class he enabled women's concerns to be marginalised within socialism. The implications for socialists of his argument were clear – 'in a sense, there was no sex question under capitalism, only one of class, and to engage in sex issues, that is feminism, would only delay the achievement of socialism and thus the resolution of the woman question'.[9] Thus a space was created to debate the Woman Question, but socialists could take up multiple positions on the subject since sex oppression was not seen as a defining issue for socialist politics. There was certainly no question of being expelled from socialist groups for expressing hostility or indifference to any aspect of the Woman Question.

This ambivalence affected both the way in which women's position was theorised by British socialist groups and also arguments about strategy. If sex oppression could be subsumed in class oppression, then it could be argued that women's emancipation should wait until after the achievement of socialism. Moreover, non-economic issues were often perceived as 'fads' which detracted from key areas of socialist struggle, while the oppression of women by men was sidestepped since it threatened to undermine class solidarity.

Debating the Woman Question in the 1880s and 1890s

During the 1880s and 1890s British socialist groups all expressed a complex range of arguments around the Woman Question. Since the SDF's view of socialism was an orthodox Marxist one, it is hardly surprising that it saw the crucial divide in society as economic and class-based while everything else, including women's emancipation, was seen as peripheral. In addition, men such as Harry Quelch and Belfort Bax, who had considerable power to influence opinion because of their access to the party newspaper *Justice*, were particularly antagonistic. Bax was overtly misogynistic in his views, claiming that women were inherently inferior and liable to hysteria, and therefore not as fit as men for 'political, administrative or judicial functions'.[10] And yet Karen Hunt has shown that the SDF as a whole should not be characterised by these attitudes.[11] A range of different views were expressed in *Justice* and women's emancipation was the subject of a lively debate. On the other hand, the SDF did not take an official stand on the Woman Question since it was seen as an issue of conscience. A variety of arguments, including those of Bax, were therefore acceptable.

In contrast, the ILP drew inspiration for its socialism from diverse political sources which ranged from Marxism to radical liberalism, and its views on the Woman Question were just as likely to be influenced by Ruskin, William Morris and Edward Carpenter as by Engels and Bebel.[12] The ILP criticised capitalism as immoral and inefficient, and it was assumed that the transition to socialism would be achieved through gradual political change rather than through class struggle. Emphasis was placed instead on the importance of persuading all members of the community to reject the injustices of capitalism in favour of a cooperative commonwealth. Socialism was defined in broad terms as bringing a transformation of personal relationships and new social, moral and artistic possibilities as well as material benefits.[13] In this context it was far more acceptable for the ILP at an official level to be supportive of women's rights and one of its leaders, Keir Hardie, was a stalwart campaigner for women's suffrage.

Nonetheless, in practice the commitment of the ILP to 'women's emancipation' was also ambivalent. The *Labour Leader* did not publish overtly misogynistic statements or arguments against women receiving political and economic equality, but it was clear that the main audience to be addressed were working men. Moreover, the ILP did not put forward very specific policies or give priority to issues of particular relevance to women. In common with the SDF there was a tendency to see non-economic issues as marginal questions which could be addressed once socialism had been achieved.[14] Indeed, the party was always reluctant to question existing gender divisions in the workplace and in the home and increasingly came to focus on women's suffrage as the measure of its commitment to women's equality and women's emancipation.

Socialist women's voice

Not all socialist women were prepared to accept such views without a challenge or to wait until 'after the revolution' to deal with issues which seemed relevant to women. They sympathised with Margaretta Hicks of the SDF, who thought that this 'would be worse than waiting for heaven. Unless we do and say something now we shall all be dead and buried before any improvement is made'.[15] Socialist women sought to ensure that debates about woman's nature, the social construction of gender and the meaning of women's emancipation would not just be left to the women's movement but would be placed on the socialist agenda.

In particular, socialist women contested the argument that women's issues were peripheral to the class struggle and questioned socialist rhetoric of equality. By asking what a woman-focused socialism would look like, they not only sought to include women in a pre-existing framework but began to reconfigure the nature of socialism itself. Thus some socialist women challenged the way in which socialism privileged production over consumption (see Chapter 6), while others argued that 'personal' issues such as marriage, family relationships and birth control should be seen as political questions which were central, rather than peripheral, to the socialist project.

Nevertheless, it was not always easy for socialist women to find a space in which to express their views. They often used poetry, short stories and novels to explore controversial questions such as personal relationships, marriage and sexuality. It may have been more acceptable in a movement based on the male worker and class exploitation to use the genre of fiction to provide a critique of marriage and to raise the possibility of independence for women.[16] Chris Waters suggests that, in the 1890s in particular, socialist women sought through their fiction to 'undermine deeply entrenched beliefs that held the "political" to be distinct from the "personal" and that marginalized the latter'.[17] Socialist women certainly saw their different forms of writing as an integral part of their role as propagandists. Waters notes, for instance, that Isabella Ford saw the rousing of discontent as one of the central tasks of her novels, while Katharine Bruce Glasier claimed that her novels were works of propaganda which aimed to awaken her readers' minds to the necessity of working to alleviate suffering.[18]

Although novels and short stories, in particular those which emphasised romance, were seen by many male socialists as a diversion from the real political struggle, they provided an important space to imagine different relationships between men and women and new gender roles. Isabella Ford's novels were directed at a middle-class audience, but other authors used romance and sentimentality to appeal to working-class women. Ethel Carnie Holdsworth, a former mill worker and daughter of an active SDF member, was a prolific writer of novels, stories, poems and journalistic items. Pamela Fox suggests that she used her romantic fiction to explore the revolutionary potential of women and to critique gender relations while at the same time refusing to 'deny the importance of love itself'.[19] Moreover, her writings, along with those of Katharine Bruce Glasier, were sold at a price that working-class women could afford.

Socialist women also used their positions as journalists to examine a range of issues arising from women's involvement in socialist politics and to challenge the conventional separation made between public and private life. In the 1890s, however, they were more likely to explore these themes through papers such as the *Clarion* and the *Labour Prophet*, the official organ of the Labour Church, which were not attached to specific socialist parties.[20] The official newspapers of the ILP and the SDF were edited and controlled largely by men and it was difficult for women to find a voice, although they frequently expressed their views through letters and, in some instances, short articles.[21] Women often combined fiction and non-fiction in their journalism. It was common, for instance, to present ideas through a dialogue between two fictional characters, a device used by Enid Stacy when debating women's potential for political activity.[22] Carolyn Steedman suggests that Margaret McMillan developed a genre of 'fictional allegory', in particular when discussing working-class childhood, in which she conveyed intense emotions in accounts which were essentially reportage of 'factual' observations, while Katharine Bruce Glasier was also skilled in engaging with the emotions of her readers.[23] It was the development of women's columns, however, which provided a regular space for women to analyse and debate a broad range of issues arising from the Woman Question.[24] The main columns included 'Matrons and Maidens' (1894–8), edited by 'Lily Bell'; 'Our Women's Outlook' (1906–9), edited by 'Iona' in the *Labour Leader*; 'Our Woman's Letter' (1895–1911) by 'Julia Dawson' in the *Clarion*; and 'Our Women's Circle' in *Justice*.[25] The women's column in *Justice* was not established until 1907 and its best-known editor was Dora Montefiore, who took over the column between 1909 and 1910. She wanted to use her column to 'concentrate on the special side of Socialist propaganda, as it affects women, and interpret everyday events from the standpoint of Social Democracy' and hoped that it would 'voice the demands and aspirations of socialist women'.[26] The way in which gender and class questions were conceptualised differed from column to column, as did the audience to which the columns were addressed, but to a greater or lesser extent they all challenged the masculinist rhetoric and practice of socialism.

Gendering socialism

It is difficult to disentangle women's attempts to develop a theoretical understanding of the relationship between feminism and socialism from their response to particular issues and to current political debates. For example, the Edith Lanchester case, when a young SDF member was committed to an asylum by her male relatives for living in a 'free love' union with a working-class man, led to a lengthy debate in the socialist press on the nature of marriage and the desirability of 'free love'.[27] Socialist women differed among themselves on the issue. Edith Lanchester argued that 'free love' unions were a higher form of marriage, where a woman would no longer be a man's property or under his control. Instead marriage would be a union of souls which would not need to be endorsed by a public ceremony.[28] Her views were greeted sympathetically by Caroline Martyn and Lily Bell, although Julia Dawson warned that freedom could bring its own chains and that bad marriage laws were better than none at all.[29]

Male writers in the socialist press expressed a similar variety of opinions, but socialist women added a different perspective. They insisted that the marriage question was a political issue which should form an integral part of the current socialist agenda rather than be left to one side until the achievement of a socialist society.[30] They also focused on the gender implications of the debate. Lily Bell, for example, agreed with those who took a libertarian view and who criticised contemporary morality, but also pointed to the way in which the case raised questions about whether women should be seen as the property of men and therefore subject to their will. She concluded that the key issue was 'the right of every woman to independent individual action, uncontrolled by her male relatives' and that this was more important than the specific debate about 'free love'.[31]

Socialist women did not just react to debates on specific issues, but also worked out their ideas in pamphlets and articles which provided space for lengthier discussion.[32] In the 1880s and 1890s they were concerned to differentiate their theoretical and strategic position from that of the 'bourgeois women's movement' with its liberal framework of ideas. Although they agreed that women should have equal rights with men on the grounds of natural justice, socialist women emphasised the material basis of women's subordination, which was rooted in the capitalist system. Thus they argued that it was only through socialism that women could achieve their full emancipation, since only socialism would provide a solution both to social wrongs and also to sex and class oppression. Quataert suggests that this contrasted with the aim of the women's movement, which was to 'assimilate females into the capitalist state as equal and responsible citizens'.[33]

Although Eleanor Marx is usually viewed as unsympathetic to the demand for women's emancipation, she was responsible for drawing the writings of European socialists on the Woman Question to the attention of a wider audience. She reviewed Bebel's book for *Commonweal* and, with Edward Aveling, for the *Westminster Review*.[34] Marx and Aveling agreed with Bebel that the Woman Question was largely one of economics and echoed his arguments that both prostitution and the difficulties faced by women in bourgeois marriage had an economic cause. They were particularly impressed by the way in which Bebel discussed the social construction of gender. Eleanor Marx welcomed his argument that 'if woman is an inferior creature today, she is only, like the proletarian, a victim of the circumstances in which she is placed' and therefore it should not be assumed that she 'is never by any chance capable of such greatness as a man'.[35] Moreover, Marx and Aveling went further than Bebel in giving some recognition to the patriarchal power of men over women.

Eleanor Marx also helped to publicise the ideas of Clara Zetkin to a British audience by reporting her speeches in *Justice*. Zetkin had an eminent position in the German Social Democratic Party and also within the Second International. From 1889 onwards she sought to build on the work of Engels and Bebel in a series of articles and key speeches at international congresses. Zetkin accepted that women were subjugated by men as well as by capitalism, but sought to differentiate between women on the basis of their class position. Although sympathetic to middle-class women who were frustrated by the restrictions on their lives and who demanded economic, social and intellectual independence, she argued that these demands were not necessarily of benefit to all women. Proletarian women already had some economic independence because they had been drawn into paid work, but in a capitalist system which treated them as cheap labour this was exacted at a price – 'neither as a person nor as a woman or wife does she have the possibility of living a full life as an individual'.[36] Thus women could only achieve liberation if they worked alongside the men of their class for the socialist revolution. Zetkin did alter her views over time, putting less emphasis on the importance of women's labour when it became apparent that it was the wives and daughters of SPD men who were joining the socialist movement in large numbers rather than women workers. Nonetheless, 'class not sex ultimately was seen to determine a woman's existence'.[37]

'Women first and socialists afterwards'

The prevailing view in most studies of the socialist movement is that when a conflict arose women put their socialism and their class interests first.[38] On closer examination, however, it is apparent that socialist women adopted a broader range of positions than this would imply. Many were concerned that women's subordination might become subsumed or forgotten altogether in an analysis based solely on class exploitation. Lily Bell stood at one end of the spectrum when she declared that:

> I hope our socialist women will never forget that they are 'women first and socialists afterwards', being socialists simply because through Socialism they hope to find fuller outlet for their womanhood; and as

womanhood cannot evolve truly except in freedom, therefore it is our *first* duty to see that its man made barriers are removed.[39]

Dora Montefiore, on the other hand, gave more primacy to the class struggle and criticised feminists who 'try to stir up a sex-war instead of preaching class-war', but she differed from many members of the SDF in wanting to ensure that women had an equal place within the organisation and was not prepared to subordinate women's interests every time there was a clash of views.[40] In trying to persuade other socialists of the importance of achieving universal adult suffrage, she argued that 'the principle of sex equality in political matters is necessarily involved in Social Democracy; and that as class distinctions gradually and evolutionally disappear, so sex distinctions … will also disappear'.[41]

Yet others, including Isabella Ford, tried to ensure that neither class nor sex was given the greatest emphasis and believed that the two could be integrated within socialist theory and practice. In common with many other members of the ILP, Ford disliked any emphasis on class conflict and assumed that men and women from all classes would be drawn to socialism once they realised the injustices and immorality which lay at the heart of the capitalist system.[42]

Socialist women used the term class in very different ways. Both Dora Montefiore of the SDF and Katharine Bruce Glasier of the ILP emphasised class in their speeches and writing. But for Dora Montefiore this was because she shared the SDF view that class struggle would be the means to achieve socialism, whereas for Katharine Bruce Glasier it was because she believed that middle-class men and women were both in a privileged position and their first duty was to help the working class, regardless of their sex. These differences are reflected in the language and tone of their writings. In explaining why she had agreed to edit a women's column in *Justice*, Dora Montefiore argued that 'women comrades must remember that we have a bourgeois press organised to misrepresent, and in order, therefore to keep clear the vital issue of the class struggle, we need every week … a re-statement and re-interpretation, from the point of view of the interests of the working man and woman'.[43] By contrast, Katharine Bruce Glasier wrote in emotional and sentimental terms about her decision to emphasise the needs of the working class rather than women's rights:

> And joyfully we early women workers in the I.L.P. who had in any way enjoyed privileged conditions, obeyed the call, to receive back in full measure and running over, our reward in the love and faith of our working men and women comrades all over the land.[44]

Others were more willing to discuss the ways in which working-class men oppressed women of their own class and gained material benefits from their subordination at the workplace and in the home. Lily Bell attacked the double standard of morality since the 'subjection of woman and the idea of her inferiority to man are just the outcome of his physical appropriation of her to his use, or rather, to his pleasure'. In urging the need for sex education for girls, she argued that 'ignorance has been the main point men have relied on to keep women in subjection to them'.[45] In a later pamphlet Ethel Snowden also argued that women were much worse off than men since they were 'economically in bondage to capitalism, spiritually to the wrong ideas and sexually to men'.[46] Similar points were made in letters to *Justice*. It was argued by one correspondent, for example, that man treated woman in the same way as capitalists treated both sexes. 'As a rule he is as much opposed to the emancipation of women from his domination as the capitalist is to the emancipation of labour'.[47] A few years later another SDF member claimed that 'the average workman ... regards his wife as a mere housekeeping automaton'.[48] Nonetheless, there was a general reluctance among women socialists to emphasise the potential for antagonism between men and women of the working class. Instead, the tendency was to blame capitalist property relations for leading to women's economic dependence and therefore for turning men into their oppressors within the home.[49]

Women across different socialist groups shared the view that men and women could only be fully human in a society organised along socialist lines, and they drew on a long-standing radical tradition of human rights to argue that it was on the grounds of their humanity that women's concerns should be an integral part of socialism. Writing in the 1890s, Enid Stacy argued that:

> the watchword of the movement in future will, I think, be no longer 'Women's Rights'. The true aim of reformers is to consider neither men's nor women's rights qua men and women, but to secure to each human being such conditions as will conduce to full development as an individual and a useful life of service to the community.[50]

Dora Montefiore reached very similar conclusions a decade later. She believed that the Woman Question had an important place within socialism not because it was a 'feminist dogma', as suggested by Belfort Bax, but because it was a 'human dogma' which was 'part of the great evolutionary demand for the social, economic and political freedom of every human being'.[51]

Caged birds

In the 1880s and 1890s 'new life socialists' aspired to another way of living and, as Sheila Rowbotham suggests in her perceptive study of the period, this provided a context in which women could imagine new gender identities and a new sense of self which was important for attracting women to socialism.[52] This utopian impulse to 'prefigure the future in the present' enabled women to challenge the power of men to decide what the socialist movement was all about, and thus they could help to shape the socialist society which they wished to see.[53] In common with members of the women's movement, socialist women developed a broad conception of women's emancipation – it would mean personal self-fulfilment, the ability to make choices about how women wished to live their lives, freedom from the constraints of conventional views of women's capabilities and an end to legal, economic and educational restrictions. Lily Bell captured the frustrations of many in describing how women's lives as a whole were restricted and constrained. In referring to caged birds she was drawing on an image which had been familiar in women's writing since the eighteenth century.

> I feel ... that we are caged birds. We long for something we know not what, and some pine and die for lack of it, and some go on living without any music in their lives. Is it to be always thus? Nay. Some day we will have the doors of our social prison burst open.[54]

Socialist women's belief in individual freedom and self-fulfilment was tempered, however, by their socialist perspective, which emphasised cooperation with others and collective needs rather than individual rights.[55] Katharine Bruce Glasier, for example, welcomed the opportunities that the socialist movement offered her to have worthwhile work as a propagandist, but also recalled that in the early days 'to many men and women for a time their sense of personal existence was all but lost'.[56] This could lead others to argue that women had duties to the community and to the needs of the socialist state and therefore there was a certain ambivalence in their views about what emancipation would mean for women. Enid Stacy's article on women's rights, published in the influential collection of socialist writings *Forecasts of the Coming Century*, provides a good example of such ambivalence. She praised the women's movement for helping to open up new areas of employment for women and gaining some legal rights, but argued that a wide range of further changes were needed in order to achieve real emancipation, including the right to choose whether or not to have children, full legal and political rights, easier divorce, freedom as workers and protective legislation which would apply to both sexes. She claimed that 'the perfect state will only be reached when each human being is doing the work she can do best, irrespective of hard and fast sex distinctions' and argued that women needed 'the right to their own persons, and the power of deciding whether they will be mothers or not'. On the other hand, she also emphasised the importance of women's role as mothers and suggested that there was a need to harmonise the 'just claims of the individual woman for power to develop and the just claims of the state on behalf of its children'.[57]

Thus socialist women faced a constant dilemma about whether women should take part in civil society as citizens and workers with rights and duties which were the same as men, or whether their special function as mothers entailed social responsibilities which overrode their own self-fulfilment while also enabling them to make a distinctive contribution to public life.[58] To some extent this mirrored debates within the contemporary women's movement,[59] but for socialist women it rested on an acknowledgement of differences between women themselves, in particular on the basis of class, as well as between women and men. Such questions were foregrounded explicitly in debates about whether, and how, women's economic dependence within the family should be addressed and the extent to which economic independence was crucial if women were to join fully in the struggle for socialism. Socialist women reached different conclusions, in particular in relation to specific issues, and their views were influenced both by the political context in which they found themselves and also by the overall theoretical perspective of the socialist organisation to which they belonged.

Marriage, motherhood and the family

In the 1880s and 1890s socialists took part in discussions around prostitution, marriage and women's position in the family, which were matters of considerable interest to contemporaries.[60] Socialists assumed that relationships within marriage had been distorted by women's economic dependence on men and therefore were based not on affection but on material need, which made marriage in many ways akin to prostitution. Emphasis was placed in this period on ending women's economic dependence through paid employment. Annie Besant, for instance, argued that women needed to enter the workplace, both to end their domestic slavery and also to ensure that they would become more class conscious.[61] It was common within the SDF to assume that paid labour would enable women to become involved in the class struggle and also that it was a precondition for their emancipation.[62] It was argued frequently, therefore, that childcare and domestic duties could be undertaken collectively to enable women to take their place within the labour force. Nonetheless, married women's employment was a controversial question and socialist women found themselves having to defend women's right to work. Writing in *Justice*, both Dora Montefiore and Elizabeth Wolstenholme Elmy, a member of the radical wing of the women's movement, not only pointed out that many married women were forced to work through economic pressure, but also argued that they should have an equal right with men to work and to gain economic independence.[63]

Many socialist women were also in this period 'actively searching for a new construction of marriage' which they could practice immediately in their own lives as well as looking forward to a future socialist society.[64] Only a small number of women, including Eleanor Marx and Edith Lanchester were prepared to consider living with men outside marriage. Both Enid Stacy and Katharine St John Conway felt that they had to distance themselves from the Fabian organiser of their lecture tour, W.B. De Mattos, because his views on free love might damage their reputations, while Hannah Mitchell expressed doubts about the propriety of two men and two women sharing a confined space when they travelled in the Clarion Van.[65] On the other hand, both Enid Stacy and Katharine St John Conway did seek a different type of marriage. They agonised for a long time before they married, fearing that it would interfere with their propaganda work and their independence, but were persuaded by the belief that they could form a new kind of partnership which would also help the socialist cause.[66]

Socialist women did not necessarily challenge gender roles within the home itself. Katharine Bruce Glasier wrote in very positive terms about the importance of women performing domestic tasks out of love for their families,[67] while even Hannah Mitchell, who disliked housework, viewed her attitudes as a matter of personal preference, rather than linking them closely into her political analysis of women's oppression.[68] Lily Bell valued family life and domestic concerns and claimed that 'judging from my own feelings in the matter it is only because men have tried to *limit* us to domestic affairs that we are inclined to rebel against them more than we should otherwise do'.[69] Socialist women still tended to see childcare as women's special province. Enid Stacy's husband looked after their child when she went on lecture tours, but she found it difficult to be absent from her son for long periods.[70] John Bruce Glasier, on the other hand, did not play an active role in looking after his children and so Katharine Bruce Glasier, in common with many middle-class women, relied on the services of a working-class woman, former mill worker Jenny Davis, and other members of her family for childcare to enable her to continue with political work.[71] Overall, therefore, socialist women did conceive of a different kind of relationship between the sexes in marriage, but stopped short of a thoroughgoing critique of gender divisons within the family and had few practical suggestions for changing the lives of those women who did not have husbands who were equally committed to change.

After the mid-1890s the ILP in particular increasingly came to emphasise the importance of women's role within the family rather than in paid employment. This was partly as a result of the influence of Morris, Ruskin and Carpenter who, in different ways, stressed the importance of household and family and drew attention to women's 'natural' fulfilment through motherhood.[72] Partly, however, it resulted from the attempt to form an alliance with the trade union movement, which led to support for the notion of a male family wage.[73] After the turn of the century a more general interest in motherhood as important for the well-being of the state and the 'development of the race' reinforced the ideology of separate spheres which equated women with the home and domestic life.[74] The ILP saw the family as central to its vision of a future socialist society, when woman would be freed from the double burden imposed by waged labour and be able to devote all her time to childcare and domestic labour.[75] Katharine Bruce Glasier, for example, expressed these views in her pamphlet *Socialism and the Home*, where she argued that the family would be re-established on a higher plane by socialism.[76]

In the hands of many socialist propagandists, including Katharine Bruce Glasier and Margaret MacDonald, this became a sentimental vision which glided over any potential conflict between the sexes and gave women little choice about their social roles or the achievement of personal and sexual autonomy. Other socialist women such as Enid Stacy, Isabella Ford, Ada Neild Chew, Ethel

Snowden and members of the Fabian Women's Group (FWG) continued to argue that women's right to work should be respected, but they too emphasised the value of motherhood. Enid Stacy argued that 'one of the most important duties a woman can fulfil is to bear and educate the state's future children', while Isabella Ford believed that trained motherhood was vital for the well-being of the community.[77]

Debates around motherhood and the family were also closely intertwined with views about women's nature. In common with their contemporaries in the women's movement, most socialist women believed that women had specific qualities, such as a caring attitude towards others, selflessness and a moral outlook, although there was a certain ambivalence about how these characteristics had been developed. Isabella Ford argued that they were 'in part innate, owing to the share they have in the production of the race' and in part acquired, through women's socialisation in domestic roles.[78] Socialist women emphasised the social construction of gender differences and therefore the potential for them to change. Yet where women lacked confidence and showed little interest in events beyond the home, they also sought to build on those 'feminine' characteristics in developing a political practice. There were considerable differences, however, in the way in which socialist women interpreted the relationship between women's nature and political activism.

At one end of the spectrum, Dora Montefiore was sceptical about the extent to which women would support specific policies simply because they were women. In response to Robert Blatchford's column in the *Woman Worker* which asked how women might prevent war, she thought that 'the answers appeared to me somewhat naive in their absolute belief that women as a sex are opposed to war'.[79] She gave examples from around the world of how women who had been enfranchised supported wars as much as men and argued, therefore, that women would have to be educated to use their votes in the right way. At the other extreme Margaret MacDonald emphasised that women would bring their caring qualities, or 'mother spirit', into politics and would be likely to support social reforms to benefit children and the home. She not only emphasised the importance of women's role within the domestic sphere, but also discouraged their engagement in paid employment.[80] Others, however, were anxious to value the qualities that women derived from the domestic sphere while not seeing this as restricting their opportunities to play a full part in political and economic life. Ada Neild Chew, for instance, advocated that women should have freedom to develop their own potential, including the right of married women to work, but discussed working women who supported their husbands on strike in the following terms: 'So, in her instinctive care for the advancement of the race, she willingly suffers that the men may win'.[81]

For most socialist women there could be positive gains in emphasising women's distinctive qualities, in particular if they were 'to enlarge for themselves and for posterity the limits of the possible'.[82] It was frequently argued, in opposition to those men who saw women as inherently conservative, that women's nature made them likely to accept the tenets of socialism. Isabella Ford, for instance, suggested that woman's subjection had so trained her to think of others rather than herself that it would bring her 'to the problems of the future with a purer aim and a keener insight than is possible for a man'.[83] It was also assumed that women's interest in children and in the home would inspire them to action if they perceived injustice. In discussing the Minority Report on the Poor Law concerning distressed mothers, Annot Robinson claimed that *'this is a woman's battle*. When trouble comes it is the woman who has to "manage" and succour the maimed and distressed'.[84]

Socialist women who argued, to a greater or lesser degree, that the sexes had distinctive characteristics raised the possibility of challenging the values which predominated in the socialist movement. Katharine Bruce Glasier, for example, claimed that:

> Women are not men, and never will be. And while we claim that women should have equal freedom with men to engage in every occupation for which they are capable, no greater reproach can be laid upon womanhood than the assumption that women should aim at men's views and ways of life. Women want freedom to be *citizens and to be women*. They don't want to copy the vices of men – their chewing, smoking, drinking, betting, fighting, and rowdyism at football matches.[85]

She went on to argue that rearing children and attending to the household 'is as noble as working in an office or a factory for an employer'.[86] In practice, however, in a context in which women's issues were marginalised, this could merely reinforce gender divisions in politics as well as in the home. As Caroline Rowan notes, women could pursue 'domestic' questions and avoid conflict over women's paid employment and the family wage. Wherever conflict did arise, it was usually the interests of male workers which predominated.[87]

Economic independence

Socialist women tended to agree that women's economic dependence in the family underpinned their personal, social and sexual subordination to men. There was less agreement, however, about how this could be addressed. A few voices, including that of Ada Neild Chew, called for housework to be better organised and for childcare to be provided on collective lines. It was argued that this would then open up a new field of paid employment for trained mothers and domestic workers.[88] Others sought economic assistance from the state and, in the immediate pre-war years, put forward a wide variety of proposals for some form of allowances. This was in a context in which fears about the health of children and the 'future of the race' had stimulated a more general interest in family poverty.[89] However, socialist women, along with members of the women's movement, were concerned to emphasise the importance of women's economic independence to these demands as well as the potential improvements in child health.

The Fabian Women's Group argued for the endowment of motherhood, which would be part of a broad programme to reform gender relations, including marriage reform. It is significant that the Fabian Society as a whole chose to adopt only the family endowment part of these proposals. The Society used the argument that women's economic independence was vital for socialism, although it could not be supported just because it might help realise individual women's autonomy.[90] SDF women also took an interest in the question. Dora Montefiore, for example, argued that motherhood should be seen as a valuable occupation. By rearing future citizens, mothers were performing a service for the state and were entitled to support and to enjoy economic independence.[91] This prefigured a socialist state in which all contributions to the community would be recognised and remunerated. Similarly, Ethel Snowden argued that in a socialist society women would receive economic support from the state which would enable them to enter marriage freely rather than because of economic necessity.[92] These arguments for economic independence led to considerable fears, in particular among male socialists, that the family wage and 'traditional' relationships within marriage would be undermined. Therefore, the demand for the endowment of motherhood/family allowances was to be a highly contentious one.[93]

Some socialist women, in particular in the pre-war ILP, shared similar fears. The issue of economic assistance for families was debated at annual conferences of the Women's Labour League and many were reluctant to support such a measure. Katharine Bruce Glasier, for example, opposed state maintenance for wives and children on the grounds that this could reduce men's responsibilities for their families. She also argued against the socialisation of housework since this would undermine the personal service aspects and duties of domestic work, replacing them by individualism.[94] From her perspective the well-being of the family, in particular the working-class family, became the focus of attention rather than 'women's emancipation'. This view was shared by Margaret MacDonald, who feared the detrimental effects of family endowment on male responsibilities, while she also opposed married women's work since 'there could be no home life for the child where the mother went to the factory'.[95]

Involvement in the pre-war suffrage movement, however, encouraged many socialist women to place their emphasis on political exclusion as the main cause of women's social and economic subordination and to argue that if women gained the franchise, their economic and social status would be raised. Charlotte Despard, Isabella Ford, Teresa Billington-Greig, Sylvia Pankhurst and Ethel Snowden all claimed that 'political freedom' was necessary before any other changes in women's position could be achieved. They argued that the vote had to be won so that women could fight for socialism on an equal basis with men and that only this would ensure that 'women's emancipation' would be central to the new socialist society.⁹⁶ Isabella Ford also assumed that once women had gained the parliamentary franchise, they would achieve a more equal position within the family.⁹⁷

Citizenship after 1918

The enfranchisement of some women in 1918, coupled with the strengthening of the Labour Party as a force in politics, provided a new context in which socialist women discussed the Woman Question. Their view of the new female citizen was a complex one, in which there was an emphasis both on the shared needs and grievances of men and women as well as a recognition that women still had specific problems to face as a sex. In her influential pamphlet *Socialism for Women*, written to provide eight short talks for women's study circles, the ILP organiser Minnie Pallister, claimed that:

> it is necessary at present to concentrate upon the women's question, because she has been more particularly injured not only by Capitalism, but by many traditions not directly connected with any system of industry. But there is nothing more unjust about the oppression of women than the oppression of men. There should be no 'women's question'. Women as women should have no special privileges, they should be equal alike in privilege and responsibility with men.⁹⁸

She believed that women now had more political and industrial weapons than they had enjoyed in the past, but argued that they still needed to achieve greater economic independence if they were to be able to take a full part in public life on an equal basis with men. Thus, she supported policies which recognised women's different social and economic interests, such as lower subscriptions for married women and separate women's groups in the ILP, as well as advocating family allowances to change women's dependent status within the family.⁹⁹

Indeed both the Labour Party and the ILP used welfare issues such as the provision of better houses, health care and education to appeal to the new women voters.¹⁰⁰ In addition, the ILP officially endorsed the demand for children's allowances as part of its Living Wage campaign against poverty. Welfare goals alone, however, did not necessarily address broader feminist aspirations. This was pointed out by the former suffragette Teresa Billington-Greig in an attack on the Labour Party.

> The promise of socialism as presented to the women boils down to more food, better clothes, houses and equipment. But no fundamental change in their status … the voice of the … Socialist is the voice of the male … nothing for women themselves as human persons: all sorts of

bribes to them as the agents of the male head of the house and *his* children.[101]

Socialist women in the ILP did give their support to the campaign for children's allowances, and they used similar arguments to those of their male contemporaries in emphasising that these would reduce poverty and improve child health and welfare. In addition, however, they also claimed that allowances paid directly to the mother would increase women's independence and personal freedom. Thus Dorothy Jewson argued that:

> In revolt against the insecurity of her home the working-class mother sees in children's allowances a means of using her new political power to save her children from the worst effects of a vicious system. For herself she will gain some recognition from the State of the value of her work in rearing children, and the increased independence that will come from greater security.[102]

Such arguments differentiated socialist women from those Labour Party women who favoured allowances in kind, such as free school meals and clothing for children. Mary Stocks claimed that this was neither 'feminist' nor 'socialist', since women in the home would still be denied the kind of economic freedom enjoyed by women in the labour market.[103]

In attempting to attract women to the ILP, socialist women went beyond the provision of welfare measures and argued that a woman-focused socialism would enable women to develop all their talents as individuals on an equal basis with men. This could only be achieved once women had gained economic as well as political freedom since, as Minnie Pallister argued:

> If a woman can only receive maintenance through her husband and has no direct claim she can never be free in any real sense ... In the past, a woman was always somebody's daughter, or somebody's wife, or somebody's mother. She was legislated for, and thought of *always* as daughter, wife or mother, *never* as just herself .... It is this idea of the necessity of *belonging* to someone, which is slavery ... socialism bestows personal freedom upon women by thinking of them as individuals quite apart from their relationship to men.[104]

She urged the importance of men and women working together to achieve a new life for women which would be 'rich and full, useful and beautiful ... because we believe that only under Socialism can there be any true freedom, morality, or comradeship, we recommend it to the new woman citizen'.[105]

Although socialist women attempted to argue for a broad conception of what a woman-focused socialism would look like, they found it increasingly difficult in the 1920s to get their views across, both in the ILP which emphasised class issues, and in the Labour Party which marginalised women and their concerns.[106] They did manage to raise the issue of women's economic independence in discussions of children's allowances, although this was never the emphasis of ILP debates on the question, but in the far more sensitive area of access to birth control information they invariably emphasised that it was a class and health question rather than one of a woman's right to sexual autonomy, regardless of their personal views on the matter. This approach had some success since the ILP officially gave support to the need for access to birth control at its conference in 1928.[107]

Throughout the late nineteenth and early twentieth centuries, therefore, socialist women made an important contribution to socialist debates around the Woman Question. Although usually characterised as putting socialism and class interests first, their writings show that they adopted a complex range of arguments about the relationship between sex and class, the meaning of women's emancipation and the balance between individual rights and social duties. There was a recognition among women across the ILP and the SDF of the positive gains to be made in emphasising women's distinctive qualities, although they differed in their emphases and in the policies which were put forward. The way in which the Woman Question was theorised was not simply an academic matter but was closely intertwined with political practice. It had an impact on the nature and extent of women's engagement in socialist politics and on the way in which socialist organisations, and also their women members, positioned themselves in relation to specific issues, strategies and tactics.

Notes

1 K. Hunt, 'Fractured universality: the language of British socialism before the First World War', in J. Belchem and N. Kirk (eds), *Languages of Labour*, Aldershot, Ashgate, 1997.
2 For example, see L. Vogel, *Marxism and the Oppression of Women*, London, Pluto, 1983; L. Sargent (ed.), *The Unhappy Marriage of Marxism and Feminism*, London, Pluto, 1981; M. Barrett, 'Marxist-feminism and the work of Karl Marx', in A. Phillips (ed.), *Feminism and Equality*, Oxford, Blackwell, 1987; R. Coward, *Patriarchal Precedents: Sexuality and Social Relations*, London, Routledge & Kegan Paul, 1983, ch. 6; K. Hunt, *Equivocal Feminists. The Social Democratic Federation and the Woman Question, 1884–1911*, Cambridge, Cambridge University Press, 1996, ch. 1.
3 This point is made by J.H. Quataert, 'Unequal partners in an uneasy alliance: women and the working class in Imperial Germany', in M.J. Boxer and J.H. Quataert (eds), *Socialist Women: European Socialist Feminism in the Nineteenth and Early Twentieth Centuries*, New York, Elsevier, 1978, p. 117.
4 S. Rowbotham, *Women in Movement: Feminism and Social Action*, London, Routledge, 1992, p. 141.
5 This discussion of Engels and Bebel is based largely on Hunt, *Equivocal Feminists*, ch. 1.
6 F. Engels, *The Origin of the Family, Private Property and the State*, London, Lawrence & Wishart, 1972, pp. 129, 137.

7 C. Sowerwine, 'The socialist women's movement from 1850 to 1940', in R. Bridenthal, C. Koonz and S. Stuard (eds), *Becoming Visible: Women in European History*, Boston, Houghton Mifflin, 1987, p. 403.
8 For a discussion of the influence of Bebel and Engels on British socialists see Hunt, *Equivocal Feminists*, pp. 29–36.
9 Hunt, *Equivocal Feminists*, p. 29. A. Bebel, *Woman in the Past, Present and Future*, trans. H.B. Adams Walther, London, Modern Press, 1885.
10 *Justice*, 19 October 1895.
11 Hunt, *Equivocal Feminists*, ch. 2.
12 J.S. Lohman, 'Sex or class? English socialists and the woman question, 1884–1914', PhD, Syracuse University, 1979, p. 166.
13 D. Howell, *British Workers and the Independent Labour Party, 1886–1906*, Manchester, Manchester University Press, 1983, ch. 15.
14 L. Ugolini, 'Independent Labour Party men and women's suffrage in Britain, 1893–1914', PhD, University of Greenwich, 1997, ch. 1; J. Hannam, 'Women and the ILP, 1890–1914', in D. James, T. Jowitt and K. Laybourn (eds), *The Centennial History of the Independent Labour Party*, Halifax, Ryburn, 1992.
15 *Justice*, 6 April 1895.
16 Wheedon makes this point for Germany (C. Wheedon, 'The limits of patriarchy: German feminist writers', in H. Forsas-Scott (ed.), *Textual Liberation: European Feminist Writing in the Twentieth Century*, London, Routledge, 1991).
17 C. Waters, 'New women and socialist-feminist fiction: the novels of Isabella Ford and Katharine Bruce Glasier', in A. Ingram and D. Patai (eds), *Discovering Forgotten Radicals: British Women Writers, 1859–1939*, Chapel Hill, University of North Carolina Press, 1993, pp. 26–7.
18 Ibid., p. 26.
19 P.A. Fox, 'Ethel Carnie Holdsworth's "revolt of the gentle": romance and the politics of resistance in working-class women's writing', in Ingram and Patai (eds), *Discovering Forgotten Radicals*.
20 For example, see the series of articles by Enid Stacy, Katharine Bruce Glasier, Caroline Martyn and Isabella Ford in the *Labour Prophet*, 1893 to 1895.
21 A small number of women owned and edited their own newspapers. For example, Annie Besant's *The Link* was published in 1888; Florence Groves' *Chelsea Pick and Shovel* appeared between 1899 and 1901; Margaretta Hicks edited *The Link* 1911–1912, while Sylvia Pankhurst edited the *Women's Dreadnought* and then the *Workers' Dreadnought* from 1914–24.
22 E. Stacy, *Labour Prophet*, February 1894.
23 C. Steedman, *Childhood, Culture and Class in Britain: Margaret McMillan, 1860–1931*, London, Virago, 1990, ch. 7.
24 For a fuller discussion of women's columns, see K. Hunt and J. Hannam, 'Propagandising as socialist women: the case of women's columns in British socialist newspapers, 1884–1914', in B. Taithe and T. Thornton (eds), *Propaganda: Political Rhetoric and Identity*, Stroud, Sutton, 1999.
25 'Lily Bell' was the pseudonym of Isabella Bream Pearce; 'Iona' cloaked the identity of Katharine Bruce Glasier; while 'Julia Dawson' was the pen name of Mrs D. Middleton Worrall.
26 *Justice*, 20 March, 27 March 1909.
27 Hunt, *Equivocal Feminists*, pp. 94–104.
28 *Labour Leader*, 15 February 1896.
29 *Clarion*, 14 August 1897.
30 This view was expressed by Edith Lanchester in a series of meetings which she addressed in 1896. See reports in *Labour Leader*, 15 February 1896; *Justice*, 22 February 1896.

31 *Labour Leader*, 2 November 1895.
32 For example, see E. Stacy, 'A century of women's rights', in E. Carpenter (ed.), *Forecasts of the Coming Century*, Manchester, Labour Press, 1899; I.O. Ford, *Women and Socialism*, London, ILP pamphlet, 2nd edn, 1906; E. Snowden, *The Woman Socialist*, London, George Allen, 1907; D.B. Montefiore, *The Position of Women in the Socialist Movement*, London, Twentieth Century Press, 1909; M. Pallister, *Socialism for Women*, London, ILP, 1925.
33 Quataert, 'Unequal partners', p. 115.
34 *Commonweal*, July 1885; E.M. and E. Aveling, 'The woman question', *Westminster Review*, January 1886.
35 *Commonweal*, July 1885.
36 C. Zetkin quoted in H. Draper and A.G. Lipow, 'Marxist women versus bourgeois feminism', *Socialist Register*, London, Merlin Press, 1976, p. 196.
37 Quataert, 'Unequal partners', p. 116.
38 See, for example, P. Graves, 'Women in British working-class politics, 1883–1939', PhD, University of Pittsburgh, 1989, p. 24; B.S. Anderson and J.P. Zinsser, *A History of Their Own: Women in Europe from Prehistory to the Present*, Vol. II, Harmondsworth, Penguin, 1990, Part IX, ch. 4; Sowerwine, 'The socialist women's movement', pp. 406–7.
39 *Labour Leader*, 13 April 1895.
40 D.B. Montefiore, *Some Words to Socialist Women*, London, Twentieth Century Press, 1908, p. 13.
41 *Social Democrat*, May 1901.
42 Ford, *Women and Socialism*; *Labour Leader*, 13 May 1904.
43 *Justice*, 20 March 1909.
44 *Labour Leader*, 9 April 1914.
45 *Labour Leader*, 30 June 1894.
46 Snowden, *Woman Socialist*, p. 6. See also Teresa Billington who argued that 'in addition to the capitalistic burdens which she shares with men, she bears burdens political, social and economic which he has placed upon her shoulders and shows no eagerness to remove' (*Clarion*, 2 November 1906).
47 *Justice*, 10 August 1895.
48 *Social Democrat*, January 1902, quoted in Lohman, 'Sex or class?', p. 280.
49 For example, see Ford, *Women and Socialism*, 1906, p. 3; Zelda Kahan in *Social Democrat*, December 1909; Sylvia Pankhurst in *Forward*, 25 May 1912; Special Suffrage Supplement, *Labour Leader*, 9 January 1913.
50 Stacy, 'Century of women's rights', p. 101. Quataert also makes this point about Clara Zetkin, who argued that woman was neither 'just a person' nor 'totally female', but 'a full human of the female sex ... with corresponding duties in the family and in public life. To neglect her humanity would cripple a woman's growth as a female and restrict her influence at home ... satisfying her needs as a woman saved her from becoming a "superficial copy of a man"' ('Unequal partners', p. 132).
51 *Social Democrat*, April 1909, p. 151.
52 Rowbotham, *Women in Movement*, p. 130.
53 Ibid., p. 135.
54 *Labour Leader*, 31 March 1894.
55 Sally Alexander suggests that this is a dilemma which feminists and socialists have yet to resolve (S. Alexander, 'Fabian socialism and the "sex relation"', in S. Alexander, *Becoming a Woman and Other Essays in 19th and 20th Century Feminist History*, New York, New York University Press, 1995, p. 169). It was a dilemma which was not confined only to socialists. Liberal women also had to juggle their demands for equal rights with notions of duty to their families and the wider community. See C.

Pateman, 'Feminist critiques of the public/private dichotomy', in A. Phillips (ed.), *Feminism and Equality*, Oxford, Blackwell, 1987.
56 *New Leader*, 18 July 1924.
57 Stacy, 'Century of women's rights', pp. 95–6. Keith Laybourn suggests that there was a split within the ILP between the collectivist/statist approach of the trade unions and a more individualistic approach in which socialism was viewed as a way to release people to enjoy a 'wholesome cultural and social life' (K. Laybourn, *The Rise of Socialism in Britain*, Stroud, Sutton, 1997, p. 36). However, we would argue that socialist women attempted to combine both perspectives and did not see them as mutually exclusive.
58 P. Beals, 'Fabian feminism, gender, politics and culture in London, 1880–1930', PhD , Rutgers University, 1989, p. 213.
59 For a discussion of the debates within the women's movement between what she labels as 'individualist' and 'relational' feminism, see K. Offen, 'Defining feminism: a comparative historical approach', *Signs*, 14, 1, 1988.
60 For a discussion of these concerns see L. Bland, *Banishing the Beast. English Feminism and Sexual Morality, 1885–1914*, Harmondsworth, Penguin, 1995.
61 Lohman, 'Sex or class?', p. 36; *Our Corner*, 1 August 1885.
62 For example, see Zelda Kahan's view, *Social Democrat*, December 1909.
63 *Justice*, 13 September, 25 October 1902.
64 K. Cowman, '"Giving them something to do": how the early ILP appealed to women', in M. Walsh (ed.), *Working Out Gender: Perspectives from Labour History*, Aldershot, Ashgate, 1999, p. 128.
65 Enid Stacy to Edward Pease, 13 May 1892, Glasier Papers, Sidney Jones Library, Liverpool University. For Hannah Mitchell, see J. Liddington and J. Norris, *One Hand Tied Behind Us: The Rise of the Women's Suffrage Movement*, London, Virago, 1978, pp. 133–4.
66 Cowman, '"Giving them something to do"', p. 126; J. Balshaw, 'Suffrage, solidarity and strife: political partnerships and the women's movement, 1880–1930', PhD, University of Greenwich, 1999, pp. 155–9.
67 For example, see her column devoted to the 'joys of spring cleaning', *Labour Leader*, 23 March 1906.
68 T. Davis, M. Durham, C. Hall, M. Langan and D. Sutton, '"The public face of feminism": early twentieth century writings on women's suffrage', in Centre for Contemporary Cultural Studies, *Making Histories: Studies in History Writing and Politics*, London, Hutchinson, 1982, p. 315.
69 *Labour Leader*, 4 August 1894.
70 Cowman, '"Giving them something to do"', p. 130.
71 Balshaw, 'Suffrage, solidarity and strife', pp. 169–70.
72 Lohman, 'Class or sex?', pp. 169–75.
73 Ugolini, 'ILP men', ch. 2.
74 A. Davin, 'Imperialism and motherhood', *History Workshop Journal*, 5, 1978.
75 Hannam, 'Women and the ILP', pp. 213–14.
76 K.B. Glasier, *Socialism and the Home*, London, ILP, 1909.
77 Stacy, 'Century of women's rights', pp. 95–6; Ford, *Women and Socialism*, 1906 edn, p. 11.
78 Ford, *Women and Socialism*, 1904 edn, p. 13.
79 *Justice*, 27 March 1909.
80 C. Rowan, '"Mothers vote Labour!" The state, the labour movement and working-class mothers, 1900–1918', in R. Brunt and C. Rowan (eds), *Feminism, Culture and Politics*, London, Lawrence & Wishart, 1982, pp. 74–5.
81 Special Suffrage Supplement, *Labour Leader*, 9 January 1913.

82 J.W. Scott, 'The imagination of Olympe de Gouges', in E.J. Yeo (ed.), *Mary Wollstonecraft and 200 Years of Feminisms*, London, Rivers Oram, 1997, p. 45.
83 Ford, *Women and Socialism*, 1904 edn, p. 14. See also E. Wolstenholme Elmy, *Woman – The Communist*, London, ILP, 1904, who argued that women were more naturally suited to a cooperative society because of their maternal and familial roles.
84 *Labour Leader*, 1 July 1910.
85 *Labour Leader*, 16 February 1906.
86 Ibid.
87 C. Rowan, 'Women in the Labour Party, 1906–1920', *Feminist Review*, 12, 1982, p. 77.
88 *Common Cause*, 6 March 1914. The SDF also supported communal childcare, but with the aim of teaching children 'collective citizenship' rather than so that women could achieve personal freedom (Rowan, ' "Mothers vote Labour!" ', p. 64).
89 S. Pedersen, *Family, Dependence, and the Origins of the Welfare State: Britain and France, 1914–1945*, Cambridge, Cambridge University Press, 1993; J. Macnicol, *The Movement for Family Allowances, 1918–1945: A Study in Social Policy Development*, London, Heinemann, 1980.
90 Beals, 'Fabian feminism', pp. 183, 197; S. Alexander, 'The Fabian Women's Group, 1908–52', in Alexander, *Becoming a Woman*, pp. 153–5.
91 *Justice*, 5 March 1910.
92 Snowden, *Woman Socialist*, ch. 7.
93 Pedersen, *Family, Dependence*, pp. 50–1, ch. 4.
94 Glasier, *Socialism and the Home*. For the views of other ILP women see Rowan, ' "Mothers vote Labour!" ', pp. 73–8.
95 Women's Labour League, *Annual Report*, 1909–10, quoted in Rowan, ' "Mothers vote Labour!" ', p. 75.
96 J. Hannam, *Isabella Ford 1855–1924*, Oxford, Blackwell, 1989, chs 6 and 7; T.B. Greig in *New Age*, 20 June 1907; Special Suffrage Supplement, *Labour Leader*, 9 January 1913; S. Pankhurst in *Forward*, 25 January 1913.
97 Ford, *Women and Socialism*, 1906 edn, p. 3.
98 Pallister, *Socialism for Women*, p. 4.
99 See Chapter 4 for a discussion of women organising separately.
100 See, for example, the leaflet *To Women Voters*, 1918, and *Why Labour Women Should Be on Town Councils*, 1921, Francis Johnson Collection, British Library of Political and Economic Science, London School of Economics.
101 Teresa Billington-Greig quoted in Lohman, 'Sex or class?', p. 297.
102 *New Leader*, 28 February 1930. See also Pallister, *Socialism for Women*, pp. 27–9.
103 *New Leader*, 11 May 1923.
104 Pallister, *Socialism for Women*, p. 6.
105 Ibid., p. 4.
106 M. Francis, 'Labour and gender', in D. Tanner, P. Thane and N. Tiratsoo (eds), *Labour's First Century*, Cambridge, Cambridge University Press, 2000, p. 199.
107 See Evelyn Sharp, *New Leader*, 9 March 1923; Dorothy Jewson, Dora Russell and Dorothy Evans, *New Leader*, 28 February 1930.

4

MIXED-SEX POLITICS

Women entered socialist politics with a sense of excitement. With no formal barriers to their participation at any level in socialist organisations, they believed that they had an opportunity for self-fulfilment as political activists and also a space in which to pursue women's collective interests as a sex. The young artist Barbara Lowrie explained that she had joined the Leeds ILP because 'I believe woman has the right to her own individuality, and to be recognised as equally important with man, in all matters. In this club I found men and women who entirely agreed with me'.[1] In practice it was difficult for women to define a new role for themselves in a mixed-sex political movement. They sought to work with men to achieve a socialist society which would end the exploitation of working-class people of both sexes, while also arguing that women suffered from a distinct oppression as a sex and needed to act together to ensure that their concerns were taken seriously. Moreover, they contested prevailing assumptions about what was appropriate political behaviour for a woman and sought equality with men within socialist organisations, but their framework of ideas was still shaped by contemporary preoccupations about gender difference.

It might seem on the surface, therefore, that socialist women had to work out their political practice within a set of dichotomous and competing positions. It will be suggested here, however, that they used a complex range of arguments, which could change over time and according to particular issues, and that it is important to be clear about the meanings that were being given to terms such as equality.[2] This chapter will explore how socialist women brought together their theory and their practice in developing their political role as women and as socialists and the ways in which they negotiated women's identity as a collective political group.

'Sex equality' in practice

As already discussed in Chapter 1, it was common for women to claim both at the time and in subsequent interviews and reminiscences that one of the reasons why they had joined the ILP in the 1890s was because it was welcoming to women and offered them an equal role in political work. Similar views were also expressed in the 1920s, when ILP women urged newly enfranchised women voters to join the socialist movement because 'the ILP has always believed in sex equality'.[3] Such statements have been taken by historians to signify that the ILP gave women a degree of equality in its organisation which was far greater than any other group.[4]

And yet this fails to take account of the competing stories told by ILP as well as by SDF women about how they experienced socialist politics. They complained about the male atmosphere of branches, where men were either hostile or patronising towards women members and speakers. Ellen Batten of the SDF commented, 'when one sees the half-contemptuous smile, or hears the slighting remark when women are mentioned as workers or speakers one cannot help feeling that those socialists are not as advanced or true to their principles as they ought to be'.[5] After the turn of the century the women's suffrage movement brought to a head the frustrations that socialist women had been feeling for many years. In the 1890s Marion Coates Hansen was critical of the misogyny that she encountered in the SDF, but after joining the ILP found that attitudes were not much better. In a letter to George Lansbury she claimed that her experience of the socialist movement had left her with:

> A passionate hopeless feeling that women don't count ... Imagine an enthusiastic boy – yourself for example ... going into a movement in the hope of becoming of use – and then finding that you did not count – that another sex only had power etc. You've got to *feel* it to know what it means.[6]

These competing versions must be understood in the context in which they were made and against the social background of the individual who expressed them. In the 1880s and 1890s socialist women were keen to differentiate their position from that of women in the Liberal and Conservative parties, whom they believed were treated simply as auxiliaries.[7] Clare Collins suggests that the pride ILP women expressed in their party and the 'equality' that they found there were ways in which they could make sense of their involvement in a mixed-sex politics which rarely emphasised gender issues.[8] The way in which women experienced socialist politics was not necessarily related to the characteristics of the particular organisation in which they were active. It was also affected by their class, their level of education and their own personality, in particular their confidence, as well as by the branch or region in which they were active.

Socialist organisations were not highly centralised in the pre-war years and branches had considerable freedom of action and distinctive characteristics.[9] In the ILP, for example, branches in Yorkshire and to some extent in Lancashire, where women's employment was widespread and where active female members were well-known feminists, were seen as particularly welcoming to women.[10] In a letter to *Labour Leader* in the 1890s one female socialist complained that the advanced women in the North would not be able to understand the servile place given to women in the London ILP,[11] while twenty years later this view was confirmed by Katharine Bruce Glasier, who claimed that in Yorkshire in the 1890s she had found an atmosphere of 'swift and eager welcome for every woman comrade and of settled conviction as to the women's equal rights of citizenship with men'. In Glasgow and London, however, 'there were, alas, a few hostile forces, even within the pale of the socialist movement itself'.[12]

Despite the favourable comparisons drawn between socialist organisations and the mainstream political parties, therefore, it was not always easy for socialist women to carve out a new political role for themselves. Women lacked visibility in both the ILP and the SDF. Approximately 10 per cent of delegates to annual conferences were women and they formed only a small proportion of branch secretaries, treasurers and candidates for elected bodies, while there were never more than one or two women on the executive committees of the two main socialist organisations.[13] The identification of the SDF and the ILP with male leaders was underlined by the illustrations produced to accompany reports of annual conferences – in a special supplement to the *Labour Leader* which commemorated the ILPs 'Coming of Age' conference, the title page pictured six chair*men*. Women were represented in a 'traditional role' in the top right-hand corner of the page, where there was an idealised drawing of a mother holding a child's hand.[14]

In common with other political parties, women were found in large numbers taking on auxiliary roles as tea makers, organisers of social events as well as canvassers and distributors of leaflets. As a member of the Ashton ILP, Hannah Mitchell noted how 'the capable women sit by with folded hands until a social or tea party is needed, when they are entrusted with the hard work of getting it ready, while the men occupy themselves in electing a chairman to preside over the evening's entertainment'.[15] Elizabeth Dean found that she was often the only active female member in the BSP club in Salford. A few 'wives' attended, but they did the washing up and the cleaning rather than taking part in more overtly political work.[16]

Only a minority of women socialists, regardless of the groups to which they belonged, were able to exercise some choice about the roles that they wished to play. They were likely to be middle-class, well-educated women or those unusual working-class women who were confident enough to overcome domestic and personal obstacles to their political activism. They may have been exceptional, but their public profile as lecturers and their role on the executive committees of the SDF and the ILP did give them a presence in socialist politics which was different from that of their counterparts in the Conservative and Liberal parties.[17] They gained a reputation as speakers, as journalists and as members of Boards of Guardians and School Boards, attended socialist conferences at home and abroad and took part in demonstrations for free speech and to help the unemployed. Some gave a full-time commitment to this work, while others combined it with paid employment in another section of the labour movement or with marriage, motherhood and domestic duties.

Women usually took on several activities at once or moved between them over the course of their political careers. This can be illustrated by two examples of women from working-class backgrounds. Margaretta Hicks of the SDF attended annual conferences, lectured on public platforms and stood as an SDF candidate for the St Pancras Board of Guardians in 1904. She was chairman of the Women's Education Committee of the SDF, set up a woman's paper, *The Link*, in 1911 and became the prime mover in the women's organisation of the BSP.[18] Hannah Mitchell, a member of the Ashton ILP, developed skills as a local speaker and was elected to the Board of Guardians. For a time she was active in the Women's Social and Political Union, suffering arrest and imprisonment. In the inter-war years she once again gave more of her time to socialist politics and was a local councillor, a magistrate and published her dialect columns in the ILP's *Northern Voice*.[19]

Socialist women enjoyed the comradeship that they experienced in working alongside men for socialism and this was reinforced by the numerous married couples, in particular in the ILP, who were active in the movement at a local and at a national level.[20] In some cases the activities of the couple tended to be gendered; Lisbeth Simm, for example, who was married to the organiser of the North East Federation of the ILP, wrote a women's column in the *Northern Democrat*, a paper edited by her husband. She was one of the leaders of the North East Women's Suffrage Society and subsequently became active in the Women's Labour League, working as an organiser between 1908 and 1918. In other cases women played a more general role. Agnes Dollan, for instance, the wife of the ILP organiser for Scotland, was a member of the executive of the Scottish Labour Party, stood unsuccessfully as an ILP candidate for parliament in the 1920s and was an ILP nominee for the executive of the Labour Party.[21]

The position of socialist women, however, was an ambivalent one. As well as working together with men, socialist women also highlighted the specific needs of women as a sex. By seeking to persuade the socialist movement to do something about this, they risked undermining the comradeship that they prized. During the pre-war suffrage campaign some socialist women chose to prioritise their solidarity with other women, but this was never an easy option and they expressed a sense of relief when such choices were no longer necessary. After an alliance had been made between the Labour Party and the National Union of Women's Suffrage Societies, for example, Isabella Ford wrote excitedly to Edward Carpenter that Labour meetings were 'so splendid that I feel comradeship, the real thing, is growing fast, just because of this battle ... I feel like bursting with joy over it at times'.[22]

'Obstreperous females'

Socialist women propagandists were conscious that they were engaged in redefining what it meant to be a political woman. They were flouting conventions in two ways, by taking part in public actions which could be viewed as 'unwomanly' and by supporting a 'subversive' political doctrine. Middle-class women, in particular, found that for the first time they were engaging in propaganda work which took them on to the streets or other public places and into the fray of direct action. They marched with female workers who were on strike, chalked pavements to advertise meetings and spoke on street corners, which Katharine Bruce Glasier described as 'an outrageous act in those days for a woman and requiring every ounce of character and courage one possessed'.[23] In the 1890s Enid Stacy joined demonstrations of the unemployed which led to clashes with the police, while similar confrontations occurred in free speech campaigns.[24] Amie Hicks was arrested addressing a crowd during a free speech campaign in Dod Street, London, in the 1880s.[25] She defended herself in the police court but was found guilty of obstruction and bound over to keep the peace for six months. In 1896 Emmeline Pankhurst was also arrested when she spoke during the free speech campaign at Boggart Hole Clough, near Manchester, where the local authorities had tried to ban socialist meetings. She threatened to go to prison rather than pay a fine, but the case against her was dismissed.[26]

Many socialist women believed that these kinds of actions both required, and helped to create, a different kind of political woman. They used the rhetoric of the 'new woman', who appeared in fiction, drama and newspapers in the 1890s, to frame their own discussions.[27] The 'new woman' was identified as someone who was able to pursue a career, often living apart from her family, held independent views and was less constrained than previous generations by prevailing notions of femininity. In their novels *On the Threshold* and *Aimée Furniss*, and in other writings, Isabella Ford and Katharine Bruce Glasier explored the relationship between the 'new woman' and socialism, arguing that socialism could emancipate middle-class as well as working-class women by providing 'new opportunities for those ... who longed for a different kind of existence'.[28] At the same time such women could also help to expand the meaning of socialism. Isabella Ford quoted approvingly the independent attitudes displayed by Ibsen's Nora and argued that 'surely the New Woman, the intelligent, questioning human being is the one we want in the Labour movement; and surely, therefore, one of the chief objects of the movement is to produce such a woman'.[29] Time and again female propagandists stressed the importance of women acting and thinking with determination and independence. Lily Bell, for example, argued that 'women have to learn to think and act for themselves independently of men, for until they can do so they cannot combine with them on a really equal footing'.[30] She described Kate Taylor, who had formerly worked for the Women's Protective and Provident League, as someone whose 'vigorous, thorough way of getting through work did not please the namby pamby women who run the show'.[31] Women's skill at putting across complex arguments went some way to undermine the view that they were frivolous or incapable of taking a serious interest in politics. Katharine Bruce Glasier described Enid Stacy as 'brilliant, incisive, logical', while John Bruce Glasier claimed that 'by her dignity and ability upon the public platform, and by her admirable grasp of political problems, she did a great deal to further the advent of women into politics'.[32]

Reactions to the independent socialist woman were, however, ambivalent. Well-known female propagandists were admired for their willingness to go into the 'thick' of the fight and for their speaking skills, which were described time and again as 'inspiring'. They were usually differentiated from each other in terms of style and the descriptions used by contemporaries were still being repeated decades later. In an obituary of Katharine Bruce Glasier, written in 1950, the *Socialist Leader* claimed that the names of the 'great women pioneers ... still ring in our ears. Enid Stacy was convincing and logical. Katie Conway was a different type of speaker, warm, emotional and deeply moving'.[33] It was recognised that women often had a greater impact *because* of their sex, which caused the SDF to express concern that it did not attract enough female speakers. Women drew large audiences and in 1892 W.B. De Mattos, lecture secretary of the Fabian Society, commented that:

> It is possible that Katharine Conway was getting more applause than a woman less young and attractive might have got, but that was all doing good to Socialism. She has a peculiar magnetic influence over her audiences, and larger audiences could be drawn for her than for almost any other lecturers.[34]

Nonetheless, it was difficult for socialists to find a language to describe the 'heroic' female political campaigner whose actions displayed qualities not normally associated with contemporary definitions of femininity. Thus, when Enid Stacy took part in a demonstration of the unemployed, she was described as clinging 'manfully to the railings', while on another occasion she was referred to as a 'Young man in a hurry'.[35]

Some socialist men were suspicious of female propagandists, in particular those from a middle-class background, because of their class and their gender. Ethel Snowden, for example, was disliked by many because she campaigned to get alcohol banned from labour clubs and was rarely tactful in her dealings with others. Alf Mattison, the Leeds engineer, noted in his diary that at a meeting to be addressed by Ethel Snowden the chairman indicated with a backward jerk of his thumb that he would speak briefly since 'this one's the object we've come to listen to', although Mattison himself described her as 'charming and gifted'.[36]

A deeper concern among socialist men was the fear that if men and women played an 'equal' part in politics, then relationships between the sexes, and in particular gender roles within the home, would be transformed. Indeed women propagandists were themselves concerned to explore how an active role in politics might have implications for their personal lives. Ellen Wilkinson, for example, never married and used her novel *Clash* to express some of the dilemmas and choices socialist women activists had to make. Joan, the central character in the novel, accepted that if a woman wanted to pursue a career as the most important thing in her life, 'she must make it a whole time job if she is to compete on equal terms with men of her calibre … She might have love affairs, even marry, but if she means to do big things, then work is in the front of the picture'.[37] Others, including Katharine Bruce Glasier, hoped to strike a balance between home life and their political activism, and therefore tried to work out how domestic arrangements could be organised so that they could continue to play a full part in socialist politics after marriage and childbirth.[38] Usually this involved the help of other women, whether paid or unpaid, rather than a fundamental change in the gender division of labour within the family, but this could still undermine the routines of family life.[39] Mrs Somerville from Manchester recalled that when her father, a police sergeant, and her mother joined the ILP, family life was completely disrupted since both parents attended meetings regularly.[40] Examples such as this caused anxiety among many men. Lily Bell claimed that in the early days, when she tried to express her views on women's rights, she was 'invariably met with the same remark, "You want to make women into men"'.[41] A report from the Salford SDF made the same point by caricaturing the lives of men whose wives attended meetings. 'Don't you know we have got the women – in Lancashire. In some of the branches the men are at home mending the stockings and nursing the baby – the best place for them – whilst the women are out in the squares and at the street corners.'[42]

Such fears meant that socialist men only seemed to be comfortable with 'independent women' if they could also emphasise that the woman propagandist had lost none of her 'womanly' qualities. Caroline Martyn was usually described as sympathetic and womanly, while Katharine Bruce Glasier was the 'beautiful angel of the revolution'.[43] Photographs in which women speakers looked particularly glamorous appeared in the socialist press and their physical appearance was often remarked on. When Ethel Annakin made her debut as a socialist speaker, she was described as a 'second Annie Besant … to her good gifts of dark eyes, golden brown hair and rich colour, nature has added a sweet singing voice and musical ability of no mean order'.[44] It was also claimed that political activism did not necessarily mean neglect of domestic responsibilities. In an interview with Emmeline Pankhurst at the time of the Boggart Hole Clough incident, she was praised as one of the 'most interesting and attractive personalities in the whole Socialist Party'. After going through a long list of her political campaigns and activities, the interviewer concluded:

> Yet she finds time to be at leisure to her friends, to look well after her bonnie daughters, and to see that Dr Pankhurst wears his flannels in due season. Her influence too has redeemed him from the baneful habits of reading metaphysics up to 3 a.m., of irregular meals or sometimes none, and shocking hours for breakfast.[45]

Socialist women themselves were not averse to using their gender if it meant that they could advance the cause of socialism, but they were reluctant to see women's political role as bounded by this. In free speech campaigns both Amie Hicks and Emmeline Pankhurst put themselves in positions where they might be arrested, since they knew that, as women, this would have a greater publicity value. Enid Stacy urged women to collect money at meetings: 'Not only have the amounts collected been larger than they would otherwise have been, but the usual silly sneers at "folks who were trying to line their own pockets" … ceased completely when the wives took up the boxes and went around'.[46] This can be contrasted, however, with a similar suggestion in *Justice* that 'half a dozen good looking girls would treble and quadruple the usual collection made at any open air meeting', where women's appearance was emphasised rather than their integrity.[47] Moreover, there was no suggestion, as there was in Enid Stacy's article, that this would be a means of encouraging women to take a more active role in socialist politics.

The enfranchisement of some women in 1918 prompted further discussion about the ideal characteristics of the active political woman. Minnie Pallister suggested that, faced with new problems in a 'modern' society, socialists both needed, and also would help to develop, a different type of woman citizen, since the 'toy woman, the slave woman, the ignorant woman has hindered the march towards progress and freedom'.[48] The term 'slave woman' was frequently used in the 1920s as the antithesis to the independent thinking woman that socialist women hoped to see. Helen Gault, who described herself openly as a feminist, reminded readers of the *New Leader* that the earlier women's movement had claimed that 'a woman was a human being' and had met 'that other hoary, cheer-evoking platitude – "Men are men and women are women" – with the sensible rejoinder – "Men and women are mankind!" '[49] Now that women were voters both the ILP and the Labour Party were keen to attract their support and appealed to the fresh, 'modern' outlook of young women.[50] On the other hand, Helen Gault reminded her readers that there were many socialist and Labour Party men who felt threatened by the new type of political woman:

> In spite of all our rhetoric, the slave mind and the craven spirit are still the qualities most highly appreciated by the men of the Party. The ideal woman is still the Victorian ideal. Independence of thought is dangerous. Originality is suspect. Fighters are taboo. Fighters are merely obstreperous females.[51]

Thus, independence of mind was encouraged if it meant that women were attracted to socialism, but not if it meant that they stood up for their own interests as a sex in the political arena and in the home.

Heroines of the socialist cause

In the late nineteenth and early twentieth centuries socialist men made sense of women's 'courage' and willingness to take direct action by representing them in ways which drew on more familiar gendered characteristics. Middle-class women were often praised for leaving a comfortable life in order to help their 'poorer sisters' and to work for socialism.[52] The effort that they put into propaganda work, which frequently undermined their health, was used as a way to shame men in the movement into greater activity. A report of Katharine Bruce Glasier's speech to the Liverpool ILP after a period of illness commented that 'if the "men" of the movement had half the courage of Mrs Glasier things would hum, and she, as well as a few others, would have better health'.[53] Humour, in which apathetic men were the subject of criticism, was also used. Commenting on Enid Stacy's speaking tour in London in 1894, the editor of the *Labour Leader* commented that:

> men have crumpled under her withering scorn. Most of them have had to pay to crumple, but this is only another proof of their intellectual woodenness. Women would be too intelligent to pay to hear themselves made the butt of humorous and scathing remarks by a man.[54]

Women were likened to famous historical figures such as Joan of Arc, an analogy which not only justified their actions but which also drew attention to their willingness to give their lives for a just cause. Caroline Martyn and Enid Stacy were canonised as martyrs because of their early deaths, which were attributed to exhaustion after constant speaking tours had sapped their strength. When Caroline Martyn died, a tribute was published in the *Labour Leader* which covered a whole page. In the middle, an idealised pen portrait of Martyn, dressed in a flowing robe reminiscent of a Roman toga, with irises growing at the front and rays of light behind her head, had the caption 'died for socialism' at the bottom, followed by a poem by J. Connell which contained the lines 'where strong men faltered with courage gone, our sister comrade marched on and on'.[55]

It could be suggested that the representation of women propagandists as champions of poorer women or as heroic martyrs for socialism was a way of bringing men and women together and emphasising their common interests at a time when the women's movement raised the possibility of sex antagonism.[56] This was certainly the way in which Katharine Bruce Glasier chose to identify the role of middle-class women in the pioneering years of the ILP.[57] This version of the pioneering days became a dominant narrative in ILP reminiscences and histories written around the period of the First World War, but it fails to capture the perspectives of women in the SDF and the ILP who struggled in the early years to raise the profile of women within their respective organisations and who were willing to criticise men in the movement for their antagonism or indifference to the female worker.

Socialist women drew examples from history, and from other parts of the world, to emphasise women's potential for political activism and their willingness to engage in revolutionary and radical politics if the conditions were right. Rather than blaming women for their political indifference or conservatism, they sought to understand their attitudes and to find a way to change them. For instance, they argued that all forms of conventional thought which taught women to be submissive needed to be challenged.[58] They also suggested that socialist men should take some responsibility for women's apathy, since they rarely gave support to enable their own wives and daughters to play a more active political role. In her column in the *Clarion* Julia Dawson despaired that 'ILP and SDF branches don't know what they miss when they do not specifically encourage the membership and attendance of women. Frequently women write to me that they don't like to offer themselves as workers, because only men are attending the meetings'.[59]

Enid Stacy used a dialogue between two male socialists to raise, and then counter, the criticisms often made that women were uninterested in politics and that they held men back from becoming socialists by their 'scolding'. After listening to complaints of this kind from his friend, Character A suggests that he should try to interest his wife by reading to her in the evening and by taking turns to go to the Labour Church and the Labour Club:

> It will be an uphill fight, and you will never succeed without trying to put yourself in her place and looking at life through her spectacles .... Show her how it is possible to make our women's lives less full of hard, uninteresting work ... I don't know what I should do in my Labour work if I had not got my wife to talk to and get help from.[60]

This was a very different angle of vision from that more commonly employed by socialists who either failed to recognise any distinction between men and women or else simply criticised women for their lack of interest.

Making socialists – a gendered model?

Socialist women propagandists drew attention to the need to make a special effort to attract women and criticised the assumptions made that the process of politicisation would be the same for both sexes. In the 1880s and 1890s both the SDF and the ILP sought to 'make socialists' by propaganda delivered in public meetings and in newspapers. It was thought that this would have the most effect on men and women who were already discontented because they had experienced poverty and injustice, or on those who had taken part in collective actions such as a strike or political campaign. The SDF, in particular, assumed that the self-educated worker would be the most receptive to the message of socialism and emphasised that education should be a continuous process after the initial 'conversion' in order to create class-conscious socialists.[61] Propaganda remained important for both groups, although the ILP's emphasis on building an electoral machinery after the mid-1890s further marginalised women's contribution to the socialist project.

Socialist women recognised that such a model of politicisation was far less appropriate for women than for men; it was argued that few working-class women had the opportunity for self-education, while an emphasis on workplace struggles and propaganda delivered in the streets made little concession to the different economic and social circumstances of women's lives.[62] Margaretta Hicks was still referring to these issues as late as 1912, when she considered what was to happen to women's organisation within the newly formed BSP:

> The difficulty is that most of the propaganda of Socialism has been carried on in terms of political economy or political action, both of which are far more used by men than by women; and beside that, we must all recognise that women who have young children find it very difficult to attend evening meetings, or meetings of any kind, if it means travelling any distance. So we must needs find other ways of propaganda. It is sure to be difficult, and there will be many comrades conservative enough to dislike variations from the regularly accepted methods of public meetings, which are considered good enough for men, and therefore should be good enough for women. We must consider, however, that the circumstances are different.[63]

In suggesting that a distinction should be made between the sexes in the project of 'making socialists', attention was drawn to women as a separate group in politics. This in turn raised questions about how far a special appeal should be made to women as women, on what basis such an appeal should be made and whether this would undermine women's ability to engage in politics on an equal basis with men, which female propagandists prized so highly. These dilemmas were revealed most acutely when socialist women debated the controversial issue of whether or not women should have a distinct space within socialist organisations, whether in the form of women's columns in the socialist press or through the establishment of separate groups.

Organising separately

The question of separate space for women was a matter of common concern for socialist groups affiliated to the Second International. The largest and most successful socialist women's group was formed in Germany in 1891 under the leadership of Clara Zetkin, who also edited its newspaper, *Gleichheit* (Equality). Women were prohibited by law from joining political organisations and therefore they had to set up their own groups outside the formal structure of the Social Democratic Party. Although Zetkin defended women's groups on the grounds that German legislation made them necessary, Karen Honeycutt suggests that she also welcomed them because she believed that they would enable women to exert more influence.[64] Zetkin argued that autonomy for socialist women would encourage them to think for themselves and to gain confidence to express their own opinions.

There was no comparable women's organisation within the British socialist movement, although there were sporadic attempts to establish women's groups, and a separate space for women within the socialist press, across the whole period from the 1890s to the 1920s. The timing and extent of women's self-organisation varied between socialist groups, but similar concerns were expressed about this development from across the movement as a whole. Debate centred on how best to politicise women and on the most effective strategy for attracting women to socialism.

In the 1890s women's columns were established in the *Clarion* and the *Labour Leader*, while ad hoc women's groups, attached to local branches, were also formed in the SDF and the ILP. There were no serious attempts to coordinate these activities at a national level, but the ILP women's groups did receive some publicity from the women's columns, which in turn stimulated further organisation.[65] SDF women, however, found it more difficult to communicate with each other, since it was not until 1907 that *Justice* published a women's column. These attempts at self-organisation caused considerable controversy within socialist groups. Many women feared that they would be seen as auxiliaries to men and that their interests would be marginalised, or else that antagonism between the sexes would be exacerbated.[66] They argued that the sexes were supposed to be equal in the socialist movement and therefore they could not see why there was a need for women to have separate space. On these grounds Lily Bell questioned whether she should edit a women's column:

> "Why", I asked, "should there be a special column for women in the *Labour Leader*? You don't set up a special column headed 'Women only' like a ladies' compartment in a railway carriage? You say you believe in the equality of the sexes and yet here you are proposing to treat us like so many children."[67]

Concern was also expressed that women's groups and women's columns would reinforce women's identification with the home and limit them to organising social events and fund raising. A number of the participants in the debate which surrounded the publication of a new women's column in the *Labour Leader* in 1906 complained that 'hitherto women's corners in the press have chiefly been filled up with pudding recipes and frivolous chatter about fashions' and they dreaded 'that sort of stuff' appearing in the *Leader*.[68] Hannah Mitchell warned against cookery recipes and dressmaking hints since 'we don't want to read about food and clothes ... our lives are one long round of cooking and sewing'.[69]

Others, however, argued that it was important to recognise that women did have an interest in domestic issues and that this could be used as a basis to engage them in socialist politics. The class dimension was crucial here. Katharine Bruce Glasier and Julia Dawson, for example, pointed out that women's groups and women's columns were not aimed at confident, female propagandists, many of whom were from educated, middle-class backgrounds, but at the wives and daughters of male socialists who up to now had received little encouragement to join socialist organisations.[70] Writing after the turn of the century, Katharine Bruce Glasier suggested that it was all very well for educated women to claim an equal position alongside men, but working-class women needed space to develop confidence and had to be reassured that socialism would address their interests in children and the home.[71] She declared that she rarely heard complaints from working-class women about covering domestic issues. 'These tiresome sayings usually come from those who place upon others the drudgery of cooking and looking after babies, but themselves wear the fine dresses and jewels'.[72]

In different ways it was hoped that a recognition of women's interests in the home could be a starting point for politicising women. Julia Dawson was willing to put household hints in her column since, by showing women an easier way to complete their domestic tasks, 'I shall be helping on Socialism. When women get the leisure they ought to have for reading, thinking and resting, Socialism will be within close reach'.[73] Although many women's groups limited themselves to a social function, Enid Stacy thought that even this had the potential to engage women in political work. By clubbing together to buy material for a banner, for instance, and then making it, women would have 'pleasant intercourse' and this would foster feelings of comradeship. Enid Stacy urged female members to take the chair when there were women speakers, since it would be 'pleasant and encouraging for a woman speaker to find a comrade of her own sex as a "chair-woman"'. It could also be a way to find fresh speaking talent among women 'which might otherwise have remained forever hidden'.[74]

Women's groups and politicisation

Thus all of these female commentators hoped that women's groups and women's columns would encourage women to take a greater interest in socialist politics. In practice, however, this was difficult to achieve. The SDF women's groups in the 1890s were set up with the backing of male socialists to encourage social aspects of branch life, rather than to broaden women's political role. This was also the case in the ILP, but there were some women's groups which sought to use their separatism to engage women more fully in political work. Mary Alice Taylor, who was instrumental in establishing a women's branch in Halifax and was later arrested for suffrage militancy, described how her group aimed to read and discuss socialist texts, since 'I want it to be something more than a "mother's meeting"'.[75] Similarly, the Glasgow Woman's Labour Party, which was active in the 1890s, aimed to educate women in the first principles of socialism, to encourage them to take part with men in general propaganda and to prepare them for a time when they would be able to exercise the vote.[76] Although the group involved women in raising funds by sewing and holding tea parties, this was to enable them to maintain their policy of voluntary subscriptions. Delegates were sent to the annual conference of the ILP in the early 1890s and the president, Mrs Harper, was the first woman to appear on a May Day platform on Glasgow Green. In 1895 the group drew up its own manifesto for distribution during election campaigns, which endorsed the general programme of the ILP but drew special attention to women's industrial grievances. The activities of the Glasgow group helped to persuade Lily Bell to change her attitudes towards separate organisation. She now thought that 'a Women's party might be a means of education to the women themselves.'[77] The outlook of the Glasgow organisation was influenced by a very active group of women, including Lizzie Glasier, Isabella Bream Pearce and Kate Taylor, who were instrumental in its formation. They were already involved in local socialist politics or the trade union movement, and were influenced by feminist ideas.[78] Where such strong-minded women were absent, it was more difficult for groups to move beyond a social function.

In the early 1900s an impetus was given to the establishment of socialist women's groups on a national basis when suffrage campaigners increased the level of their activities. The formation of the Women's Social and Political Union, in particular, was seen as presenting a rival for the allegiance of working-class women, and it was in this context that the SDF supported the formation of a national women's organisation for the party.[79] In 1904 it was announced that Women's Socialist Circles would be established at a local level to organise the 'wives, daughters and sisters' of male comrades and that there would be a National Women's Committee, later entitled the Women's Education Committee, to coordinate their work.[80] The most rapid growth took place after 1907 with the number of Circles reaching a peak of thirty in 1909.

Although the Circles began by emphasising social activities, leading female members of the party, including Dora Montefiore, Clara Hendin and Rose Jarvis, tried to ensure that they would have a broader function. Dora Montefiore, in particular, disliked women's identification with fundraising and made it clear that 'I never on principle associate myself with bazaars; I very much deprecate the loss of time, money and energy which they entail'.[81] By 1907 the Circles were seen much more as training grounds for socialism and their educational work was underlined by the setting up of a women's column in *Justice* in the same year. Dora Montefiore claimed that the Circles would 'organise and educate women in the principles of Social Democracy with a view to their becoming members of the SDF and to stand side by side with the men to bring about the abolition of capitalism'.[82]

Social and educational work were not necessarily distinct. Rose Jarvis, for instance, recognised that branch practices were often unappealing to women and encouraged Circle organisers to invite women to their homes in the afternoons. Once they were comfortable, they could then be encouraged to join the branch.[83] The Northampton Women's Circle tried to make its afternoon meetings accessible to working-class women by including songs and refreshments as well as lectures, but also aimed to ensure that its members would become political activists and to challenge the view that women's place was in the home.

They did not view separate organisation for women in the same way as male members of the SDF – as useful for the branch or to prevent women hindering their husbands' work for socialism – but as a means of empowering women themselves. There was a balance between social and educational work and the former was seen in a positive light as a way in which women could give each other valued mutual support. The Circle also took up issues which contested women's unequal social position, notably the suffrage campaign, and members of the Circle led a meeting in the local SDF branch on 'The Emancipation of Women'.[84]

In 1908 Fabian women also established a separate organisation, the Fabian Women's Group, which at its peak in 1912 had a membership of 230.[85] In contrast to other socialist women's organisations, the FWG did not seek specifically to target working-class women. Its members were drawn from well-educated professional women such as teachers, clerical workers and secretaries, or from those with independent means.[86] Fabian women were inspired by the militancy of suffragettes to organise together in a separate group so that they could focus on 'women's social welfare and political rights' and give the Woman Question a higher profile within the Fabian Society. The FWG had some success in encouraging women to stand for election to Poor Law Boards and local councils in London and also contributed to debates around women's social welfare through the publication of books, pamphlets and tracts. The emphasis of the FWG was on the need for women, in particular mothers, to be economically independent, and its members argued consistently for social reforms which would provide a state endowment of motherhood.

The ILP, however, took a different route. There was little demand for branches to set up women's organisations in a systematic way or for a national body to coordinate their activities. The issue was not debated explicitly, but the views of some leading women can be assumed from their reaction to the establishment in 1906 of a new women's column in the *Labour Leader*. The most ardent critics of the column were those most closely identified with suffrage activism. It was feared that a separate space would imply marginality. Ethel Snowden asked 'for whose benefit is the remainder of the *Labour Leader*? If for men only, why so much more space for men than for women? If for both men and women, why a special column for women?'[87] Echoing these views, Isabella Ford argued that 'I thought the day had gone by for the separate treatment of men and women's interests'.[88] At a time when she was steeped in suffrage politics, Ethel Snowden accepted that men and women might have 'different tastes and desires in many cases; but in matters of citizenship and on questions of reform there need be nothing in the way of specialisation for either of the sexes'.[89]

The widespread belief that the ILP offered equality for women meant that even those who supported a women's column were not inclined to seek a separate organisation for women within the party. Instead, many ILP women put their energies into the formation of the Women's Labour League in order to encourage women to support the Labour Party. This development was not welcomed by all female members of the ILP. Some local women's groups attached to ILP branches were concerned that they might lose their independence and also their members to the WLL.[90] Edna Penny from Sheffield, the wife of an ILP organiser, complained that too many men and women were being drawn to work for other movements, which deprived the ILP of their services:

> I suppose if it is necessary to have a Women's Labour League so that women can work without the hampering influence of men, the men folk will soon find it necessary to set up a Men's League so that men can work without the hampering influence of women. Then if one takes the women and the other men, the ILP will be snuffed out altogether. My ideal is that men and women should work together for the common good, and the good old ILP is the ideal organisation where the combination is effective.[91]

Organising ILP women in the 1920s

In the immediate post-war period it seemed as if some of these fears had been realised. Women were joining the newly established Labour Party's women's sections in considerable numbers but did not appear to be attracted in the same way to the ILP. This led the National Administrative Council to reverse the practice of equal subscriptions for men and women, which many had taken pride in as the symbol of women's equality within the party. Some branches had already operated a differential rate for women before a reduced subscription for married women was debated and agreed as an experiment by the party's 1924 conference.[92] Many of the opponents of change were women. Mary Cross from St Pancras argued that her branch had a large female membership and therefore finances would suffer, 'but more important than that, it was bad to differentiate between the sexes'. This view was supported by Emma Sproson from Wolverhampton, who said that 'women must not accept favours, in view of their stand for sex equality'.[93] Minnie Pallister, however, who usually agreed that women should have no special favours (or privileges), supported the proposal on the grounds that

> [t]he woman's case surely is, rather, that while she bears equal burdens she has not received equal privileges ... while the economic freedom of the married woman is something which ought to exist, it does not yet exist ... Anyhow, need we add to the woman who has the disability of being married any other disability?[94]

A similar range of views was expressed over the proposal that a more systematic attempt should be made to form women's groups. It was not just that women were failing to join the ILP in large numbers, but also that they appeared to have a lower profile in the party than in the pre-war years. In 1924 leading women members, including Dorothy Jewson, Minnie Pallister and Annot Robinson, wrote to the party's paper, *New Leader*, concerned that 'at the present moment women are not taking the part they should in the life of the movement'. They pointed out that there were no women on the NAC and women comprised only nine of the 129 Divisional Council representatives, only seven of the 146 delegates to the 1923 ILP Conference and only three of the ninety-one ILP candidates at the last general election. In a rather understated way the signatories claimed: 'This is anything but satisfactory, especially when we remember that much of the actual branch work is done by women'.[95] It was in this context that the NAC, concerned that the ILP should not lose its self-image as 'woman friendly', called for branches to establish separate women's groups as a matter of policy.

In an attempt to coordinate the work of local groups at a national level, a Women's Advisory Committee was established and Dorothy Jewson also edited a *Monthly Bulletin* as a way to keep the groups in touch.[96] The NAC declared that the first Sunday in February, beginning in 1925, should be designated as socialist women's day.[97] This later expanded into an annual women's weekend, when rallies were held and conferences organised to debate a variety of topics, ranging from social welfare issues to married women's right to work.[98] Response to this initiative was slow at first, but 135 groups had been formed by 1928.[99] The bulk of the membership was in Scotland, where there were few Labour Party women's sections to provide competition. In Glasgow in particular, where there had long been a tradition of ILP women organising, women's groups were popular, numbering twenty-three in 1924.[100] Elsewhere there was reluctance to follow the NAC's advice. The Divisional Council for London and Southern Counties reported in 1927 that it, 'in accordance with the repeated decisions of conference [,] has not encouraged such development, believing that the segregation of ILP women into separate groupings is not in the best interests of the movement'.[101] The London Divisional Council had also been among the most vociferous critics of lower subscription rates and prided itself in taking the lead on sex equality. On the other hand, it was pointed out in *New Leader* that few women attended the London Divisional annual conference and that a theoretical interest in equality needed to be put into practical effect by choosing female delegates.[102]

Thus women's separate organisation remained a contentious subject within the ILP. As early as 1923 Agnes Dollan had argued for women's sections in terms which were familiar from other socialist organisations but which had been resisted so far in the ILP. She claimed:

> The branches now organised are not suitable for training women in the home and domestic questions arising from the consideration of Socialism. In the main the branches are concerned with routine administration, advanced politics, and industrial economics. Some women are

able to revel in these subjects because of special training or occupation. For the great majority, however, the branch meetings are abstract and dull .... Women, therefore, do not get the training which they require to enable them to work out Socialism in its relation to home, family life and kindred problems. These are almost specialist problems requiring special study, and could be best considered at meetings of women. This means a section for women members with autonomous rights on all matters affecting the discussion of women and Socialism.[103]

Here she raised questions which were vital for socialist women. How far did they seek to reconfigure the meaning of socialism and what did they see as the purpose of separate women's groups? Some women, echoing views which had been expressed as long ago as the 1890s, reasserted the importance of equality between the sexes within the ILP and refuted the idea that any differentiation should be made between the interests of men and women. Hannah Mitchell refused to join the Labour Party's women's sections in the inter-war years, since

> I believe in complete equality, and was not prepared to be a camp follower, or a member of what seemed to me a permanent Social Committee, or official cake-maker to the Labour Party. So in the I.L.P. with its open membership of both sexes I found my spiritual home.[104]

Emma Sproson, a former suffragette, agreed and argued that women's auxiliaries usually

> get an official backing with women of the half-box cookery type of politician, who happen to be the wives and daughters of the men leaders. Result: feeding bottles, birth control, divorce law reform ... the question of sex should be eliminated from the socialist movement.[105]

For others, such as Helen Gault and Dorothy Jewson, these were exactly the sort of questions that women's groups should deal with or otherwise, they argued, such issues would not be taken seriously by the ILP.[106] When a male delegate to the ILP Conference of 1930 suggested that women's groups should be abolished, since subjects such as maternity were of as much interest to men as to women, Winifred Horrabin defended their continued existence in her women's column in the *New Leader*. She claimed that it was 'only by "persistent nagging" – I use the phrase because it is one that men will be able to understand – that women have at last forced men to consider these questions as serious and vital political issues'.[107] This raised the possibility that separate organisations might be used not just as training grounds for women socialists, but as pressure groups to ensure that socialist organisations would do something about women's subordinate economic and social position.

Effectiveness of women's groups

How effective were socialist women's groups, either in politicising women or in pushing forward women's own interests? Melville Currell claimed in 1974 that women-only groups in political parties implied an 'institutionalisation of inequality', a conclusion which has been endorsed more recently by Pamela Graves, who suggests that women's sections in the inter-war Labour Party and their separate women's conference marginalised women and their concerns.[108] By organising separately women could certainly find themselves excluded from access to resources and power within the socialist movement as a whole. However, there were no automatic gains when they did become more integrated into their respective parties. When a change in the law in Germany meant that women could take part in mixed-sex political organisations, there was a rapid increase in female membership of the Social Democratic Party but a loss of autonomy.[109] Women found that they had very little power in the decision making process and the one female member on the national executive, Louise Zietz, 'appeared to interpret her task more as representing to the socialist women the interests of the party executive than vice versa'.[110] Similarly, in America the organisational autonomy of socialist women was ended in 1908 with the formation of the Woman's National Committee, which was elected by the national convention of the Socialist Party of America.[111] The Committee was given extra resources but had little power over the membership as a whole. Local branches could set up their own women's committees but this enabled them to gain control over women's activities and they did not put a great deal of effort into encouraging women to join the movement.

At particular moments women's groups in the SDF and the ILP did have some success in attracting women into socialist politics. Between 1909 and 1911 the SDF women's groups flourished and were able to provide women with mutual support, as well as developing their potential for political work. They were more than simply auxiliaries to the SDF, although they did benefit the party in terms of recruitment and an improvement to its image.[112] Similarly, in the ILP in the mid-1920s women began once again to take a higher profile in the party. They were elected onto the NAC and attendance at conferences increased so that approximately 16 to 20 per cent of delegates were women after 1925.[113]

There is less evidence that socialist women's groups were able to make an effective challenge to the masculinist theory and practice of socialist organisations. Linda Walker has argued that groups such as the Women's Liberal Federation, the Women's Labour League and women's sections in the Labour Party showed the desire and ability to challenge male power and authority if they thought women's interests were not being acknowledged.[114] It was difficult, however, for socialist women's organisations to gain access to power within their parties or to overcome deep-seated views about which spheres of activity and which issues were appropriate for women. The extent to which they were prepared to make such a challenge depended on the characteristics of the women's organisation rather than simply on the fact that women were organised together as a separate group. It could also depend on the framework of an individual woman's politics. Thus Annot Robinson, who had been a member of the WSPU before joining the ILP, took a leading role in the WLL, a group which is usually seen as reluctant to cause any disunity within the Labour Party. Nonetheless, she argued consistently that women should 'attend to their own business' and suggested at the 1910 ILP conference that if the party did not become more active in pursuing the claims of women, then she would have to follow the lead of the Pankhursts and devote herself to suffragism.[115] She agreed that women had different values from men but thought that the WLL was not just a women's complement to the Labour Party, but was an organisation which was necessary because Labour men could not be relied upon to fight for women's rights.[116]

ILP women in the 1920s were highly critical of the Labour Women's Conference. Helen Gault claimed that it was the 'greatest organised futility in politics. Elephantine in size, microscopic in influence! But it gives the rank and file the *illusion* of power'.[117] In similar vein Winifred Horrabin argued that it 'gets more and more like an overgrown Mothers' meeting holding a garden party with the Vicar in attendance, and … it is just about as effective in the political life of the movement'.[118] Dorothy Jewson, in particular, tried to persuade the Women's Conference to call on the Labour Party to empower it to submit resolutions to the main party conference and to play a direct part in electing women to the reserved seats on the executive.[119] ILP women were also critical of Labour Party women themselves for failing to act independently. In a report of the 1928 International Conference of Socialist Women, Dorothy Jewson expressed regret that it was the opposition of British Labour Party delegates which had prevented a discussion on birth control:

> From the chair of the commission, Miss Susan Lawrence declared that the question of preventive measures should not have been raised. 'If they had known it would be raised, I doubt if our own men would have let us come' – a statement which was rather strange in view of the fact that the official resolution sent in by the Labour Party contains a paragraph asking for an inquiry into 'the effect upon maternal health of methods of family limitation'.[120]

Helen Gault was more hard hitting in her response. She deplored the fact that women leaders were taking such a position. 'Do they really accept it, or are they practising a kind of blacklegging against the sex in order to win some petty prestige or "honour"?'[121]

Socialist women in the ILP thought that their own groups should take a lesson from the Labour Women's Conference and ensure that they not only persisted in pressurising the party as a whole to take questions such as birth control more seriously, but that they should see their groups as providing women with a base from which they could be 'trained to push forward to militant working-class action'[122] Winifred Horrabin asked,

> Can we develop really active groups which will not only help us to rope in the women and train them as Socialist propagandists, but will also give us some real power inside our organisation? Can we put some punch behind our resolutions, so that our work will be a contribution to Socialism as well as to our special party organisation?[123]

On the other hand, Helen Gault expressed the views of many others when she claimed that she did not put her faith in structures alone and urged women generally to develop a more 'militant psychology' if they were to have a real effect and influence.[124]

Separate women's groups and women's columns did provide women with space to express their views as women and to debate the theory and practice of the socialist organisations of which they were a part. Nonetheless, it was difficult for women to make an impact in groups for whom class issues remained central and the Woman Question was still viewed as of marginal concern. Many male socialists continued to doubt women's potential as political activists and to assume that they were particularly suited to a limited range of gender-specific roles. It was comfortable for the leaders of socialist organisations to see women's groups as a valuable way to attract women to work for socialism, but not to recognise that they could be a vehicle to pursue women's collective interests as a sex. In the ILP, for example, women's groups were viewed as 'training centres' for women speakers and administrators and in 1927 it was suggested that there should be a special women's campaign to interest housewives in the party's Living Wage policy.[125] Socialist women themselves saw the groups as having varied functions, which could differ according to the political context. In the 1920s, for example, socialist women in the ILP were as concerned as their male comrades to push forward the cause of socialism, in particular in the Labour Party. They shared the view of the leadership that women's groups could attract women to socialism and also provide an organisational base which would make ILP women more effective in arguing for ILP policies at the Labour Party Women's Conference. At the same time, however, they also tried to persuade men of their own party to develop a more woman-focused theory and practice.[126]

In attempting to carve out a role for themselves within mixed-sex politics, socialist women found it difficult to negotiate between their desire for equality and the recognition that existing gender inequalities meant that women could not be expected to approach their politics in exactly the same way as men. They identified that the practices of socialist groups were gendered, but differed amongst themselves about how to deal with this and whether to seek to transform the nature of socialism itself. The way in which they worked out their position as women and as socialists, and the effect that this had on their practice as socialist women, will be explored in the three case studies which follow.

NOTES

1. J. Clayton (ed.), *Why I Joined the Independent Labour Party*, Leeds, Leeds ILP, c.1896. For other examples see Isabella Ford's comments in *Yorkshire Factory Times*, 20 January 1893; Lily Bell in *Labour Leader*, 1 December 1894.
2. In her discussion of the women's movement in the 1920s, Cheryl Law also argues that it is unhelpful to draw rigid distinctions between equality and welfare feminists (C. Law, *Suffrage and Power: The Women's Movement, 1918–1928*, London, I.B. Tauris, 2000, ch. 8).
3. *New Leader*, 8 February 1924. Jean Mann of the Glasgow ILP argued that women in the ILP had long had 'equality with men in the branches' and therefore did not need separate women's groups (*New Leader*, 25 March 1927). See also M. Pallister, *Socialism for Women*, London, ILP, 1925; Mrs P. Snowden, *The Real Women's Party*, Glasgow, Reformers' Bookstall, 1920.
4. See discussion in Chapter 1.
5. *Justice*, 2 September 1893.
6. M. Coates-Hansen to George Lansbury, 30 October 1907, quoted in C. Collins, 'Women and Labour politics in Britain, 1893–1932', PhD, London School of Economics, 1991, p. 86.
7. See, for example, the frequent references to the Women's Liberal Federation in Lily Bell's column 'Matrons and Maidens'. For example, *Labour Leader*, 19 May 1894; 13 April 1895.
8. Collins, 'Women and Labour politics', p. 69.
9. For the different views of women in SDF branches, see K. Hunt, *Equivocal Feminists. The Social Democratic Federation and the Woman Question, 1884–1911*, Cambridge, Cambridge University Press, 1996, ch. 7.
10. Isabella and Bessie Ford were leading members of the Leeds ILP in the 1890s and had the support of male socialists, such as Tom Maguire, who were sympathetic to women's interests. Emmeline Pankhurst was active in the Manchester ILP in the same period.
11. *Labour Leader*, 6 October 1894.
12. *Labour Leader*, 9 April 1914.
13. Hunt, *Equivocal Feminists*, p. 213; Appendix 2 provides a comparison of women delegates at ILP and SDF conferences. In the ILP in 1907, 10 out of 557 local branch secretaries were women and in 1909, 16 out of 800 (P. Graves, 'Women in British working-class politics, 1883–1939', PhD, University of Pittsburgh, 1989, p. 56).
14. Conference supplement, *Labour Leader*, 9 April 1914.
15. *Labour Leader*, 18 July 1903, quoted in J. Liddington and J. Norris, *One Hand Tied Behind Us: The Rise of the Women's Suffrage Movement*, London, Virago, 1978, pp. 128–9.
16. C.A.N. Reid, 'The origins and development of the Independent Labour Party in Manchester and Salford, 1880–1914', PhD, University of Hull, 1981, p. 651.
17. Collins, 'Women and Labour politics', p. 60.
18. Hunt, *Equivocal Feminists*, Appendix 5. See also Chapter 6 for Hicks and the politics of consumption.
19. H. Mitchell, *The Hard Way Up: The Autobiography of Hannah Mitchell, Suffragette and Rebel*, London, Virago, 1977; O. Banks, *Biographical Dictionary of British Feminists, Vol. 1: 1800–1930*, Brighton, Wheatsheaf, 1985.

20 National couples included Amie and William Hicks, Katharine and John Bruce Glasier, Eleanor Marx and Edward Aveling, Mary Macarthur and William Anderson, Ethel and Phillip Snowden. For local examples, see Reid, 'The origins and development of the ILP'; C. Collette, *For Labour and for Women: The Women's Labour League, 1906–18*, Manchester, Manchester University Press, 1989, Appendix 1; D. Neville, *To Make Their Mark: The Women's Suffrage Movement in the North East of England, 1900–1914*, Newcastle upon Tyne, History Workshop Trust/North East Labour History Society, 1997. The extent to which men and women from the same families were involved in groups affiliated to the Second International is discussed in C. Sowerwine, *Sisters or Citizens? Women and Socialism in France since 1876*, Cambridge, Cambridge University Press, 1982.
21 *ILP Annual Conference Reports*, 1924–1930.
22 Isabella Ford to Edward Carpenter, 25 August 1913, Carpenter Collection, Sheffield Reference Library.
23 *Labour Leader*, 9 April 1914.
24 A. Tuckett, 'Enid Stacy', *North West Labour History Society*, Bulletin 7, 1980–1, p. 42.
25 J. Bellamy and J.A. Schmeichen, 'Amie Hicks', in J. Bellamy and J. Saville (eds), *Dictionary of Labour Biography*, Vol. 4, London, Macmillan, 1977; G. Pearce, 'Mrs Amie Hicks: an interview', *Woman Worker*, 30 June 1909.
26 *Clarion*, 4 July 1896.
27 S. Ledger, *The New Woman: Fiction and Feminism at the Fin de Siècle*, Manchester, Manchester University Press, 1997; A. Ardis, *New Women, New Novels: Feminism and Early Modernism*, New Brunswick, Rutgers University Press, 1990.
28 C. Waters, 'New women and socialist-feminist fiction: the novels of Isabella Ford and Katharine Bruce Glasier', in A. Ingram and D. Patai (eds), *Discovering Forgotten Radicals: British Women Writers, 1859–1939*, Chapel Hill, University of North Carolina Press, 1993, pp. 28–9. Isabella Ford, *On the Threshold*, London, Edward Arnold, 1895; Katharine Bruce Glasier, *Aimée Furniss, Scholar*, London, Clarion, 1896.
29 *Labour Prophet*, December 1894. For a discussion of the new woman and the ILP see K. Cowman, '"Giving them something to do": how the early ILP appealed to women', in M. Walsh (ed.), *Working Out Gender: Perspectives from Labour History*, Aldershot, Ashgate, 1999.
30 *Labour Leader*, 21 April 1894.
31 *Labour Leader*, 14 April 1894. Kate Taylor was secretary of the Glasgow Woman's Labour Party.
32 *New Leader*, 18 July 1924; *Labour Leader*, 19 September, 1903.
33 *Socialist Leader*, 24 June 1950.
34 Quoted in L. Thompson, *The Enthusiasts: A Biography of John and Katharine Bruce Glasier*, London, Victor Gollancz, 1971, p. 72. See also similar remarks in a letter from J.B. Glasier to K. Conway, May 1893, where he notes that 'you have many limitations as an orator which the charm of your youthfulness and marvelous woman vitality abundantly make up for' (Glasier Papers, 1/2/2–1/2/3, Sidney Jones Library, Liverpool University).
35 *Clarion*, 16 February 1895; *Labour Leader*, 17 November 1894; K. Hunt, 'Fractured universality: the language of British socialism before the First World War', in J. Belchem and N. Kirk (eds), *Languages of Labour*, Aldershot, Ashgate, 1997.
36 *Labour Leader*, 30 May, 13 June, 1 August, 22 August 1904; A. Mattison, Diaries, Brotherton Library, Leeds University.
37 Extract from E. Wilkinson, *Clash*, London, Harrap, 1929, quoted in B.D. Vernon, *Ellen Wilkinson*, London, Croom Helm, 1982, p. 122.
38 See, for example, J.B. Glasier to K.B. Glasier, May 1893, Glasier Papers, 1/2/2–1/2/3; Mitchell, *The Hard Way Up*, p. 125.

39 See J.M. Balshaw, 'Suffrage, solidarity and strife: political partnerships and the women's movement, 1880–1930', PhD, University of Greenwich, 1999, for a discussion of the personal and political lives of Katharine and John Bruce Glasier, Annot and Sam Robinson, and Emmeline and Fred Pethick Lawrence.
40 Reid, 'The origins and development of the ILP', p. 616.
41 *Forward*, 10 November 1906.
42 *Justice*, 23 September 1893.
43 *Labour Leader*, 4 May 1895; 3 November 1894.
44 *Labour Leader*, 17 March 1905.
45 *Labour Leader*, 4 July 1896.
46 *Labour Prophet*, August 1893.
47 *Justice*, 29 July 1893.
48 Pallister, *Socialism for Women*, p. 4.
49 *New Leader*, 5 September 1930.
50 See, for example, *New Leader*, 18 May 1928, where the front-page headline is 'Lord Rothermere prophesies that "Votes for Flappers" will mean a Socialist Victory in the General Election'. The accompanying cartoon depicts a young woman, St Georgette, who represents socialism, slaying the dragon of capitalism.
51 *New Leader*, 7 September 1928.
52 For example, see Ben Turner's portrait of Isabella Ford in *Yorkshire Factory Times*, 1 November 1889.
53 *Labour Leader*, 1 December 1894.
54 *Labour Leader*, 17 November 1894. See also in *New Leader*, Ellen Wilkinson's regular column on parliamentary politics in the mid-1920s and Winifred Horrabin's women's column in 1930, which adopted a humorous tone.
55 *Labour Leader*, 1 August 1896.
56 A similar point is made in M. Cross, 'Flora Tristan's socialist propaganda in provincial France, 1843–1844', in B. Taithe and T. Thornton (eds), *Propaganda: Political Rhetoric and Identity, 1300–2000*, Stroud, Sutton, 1999, pp. 159–60.
57 *Labour Leader*, 9 April 1914.
58 See, for example, Enid Stacy in *Labour Prophet*, March 1893; Isabella Ford in *Labour Leader*, 13 May 1904.
59 *Clarion*, 24 July 1897.
60 *Labour Prophet*, February 1894.
61 Hunt, *Equivocal Feminists*, ch. 7; K. Hunt, 'Making socialist woman: politicisation, gender and the Social Democratic Federation, 1884–1911', paper to Ninth Berkshire Conference on the History of Women, Vassar College, 1993.
62 It has been suggested that the Glasgow ILP was successful in involving women in socialist politics after 1906 because of an emphasis on community struggles. See J. Smith, 'Taking the leadership of the labour movement: the ILP in Glasgow, 1906–1914', in A. McKinlay and R.J. Morris (eds), *The ILP on Clydeside, 1893–1932: From Foundation to Disintegration*, Manchester, Manchester University Press, 1991; E. Gordon, *Women and the Labour Movement in Scotland, 1850–1914*, Oxford, Clarendon Press, 1991, ch. 7.
63 *Justice*, 27 January 1912.
64 K. Honeycutt, 'Clara Zetkin: a socialist approach to the problem of women's oppression', in J. Slaughter and R. Kern (eds), *European Women on the Left*, New York, Greenwood Press, 1981.
65 Hunt, *Equivocal Feminists*, p. 226. For example, the secretaries of the Woman's Labour Party in Glasgow, the Newcastle Women's Labour Association and Halifax Women's Branch of the ILP all wrote to Lily Bell to publicise their activities (*Labour Leader*, 14 April, 2 June 1894; 6 April 1895).

66 See, for example, the views of Mrs Harker of the Manchester ILP (*Labour Leader*, 11 April 1896) and Annie Oldacre of the SDF, who argued that women's groups would 'pander to this feeling of exclusive sex interests' (*Justice*, 16 April 1904).
67 *Labour Leader*, 31 March 1894.
68 *Labour Leader*, 23 January 1906.
69 Ibid.
70 This was certainly Enid Stacy's view (*Clarion*, 10 February 1894).
71 *Labour Leader*, 16 January 1906; 23 October 1908. See also Moira's column in the *Leeds Weekly Citizen*, 16 August 1912, which complained that the Labour Party did not make enough appeal to women's interests at election time.
72 *Labour Leader*, 23 March 1906.
73 *Clarion*, 24 April 1897.
74 *Labour Prophet*, August 1893.
75 *Labour Leader*, 6 April 1895.
76 Report by Lizzie Glasier in *Labour Leader*, 13 April 1895.
77 *Labour Leader*, 21 April 1894.
78 Lizzie Glasier, the sister of the ILP leader, John Bruce Glasier, became very active in the Socialist Sunday School movement, while Kate Taylor had been an organiser for the Women's Protective and Provident League.
79 For a detailed account of SDF Women's Socialist Circles, see Hunt, *Equivocal Feminists*, ch. 9.
80 *Justice*, 19 March 1904.
81 *Justice*, 11 March 1905.
82 *Justice*, 27 April 1907.
83 *Justice*, 23 April 1904. Minnie Pallister made the same points about the ILP in the 1920s: 'It is surely reasonable to suppose that many a woman who does not attend the ordinary political meeting ... would be inclined to attend a meeting held near her home at a convenient time if she had been personally invited to come and was sure that it was to be held in a comfortable room' (*The Orange-Box. Thoughts of a Socialist Propagandist*, London, Leonard Parsons, 1924, p. 49).
84 *Northampton Pioneer*, March 1909. For a full account of the Northampton Circle, see Hunt, *Equivocal Feminists*, pp. 241–7.
85 P. Beals, 'Fabian feminism, gender, politics and culture in London, 1880–1930', PhD, Rutgers University, 1989; S. Alexander, 'The Fabian Women's Group, 1908–52', in S. Alexander, *Becoming a Woman and Other Essays in 19th and 20th Century Feminist History*, New York, New York University Press, 1995.
86 Alexander, 'The Fabian Women's Group', p. 152.
87 *Labour Leader*, 23 March 1906.
88 *Labour Leader*, 2 March 1906.
89 *Labour Leader*, 23 March 1906.
90 Collette, *For Labour and for Women*, pp. 62–3.
91 *Labour Leader*, 30 April 1914.
92 One branch secretary reported: 'One of the greatest obstacles to women membership is the question of contributions, but we solved this years ago by admitting women for a contribution of one shilling a year and allowing them to have the same voting power and status as men' (*Labour Leader*, 20 April 1922). For a report of the 1924 conference discussion see *New Leader*, 25 April 1924. The 1926 conference amended the ILP constitution to empower branches to admit women at half subscription rates (Conference supplement, *New Leader*, 9 April 1926).
93 *NAC Annual Report*, 1924.
94 Letter from Minnie Pallister, *New Leader*, 10 October 1924.
95 *New Leader*, 8 February 1924; *NAC Annual Report*, 1925. Patrick Dollan estimated that there were five men to every one woman in the branches.

96 *NAC Annual Report*, 1924, 1928.
97 *New Leader*, 5 September 1924.
98 See, for example, *New Leader*, 1 March 1929.
99 *NAC Annual Report*, 1928.
100 *New Leader*, 22 August 1924.
101 Only six women's groups had been formed in the area and there was no general demand for the initiative from the branches (*NAC Annual Report*, 1927).
102 *New Leader*, 20 February 1925.
103 *New Leader*, 9 November 1923. Similar views were expressed by her husband, Patrick Dollan, who argued that women needed to 'thrash out a socialist domestic policy' in the same way that trade unions discussed industrial policies (*New Leader*, 22 August 1924).
104 Mitchell, *The Hard Way Up*, p. 189.
105 *New Leader*, 21 August 1925, quoted in Collins, 'Women and Labour politics', p. 277.
106 *Forward*, 9 May 1925; *New Leader*, 6 May 1927. Stella Browne, for example, commenting on the Labour Conference of 1928, said that at last sex questions, marriage and maternity had 'crossed the political threshold' (*New Leader*, 2 March 1928).
107 *New Leader*, 24 April 1930.
108 P. Graves, 'An experiment in women-centered socialism: Labour women in Britain', in H. Gruber and P. Graves (eds), *Women and Socialism. Socialism and Women*, Oxford, Berghahn, 1998; M.E. Currell, *Political Women*, London, Croom Helm, 1974, p. 37.
109 The SPD gained 150,000 women members between 1908 and 1914 (J.H. Quataert, *Reluctant Feminists in German Social Democracy, 1885–1917*, New Jersey, Princeton University Press, 1979, p. 148).
110 Honeycutt, 'Clara Zetkin', p. 43.
111 M.J. Buhle, *Women and American Socialism, 1870–1920*, Urbana, University of Illinois Press, 1983, pp. 146–52.
112 Hunt, *Equivocal Feminists*, pp. 241–2.
113 Calculated from delegate lists, *ILP Annual Conference Reports*, 1925–9.
114 L. Walker, 'The women's movement in England in the late nineteenth and early twentieth centuries', PhD, Manchester University, 1984, p. 11. For a positive view of the effectiveness of the WLL, see Collette, *For Labour and for Women*, Conclusion.
115 Collins, 'Women and Labour politics', p. 124. For Annot Robinson's life, see K.A. Rigby, 'Annot Robinson: socialist, suffragist, peacemaker. A biographical study', MA, Manchester Polytechnic, 1986.
116 Collins, 'Women and Labour politics', p. 123.
117 *New Leader*, 7 September 1928.
118 *New Leader*, 2 May 1930.
119 *New Leader*, 25 May 1928; 3 May 1929.
120 *New Leader*, 24 August 1928.
121 *New Leader*, 7 September 1928.
122 *New Leader*, 2 May 1930.
123 Winifred Horrabin in *New Leader*, 2 May 1930.
124 *New Leader*, 7 September 1928.
125 *New Leader*, 26 September 1924; 24 June 1927.
126 *NAC Annual Report*, 1924, 1928.

5

SOCIALIST WOMEN AND THE SUFFRAGE

An examination of the engagement of socialist women and men in suffrage politics provides a lens through which to explore many of the themes raised in this book. The suffrage movement brought into sharp relief issues around an individual woman's political identity and hence her collective loyalty, in particular towards her sex, her class and her party. In the late nineteenth and early twentieth centuries socialism and feminism came into greatest tension over women's suffrage. Suffrage made the apparently simple dichotomy of 'sex versus class' no longer just part of the mantra of the socialist construction of the Woman Question, or a matter to be unpicked once the socialist commonwealth had been achieved, but central to the negotiation and renegotiation of a socialist woman's political practice. For many socialist women this issue exposed the fragility of any possible alliance, let alone identity, between the two movements. In particular, the gap between the rhetoric and the practice of many socialist organisations was exposed and resisted by women who were determined to sustain a woman-focused socialism within socialist parties.

As the campaign for women's suffrage moved to centre stage in the early years of the twentieth century, many socialist women felt they were being forced to choose between their suffragism and their socialism. These dilemmas were not only a matter of personal anguish but were brought into the public domain in the form of passionate debate on the proper and practical relationship between socialism and suffragism. Individuals made different choices both within the complex politics of suffrage and also when it came to prioritising their suffragism or their loyalty to party. Changes in the broader political context help to explain the nature of the arguments put forward by socialist women. As the issue changed within parliament, so the suffrage question took on different polemical forms and had a range of personal consequences. For some suffrage drove a wedge between their socialist and women's politics to the point where they adopted outright hostility to socialism. Yet for others suffrage was the issue that not only most obviously expressed the tension between socialism and feminism but which also provided the catalyst to build a self-consciously woman-focused socialism, albeit at the margins of the socialist parties of the day.

Reinterpreting the suffrage movement

The suffrage movement has long excited the interest of historians. A number of recent texts have sustained this interest by providing an extensive reinterpretation of the campaign.[1] Nonetheless, earlier studies by Jill Liddington and Jill Norris, and by Sandra Holton, still remain as the standard accounts of the relationship between the suffrage and labour movements, and little new attention has been given to socialist women's perspective on the suffrage.[2] And yet, as Karen Hunt's work on the SDF and on the suffrage politics of Dora Montefiore has shown, an examination of that perspective leads to a reappraisal of British suffrage politics.[3] Any reassessment must necessarily involve revisiting the demand for adult suffrage from the socialist woman's point of view. In so doing, some of the easy judgements made in both labour and suffrage histories are challenged. These histories emphasise the ILP's support for a limited franchise for women, which is compared, favourably, to the adult suffrage position of the SDF.[4] And yet the question of which demand to adopt was fiercely contested within the ILP and continued to be a matter of debate despite conference resolutions which supported demands for a limited franchise.[5] The complex range of positions taken by socialist women, and the changes in their views over time, are often overlooked in mainstream studies which polarise the demands for adult and limited suffrage.[6]

Jill Liddington, Jill Norris and Sandra Holton *do* draw attention in their work to a variety of views expressed by women who pursued their suffragism within the context of labour politics. Nonetheless, they also identify a distinct approach which differentiated such women from the mainstream suffrage movement. Jill Liddington and Jill Norris describe the Lancashire working-class women who took an interest in the suffrage as 'radical suffragists' because they shared 'considerable industrial experience and a political radicalism which set them apart from other non militants'.[7] As members of trade unions, socialist groups and the Women's Co-operative Guild, they wanted the vote to improve work and home conditions for women like themselves and sought to achieve this by working at a grass roots level through the organisations of the labour movement.[8]

Sandra Holton is concerned to chart the emergence after 1910 of a group of younger women within the National Union of Women's Suffrage Societies who sought closer links with the labour movement. She labels them 'democratic suffragists', a term originally used by Margaret Llewelyn Davies, president of the WCG, to describe those who campaigned for women to have the vote but combined this with 'the democratic demand that the suffrage should be placed on a human and not a property basis'.[9] Holton argues that, as socialists or progressive liberals, democratic suffragists believed in the principle of universal suffrage based on a humanist perspective. They supported women's suffrage, however, because they feared a manhood suffrage bill would exclude women. Holton traces attempts to bring labour and suffrage together at a local level from 1900 onwards, but argues that only after 1909, when democratic suffragists attained leadership positions in the NUWSS, did an alliance with the Labour Party become more acceptable.[10]

By recognising that women involved in labour politics had complex attitudes towards the enfranchisement of women, such studies have added to our understanding of the features of the suffrage movement as a whole. On the other hand, there can be drawbacks to placing women too neatly into particular categories, which tend to be accepted uncritically in other texts.[11] For instance, the terms 'radical suffragist' and 'democratic suffragist' can mask differences between women, in particular between socialist and non-socialist women, but also between socialist women themselves, who often adopted a variety of arguments and tactics which changed over time. Moreover, the demand for a full, democratic franchise based on the rights of the individual rather than on the possession of property was a long-standing one among socialists. It is unclear, therefore, how socialist women with this perspective differed from the democratic suffragists of the immediate pre-war period.

Not only do suffrage histories tend to neglect socialist women, but they also rarely give much space to a discussion of adult suffrage. When they do, it is usually assumed that limited suffragists were the only ones who were really committed to achieving the franchise for women, while adult suffragism is seen as the least progressive and the least feminist demand to adopt.[12] Sandra Holton, for example, devotes a chapter in *Feminism and Democracy* to adult suffrage.[13] She gives a valuable account of the main arguments put forward and charts the development of the People's Suffrage Federation (PSF) after 1909. This provides an important reminder of the range of individuals and organisations who supported an adult suffrage position, but the demand for adult suffrage is viewed through the perspective of women's suffragists, in particular members of the constitutionalist NUWSS. Thus the judgements made by contemporaries that adult suffrage was really a demand for manhood suffrage form the basis for Holton's own assessment:

> The formulation 'adult suffrage' remained ambiguous in the context of a property-based franchise. It could connote either universal suffrage with both the property and sex disqualifications removed, or merely the extension of the existing sexually exclusive franchise to all adult males. Women suffragists believed, with good reason, that the political ambitions of many within the labour movement would be satisfied by a reform limited to manhood suffrage.[14]

Moreover, Holton's discussion of adult suffrage forms a backdrop to the main focus of her chapter, which is to explore the emergence of democratic suffragism within the NUWSS.

It is argued here, however, that adult suffrage needs to be considered as a long-standing demand in its own right and should be viewed from the perspective of its supporters rather than simply through the eyes of opponents. This chapter, therefore, will identify the different moments when adult suffrage became a key issue for socialist women and will chart changes in the position of organisations and of individuals over time. It not only aims to explore the tactical considerations which underpinned differences between adult and limited suffragists, which in themselves illuminate deeper tensions over political priorities and loyalties, but also seeks to interrogate the arguments used, the meanings that lay behind them and the language in which they were framed.

Support for adult suffrage

Adult suffrage had been an issue for ILP and SDF socialists from the 1890s, well before the women's suffrage movement came into public prominence after 1905. The SDF discussed and campaigned around the subject and from the earliest days advocated universal adult suffrage. The Annual Conference of the ILP in 1895 also committed the party to pursuing a policy of extending electoral rights for both men and women. This position was reinforced at the Glasgow May Day celebrations, when a resolution was passed on the following lines:

> That as the present limitation of the franchise debars all women and a large number of the male workers of the nation from having any voice in its government, this meeting expresses its sympathy with, and pledges itself to support the principle of manhood and womanhood suffrage.[15]

The goal of universal adult suffrage had widespread support, since it was argued that a more limited franchise would benefit only propertied women. Mary Gray of the SDF proclaimed that a limited women's franchise bill, introduced in 1892, was 'a fraud and a snare for the working women of England', while the Manchester ILP member Elsie Harker argued that it would mean an extension of power to the middle and upper classes.[16] In the 1890s, there was no particular pressure to decide between a limited and adult suffrage demand as the issue of the suffrage did not as yet have a high political profile. The differences between socialist women, therefore, tended to revolve around whether franchise reform should be given priority in socialist politics and the extent to which the claims of women should be emphasised as part of an adult suffrage demand.

A number of women across the different socialist groups were not convinced that franchise reform should take priority, including the leading SDF members Amie Hicks and Mary Gray, and Julia Dawson of the *Clarion*, who took little interest in the subject until 1898.[17] Others, however, believed that it was crucial for a socialist movement to campaign to extend voting rights and began to express doubts about whether some male socialists were really committed to adult suffrage. Enid Stacy commented on the 'half defined instinctive antipathy' of several male members of the ILP to adult suffrage even though it was part of the party programme.[18] There is little evidence of widespread hostility to adult suffrage among socialist men, but rather more indication that the SDF and the ILP were indifferent to pursuing franchise reform with any vigour in the 1890s.[19]

In this context socialist women such as Enid Stacy sought to highlight the need for women to be included in any franchise reform, but framed their arguments carefully in order to locate women's suffrage within a broader socialist perspective. Speaking to a women's suffrage meeting in Manchester on the same platform as the NUWSS leader, Millicent Fawcett, Enid Stacy argued that, while it was hard for women of 'culture and refinement not to have their civil rights ... it was worse for those women who were deprived both of their civil rights and the fruits of their labour'. She wanted the suffrage for them so that they could have 'the power to better their condition all round, and in ways that many of those present had no need of'.[20] However, she avoided any precise definition of the basis on which the suffrage should be demanded.

Even at this early stage, however, there were dissentient voices from this approach. Isabella Ford, a member of the Leeds Women's Suffrage Society and ILP, argued consistently that women should have votes on the same terms as men, while Isabella Bream Pearce claimed that the principle of women's suffrage was all important, even if initially only some women achieved the vote.[21] She argued that the removal of sex inequality from the franchise should be the main priority and, as Lily Bell, used her column in the *Labour Leader* during the 1890s as a platform for her views. By 1897 she was arguing that 'women's suffrage is not at present a class question, but a sex question. It is not really a question as to what women shall or shall not be enfranchised, but as to whether women, as women, are entitled to share in the government of the country'.[22]

Adult versus limited suffrage

Until at least 1905 socialist women who were committed to pursuing women's suffrage as a priority within their politics were still arguing explicitly that their demand was compatible with an adult suffrage position, and indeed that the two things should not be seen as separate. In debating the Women's Enfranchisement Bill in 1904–5, Teresa Billington of the ILP and the WSPU argued that it was false to oppose women's suffrage and adult suffrage since one was part of the other.[23] Emmeline Pankhurst also claimed that the Enfranchisement Bill was not a limited but an equality bill and that adult suffrage was the position that 'we all desire and strive for'.[24] Similarly, Dora Montefiore of the SDF and the Women's Social and Political Union argued that a limited suffrage demand was only a tactic towards full adult suffrage.[25]

The positions taken on adult and limited suffrage became gradually more polarised, however, from the end of 1904. A series of outside events, in particular the introduction of suffrage bills in parliament, prompted debates on franchise reform which encouraged the view that the two approaches were irreconcilable. A heightened sense of rivalry was exacerbated by the establishment of groups which had links with the labour and socialist movements, but which had differing perspectives on the suffrage. Two women's suffrage groups were formed in 1903, the WSPU, whose members were initially drawn from the Manchester ILP, and the Lancashire and Cheshire Textile and Other Workers' Labour Representation Committee (LCTOWLRC), both of which were seen as potential rivals for the allegiance of working-class women.[26] In the autumn of 1904, following on from the Trades Union Congress of that year, an Adult Suffrage Society (ASS) was established which was open to all men and women who were prepared to fight for adult suffrage. Although the ASS has often been seen as an SDF dominated organisation,[27] its active members included not only SDF women such as Margaret Bondfield, Clara Hendin and Kathleen Kough, but also a number of ILP members, including Ada Neild Chew, Mary Macarthur and Jennie Baker.

Accusations were made in the ILP that the ASS was 'engineered by an astute radical politician', but this was vehemently denied by Margaret Bondfield, Ada Neild Chew and Jennie Baker, an ILP activist from Stockton, who claimed that the Adult Suffrage League, as they described it, was the initiative of socialist women.[28] ILP women who joined the ASS were disillusioned with the ILP's willingness to support the Women's Enfranchisement Bill, described by Ada Neild Chew as a 'mischievous' and 'a class and property measure' which was inappropriate for a socialist party to pursue.[29] The debate continued at the ILP Annual Conference in 1905, when Mary Muir from Bradford declared that when she had joined the 'Socialist Party she understood that the party were in favour of complete and equal rights for all women and all men'. The Women's Enfranchisement Bill, however, would not enfranchise poor working-class women, and she thought that 'if the same enthusiasm had been put into an Adult Suffrage Bill, a one clause bill could have been carried through the House of Commons'.[30] The controversies surrounding the formation of the Adult Suffrage Society embittered relationships between its members and supporters of the Women's Enfranchisement Bill. Each side then misrepresented the other's views. In observing this, Julia Dawson claimed that 'some advocates of adult suffrage accuse the women's enfranchisers of wire pulling and intriguing. Not to be outdone, some advocates of the Women's Enfranchisement Bill accuse adult suffragists of not being sincere, and of really being opposed to women having the franchise at the bottom of their black hearts'.[31]

The arguments advanced by contemporaries that adult suffragists were at worst hostile to women's suffrage, or at best doing little to achieve it, have had a long-lasting influence on the perspective adopted by suffrage historians. When Charlotte Despard resigned from the ASS in 1906, she claimed it was because the organisation had little enthusiasm and no hope. 'I am aware also of the fact that these Socialists, who are really a minority, are not earnest about Adult Suffrage'.[32] Her views have then been quoted without comment in many texts dealing with this question and have come to represent all that was wrong with the ASS.[33] The open hostility to women's suffrage expressed by male socialists such as the SDF member and trade unionist Harry Quelch, and the lack of action taken by the SDF as an organisation to achieve adult suffrage, are then seen as reinforcing Despard's conclusions.[34] And yet it is difficult to find anyone else who resigned from the ASS on the same grounds as Charlotte Despard, while there were many male socialists who viewed adult suffrage as meaning the enfranchisement of both sexes. The ASS was only a small organisation and did not have a great deal of impact in its early years. In 1906, for instance, Margaret Bondfield agreed that the ASS had not been very active, but explained that this was because the organisation could not identify with a limited bill and did not want to accentuate the differences which already existed among socialist women about the basis on which the franchise should be demanded.[35] Nonetheless, leading ASS members such as Margaret Bondfield, Jennie Baker and, later, Dora Montefiore were enormously energetic in arguing the adult suffrage case. Along with Ada Neild Chew, Jennie Baker played a particularly important part in arguing for support for an adult suffrage measure in the debates within the ILP on this issue between 1904 and 1907.[36]

Debates on an adult versus a limited franchise demand were at their keenest in 1904/5, when the Women's Enfranchisement Bill was before parliament; in 1907, when the Labour Party failed once again to support women's suffrage at its annual conference and when the Second International meeting at Stuttgart confirmed unequivocally its stand on universal adult suffrage; and in 1909, when the government suggested the possibility of an adult suffrage bill. All of these events stimulated discussion in the socialist press. A variety of views were expressed by socialists regardless of their organisational affiliation, despite the fact that the SDF and the ILP held different official positions on the question. Moreover, the balance of debate within the two parties, and within their various newspapers, did change over time.

The socialist press and the suffrage debate

Socialist newspapers are central as a source for understanding socialist women's outlook on the suffrage. They were thought by contemporaries to have a key role not only in spreading socialist propaganda, but also in helping to shape the ideas of men and women who were already socialists.[37] The views expressed within them depended on a complex relationship between the outlook of the editor, the official policies of specific organisations and individual women journalists. The existence of a women's column could also make a difference to the extent to which newspapers debated women's suffrage and to the arguments put forward.[38]

From 1905 coverage of the suffrage issue increased markedly in *Justice*, with over two-thirds of the editions in 1907 containing suffrage items. Although there was a decline in interest in 1909, the issue was taken up by the party's monthly journal, *Social Democrat*, which had items on suffrage in ten out of the twelve editions of that year. *Justice* continued to include material on suffrage, however, and coverage always remained higher than in the years before 1905.[39] The official line of the SDF was to support adult suffrage, but the activities of the Adult Suffrage Society received little coverage in *Justice* before 1907. It was also still possible for dissenting voices to be heard; Dora Montefiore, while a member of the SDF executive and the WSPU, was instrumental in stimulating debate around women's suffrage. In 1907, however, Montefiore moved from the WSPU to the ASS and there was no longer space for a limited suffrage position within SDF publications. Moreover, increasing rivalry between the party and the WSPU for potential supporters helped to polarise the debate. In the same year, after the meeting of the Second International in Stuttgart put pressure on its members to undertake a systematic campaign for adult suffrage, the SDF at last produced a manifesto which called on all its branches to give prominence to the campaign for adult suffrage.[40] Nonetheless, given the continuing ambivalence of the SDF towards the Woman Question more generally, it was still left largely to individuals to pursue the cause with any degree of enthusiasm.

The suffrage question was even more complicated within the ILP. The official stand of the party, confirmed at annual conferences and maintained despite the resolution passed at Stuttgart, was to support the enfranchisement of women, even on a limited basis, as a step towards full adult suffrage. Nonetheless, this position was contested within the party both at a leadership and at a rank and file level. The *Labour Leader* did make reference to the suffrage campaign during the 1890s, but coverage of the issue was only sporadic. The most systematic argument for the need for the ILP to give priority to women's suffrage was made by Lily Bell in her women's column. This can be contrasted with the long-lived 'Our Women's Letter' in the *Clarion*, which was slow to take up the question. In the late 1890s Julia Dawson, its editor, claimed that she was a 'recent convert to Women's suffrage', but by the early 1900s she had become an important advocate of adult suffrage, which may explain why the activities of the ASS were frequently reported in the paper.[41]

As in the case of *Justice*, coverage of the suffrage question increased in the *Labour Leader* in the early 1900s, in particular from the end of 1904, when there was a fierce debate in the letters page over the Women's Enfranchisement Bill. The committed suffragists Emmeline Pankhurst and Isabella Ford were both on the National Administrative Council at that time and encouraged the party to give more attention to suffrage. Isabella Ford, for example, wrote glowing reports in the *Labour Leader* about the revived women's suffrage movement and the new enthusiasm being displayed for the women's cause.[42] After 1907, however, when the WSPU severed its ties with the ILP at a national level, and many of the most active suffragists decided to give a full-time commitment to the suffrage campaign, the *Labour Leader* gave far less coverage to the suffrage question. It still, however, maintained its support for a limited franchise as a stepping stone to adult suffrage. The issue was frequently raised in the women's column edited by Iona from 1906 to 1909. She expressed support for a limited franchise, but argued increasingly that other reforms were more important for socialists. Interest in the subject only revived after 1911 when, in a context in which the government proposed that there should be a manhood suffrage bill, the new editor of the *Labour Leader*, Fenner Brockway, launched a political equality campaign. The alliance between the Labour Party and the NUWSS then led to an outpouring of articles and letters in the paper on women's suffrage between 1912 and 1914.

It is crucial to look beyond the national press, however, to understand the full range of perspectives on the suffrage which were advanced within the ILP.[43] For example, Tom Johnston, editor of the influential Glasgow ILP newspaper *Forward*, was an active supporter of women's suffrage and ensured that the paper maintained a keen interest in the suffrage question from its launch in 1906 up until the outbreak of war.[44] Items on the franchise appeared almost every week and in 1907, when Keir Hardie introduced a women's suffrage bill in parliament, there was an extensive debate in *Forward* between adult and limited suffragists. In contrast to the *Labour Leader*, *Forward* was sympathetic towards the militant suffrage movement. A women's suffrage column was edited between 1906 and 1909 by WSPU members from Glasgow, including Lily Bell and Mary Phillips. There was no column from 1910 to 1912, but it reappeared in 1913, when it was once again edited by local WSPU members such as Janie Allan and Helen Crawfurd. In this later period Sylvia Pankhurst was also a regular contributor to the paper, writing a series of articles on why women needed the vote.[45]

What this brief survey suggests is that despite the official position taken by the different socialist groups, views around how to frame the demand for the suffrage and whether to pursue the question vigorously varied both within and across those organisations. The complex ways in which participants in the debate approached the suffrage question and the arguments they used will be explored in the next section. It will be argued that the debate between an adult and a limited suffrage position should not be seen simply as an anti-woman stance versus a pro-woman stance, which is how the two sides are often portrayed in the secondary literature. Instead, an attempt will be made to explore the arguments of those who took an adult suffrage position and to suggest that they made their arguments as socialists rather than as anti-feminists and that their position on the suffrage question was yet another area in which women had to work out their identity as women, as socialists and as party members.

Tactical arguments

One thread running through socialist women's attitudes to political enfranchisement was the extent to which franchise reform should be seen as a key issue for socialists, irrespective of the basis on which it might be granted. During the 1890s in particular, in the context of debates around the relative importance of political versus economic power, many women were not convinced that they should emphasise the need for the vote.[46] As the suffrage movement gained momentum it was difficult to ignore the issue, although individual women still took it up only with reluctance. Kathleen Kough of the SDF, who had previously been sceptical about franchise reform, was persuaded that socialists should campaign to achieve adult suffrage by the increasing interest shown by all classes of women in the suffrage. She believed that if the issue were settled, more important matters would then receive attention, and that once women had the vote it would 'show them of what very little use, comparatively speaking, political power can be'.[47]

Not all of those who were committed to achieving women's enfranchisement, either through an adult or a limited measure, were prepared to give it priority. Katharine Bruce Glasier, for example, in common with many other ILP women who were active in the WLL, supported the demand for a limited franchise but argued that this should not detract from social and economic reform campaigns which would benefit working-class mothers. She often drew attention to questions of class power, arguing in 1912 that 'I don't think I ever confused freedom with the mere possession of the vote'.[48] Looking back on her student days, she claimed that even without the vote, as a middle-class, well-educated woman, she had been able to exert more influence and to exercise more choice in her life than agricultural labourers who had recently been enfranchised.

For some women, however, the extent to which priority should be given to the vote *was* tied up with the basis on which it was demanded. Mary Muir, for instance, argued that anything short of adult suffrage was not worth the serious attention of socialists, but that the diversion of energy from important questions such as the feeding of schoolchildren or medical inspection in the direction of *any* suffrage bill was 'a doubtful step in the interests of the human race'.[49] In similar vein, Julia Dawson believed that the suffragette slogan should read: 'Votes for some women – they talk as if granting suffrage will alter poverty, unemployment etc when we know only socialism can do that'.[50] She argued with increasing frustration that socialists had no business in wasting their time on votes for some women. 'During this coming winter, when the question of actual meat and drink presses, I doubt even whether adult suffragists ought to spend more time on their more sensible propaganda'.[51] Although she agreed that votes for all women was an admirable demand which all should support, she still thought that 'we must not let it carry away our sense of proportion'.[52] Regardless of their position on the basis on which to ask for the vote, therefore, there were some suffragists who were reluctant to prioritise the suffrage question in their day-to-day politics, although it is adult suffragists who are usually characterised as having far less commitment to pursuing the measure.

Socialist women who *did* seek to prioritise women's suffrage, either through a limited or an adult demand, had a variety of reasons for doing so. Zelda Kahan, a member of the SDF and an adult suffragist, argued that, although there were more urgent questions, adult suffrage was an important agitation in which Social Democrats should take the lead and capture the movement from the hands of middle- and upper-class women. For her, the vote was important because it would enable men and women to fight together against capitalism.[53] Lily Bell, on the other hand, claimed that, while votes in themselves were unlikely to bring about sweeping social changes, they were important as 'symbols of that freedom from male domination that we demand as our right'.[54] This emphasis on 'women's emancipation' was a far cry from those such as Katharine Bruce Glasier and Margaret MacDonald who believed that the vote would enable working-class women to exert an influence on politics from their perspective as wives and mothers. Isabella Ford stood somewhere between the two, emphasising both how the vote would make women at last 'fully human' and also that it was necessary so that women could fight alongside men for socialism and help to shape the new society. 'Perhaps even more. It is political equality, too, which alone will bring economic equality, equal pay for men and women, and men know this perfectly well and are teaching it to the women'.[55]

Socialist women invariably claimed that their ultimate goal was full adult suffrage, but they differed over the tactics which should be employed to achieve this aim. In the early 1900s members of the Lancashire and Cheshire Textile and Other Workers' Labour Representation Committee and of the Women's Co-operative Guild called for a measure of womanhood suffrage, that is votes for all women over the age of 21, which 'in effect was a demand for adult suffrage, but it placed all its stress on the claims of women'.[56] On the other hand, the LCTOWLRC were prepared to support any measure which enfranchised women and believed that even under a limited bill many working-class women would be able to vote.[57] One of the group's leading members, Selina Cooper, argued on behalf of the ILP at the 1905 LRC Conference that the Women's Enfranchisement Bill was the only possible practical step towards adult suffrage. At the same conference Keir Hardie also claimed that the Bill was not an alternative to adult suffrage 'but clearing the way to that ideal'.[58] This argument was frequently used. In the same year several women who were members both of the ILP and the WSPU signed a petition in support of the Bill, arguing that 'it simplifies the position with regard to adult suffrage by leaving only the property basis to be removed' and 'it is a stepping stone to adult suffrage, not an alternative to it'.[59] In giving their support to the Women's Enfranchisement Bill, however, many ILP women agreed with Jane Ford that:

> we can only hope that ... the LRC will give its wholehearted support to the principle of Women's Suffrage, and at the same time see to it that the agitation for Adult Suffrage, which I need hardly say has the active support of every genuine Woman Suffragist, is more effectively carried forward in the House of Commons than has hitherto been the case.[60]

Later in the period, in particular after 1907, when the Labour Party Conference once again failed to support the women's suffrage resolution and the WSPU split from the labour movement, there was a far greater antagonism from limited suffragists towards the expression of the adult suffrage demand. Isabella Ford, for example, argued that adult suffrage bills were a 'snare led to entrap us and turn us away from our object. I wish people would look at politics as they really are, and not as they think they ought to be'.[61]

The debate in 1905 frequently revolved around whether support for full adult suffrage was a realistic demand. Julia Dawson could not accept that it was more difficult to gain adult suffrage than to gain the vote for 'widows and single women who are sufficiently well off to qualify for the Women's Enfranchisement Bill'.[62] She argued that:

> I think we should in justice wait for the whole loaf. But even if we take it for granted that it would be expedient to be content with half the loaf at first, why choose the top half? Should not the claims of the bottom crust come first which, as everybody knows, supports the upper.[63]

Protagonists on both sides were fond of using the metaphor of a loaf of bread to get their point across. Marion Coates Hansen, for example, claimed that they were going at once for what 'appears to some a "half loaf" for we are starving'.[64] Helena Swanwick, who in 1908 was an active member of the North of England Society for Women's Suffrage, claimed that her own society did not oppose adult suffrage but that adult suffragists did oppose the enfranchisement of women. 'Can you wonder if we women rather suspect a generosity which offers the whole loaf (in the distant future) but refuses the half?'[65] Dawson replied that she wanted the whole loaf now, not in the distant future, and she did not see 'why they should be content with a half when they can get the whole just as easily'.[66]

Socialist women frequently changed their tactical position, while maintaining that their commitment to women's suffrage within the framework of adult suffrage remained the same. Charlotte Despard resigned from the Adult Suffrage Society in 1906 and in the following year helped to establish the Women's Freedom League, but claimed that adult suffrage was still her objective.[67] Ada Neild Chew, who was involved in the Women's Trade Union League and then in the Women's Labour League, played a particularly important part in the 1905 debate around the Women's Enfranchisement Bill, arguing from an adult suffrage position. In 1911, however, she became an organiser for the NUWSS. She explained in the *Common Cause* that she had always thought that women trade unionists were disadvantaged by not having a vote, but:

> I could not see that anything less than Adult Suffrage would be of any use to the working woman .... After many months of anxious thinking, I have come to the conclusion that we cannot get on whilst women have *no* means of even presenting their point of view, and that we shall be at a standstill till this necessary 'first step' is taken; and that to be determined to wait until all women can vote is as reactionary and

impracticable as to oppose all reform because it does not go as far on our way as we wish it to go.[68]

Nonetheless, she felt more comfortable once the Labour Party had made an alliance with the NUWSS and argued that working women distrusted the suffrage societies because they were run by 'fine ladies'.[69] Not all socialist women moved from an adult to a limited suffrage position. Dora Montefiore of the SDF was an active member of the WSPU before joining the ASS in 1907. She had always focused on a democratic and inclusive measure, but now felt that the strategy of using a limited franchise as a stepping stone to full adult suffrage was no longer tenable, since 'few working men's wives would be enfranchised, which would place them in an unfair position'.[70]

Class versus sex

Given the emphasis of the historiography on the tactical differences between adult and limited suffragists, and the relative neglect of the perspective of socialist women, little attention has been paid to the arguments which were put forward and to the subtle differences between socialist women in their understandings of the meaning of citizenship. Class was seen as a fundamental issue in debates over the suffrage, but the way in which it was used could vary depending on the audience which was being addressed. So much of the debate on suffrage was about persuading specific groups, for example their own parties, unaligned socialists, suffragists and the public, including the male voter and the unenfranchised woman. Each audience might have very different understandings of class. Thus, the appeal to class war might work for an SDF conference, but it was more risky for an ILP meeting and was likely to be inappropriate for a suffragist audience.

On one level, the debate between adult and limited suffragists brought to the fore the question of class versus sex. Men and women in the SDF and ILP frequently expressed the fear that the women's suffrage movement would draw attention to sex, rather than class, inequalities and also that it would exacerbate antagonism between the sexes.[71] William Anderson of the ILP, for example, claimed that it was inconsistent for a 'Socialist party to lend its support to a movement which is deliberately attempting to distract the attention of women workers from the wrongs of their class to the wrongs of their sex'.[72] He feared that women workers, in particular textile workers, were being taught to think that all their problems stemmed from their voteless condition rather than from their status as waged workers. At almost the other end of the spectrum Lily Bell, by now a member of the WSPU and the ILP, wrote in *Forward* that:

> Sex autocracy is even more tyrannical than class autocracy, and to end its rule women must stand together as women irrespective of class, determined to insist upon the principle of sex equality being fully

recognised and established. Let them heed not the men who seek to inflame class prejudice.[73]

Most socialist women were not prepared to emphasise sex autocracy at the expense of the class dimensions of suffrage. Ada Neild Chew cited an ILP lecturer who, in referring to suffrage campaigners, said ' "We must trust these wealthy women". I submit sir, that this is not an answer which will convince any woman who is not blinded by the wrongs of sex to all other considerations'.[74] The extent to which middle-class women could be trusted to help other women was a constant theme in the speeches and writings of socialist women, irrespective of their party affiliation. Amie Hicks of the SDF, for example, in seconding an adult suffrage resolution, recalled her father's work as a Chartist and the way in which the agitation of the workers was made use of by the middle classes, who then reaped the sole advantage when the Reform Act was passed in 1867.[75] On the other hand, in keeping with the ILP's attempt to downplay class conflict and to emphasise cooperation between classes, Julia Dawson hoped that the ASS would have 'a large following among all classes of women'.[76]

The potential for female solidarity raised by the women's suffrage campaign could cut across and conflict with the comradeship between the sexes which was held up as an ideal within the socialist movement. The question was often asked about how far socialist men could be trusted to support women's interests. Thus, when Edith How Martyn of the WSPU asked what precautions adult suffragists had taken against betrayal by men, Julia Dawson was quick to reply that personally she trusted men and that the best precaution against any such betrayal was to ask for votes for all women.[77] In contrast, using her usual belligerent tone, Lily Bell claimed that 'a study of the history of the relations between men and women in the past will show ... that the interests of women cannot be left safely in the hands of men'.[78]

The class of women who would be enfranchised under a limited suffrage bill was a matter of considerable importance to socialist women, and in 1904 a number of surveys were conducted by the ILP, the Lancashire and Cheshire Textile and Other Workers' Labour Representation Committee and the Women's Co-operative Guild to determine what proportion of working-class women would be enfranchised under the Women's Enfranchisement Bill.[79] A controversy then developed over the question of class definitions which demonstrated the difficulty that socialists had in fitting women into a conventional class analysis. Jennie Baker, for instance, challenged the wide definition being given to the term working women in the ILP survey, since she did not agree that shopkeepers should be seen as working class. Marion Coates Hansen, however, argued that widows running tiny backstreet shops with housework on their minds should not be characterised as lower middle class.[80] The term 'working women' was used far more frequently than 'working-class women', but again there was little consistency in the way it was defined. When they gave papers to the Annual Conference of the National Union of Women Workers in 1906, Katharine

Bruce Glasier and Selina Cooper both discussed the need for working women to have the vote, but they used the term differently. Katharine Bruce Glasier included both women wage earners and women wage spenders, in particular members of the Women's Co-operative Guild, whereas Selina Cooper referred on that occasion only to textile workers.[81] Agnes Pettigrew, secretary of the Glasgow branch of the Shop Assistants' Union and a member of the Adult Suffrage Society, in discussing who would be enfranchised by a limited bill, claimed that her reference to working women:

> was in the narrower sense, meaning wage earners, although working-men's wives are entitled to be included in the term ... In reply to the statement that more working-class women would be eligible to vote than women of the other classes if the sex disability was removed, I fear there are women included in this estimate who would object at any other time to being so classed.[82]

The language of property was frequently used by adult suffragists when explaining their objections to a limited franchise. This might have been an easier way to discuss class distinctions than the language of class itself, in particular when women were the subject of the debate. The limited demand was often characterised as a means to extend the 'powers of property'.[83] As early as 1895 Elsie Harker argued that 'many of the advanced women who are now agitating make the fact that they own property one of their chief arguments, losing sight of their own argument of womanhood ... What are they going to do for those who have no property?'[84] In 1905 Ada Neild Chew complained that the Women's Enfranchisement Bill would enfranchise women of property,[85] while two years later Margaret Bondfield argued that, if property were used as a qualification for the suffrage, then only wealthy women would be enfranchised. She thought that the right to vote should be on a 'human' basis and should not involve 'bricks and mortar'.[86] Agnes Pettigrew further claimed that the interests of working-class women would be no safer in the hands of propertied women than in those of propertied men.[87] Limited suffragists countered this view by pointing out that whether the franchise was based on a property qualification or not was irrelevant, since it was a question of 'sex equality' and not one of property.[88]

Regardless of their views on a limited or an adult suffrage position, socialist men and women could use their opposition to property owning to support the actions of the militants. Margaretta Hicks, for instance, encouraged Social Democrats to support suffragette window smashing because

> it is impossible for women to use either the industrial strike or the vote to enforce their claim to the franchise. This is the age of property, therefore an attack on the face of property is the most effective way of

declaring rebellion against a society which does not recognise them as citizens.[89]

Thomas Johnston, in an article entitled 'The Woman Militant', praised the WSPU for their brave actions. 'Open war on Property (that great Seventeenth century fetish) has been declared. The women know the risks they run: these risks they are prepared to face.' He also argued that women were unable to use the ballot box and reminded his readers about the Chartist period, 'the burning of hay ricks, the smashing of the weavers' looms', concluding that although he disapproved of some actions 'surely we can admire ... the spirit, the fearlessness, and the courage of the Woman Militant who has arisen among us'.[90]

Language of democracy and rights

Those on all sides of the debate laid claim to terms such as democracy, equality and rights, which they saw as an integral part of their socialist beliefs. Jennie Baker, for instance, argued that the Women's Enfranchisement Bill (WEB) 'makes no provision for those who most need to have a voice in the laws of the country' and suggested that it was not in the best interests of democracy to merely extend the property qualification.[91] A few years later M. (Maud) M.A. Ward, secretary of the Adult Suffrage Society 1908–9 and close friend of Margaret Bondfield, talked of adult suffrage as *the* 'democratic aim', while Margaret Llewelyn Davies saw her adult suffrage position as democratic since a limited franchise bill would enfranchise only one in seven or eight working women 'and those that are will not be representative of either the great class of married working women or of factory workers'.[92] On the other hand, limited suffragists countered with the argument that *their* position was the most democratic since they wanted votes on the same terms as men.[93] Such arguments were questioned by the ASS, since it was claimed that the exact nature of votes for women on the same terms as men was never explained by its supporters.[94]

Protagonists on both sides of the debate also claimed that it was *their* demand which would bring equality for women. In 1905 supporters of the WEB argued that they sought equality before the law and 'equal voting power with their brothers'.[95] In contrast, the adult suffragist Mary Muir argued that if it was an equality bill, then all women would be in it.[96] Beyond the debates over the clauses, and potential consequences, of specific legislation, contributors to discussions on women's suffrage also employed the language of equality to describe the importance of the suffrage itself. An editorial in the *Labour Leader*, reflecting on the defeat of the Women's Enfranchisement Bill in 1905, suggested that it was a hopeful sign that women's suffrage was now part of socialist agitation in Britain, since 'the equality of women as citizens will be raised to the forefront of politics'.[97] The language of rights was also used, but it is unclear if this was evidence of residual liberalism or a more common framing of socialists' demands such as the Right to Work. Again in the 1905 debate Katharine Bruce

Glasier talked of the present splendid stand made by the ILP on the broad principle of 'women's rights as citizens to the vote'.[98] And yet from an adult suffrage perspective Ada Neild Chew turned this on its head. She argued that a limited bill would make citizenship for women a privilege when 'we want rights not privileges'.[99]

Thus socialist men and women who took different positions on the suffrage argued their case using similar terms, which in turn could make it appear that their own views were the more 'democratic', 'equal' or supportive of working/working-class women. They also claimed that their *own* stand on the suffrage represented the best way forward both for the achievement of socialism and also for women's overall 'emancipation'. Throughout all the changes of tactics, alliances and organisational affiliations most socialist women who participated in the debate could not see a real separation between their 'feminist' and their socialist goals, which to their minds were inextricably linked. A few women, such as Lily Bell, Mary Gawthorpe and Emmeline Pankhurst, were so committed to the suffrage movement at all costs, and disenchanted with the level of socialist and Labour Party support, that they were lost for good to socialism. The majority, however, continued to juggle their interests as they worked through their priorities as socialists and as women.

When the WSPU failed to support the Labour Party candidate at the Cockermouth by-election of 1906, Julia Dawson claimed that it 'shows how the mighty have fallen. They used to work for Socialism'.[100] Teresa Billington, however, countered with the argument that 'in the best interests of Socialism, as well as for women, we must demand and win equal human rights for our sisters'. She accepted that 'Socialism includes sex equality. True. But the official socialist parties ignore it as much as possible'.[101] The methods of these parties forced her to step down from the socialist platform at the beginning of the year since she saw working for the vote as a way to bring women to socialism, but she remained a member of three ILP branches. Others appeared to reverse priorities and strategies. Mabel Hope of the SDF thought that 'only under Socialism will justice ever be done to women. Piecemeal legislation is therefore a waste of valuable time', while Julia Dawson, commenting on the ILP conference of 1907, when there was criticism of the political actions of the WSPU, feared that the suffrage had made mischief in the ranks of socialism and was likely to make more. She felt that the question was not one of adult versus a limited suffrage 'but the sentimental one as to whether certain women who long ago won the hearts of the ILP by their noble work, were to be retained in the movement, or lost to it'.[102] Later she preferred to support a socialist group to which she did not belong rather than women suffragists: 'The SDP is taking up the cudgels for a Franchise Measure which would give justice to ALL. More power to it!'[103]

These complex arguments, which cut across the adult/limited suffrage divide, should make us wary of neatly categorising socialist women as adult suffragists who were not really very interested in women as a political group, or as limited suffragists who took a 'feminist' perspective and prioritised sex disabilities in their politics. Regardless of their position on the form that the demand for the suffrage should take, socialist women could share the view that women as a political category needed a voice in order to change their subordinate position. Jennie Baker, for example, was inspired by the actions of Christabel Pankhurst and Annie Kenney when they disrupted a meeting at the Free Trade Hall in Manchester in 1905 and claimed that full adult suffrage needed support since 'every woman in the country [must feel] that the battle is for personal and individual rights'. She argued that women had 'practised self effacement quite long enough'.[104] On a tactical level individuals such as Margaret Bondfield might choose to see the interests of the socialist struggle as so important that they were unwilling to be too confrontational, whereas others were willing to make women's suffrage a resigning issue. Dolly Lansbury, for example, suggested that, if women were not included in Asquith's reform bill, 'we ILP women will have to give, not some but all of our time to the cause of Votes for Women. We do not want to do this. It is up to the ILP men to make sure that we shall not find such a step necessary'.[105]

Women's position could alter over time as the context in which they framed their strategies changed. Margaret McMillan, for example, was a member of the National Administrative Council of the ILP in 1906 and joined with Isabella Ford in seeking to conciliate between the ILP and the WSPU after the Cockermouth incident. She claimed that women had good reason to be discontented with the ILP, since 'women were still political outcasts and stood in an entirely different relation to the political issues of the day than men did'.[106] Unlike other leading ILP suffragists, however, she chose to remain on the NAC and to give her energies to the ILP, rather than giving a greater commitment to the suffrage campaign, because she thought that the ILP provided the best platform for her main political agenda, the medical inspection of schoolchildren.[107] Nonetheless, McMillan continued to take an interest in the vote and at various times belonged to both the Women's Freedom League and the People's Suffrage Federation. She emphasised the importance of enfranchising working women, amongst whom she included herself, since she saw them as 'the creators of civilisation and of the elements of that political life from which they are now excluded'.[108]

The People's Suffrage Federation

The immediate pre-war years brought a new political context to the suffrage campaign. In 1909 the Liberal Prime Minister, Asquith, announced that a manhood suffrage bill would be introduced which could be amended to include women's suffrage. This prompted the establishment of a new organisation, the People's Suffrage Federation (PSF), whose founders included Margaret Llewelyn Davies, Mary Macarthur and Margaret Bondfield, now an ILP activist. The aim was to draw together all those who sought a broad franchise, including progressive liberals, to demand a government measure which would enfranchise both sexes and to gain support for adult suffrage from organised bodies.[109] Sandra Holton claims that it was the fear that adult suffragists would not remain firm for sex equality which led to the formation of the PSF. But letters and articles written by PSF leaders at the time suggest that they believed that, since Asquith's announcement, a demand for a limited bill, such as the Conciliation Bill, was futile and would mean opposition to a wider, more democratic franchise.[110] Margaret Llewelyn Davies admitted that in the past there were grounds to fear that adult suffrage might mean manhood suffrage, but the work of suffrage societies and the growth of democratic feeling, along with 'the building of such an organisation as the PSF is making the betrayal of women a practical impossibility'.[111] She thought that the time was now ripe to press for a 'democratic measure of reform' which would enfranchise all men and women on the grounds of 'common humanity'.[112]

The PSF had close links with the ILP and the Labour Party and also found that it could work with the Women's Labour League.[113] Its female leaders were members of the ILP, while Arthur Henderson of the Parliamentary Labour Party was one of the honorary treasurers and William Anderson, chairman of the ILP, was on the general committee. By the end of its first year 336 societies and branches had affiliated or passed adult suffrage resolutions, including 126 branches of the ILP and 66 Women's Co-operative Guild groups.[114] To some extent, therefore, adult and limited suffragists in the socialist movement found that their positions were less polarised, but there was still considerable suspicion between them. The *Labour Leader* gave little coverage to the work of the PSF and consistently reminded its readers that the official position of the ILP was support for a limited franchise. In a letter to the paper Margaret Stockman also expressed surprise to find that, given the policy of the ILP that the immediate aim should be a measure of sex equality, there was a proposal on the Annual Conference agenda that ILP branches should affiliate to the PSF, an organisation which would 'oppose such a measure'.[115]

There was also little cooperation between the PSF and the Adult Suffrage Society. The ASS had become more closely associated with the SDF once the latter had adopted its adult suffrage manifesto in 1907 and Dora Montefiore had become honorary secretary of the ASS in 1909.[116] It seems likely that the PSF was formed to distance the campaign for adult suffrage from the SDF, since the ILP, with its increasing parliamentary focus, sought to accentuate differences between itself and the SDF. The ASS also remained aloof from the PSF because the Federation was willing on occasion, for tactical reasons, to support measures which did not include full adult suffrage.[117] Thus when Margaretta Hicks of the BSP organised an adult suffrage demonstration in 1913 intended for trade unionists, the *Daily Herald* urged that 'it is the duty of every socialist worthy of the name to be there', but there is little evidence that it had the support of either the PSF or the ILP.[118]

As early as 1907 the ASS had argued that only two forces could prevent the adoption of manhood suffrage – the labour and socialist movement pledged to adult suffrage and Members of Parliament pledged to women's suffrage.[119] The suggestion that the support of the labour movement was the only way to achieve women's suffrage became central to the arguments of the PSF and the ILP after 1910. Margaret Bondfield claimed that there had never been such a good opportunity to fight for what they wanted, 'adult suffrage straight and clear', a cause which all labour and socialist women could work for together. She urged women from the ILP and the WLL to be in the van of this campaign, arguing that the only cry for them was 'not manhood, but Adult Suffrage, and that quickly'.[120]

After an alliance for electoral purposes had been made between the Labour Party and the NUWSS in 1912, ILP women, regardless of whether they had been linked to a women's suffrage group or to the PSF, put their energies into ensuring that the Labour Party would keep to its pledge that it would not support any franchise bills which failed to include a measure of women's suffrage.[121] In a special suffrage supplement in the *Labour Leader* Isabella Ford, Annot Robinson, Margaret Llewelyn Davies, Marion Phillips, Ada Neild Chew and others urged men to stand by women as the latter had stood by them in times of labour struggles.[122] Ada Neild Chew argued that men must support women as the only way to progress towards a socialist state, while Isabella Ford claimed that every labour man would see that his salvation depended on political freedom for women. It was at this juncture that the history of the ILP as steadfast supporter of the women's suffrage cause began to be created. Annot Robinson set the tone when she argued that the ILP had always been 'the women's friend' and that suffragists were 'hugely indebted to the ILP'.[123] In a series of articles in 1912 on the ILP's attitude towards the women's movement William Anderson claimed that the ILP had always been active in 'pressing the industrial, social and political claims of women. The Party believes that man cannot be free whilst woman remains in subjection'.[124] In a reversal of his stand in 1904 he claimed that it would be dreadful if women were excluded from the new suffrage bill and urged the labour movement to do all in its power to prevent this.[125]

Suffrage and War

With the outbreak of war women's suffrage seemed less important for socialist women than working for peace. Nonetheless, when franchise reform became an issue in 1916, socialist women again took part in the campaign to ensure that women would be included in any new bill. They found, however, that the nature of the debate and the alliances made were different from the pre-war years. The initial reaction of the *Labour Leader* was that women's suffrage could be demanded with greater confidence since all of the appeals for women's help during the war had dispensed with the feeble arguments once used to exclude them from the vote. The editorial ended with 'the only democratic solution is, of course, adult suffrage'.[126]

Women and men from a range of labour and socialist organisations took an active part in the campaign to secure women's enfranchisement.[127] At the Labour Party Annual Conference, held in January 1916, there was a week long campaign for the suffrage which ended with a meeting addressed by Charlotte Despard, Catherine Marshall of the NUWSS and Sylvia Pankhurst, who had all been active in different suffrage organisations before 1914. The meeting called for the inclusion of women in any franchise extension.[128] Numerous demonstrations were held for 'votes for all men and women' and a new language was used in which to demand the vote. PSF members had increasingly begun to talk about a human franchise just before the war and this language was now frequently used in the *Labour Leader*. The Workers' Suffrage Federation, led by Sylvia Pankhurst, held demonstrations to demand Human Suffrage and urged workers to come in crowds: 'You will need the vote after the War to get back the liberties you have so freely surrendered, whether you are a man or a woman'.[129] In July 1916 a letter was sent from the WSF to Asquith and other MPs which was signed by prominent Labour Party and ILP women, including Margaret Bondfield, Isabella Ford, Susan Lawrence and Marion Phillips.[130] Meanwhile, in October 1916 a National Council for Adult Suffrage was established to urge that the next parliament should be representative of men and women. Former members of the PSF such as Margaret Bondfield and Mary Macarthur were on the executive committee, along with NUWSS members such as Maude Royden and Helena Swanwick.[131]

Nonetheless, as proposals for franchise reform began to be made by the Speaker's Conference, an all male committee established in 1916 to deal with electoral change, divisions began to appear between supporters of a full democratic suffrage. Once again, however, these did not fall neatly along organisational lines, nor did they necessarily correspond to positions taken before the war. The main concern of the ILP appeared to be to oppose the strong lobby which now existed to enfranchise those who had fought in the war, which would make military service the basis for the franchise. In contrast the ILP sought to maintain the civil basis of the franchise as part of a rejection of militarism.[132] Further, when it became clear that the Speaker's Conference intended to introduce adult suffrage for men and a more limited measure for women, an interesting variety of positions was taken. Ethel Snowden felt that although womanhood suffrage was the ideal, even a measure which was not equal to the male franchise at least established the principle of women's suffrage. On the other hand, in a reversal of her pre-war stance, she would not commit herself to an opinion on what the ILP should do if women's suffrage were left out, since in the context of war it was important to increase the male franchise.[133] The *Labour Leader* and many ILP MPs expressed relief that military service was not to be the basis of the reform and were reluctant to jeopardise the gains for 'democracy' by seeking a full adult suffrage. Philip Snowden, for example, argued that there was 'not the slightest chance of universal suffrage in this country'. By compromising, he argued, six or eight million women would get the vote, otherwise women might end up excluded altogether. 'In his opinion it conformed with the ILP policy to accept a limited suffrage without in any way receding from their ideal of adult suffrage'.[134]

On the other hand, there was a groundswell of support for the view that the ILP, the Labour Party and their MPs should exert pressure to ensure that all women as well as all men would have the vote. Patrick Dollan of the Glasgow ILP cited the demand for universal suffrage made by revolutionaries in Russia and Germany, while local labour and socialist groups held meetings to demand an adult suffrage measure. In April 1917, for example, Woolwich ILP, Richmond ILP, Leicester ILP, Stratford branch of the National Union of Railwaymen, Bradford Women's Humanity League and East London BSP all met to pass a resolution that the proposals in the Speaker's Conference were unsatisfactory and were unacceptable to the working class unless they were to provide for 'complete adult suffrage for men and women'. Moreover, the meetings were determined to oppose any measures which did not 'include women on the terms proposed for men'.[135]

In the early 1900s opponents of the Women's Enfranchisement Bill had argued that married working-class women would be excluded from the franchise and yet they were the ones who needed a political voice.[136] In 1917, however, the position seemed to be reversed when it was proposed that women over 30 should be given the vote. Margaret Llewelyn Davies gave her support to the many trade union women who argued that it was young women who had worked during the war and that they needed to vote and express their views – as did younger married women.[137] This sentiment was echoed by Dora Montefiore, who was scathing of those suffragists, such as Charlotte Despard and Millicent Fawcett, who were willing to accept such a limited measure and were eager 'to betray the interests of working women'.[138] She complimented Ellen Wilkinson for her speech at the Labour Women's Conference, where she represented young, industrially organised women who were shut out from political expression and who were demanding 'all the new freedoms'.[139] Dora Montefiore claimed that the Adult Suffrage Society, the old SDF and the BSP had always supported such women but they had been let down by J.R. Clynes MP, representative of the Labour Party on the Speaker's Conference committee. In the event, it was the far more limited measure which was adopted by the government in the Representation of the People Act of 1918.

After the vote – the 1920s

The ILP claimed immediately that the Act was unjust to women by denying them the right to vote on the same terms as men and pledged itself to continue working for the only permanent and simple solution, adult suffrage.[140] As an organisation, however, the ILP was not at the forefront of suffrage agitation during the 1920s. It was far more concerned to work out its relationship with the Labour Party and to pursue the demand for a Living Wage. Nonetheless, individual socialist women were actively involved in putting pressure on the Labour Party, in particular when it formed a government in 1923–4, to act on its manifesto pledge to support votes for all adult women. Dorothy Jewson's maiden speech after her election as an MP was to second a resolution in favour of the women's suffrage bill before parliament. She expressed the 'disappointment' felt by women that the Prime Minister, Ramsay MacDonald, had said that 'the government had not had time to consider this important question'.[141] Ellen Wilkinson commented frequently on the progress of women's suffrage in her regular parliamentary column in the *New Leader*, while, along with Dorothy Jewson, who was a member of the Women's Freedom League, and Margaret Bondfield, she worked closely with women's suffrage groups. Cheryl Law claims that Margaret Bondfield's vigour in campaigning for the franchise confounded her contemporaries, who did not recognise her as a committed feminist.[142] Nonetheless, it was consistent with the stand she had taken on the suffrage since she joined the Adult Suffrage Society in 1904.

Apart from the need to campaign to extend the franchise, socialist women also turned their attention to a consideration of what citizenship meant to women. They had to do this in a context in which both the ILP and the Labour Party sought to attract women voters to strengthen their political position. In 1918 the ILP, through the *Labour Leader* and the National Administrative Council, congratulated women on receiving justice at last and expressed regret that so many able women had been excluded in the past from helping with administrative and legislative reforms. It was hoped that now women had the vote they would quickly learn to use it to further domestic, social and industrial reforms. There was little mention here of women using political equality to challenge other aspects of their unequal role. Rather the stage was set for the Labour Party to incorporate women into its framework and to identify them with social reforms. This was summed up in the report of the Labour Party Conference of 1918 in the *Labour Leader*:

> The political enfranchisement of the sex has brought an invaluable aid to the male electorate for the work of social reconstruction. It was gratifying to find that the women realise the importance of working in cooperation with political organisations not exclusively confined to women. This does not mean that the need for special organisations of women for special work will be unnecessary, but it would tend to greatly weaken the effective power of social reformers if men and women were organised in separate parties.[143]

Socialist women also set out to persuade women to become socialists, but not simply so that they could improve social and economic conditions. Many of them also argued that the right to vote was only a first step to a more complete emancipation which could only come with socialism. In 1919 Gladys Pilchard claimed that the 'woman enfranchised' was not the same as the 'woman emancipated', who would need economic freedom, while Constance Borrett, a member of the Welsh ILP, also argued in 1928 that, although women were on the eve of political freedom, this did not equal economic liberty, which the achievement of socialism would bring.[144] Minnie Pallister assumed that younger women would be more easily open to socialist propaganda since their minds were 'not bound by tradition'. Constance Borrett echoed the arguments of some of the pioneer ILP women when she claimed that women had been practising socialism in the home 'before men thought of it' and therefore they should also be socialists in the wider political world.[145]

Once the demand for women's suffrage was no longer a divisive issue, it was easier for socialist groups to argue that men and women should work together to achieve socialism and that socialist women should not give their energies to separate women's groups which were outside the labour movement. Although many socialist women did continue to be involved in women's groups, in particular the WFL, and took part in joint campaigns over issues such as birth control, they did find it increasingly difficult to agree with women who did not share their broader political perspective. Nonetheless, in a context in which class divisions, the needs of the organised male waged worker and economic questions such as unemployment predominated, socialist women found it difficult to ensure that issues which could challenge women's subordinate position were given any real priority.

The suffrage campaign brought to the surface all the underlying tensions experienced by women who struggled both for socialism and for the emancipation of their sex. Issues which had been considered as part of theoretical debates were now pushed to the forefront of practical politics. During the struggle for the suffrage socialist women worked with other women, both inside and outside the socialist movement, in a common cause on behalf of their sex. For many socialist women, however, it was difficult to accept wholeheartedly the demands of the women's movement for a limited franchise. Instead, they approached the issue as socialists and sought to pursue women's interests through the demand for an adult suffrage measure. In doing so they did not see themselves as taking an anti-feminist position, or showing a lack of interest in the needs of women, but as adopting a socialist perspective which would help working-class women and men to take a full part in political life. Socialist women adopted a range of positions, both on the nature of the demand to be made and in the arguments which they used to support their case. They also differed in the extent to which they were willing to prioritise sex disabilities over loyalties to class and party. Nonetheless, to a greater or lesser degree the suffrage campaign provided a key site for socialist women to raise women's particular interests as a sex and to give weight to their attempts to develop a more woman-focused socialism. Once the vote was won, however, it was difficult to overcome the view that the newly enfranchised woman's main role was as a canvasser and fund-raiser for the ILP and the Labour Party, since the gender division of labour in the workplace and in the home was reinforced rather than weakened in the economic and political context of the inter-war years.

NOTES

1 For example, see C. Eustance, J. Ryan and L. Ugolini (eds), *A Suffrage Reader: Charting Directions in British Suffrage History*, London, Leicester University Press, 2000; S.S. Holton, *Suffrage Days: Stories from the Women's Suffrage Movement*, London, Routledge, 1996; J. Purvis and S.S. Holton (eds), *Votes for Women*, London, Routledge, 2000; M. Joannou and J. Purvis (eds), *The Women's Suffrage Movement: New Feminist Perspectives*, Manchester, Manchester University Press, 1998; M. Pugh, *The March of the Women: A Revisionist Analysis of the Campaign for Women's Suffrage, 1866–1914*, Oxford, Oxford University Press, 2000.
2 J. Liddington and J. Norris, *One Hand Tied Behind Us: The Rise of the Women's Suffrage Movement*, London, Virago, 1978; S.S. Holton, *Feminism and Democracy: Women's Suffrage and Reform Politics in Britain, 1900–1918*, Cambridge, Cambridge University Press, 1986.
3 K. Hunt, *Equivocal Feminists. The Social Democratic Federation and the Woman Question, 1884–1911*, Cambridge, Cambridge University Press, 1996; K. Hunt, 'Journeying through suffrage: the politics of Dora Montefiore', in Eustance, Ryan and Ugolini (eds), *A Suffrage Reader*.
4 See earlier discussion in Chapter 1.
5 L. Ugolini, 'Independent Labour Party men and women's suffrage in Britain, 1893–1914', PhD, University of Greenwich, 1997.
6 For example, see B. Caine, *English Feminism, 1780–1980*, Oxford, Oxford University Press, 1997, pp. 157–8; A. Rosen, *Rise Up Women! The Militant Campaign of the Women's Social and Political Union, 1903–1914*, London, Routledge & Kegan Paul, 1974, ch. 3; L. Garner, *Stepping Stones to Women's Liberty: Feminist Ideas in the Women's Suffrage Movement, 1900–1918*, London, Heinemann, 1984, p. 4.
7 Liddington and Norris, *One Hand Tied Behind Us*, p. 15.
8 Ibid., p. 25 and ch. 13.
9 *Common Cause*, 21 October 1909, quoted in Holton, *Feminism and Democracy*, p. 65.
10 Holton, *Feminism and Democracy*, pp. 65–9.
11 See, for example, Caine, *English Feminism*, pp. 156–8; M. Joannou and J. Purvis, 'Introduction', in Joannou and Purvis (eds), *The Women's Suffrage Movement*, p. 6.
12 The following give consideration to adult suffrage: S.S. Holton, *Feminism and Democracy: Women's Suffrage and Reform Politics in Britain, 1900–1918*, Cambridge, Cambridge University Press, 1986, ch. 3; Liddington and Norris, *One Hand Tied Behind Us*, pp. 179–86 and ch. 13; L. Barrow and I. Bullock, *Democratic Ideas and the British Labour Movement, 1880–1914*, Cambridge, Cambridge University Press, 1996, pp. 153–61; M. Pugh, 'Labour and women's suffrage', in K.D. Brown (ed.), *The First Labour Party, 1906–14*, London, Croom Helm, 1985.
13 Holton, *Feminism and Democracy*, ch. 3.
14 Ibid., p. 54. This judgement is then repeated in other suffrage histories. For example, see J. Purvis, 'Christabel Pankhurst and the Women's Social and Political Union', in Joannou and Purvis (eds), *The Women's Suffrage Movement*, p. 164.
15 *Labour Leader*, 20 April 1895.
16 *Justice*, 14 May 1892; *Labour Leader*, 13 April 1895.
17 Hunt, *Equivocal Feminists*, p. 157; *Clarion*, 25 June 1898. See also Elsie Harker, who claimed that 'there are other questions more pressing' (*Labour Leader*, 13 April 1895).
18 *Clarion*, 12 January 1895.
19 L. Ugolini, '"It is only justice to grant women's suffrage": Independent Labour Party men and women's suffrage, 1893–1905', in Eustance, Ryan and Ugolini (eds), *A Suffrage Reader*, p. 127; Hunt, *Equivocal Feminists*, pp. 154–5.
20 *Labour Leader*, 30 June 1894.

21 J. Hannam, *Isabella Ford, 1855–1924*, Oxford, Blackwell, 1989, pp. 84–5; *Labour Leader*, 20 April 1895.
22 *Labour Leader*, 26 June 1897.
23 *Clarion*, 3 February 1905.
24 *Labour Leader*, 3 February 1905; *Clarion*, 24 February 1905.
25 *Justice*, 15 September 1906.
26 For example, see the comments of William Anderson in *Labour Leader*, 18 November 1904.
27 For example, C. Porter, *Alexandra Kollontai*, London, Virago, 1980, p. 165.
28 *Labour Leader*, 11 November, 25 November, 2 December 1904. Jennie Elam married John Baker of the Steel Smelters' Union in the late 1890s. They were both active in the Stockton ILP and Labour Party up to 1913, when they moved to London (C. Collette, *For Labour and for Women: The Women's Labour League, 1906–18*, Manchester, Manchester University Press, 1989, Appendix 1).
29 *Labour Leader*, 11 November 1904. Jennie Baker also thought the ILP had 'abandoned' married women, in particular the wives of working men (*Labour Leader*, 30 March 1906).
30 *ILP Annual Conference Report*, 1905, p. 37.
31 *Clarion*, 12 May 1905.
32 *Clarion*, 16 November 1906.
33 Holton, *Feminism and Democracy*, p. 54; D. Morgan, *Suffragists and Liberals*, Oxford, Blackwell, 1975, p. 47; A. Linklater, *An Unhusbanded Life*, London, Hutchinson, 1980, p. 94; Liddington and Norris, *One Hand Tied Behind Us*, p. 236.
34 Liddington and Norris, *One Hand Tied Behind Us*, p. 186; Holton, *Feminism and Democracy*, p. 54; Caine, *English Feminism*, p. 157; J. Liddington, *The Life and Times of a Respectable Rebel: Selina Cooper, 1864–1946*, London, Virago, 1984, pp. 164–6.
35 Hunt, *Equivocal Feminists*, pp. 176–7.
36 For example, she wrote numerous letters to the *Labour Leader* in the debate over the Women's Enfranchisement Bill between November 1904 and January 1905. She seconded a resolution on adult suffrage at the ILP Annual Conference of 1906, while John Baker spoke for adult suffrage at the 1907 Conference (*ILP Annual Conference Report*, 1906, 1907).
37 For the importance of socialist newspapers see D. Hopkin, 'The socialist press in Britain, 1890–1910', in D. Boyce, J. Curran and P. Wingate (eds), *Newspaper History: From the 17th Century to the Present Day*, London, Constable, 1978; K. Hunt and J. Hannam, 'Propagandising as socialist women: the case of women's columns in British socialist newspapers, 1884–1914', in B. Taithe and T. Thornton (eds), *Propaganda: Political Rhetoric and Identity*, Stroud, Sutton, 1999.
38 Hunt and Hannam, 'Propagandising as socialist women', pp. 178–80.
39 For more details on this see Hunt, *Equivocal Feminists*, p. 160.
40 *Justice*, 14 December 1907.
41 *Clarion*, 18 February 1899.
42 *Labour Leader*, 19 May, 27 October 1905.
43 For a discussion of the range of ILP newspapers see D. Hopkin, 'The newspapers of the Independent Labour Party, 1893–1906', PhD, University of Aberystwyth, 1981.
44 For an account of *Forward*'s influence see J. Smith, 'Taking the leadership of the labour movement: the ILP in Glasgow, 1906–1914', in A. McKinlay and R.J. Morris (eds), *The ILP on Clydeside, 1893–1932: From Foundation to Disintegration*, Manchester, Manchester University Press, 1991; E. Gordon, *Women and the Labour Movement in Scotland, 1850–1914*, Oxford, Clarendon Press, 1991, pp. 271–8.
45 For example, see *Forward*, 25 May, 29 June 1912; 2 January, 15 February 1913.
46 J.S. Lohman, 'Sex or class? English socialists and the woman question, 1884–1914', PhD, Syracuse University, 1979, pp. 285–6 and ch. 2.

47 *Social Democrat*, October 1907.
48 *Labour Leader*, 18 July 1912.
49 *Clarion*, 4 January 1907.
50 *Clarion*, 24 August 1906.
51 *Clarion*, 9 October 1908.
52 *Clarion*, 30 April 1909. See also J. Dawson, *Why Women Want Socialism*, London, ILP pamphlet, 4, 1909.
53 *Social Democrat*, December 1909.
54 *Forward*, 15 December 1906.
55 *Labour Leader*, 9 January 1913.
56 Liddington and Norris, *One Hand Tied Behind Us*, p. 182; *Clarion*, 30 December 1904.
57 Liddington and Norris, *One Hand Tied Behind Us*, p. 182.
58 *Labour Leader*, 3 February 1905.
59 *Labour Leader*, 21 April 1905.
60 *Labour Leader*, 27 January 1905.
61 *Labour Leader*, 17 February 1911.
62 *Clarion*, 23 March 1906.
63 *Clarion*, 23 September 1904.
64 *Labour Leader*, 21 January 1905.
65 *Clarion*, 9 October 1908.
66 Ibid.
67 *Clarion*, 16 November 1906.
68 *Common Cause*, 16 February 1911, quoted in Liddington, *The Life and Times*, p. 210.
69 D.N. Chew, *Ada Nield Chew: The Life and Writings of a Working Woman*, London, Virago, 1982, p. 43. This book, compiled by Chew's daughter, says little about her adult suffrage views.
70 *The Vote*, 12 March 1910.
71 *Justice*, 21 January 1905; M. Bondfield, *The Women's Suffrage Controversy*, ASS leaflet 1, nd (1905?).
72 *Labour Leader*, 18 November 1904; see also H.S. Wishart from Woolwich, *ILP Annual Conference Report*, 1905.
73 *Forward*, 18 May 1907.
74 *Clarion*, 30 December 1904.
75 *Clarion*, 19 May 1905.
76 *Clarion*, 30 December 1912.
77 *Clarion*, 4 January 1907.
78 *Forward*, 18 May 1907.
79 Liddington and Norris, *One Hand Tied Behind Us*, pp. 180–1.
80 *Labour Leader*, 6 January, 21 April, 28 April 1905.
81 *National Union of Women Workers Annual Conference Report*, 1906, pp. 88–94.
82 *Forward*, 8 June 1907. Marion Phillips claimed that the demand was 'votes for women who work', while Teresa Billington included university women in her definition of women workers (*Labour Leader*, 16 December 1910; *Forward*, 2 February 1907).
83 *Social Democrat*, December 1909.
84 *Labour Leader*, 13 April 1895.
85 *Clarion*, 20 January, 3 February 1905.
86 *Forward*, 2 February 1907. The phrase 'bricks and mortar' was also used by Mr Mitchell at the ILP Annual Conference in 1905 (*Labour Leader*, 28 April 1905).
87 *Forward*, 25 May 1907.
88 Thomas Johnston editorial in *Forward*, 2 February 1907. See also Lily Bell, *Labour Leader*, 20 April 1895.
89 *The Link*, April 1912.

90 *Forward*, 1 March 1913.
91 *Clarion*, 17 February 1905; *Labour Leader*, 28 April 1905.
92 *Labour Leader*, 29 October 1909; *Labour Leader*, 12 November 1909.
93 For example, see letters from M.P. Stanbury, *Labour Leader*, 2 December 1904, and G.R.S. Taylor of the WSPU, *Clarion*, 13 December 1912.
94 ASS, *To the Democracy*, leaflet 3, 1907.
95 *Labour Leader*, 21 April 1905.
96 *Labour Leader*, 28 April 1905.
97 *Labour Leader*, 19 May 1905.
98 *Labour Leader*, 20 January 1905.
99 *Clarion*, 17 February 1905.
100 *Clarion*, 24 August 1906.
101 *Clarion*, 2 November 1906.
102 *Clarion*, 12 April 1907.
103 *Clarion*, 26 June 1908.
104 *Labour Leader*, 27 October 1905, quoted in C. Collins, 'Women and Labour politics in Britain, 1893–1932', PhD, London School of Economics, 1991, p. 89. Collins also notes that Baker, despite her stand for adult suffrage, signed the ILP manifesto in support of WSPU prisoners in December 1906 (p. 130, fn. 47).
105 *Labour Leader*, 12 December 1911. See also Annot Robinson's threat to give more commitment to women's suffrage unless the ILP acted more vigorously (*ILP Annual Conference Report*, 1910). Ethel Snowden resigned from the ILP in 1909 because the NAC contained adult suffragists (*Labour Leader*, 5 November 1909).
106 *ILP Annual Conference Report*, 1907.
107 C. Steedman, *Childhood, Culture and Class in Britain: Margaret McMillan, 1860–1931*, London, Virago, 1990, p. 138.
108 M. McMillan, 'The Case for the Industrial Woman', Men's League on Women's Suffrage handbook, 1912, quoted in Steedman, *Childhood, Culture and Class*, p. 139. See also the case of Dora Montefiore in Hunt, 'Journeying through suffrage'.
109 PSF, *First Annual Report*, October 1909–10, p. 3.
110 Letters from M.M.A. Ward and Margaret Bondfield in *Labour Leader*, 29 October 1909.
111 *Labour Leader*, 12 November 1909.
112 *Labour Leader*, 8 April 1910.
113 *Labour Leader*, 1 July 1910; *League Leaflet*, January 1911.
114 PSF, *First Annual Report*, October 1909–10, p. 3. There were also 3,000 individual members.
115 *Labour Leader*, 25 February 1910. See also Isabella Ford's fears about adult suffrage bills (*Labour Leader*, 17 February 1911).
116 Hunt, *Equivocal Feminists*, pp. 178–9.
117 *Justice*, 27 November 1909, 16 July 1910; PSF, *First Annual Report*, October 1909–10, p. 2.
118 *Daily Herald*, 1 January 1913.
119 ASS, *To the Democracy*.
120 *Labour Leader*, 8 December 1911.
121 For a full discussion of the alliance, see Holton, *Feminism and Democracy*, ch. 4.
122 *Labour Leader*, 9 January 1913.
123 Ibid.
124 *Labour Leader*, 18 July 1912.
125 *Labour Leader*, 17 May 1914. See also the article by Isabella Ford which claimed that the ILP was 'the party for women' (*Labour Leader*, 1 May 1913).
126 *Labour Leader*, 1 June 1916.

127 For a full discussion of the suffrage campaign during the war, see C. Law, *Suffrage and Power: The Women's Movement, 1918–1928*, London, I.B. Tauris, 2000, ch. 2.
128 Ibid., p. 32.
129 *The Call*, 6 April 1916.
130 Law, *Suffrage and Power*, p. 33.
131 *Labour Leader*, 5 October 1916.
132 *Labour Leader*, 9 November 1916.
133 *Labour Leader*, 1 March 1917.
134 *ILP Annual Conference Report*, 1917.
135 *Labour Leader*, 25 April 1917.
136 For example, see the views of Mary Muir and Jennie Baker (*Labour Leader*, 28 April 1905; 30 March 1906).
137 *Labour Leader*, 12 April 1917.
138 *The Call*, 15 March 1917.
139 *The Call*, 24 October 1916.
140 *ILP Annual Conference Report*, 1919.
141 *Labour Woman*, 1 April 1924.
142 Law, *Suffrage and Power*, p. 184.
143 *Labour Leader*, 5 December 1918.
144 *Labour Leader*, 1 May 1919; *New Leader*, 6 January 1928. See also M. Pallister, *Socialism for Women*, London, ILP, 1925, pp. 4–7.
145 *New Leader*, 12 October, 6 January 1928.

6

SOCIALIST WOMEN AND A POLITICS OF CONSUMPTION

This chapter looks at one of the political spaces in which a socialist woman's politics could be made – consumption.[1] In that sense its subject matter is rather different from the other case studies in this book, as it is as much concerned with considering possibilities for a woman-focused politics as with recounting the actual practice of socialist women. Fundamental to the argument made here is the observation that, in its theory and its practice, socialist politics have centred on the realm of production: on workers, wages, the workplace and the economy. In contrast, consumption has had a marginal place within socialist strategy. Yet this is precisely the arena in which socialist women *could* make a woman-focused politics by renegotiating the boundaries of 'the political'.

Production was central to those socialists influenced by Marxism. After all, the classic Marxist view of the Woman Question was that women could only participate in their own emancipation once they entered the workforce. Only then did they acquire a class position in their own right and thus a place in the class struggle. But production was also crucial for non-Marxist socialists because of dominant views of what constituted the domain of politics, which were based on particular understandings of the 'public' and the 'private'. Over the period under scrutiny here, the 1880s to the 1920s, changing ideas about the role of the state ensured that the boundary between the public and the private shifted in favour of the public. More private matters, particularly those within the family such as the bringing up of children and the practice of motherhood, became public matters as collectivist social policies slowly developed. But although the margins of 'the political' expanded within political discourse, the sphere of production remained central to the public domain, while consumption was rarely regarded as a matter which transgressed the arena of politics.

Broadly speaking, socialists did not challenge the common sense of what constituted 'the political'. The issue for socialist women was to what extent this notion of what constituted the political agenda gave due recognition to the degree to which everyday life was gendered and hence the importance of what came to be seen as 'women's issues'. Pat Thane, when considering Labour women over the period 1906 to 1945, has argued that their desire for a revaluing of the domestic constituted a challenge to the priorities of politics, at least in terms of welfare isues.[2] She does not mention consumption within this discussion, although it has been argued by others that the inter-war period saw Labour Party women, including socialist women, putting pressure on local Labour parties and Labour councillors to make housing a party political issue.[3] Housing, as we will see, can be represented as a welfare issue – when the focus is on living conditions – but can also be seen as a part of consumption – when the focus is on rent.

This chapter concentrates on two aspects of consumption. One is everyday household shopping, particularly for food, and the other is rent. The argument centres on the extent to which the early generations of British socialist women were able to construct what could be called 'a politics of consumption', that is, organising as consumers *in order to* achieve political goals. Here a distinction is being made between organising as consumers to achieve consumerist goals and the use of consumption as a lever in a broader political campaign.[4] Could socialist women use consumption as a gateway to the experience of ordinary women and in so doing create a socialist politics through these everyday issues? The final part of the chapter revisits the debate about the place of consumption in the politics of socialist women by considering two separate events: the ILP's debate on the Living Wage in the 1920s and the publication of Teresa Billington-Greig's book *The Consumer in Revolt*. In both cases the issue remains the extent to which socialist women were able to reconfigure the socialist agenda to create a politics of consumption.

Identifying a politics of consumption

Socialism and shopping are not words or practices which are usually seen as connected. Shopping for the requirements of a household, particularly for food, rarely features in discussions of socialist strategy. Its mundanity and associations with the domestic world seem to isolate shopping from what is generally understood as political action. Certainly this seems to be the case when you consider socialists of the late nineteenth and early twentieth century. Although these socialists were often to be found in local market places, they were there to drum up a crowd, to make propaganda and to sell their newspapers rather than to do the household shopping. So why does socialism and shopping seem so antipathetic? This may be because the prevailing, albeit often unconscious, image of the socialist was that of a man while day-to-day shopping was largely a female activity.[5] Moreover, part of the common-sense understanding of what it was to be a political activist, whether male or female, was of someone who was too busy to do the domestic shopping. Yet the question for socialist women was: how were ordinary women shoppers to be engaged by the socialist project? Did shopping have any connection with socialism?

Shopping, particularly for food, has been the focus for community action ever since the advent of a market economy. The extent to which protest prompted by food shortages and price rises is a gendered activity is dependent on the historical context, but few would claim that, even at the height of these popular protests, the food riot constituted a politics of consumption as defined here.[6] Food riots, whether in the eighteenth century or during the First World War, were predominantly concerned with short-term goals, and in particular achieving a fair price for food and preventing profiteering, rather than as a lever for wider political change.

In relation to the cost of living protests which spread across the globe in the First World War, some evidence has been presented by historians that 'everyday life became a political process, and that through that process women's awareness grew'.[7] Were these protests examples of socialist women practising a politics of consumption? In Berlin there is evidence of women's short-term empowerment but the focus of the protests remained on the supply, distribution and price of food.[8] In contrast to Berlin, the cost of living demonstrations in Melbourne in 1917 involved socialist women in a leading role. Adela Pankhurst and Jennie Baines (formerly of the British ILP and the Women's Social and Political Union), as leaders of the largely female crowd, did make political claims beyond the immediate issue of food prices, but Judith Smart concludes that ultimately the women who participated in these protests 'concentrated on domestic issues'.[9] The riots did not succeed in the politicisation of women or prevent the move to conservatism in the inter-war years. There is nevertheless some suggestion of a politics of consumption in Melbourne in 1917, albeit an unsuccessful one. Moreover, Temma Kaplan, in her study of working women's activity in the political street life of Barcelona between 1910 and 1918, contends that women 'felt they had special responsibilities and so demanded special rights to protect their families and communities against extinction'.[10] This she calls 'female consciousness'. She argues that, by collective action based on female consciousness, Barcelona's working women broadened their concerns from consumption to wider political issues and therefore made a politics of consumption. This was most apparent in the 'women's uprising' of 1918 which united housewives and waged women, although unlike in Melbourne there was no involvement of socialist women. Kaplan concludes that: 'Female consciousness, though conservative, promotes a social vision embodying profoundly radical political implications'.[11] Together these interpretations of various wartime cost of living protests show that consumption became a political issue in this period and in so doing legitimised women's interventions in the public world, but only the Melbourne example suggests the short-lived possibility of a *socialist* politics of consumption.

Certainly there had been British women who used consumption as a political lever before the 1880s. Some Chartist women employed the tactic of 'exclusive dealing', that is the boycotting of shopkeepers who refused to support the cause, as did some radicals in the middle years of the nineteenth century.[12] Women's anti-slavery campaigners led various drives to ensure abstention from eating as well as buying slave-produced sugar. In so doing, Clare Midgley claims that 'women campaigners blurred the boundaries between "masculine" public and "feminine" private spheres'.[13] These are all examples of women capitalising on their power in the market place to pressurise for a specific political goal. In that sense these tactics differ from the more well-known example of organised women consumers, the Women's Co-operative Guild (WCG).

By the end of the nineteenth century the WCG, an organisation of the wives of male cooperators, saw its role as a 'trade union for married women'.[14] Margaret Llewelyn Davies, secretary of the WCG from 1889 to 1921, defined the power of the organised housewife: 'Isolated in their own individual homes, it is through their common everyday interests as buyers that married working-women have come together, and find their place in the labour world and national life'.[15] Although represented by the image of the 'Woman with the Basket'[16] – the quintessential shopper – the Guild rarely used their collective power as consumers for wider political ends, using instead more conventional pressure group tactics. Although, as Gill Scott has shown, the WCG constituted a powerful voice for working-class housewives, even a working-class feminism, it does not provide a clear example of a politics of consumption.

So where are we to find examples of a politics of consumption? Those who have explored particular examples have tended to focus on the labour, essentially the trade union, movement rather than on the practice of socialists. The political goals are more likely to be a rather vague sense of solidarity and, sometimes, a challenge to employers more generally. A socialist politics of consumption, should it exist, would pose a more fundamental challenge to the social order, exposing the nature of the capitalist system and seeing consumer action as a tactic in the class struggle.

Dana Frank has explored consumer-based organising by the Seattle labour movement in the 1920s – such as the use of boycotts, cooperatives, labour-owned businesses and the promotion of the union label. Although for a time apparently successful, these initiatives had serious limitations, not least because a number of the tactics intensified housewives' labour as consumers.[17] It was therefore hard to build lasting support for this attempt to politicise consumption. As importantly, energy was not put into persuading housewives of the reasons, both pragmatic and political, for supporting these campaigns. Although an attempt to build solidarity beyond union members to their wives and families, these consumer-based activities were initiated by the male-dominated trade unions and were largely organised on their terms. In a movement where the sexual division of labour was strong, these consumer-focused initiatives were seen as giving a role to unorganised women whose workplace was the home. But this was not a politics which in any real sense politicised the domestic sphere or empowered women.

In contrast, Susan Levine, in her work on the women who built the skilled trade auxiliaries in the America of the 1920s, suggests that: 'By asserting the central role of standard of living in labor's ambitions, these women also implicitly challenged the labor movement to assert itself beyond the shopfloor'.[18] Here, she argues, is an example of consumption being forced onto the agenda of the labour movement, but it is not a politics of consumption where consumers are organising to achieve wider political goals. It was this kind of activity which was briefly apparent in New York in 1917 during the cost of living protests.[19] Here, according to Dana Frank, an independent working-class housewives' movement erupted into violent street protests against the high cost of living. Although this uprising did not fit neatly into the Socialist Party's traditional areas of work – electoral work and trade union organising – these socialists seized the opportunity for agitational work presented by the uprising and organised a series of cost of living protests designed to direct the movement towards socialist goals. She concludes that:

> While some Socialists did view price protests as a direct step towards socialism through demands for a reorganisation of the city's food economy, most Socialists – both female and male – ultimately sought to divert the cost-of-living movement into alternative channels of protest – antiwar, suffrage, or wage struggles. Mobilized consumers, they believed, should eventually be directed away from consumer issues.[20]

Thus we have some American examples of a range of different ways in which the labour movement, and even the socialist movement, responded to consumption as an issue which could provide the means to incorporate unorganised women – the problematic housewife – into the movement. None of these examples show any sustained success in destabilising the traditional priorities of labour and creating a politics of consumption that was equivalent to the dominant politics of production.

Socialism and shopping

Socialism and shopping were connected for British socialists in a number of different ways. For some socialist men the distractions of consumption – of 'frocks and bonnets and fashions' – kept women from empathising with socialist politics.[21] This view did not go unchallenged: 'I feel sure those women who care about fashions and the like will hardly give their minds to our cause. It is those who are striving and struggling to try to make both ends meet (which they never can) whose sympathy and help we want to get'.[22] But how were socialists to embrace the practical issues which consumption raised? One way was to accept and even accentuate the existing sexual division of labour and to mobilise consumption as a 'women's issue'; thus: 'To take advantage of the shopping, millinery and upholstery proclivities of women, is surely, under the circumstances, not an unreasonable method of exciting the interest of women in Socialism'.[23] This was argued by the same man, the 'Sage of the Northern Heights', who in debating how to 'induce' women to become socialists suggested:

> To men, as producers of wealth, we shall lecture on the economics of social production; to women, as purchasers and consumers, we shall apostrophise the bountiful side of distributive communism .... Now if we were to constantly point out to women that under Socialism family life would have their first claim; that in all probability their chief duties would consist of 'shopping', and selecting articles which would beautify themselves and their homes, ... we should soon get them on our side.[24]

This idea of the future socialist society as a shopper's paradise does not seem to have captured the imagination of other socialists, particularly as the vision of 'shopping for pleasure' was so unlike most working-class women's experience of 'shopping for survival'. Yet shopping still had a role to play in day-to-day socialist politics.

The socialist press[25] carried adverts for a number of different ventures where goods were produced or distributed in aid of the party/movement. Socialists were urged to buy their footwear from the Pioneer Boot Factory, their clothing from various socialist tailors and even their confectionery from the Red Flag Toffee company. But these were never going to entirely provide for the consumption needs of socialists and their families, let alone form the means to bring socialist ideas to the unpersuaded. The idea that motivated these activities was the support of fellow socialists, often those already victimised for their politics and seeking an alternative form of employment. In addition, 'profits' derived from these small-scale producers could benefit the movement.

There were also attempts within ILP and SDF branches to introduce a form of socialist or 'democratic' trading. Trading departments would be set up, often in the hands of women members, where tea, coffee, cocoa and tobacco, for example, could be bought. Some socialists saw systematic democratic trading as more than another method of fundraising.[26] In 1901 it was suggested within the SDF that a Socialist Trading Store should be opened in London. Clara Hendin was enthusiastic, particularly as she was already active in the WCG – although, as Peter Gurney has shown, many socialists were highly ambivalent about the Co-operative movement.[27] She saw the potential for such trading to provide opportunities for reaching and politicising women which other aspects of socialist fundraising had failed to do. In particular, she meant the bazaar, which was the usual method of raising money for the socialist cause. This was seen as women's province in terms of providing a volunteer workforce to sew and cook in aid of the party, although the national organisation of such activities remained in male hands. For Hendin, consumption was definitely a women's issue:

> When our store opens, I should like to see comrades of the SDF encourage the women to deal there by offering to stay at home while their wives go to the store to do the shopping, and if there should be a meeting on (which I hope there will be for the women) she could go to it

while her goods are being got ready for her, but not for the husband to growl, when she arrives home, because she is a long time gone .... Remember that the Women's Cooperative Guild are an organised band of nearly 13,000, and if the wives of cooperators can organise themselves why not the wives of Social Democrats?[28]

Other socialists, including women who had tried to run trading departments in their own branches, were not so optimistic[29] and *Justice*'s columnist the Tattler even suggested that women themselves would constitute the main obstacle to a successful socialist trading scheme. The chief difficulty, he thought, was that a woman 'is always suspicious of buying where he wishes her to, especially if she thinks some movement with which he is concerned is going to benefit in any way. Then she is quite sure she is being cheated'.[30] Consumption was certainly assumed to be women's business, but it was seen by many as a private, or domestic, matter which therefore provided no scope for socialist organising – it could not be politicised. There is certainly a domestic feel to the way in which socialists wrote about consumption, revealing at the same time some sense of the domestic negotiations which underlay any political activism.

Gendering the politics of consumption?

Yet there was an initiative in the immediate years before the First World War which sought to bring consumption into the realm of politics in a specifically gendered way. Although the Socialist Women's Circles of the SDF had had 'Rent, Food and Laundries' on their syllabus for discussion in 1910–11, the party's women's organisation did not foreground consumption in political activities. It was only when the successor organisation, the British Socialist Party, formed its women's organisation with Margaretta Hicks as its organiser that a new approach began to women's self-organisation. Even before the Women's Council of the BSP was formally constituted, Hicks was beginning to air her thoughts on a new focus for socialist women's organisation.[31] In July 1912 she pointed out to the readers of the women's column of the socialist monthly *The Link* (later subtitled 'The Organ of the Women's Socialist Movement') that:

> Women have power as consumers. They are pre-eminently *the* purchasers. A strike for better terms is of no utility if the price of bacon and cheese, milk, coal and rent goes up. There is a 'hole in the pocket' which must be mended, even as the Edmonton women struck against the rise in the price of milk, and used condensed until it came down.[32]

A few months later she suggested that women, as purchasers, should be organised to keep prices down and to prevent adulteration. She cited the example of the WCG's unsuccessful campaign to get a minimum wage for women employees of 'the Co-op'. Hicks suggested that a more effective tactic would have been a boycott of any goods on which workers had been paid less than a minimum wage. She noted that such a strategy would open up a wide field of work that had not yet been touched on and which would provide a means for every woman to take her part in the industrial struggle.[33] Here, at an early stage, were some of the significant features of what Hicks would try to develop into a politics of consumption. She focused on ordinary women shoppers, rarely the target of socialist propaganda, and linked her ideas to the practices of other women's organisations, such as the Guild, with which she was clearly familiar. Most challengingly, in terms of socialist strategy, she sought to tie together day-to-day domestic concerns with the industrial struggles of the workers. Consumers could play their part in the class struggle too. Indeed, 'co-operation of the workers as purchasers is the other end of the industrial screw. It is no use screwing up wages to make ends meet unless the other end remains firm; the workers must control both ends – wages and prices'.[34]

By the autumn of 1912 the Women's Council of the BSP was in action and Margaretta Hicks took her ideas into the pages of *Justice*. She began to suggest that women, as the domestic 'chancellors of the exchequer', should be organised properly 'as buyers'. If organised, women would be able to control prices as well as the quality and purity of food and clothing. To this end, she suggested organising as buyers in cooperative clubs.[35] To the readers of *Clarion* the new initiative was explained as an organisation of housekeepers which would focus on everyday matters 'so that all women shall understand how they are affected by Socialism'.[36] As she elaborated this idea, a number of distinctive features of her proposal became apparent. First, she was clear that this was a way of politicising women which started from an understanding of the realities of working-class housewives' lives – that is unorganised women. So:

> We must take up the petty worries of their lives, and show how even the haggling to get the best value for every penny is not mean, but is part of the great fight to get the best conditions of living. In combination with other women, it is this same spirit of sharp economy that will watch over the welfare of the whole working class. The greatest need of the present moment is to enlarge the outlook of working women from the individual to the social point of view.[37]

The key was organisation, but around an issue which was crucial to women's daily lives – consumption. She saw the cooperative clubs as providing 'a common interest in which all can take part, and which will help us to retain our membership'.[38] To begin with it was emphasised that organising as consumers was a way to 'assist the industrial struggle by endeavouring to maintain the standard of living' as well as giving financial support to socialist activities, as earlier socialist trading had promised.[39] At this stage this was not a challenge to existing socialist strategies, merely a complement, which had the added benefit of raising money for the movement. Later it was suggested that the discount on cooperative buying should be used to pay the wages of a woman organiser,[40] thus this organisation of women as consumers would no longer merely be an auxiliary to the parent party but a self-governing and self-financing organisation.

One of the empowering aspects of this idea was the stress that Margaretta Hicks gave to the strength that women could gain from collective action. For example, speaking in Shoreditch in 1913, Hicks said that 'women must realise that combined force or a boycott against the higher price would ultimately result in the master bakers giving way'.[41] Could this power be used for more than narrow consumer ends? Hicks seemed to think that it could be, and more importantly should be, presented in this light: 'we shall use practical household economies to assist women to unite for the realisation of Socialism'.[42] The cost of living was increasingly presented as, first, a political issue and, second, a campaign in which socialist women must take the lead.[43] The National Women's Council (NWC), as the BSP's women's organisation was now called, declared: 'It is not enough to fight the employers; we want to collectively own and control the means of living, and our food supply'.[44] In the *Daily Herald* this work was described as the forming of a 'trade union of housewives' for if women were organised as buyers, they would control the markets. 'It would be a brave shopkeeper who would dare to raise prices when all his customers were organised.'[45] As 1914 began, Margaretta Hicks made it clearer that the politics of consumption was as important as the traditional sites of class struggle. She declared that:

> The trade unions of men and women are industrial organisations of the producers, up to the point when they receive their wages in coin; but we must never forget that we do not work for money, but for what that money will buy. Therefore the economic organisation of working women, to get as much as possible in quantity and quality for the wages we spend, is the fellow-half to the trade union movement. Each half must support the other to obtain the necessaries of life. Within the next twelve months we may hope to see a powerful organisation of working women that shall make itself felt rather than heard.[46]

The next twelve months were to be crucial for the politics of food but not in the way that Hicks had hoped. Before turning to the effect that the advent of war had on these nascent politics of consumption, let us first consider the practice that accompanied the arguments developed by Hicks and the NWC.

Practising a politics of consumption

This was *not* a campaign that involved large numbers of women. It certainly did not rival the WCG or the Women's Labour League, which in differing ways, and to varying extents, organised around consumption but did not have an equivalent politics of consumption. For, unlike the BSP women, neither of these organisations saw their goal as making socialist politics or creating socialist women through organising around consumption issues.

In early 1913 the NWC organised meetings for working women in various parts of London under the slogan 'Keep Prices Down'.[47] By June it was claimed that a range of trade unions, from the Shop Assistants' Union to the Gasworkers' and General Labourers' Union, had indicated their support for the campaign against the rising cost of living and eighteen Women's Circles had been formed.[48] A leaflet on the cost of living was published which claimed that over the period from 1901 to 1911 trade unions had only been able to raise wages by about a penny in the pound, while for the same period the price of food had risen by nearly 2s 4d in the pound.[49] The Council's principal activity was organising cooperative clubs, primarily in the London area, where Hicks herself was particularly energetic as a galvaniser of activity. Initially socialists were encouraged to buy their coal through the NWC.[50] In November 1913 there were five cooperative clubs, which included fuel and drapery among their activities. After less than nine months in existence, they had raised nearly five guineas.[51] Not only the BSP but also a number of trade unions circulated their members in an effort to organise their wives against the increased cost of living.[52]

The NWC was also keen to work with other women's organisations. In March 1914 it convened a conference on the 'Increased Cost of Living' with speakers from the WLL and Women's Industrial Council as well as from the NWC. Nearly a hundred societies were represented at the conference, including the Fabian Women's Group, WCG, Women's Adult Schools, BSP, ILP, London Trades Council, as well as trade unions and Daily Herald Leagues. Margaretta Hicks reported that: 'It was a great Conference, and worthily upheld and supported. We stood for the interests of the whole of the workers and their homes. Our women rose to the occasion. It was not academic; it was a real expression of thought and feeling.' She concluded her report: 'Now that we have the opportunity for effective work we need the solidarity and full support of our fellow comrades. Let our work be felt as one power.'[53]

When war broke out, the NWC took part in the protests against the war and issued a manifesto noting that the outbreak of war had been 'used by unscrupulous moneymakers on the market as an excuse for robbing the workers by raising the price of food and other necessities'. They charged men and women to unite and fight these demands and urged women to canvass in their neighbourhoods to oppose any rise in the price of food.[54] In August 1914 they began to organise a petition to government that it take over the food supply. They also urged their own members to get elected to the newly formed Citizen Committees. The question of the food supply and the increased cost of living were seen as the issues which would mobilise women within their communities, and socialist women should seek to build on this.[55] Effective organisation was now more important than ever. Daily Herald Leagues urged their members to sign the NWC petition to 'nationalise' the production and distribution of food, and within less than a month 16,000 had signed the petition.[56] By the end of 1914 the NWC was a distinct organisation, no longer the BSP's women's section, and it was reported to be doing good work by directing the attention of housewives to the need for national control of the food supply.[57]

The First World War and the politics of consumption

But the war had changed everything. Consumption, particularly the question of the food supply, was no longer seen as a women's issue. The socialist press could now regularly discuss the cost of living without ever referring to the women who were struggling to make ends meet. Food had now ceased to be a domestic matter but was one around which state action was being demanded by male socialists and through the organised voice of Labour and Socialism, the National Workers' War Emergency Committee.[58] Hyndman represented the BSP on this committee and its few women members represented various labour organisations. There was no space for the kind of socialist politics of consumption which Margaretta Hicks had been beginning to develop. Women played little part in developing the War Emergency Committee's policy on food.[59] The Committee called for official controls on the purchase and storage of food; on the fixing of maximum prices of food and necessities; and on the distribution of food. However, according to Royden Harrison, 'the Committee over-estimated popular interest in food controls'.[60] The socialist press covered the activities of the Committee, its publications and conferences but women were almost entirely absent from these discussions, either as subject matter or as discussants.

One space where these matters did continue to be aired was in a corner of *Justice* where, until November 1915, Margaretta Hicks wrote a column under the innocuous title 'National Women's Council'. Here she continued to write about the 'food question' from a socialist woman's point of view, sharing her own feelings about the progress of the war and the women's campaigns. Her focus was practical and unsectarian. In January 1915 she named a range of women's organisations which were cooperating over the issue of the food supply. These included the WIC, Women's Fabian Group [sic], East London Federation of Suffragettes (ELFS), London Kitchen Gardens, Women's Branch of the Printers', Warehousemen and Cutters' Trade Union, National Aid Corps, National Food Fund, some representatives of Child Care Committees, some WCGs, Railway Women's Guild, Girl's Club Dinners and the Food Reform Association. Sub-committees had been formed to campaign around issues such as milk depots; cost price restaurants; meals for schoolchildren; prices; and food production.[61] There was a sense of real activity and an attempt to network more broadly, although the absence of the WLL is noticeable. A few of the activities of the NWC, such as the conference on the increased standard of living held in March 1914, gained some coverage in the *Labour Leader*, but from autumn 1913 the WLL had also started to raise the food question.[62] WLL Executive minutes of the period confirm their desire to keep their distance from any initiative taken by BSP women.[63] Although many of the practical activities undertaken by the WLL in this area were similar to those of the much smaller NWC, there was no equivalent argument about the empowerment of consumers or the specific role that consumption could have in the politics of socialist women.

Others found that they could cooperate with the NWC. Sylvia Pankhurst's ELFS took up the food question as soon as war was declared. Various radical tactics were considered: rent striking until the government introduced controls on the food supply; or only paying the old prices for food and, if shopkeepers refused to comply, taking the goods forcibly.[64] But instead the Federation decided to employ more orthodox tactics, joining in the work of the Joint Food Supply Committee with the NWC, organising meetings, deputations and conferences. For Margaretta Hicks the Joint Food Supply Committee, formed in November 1914 by the NWC, provided an opportunity for organisation and for leadership – 'It is the proud work of Socialist women who believe in the collective ownership and control by the people of the means of living to take the lead in this national work.'[65] Indeed, Hicks was clear that it was as socialist women that she and others should seek to organise consumers. Relief work, which other women's organisations had turned to at the outset of war, could have a political purpose: 'we can thus teach the first lessons of the common good'.[66] Moreover: 'As Socialist women our work lies in guiding the first efforts at social reconstruction for the new world .... We want to rouse working women on these points'.[67] There was much to rouse women about: from August 1914 to the end of 1916 food prices rose by 87 per cent.[68] Even male BSPers wedded to the politics of production could recognise the urgency of the food question, particularly for women. H.W. Lee, editor of *Justice*, observed:

> we have got to get down into the streets. Thus and thus only will the people be stirred. And there are the women to be influenced. They are quite as important as the men, if not more important, on the question of food prices and the cost of living. All this is work in which we Socialists can take part. It is work which we are particularly called upon to undertake, inasmuch as our knowledge of the economic effects of capitalist production enable us to speak with knowledge and clearness.[69]

This was not a call for socialist-led food riots. Margaretta Hicks, though sympathetic to the feelings that prompted riot, did not support these tactics. She felt that 'smashing a few shops only makes things worse'.[70] Instead, 'as Socialist women, it is our work, not only to watch keenly all the economic changes that are taking place, but to lead and guide the first ideas and experiments'.[71] But as the war proceeded it was harder to see how her 'first ideas and experiments' on a politics of consumption were going to be sustained. Ironically Hicks herself became so convinced of the importance of the food question that rather than sustaining it as part of a politics of consumption, in November 1915 she announced her resignation as secretary of the NWC. She had become convinced that 'the great question of the future will be the agricultural one', particularly the necessity for domestic food production in which women, she believed, had a significant role to play. To this end she moved out of London into the country, where she became involved in agricultural work, subsequently taking on a small farm of her own.[72] Almost immediately the 'National Women's Council' column disappeared from *Justice*. Margaretta Hicks' interest in consumption, specifically food, had taken her back to the issue of production, albeit food production. Her own political journey seemed to show that at this particular moment a politics of consumption was no longer viable and was once again barely imaginable.

As the war continued, the socialist press reported organised protests against food prices,[73] but these were not particularly woman-focused in their appeal – it was more that men should organise to prevent their wives and children from starving. Women seemed to no longer have the space to be actors in their own right. Food had shifted, at least in socialists' minds, from being a gender issue to one of class. Food was now a lever in the class struggle, but not in the kind of way that Hicks had been arguing before the war. In 1917 *The Call* suggested that:

> the women have had about enough. Their patience is nearly exhausted. Their temper is such that any sudden change in prices or apparent evidence of unfairness in the treatment of customers is likely to lead to 'scenes' .... It is the duty of Social Democrats to so organise and concentrate that resentment that it will sweep the swindling away for ever.[74]

Agitation around food provided 'splendid opportunities of implanting in the minds of the workers the principles of social democracy and prepar[ing] them for the task of overthrowing the capitalist system'.[75] There was some suggestion of tying back together production and consumption – workplace and home – when the Parkhead shopstewards supported food demonstrations in Glasgow by telling the Corporation 'that unless food supplies were so regulated that the workers' wives would be saved from the queues, the workers were prepared to get out into the street and stand in the queues'.[76] Indeed there were examples of workers taking direct action over food prices and food queues. One of the first instances of a Saturday protest strike against food prices and food queues occurred in Coventry in December 1917, when men making munitions left work in order to take the places of their wives in the food queues.[77] In January 1918 men and women from eight of the largest munition factories in Manchester stopped work for three hours and marched to Albert Square to protest against the queues and to demand a national system of rationing with equal distribution of food amongst all classes. Undoubtedly traditional forms of protest were being used to make demands around consumption. More challengingly for the gendering of consumption, in January 1918 all of the engineers employed at Vickers in Erith took a Saturday morning off to do their family shopping.[78]

Generally the war had transformed consumption into an unequivocally political matter for socialists. The creation of the Consumers' Council in January 1918, with Hyndman a member, might be cited as evidence of just how far socialists had travelled.[79] Yet this did not reflect a gendered understanding of consumption either at a state or socialist party level. The distance between the Consumers' Council and the ordinary woman shopper was demonstrated by those appointed to it to represent the unorganised consumer: Lord Rathcreedan, the Countess of Selbourne and Sir William Ashley![80]

The nuances of the argument and the tentative practice that Margaretta Hicks and the NWC had been developing before the war had been overwhelmed by the different overarching agenda of socialists in wartime, divided as they were as to how to respond to a war which seemed to take them by surprise. Although women spontaneously organising around the cost of living, and particularly over the availability of food, was to provoke some disorder in Britain, there seems to have been nothing equivalent to the New York protests of 1917 or, of course, the Russian Revolution. Interestingly, in the meetings called by British socialists to greet the Russian Revolution, no mention was made of the role of food riots as a trigger to more widespread social protest.[81] The moment in which it seemed it might be possible to argue for consumption and production as complementary and equally necessary spheres for socialist politics had passed. The actual relationship between socialism and shopping had not been resolved – could shopping be a useful and politicised activity for socialists and thereby empower socialist women or was shopping to be left as the aspect of a future socialist society which would tantalise women into becoming socialists? For a fragile moment some socialist women had started to imagine one way in which the border between the 'domestic' and the 'political' could be dissolved so that a socialist strategy could be forged which no longer privileged production over consumption.

Housing as consumption

If everyday shopping for food is one area of consumption which could have provided a focus for socialists to make a woman-focused politics, another aspect of day-to-day consumption which had clear political leverage was rent. The rent strike has an undeniable political pedigree for the British Left with the most famous example being the Glasgow Rent Strikes of 1915. As part of the historiography and hagiography of 'Red Clydeside', the rent strikes have entered the mythology of the Left, contributing an image which, unusually, is peopled with female faces.[82] The issue here is not to add to the extensive and often combative literature on 'Red Clydeside', but rather to consider the extent to which socialist women identified a gendered politics of rent. Can it be argued that rent provided a focus for a politics of consumption for British socialist women?

Housing, particularly housing conditions, had been an issue for socialists long before the famous rent strikes of the First World War. Socialist demands for better housing were focused through the Workmen's National Housing Council (WNHC), formed in 1898 by three SDFers.[83] It was not an SDF 'front' organisation but gained broad-based support across and beyond the socialist and labour movements,[84] but it is striking that no women were visibly identified with its work. The approach of the Council was to treat housing as a political issue, campaigning as a conventional pressure group for municipalisation. It eschewed more radical tactics such as the use of the rent strike as a weapon in the battle for housing reform.[85]

Much socialist discussion of housing was concerned with housing conditions and the need to ameliorate them. Here housing was an issue of social policy rather than one of consumption. Slum conditions illustrated the failings of the capitalist system and the need for change. But it was through domestic rents that housing became part of consumption. Yet these two aspects of housing – social conditions and rent – often fail to be untangled by historians. This makes it more difficult to identify when the issue of housing constituted a possible site for a politics of consumption.

Rent was an issue for socialists. Yet generally, when rent was discussed, it was in terms of an economic analysis of capitalism and the role that rent played as an unearned source of income to the landlord class. In contrast, rent as a part of the ordinary household budget was a very different matter and was rarely aired as a topic for socialist discussion. Nevertheless, the WNHC did argue that rent should be related to the tenant's ability to pay and therefore campaigned for local fair rent courts. Here was the equivalent to the idea of a fair price for food, and the call for fair rent courts was to be taken up in the later rent strikes. But to what extent was housing, and specifically rent, seen as a gendered issue by socialist women?

When Julia Dawson set out the reasons 'Why Women Want Socialism', she included 'good homes for all' in her list.[86] The Social Democratic Party's Women's Committee did not disagree. In its pamphlet 'Some Words to Socialist Women' the desires of working-class mothers were described as including the building of 'houses for the use of the people'.[87] Dora Montefiore's assertion that: 'Amongst all the social problems there is none that touches women more keenly than that of housing'[88] would hardly have been seen as contentious. Yet campaigning for housing reform was not a central feature of socialist women's activities before the First World War. There were occasional discussions within the socialist press of the drudgery of housework and some talk of collective solutions for cooking, cleaning and mending,[89] but there was little focus in this period on the fabric of the home or on its design as a workplace for women. As Lisbeth Simm complained in 1914:

> we cannot expect to make good homes unless we see there are good houses. ... In our Women's Conferences we often discuss housing conditions, but, as everyone knows, the indifference and apathy of householders is a great stumbling block and hinders improvement.

> Many working women – model housewives perhaps – would rather spend their time in patching and polishing inside bad houses, than come out for one hour or so to learn how to unite to demand good houses.[90]

The more gendered reading of the home as the workplace of women was to become much more apparent in the years of reconstruction immediately after the war and in the discussion of the specific form that the new municipal housing should take.[91] In the 1920s housing was an area where there was relatively little to distinguish between the emphases within the arguments of labour and socialist women. The differences that were often apparent between these women and labour and socialist men were less about the consensus that housing could be a 'woman's issue' than its relative place on the political agenda.[92] Women continued to be defined primarily as wives and mothers by labour and socialist men and, despite the enfranchisement of women over 30 in 1918, definitions of 'the political' were slow to change. As housing reform became a more pressing issue in the inter-war years, coupled with feminist and other attempts to revalue the housewife as a worker, so aspects of the housing issue moved from the private to the public arena. But not all socialist women in the 1920s, principally women in the ILP, were at ease with the argument that housing was a woman's issue, as they felt sex differentiation was anti-socialist. There was also a real worry, learnt from experience, that a woman's issue necessarily implied marginality for the issue and its proponents.[93] That of course did not mean that housing, or rent, were not gendered issues but what was crucial for socialist women and their politics was how women chose to *represent* these issues within the broader political discourse of the time.

Rent was certainly a woman's concern even if it was not always recognised as a woman's issue. It was generally understood that the paying of household rent was part of the wife's responsibility as manager of the household budget,[94] even though tenancies would usually be in the husband's name. In that sense rent was a gendered issue, with the day-to-day responsibilities and anxieties, as well as the potential for direct action, falling to women. The associated language of housing and rent was also gendered in that those who paid rent were 'tenants' who were presumed to be male within the socialist press as much as anywhere else.[95] What there was less consensus over was the extent to which rent was an issue for socialist women. Although some did feel that rent was a relevant topic for them, this, of course, did not mean that rent was seen as an arena in which a politics of consumption could be made. For this to happen the rent strike had to be recognised as a political weapon in the fight to create a socialist society.

The rent strike as a politics of consumption

Rent strikes have tended to be employed by tenants in protest against what are seen as unjustified rent rises and as part of the pursuit of a 'fair rent'. David

Englander has traced a series of rent strikes across Britain, particularly in the years immediately preceding the First World War.[96] They were rarely successful because, as he suggests, 'the cult of home is a factor which cannot be cursorily dismissed when considering working-class reluctance to engage in rent strikes'.[97] He concludes that these rent strikes were rarely the preliminary to continuous organisation. Rather, they were indicative of the desperation to which the participants were reduced. Nevertheless, in 1912 George Lansbury asked in the *Daily Herald*: 'Has not the time come for organising a strike against paying rents to slum landlords?' A year later he felt that there were real signs of an impending rent strike, which he saw as 'a war against the House Bosses'.[98] At a time of increasing industrial unrest, some socialists saw the rent strike as a further weapon in the battle against capitalism. They did not appear to see it as a weapon particularly suited to women. Most rent strikes of the pre-war years seem to have been organised by men, although occasionally the existence of a female crowd (rent strikers and supporters) and the nature of their participation was commented on. The *Women's Dreadnought* reported of the Leeds rent strike of 1914: 'The women, it is said, are marching about the streets brandishing pokers, rolling pins, and toasting forks, to show that they intend to protect their homes.'[99] This sounds a little like the female food rioters of earlier generations.

Although there were some rent strikes scattered across the country from the beginning of the First World War,[100] the most famous example occurred in Glasgow in 1915, largely because it was seen to be successful. Some have chosen to see the Glasgow rent strikes as 'a class victory', as 'a militant, oppositional and thoroughly political struggle' in which all the leaders theorised the rent struggle in class terms.[101] Others have been struck by the high level of participation of women and have endorsed Helen Crawfurd's assessment that is was a 'women's fight'.[102] It has even been observed that there was a sexual division of politics on 'Red Clydeside', with the women fighting higher rents (an issue of consumption) while men fought the Munitions Act (an issue of production).[103] In terms of the argument here, it is the practice of socialist women in relation to the strikes which is most relevant to the consideration of the possibilities of a politics of consumption. Yet this is peculiarly difficult to ascertain.

Women's involvement in the fight for housing reform in Glasgow was channelled through the Glasgow Women's Housing Asociation (GWHA), which had been formed in 1914 with ILPers such as Agnes Dollan and Helen Crawfurd among its leading members. As the activities of the GWHA became more apparent to the readers of *Forward*, so there were calls for the locus of politics to shift a little: 'our campaigns need to be carried out in the backcourts – perhaps with a bit of music thrown in'.[104] Although the President of the GWHA, Mrs Mary Laird, addressed ILP meetings on 'Woman and the Home',[105] little of the flavour of any particular 'woman's view' of the rent problem filtered into the paper. The women were congratulated and even encouraged but it was all from a distance and rarely in the women's own words.[106] At a Women's Labour League Conference in Glasgow in November 1915 the rent strikes were claimed to demonstrate the 'immense Womanly potentialities in collective effort', and it was hoped that one result of the agitation would be the election of women members to town councils.[107] Yet there was little sense of why in particular this was a woman's issue. Maybe the decision of the GWHA to retitle itself the Glasgow Workers' Housing Association in May 1916 was indicative of a more general desire to downplay the gendered aspects of the politics of rent.[108]

Through Patrick Dollan's reports in *Labour Leader* socialists across the whole country learnt not only of the rent strikes in and around Glasgow but also of those well beyond the Clyde.[109] In his accounts these strikes were the prelude to wider class action – it was like a volcano whose 'eruption will destroy more than increased rents'.[110] Increasingly Dollan's reports highlighted the significance of the participation of women in the rent strikes:

> The enthusiasm of the women is marvellous .... The women are absolutely lacking in fear, and have reached that mental state when they are prepared to defy the houseowners and the authorities to do their worst. Such splendid women would make any movement a success. They remind me of the Paris women who marched on Versailles in 1789. No power can daunt them: not even force.[111]

Yet, ironically, the voices of the women themselves, whether leaders or rank and file, were rarely heard in the socialist press. Their speeches were sometimes reported. A range of arguments could be found, including the threats that 'the housewives would allow the munition workers to sleep in for a morning or two' and that their soldier sons would desert from the front if necessary in order to prevent evictions or that they would not allow their sons to bear arms unless their homes 'were protected against the rapacity of the house-owners'.[112] Even experienced socialist women such as Agnes Dollan and Helen Crawfurd, both office holders in the key GWHA, did not break into the male-dominated columns of the national socialist press or even the local Glasgow *Forward*. Advertisements for local meetings give some evidence of the scope of their activity, and that of other socialist women, in supporting and participating in the rent strikes but their particular arguments, including any specifically gender-based arguments, are lost. In addition, most of the memoirs of these events were written by men, such as William Gallacher and Tom Bell, who praise the action of working-class women like Mrs Barbour of Govan but nevertheless reinforce the sense of silent 'otherness' of the women strikers.[113] *The Herald*, formerly the *Daily Herald*, also reported the rent strikes – 'a splendid example of what women can do'. It was stressed that there was activity beyond Scotland, specifically in Tooting, West Ham and East London, and it was hoped that 'as an outcome of this effort our women readers will understand that a very little organisation and very little work on the part of each one of them would very soon compel the Government to take action in order to reduce food and coal prices'.[114] Soldiers' wives were urged to contact 400 Old Ford Road, although it was not noted that this was the address of Sylvia Pankhurst, a socialist woman who had already argued for the rent strike as an important political weapon for women. Indeed Sylvia Pankhurst was someone who argued for the rent strike as a politics of consumption.

Late in 1913 Sylvia Pankhurst and other members of the East London Federation of the WSPU began to argue for a new tactic in the fight for women's enfranchisement – No Vote No Rent. Because '[t]he working woman feels the burden of rent probably more than any other', here was a way of politicising a key aspect of women's day-to-day responsibilities as a consumer. It was suggested that the rent strike was 'a weapon which can be used at will' but that it needed to be prepared for with careful organisation.[115] Mrs Gough sought to persuade a Glasgow audience of the power of the 'No Vote No Rent' tactic. It would not be possible to evict several thousand families in a city and, she assured her audience, 'if any attempt were made to victimise a family the "Peoples' Army" would be brought along to help them'.[116] Pankhurst suggested that this tactic was the women's equivalent of the tax resistance and withdrawing of gold from the banks practised by men in 1832 'for in working class homes, as everyone knows, it is the woman who spends the wages and pays the rent'. She suggested that there were recent examples of the successful employment of the rent strike as a political weapon, citing the Chicago garment workers' strike of 1912.[117] The No Rent strike would, Pankhurst promised, 'be absolutely irresistible if women will but trust each other'. Indeed, '[i]f women will but adopt in sufficient numbers the No Vote No Rent strike, it will create an overwhelming deadlock, with the power to checkmate the Government and force them to give us the vote'.[118] Other women were not so convinced. Edith Watson argued in the *Daily Herald*:

> To hope for revolutionary direct action on the part of unorganised, neglected (in the sense of not being taught rebellion) wives, sisters and mothers of men who cannot themselves organise decently is to hope for the moon. Rent strikes, consumers' leagues, etc, are only just peeping into daylight and are too weak for much 'direct action' yet.[119]

Yet Margaretta Hicks and Sylvia Pankhurst were both trying to create a politics of consumption at this time. Interestingly, in Pankhurst's 1931 account, *The Suffragette Movement*, this strategy was presented as only a means to housing reform, albeit once the vote was achieved. She also recalled why it failed as a short-term strategy:

> We announced that the strike should not begin till a formidable number of pledges to join it had been received. The pledges came in slowly. A house-to-house canvass revealed the deep-rooted fear amongst the women of 'losing the home'. ... The risk of it was so terrible as only to be faced in some desperate crisis. I saw that whilst we might continue to

propagate the idea, it could only be realized as the result of some crisis.[120]

A politics of consumption, based on rent, was easier to imagine than to put into practice precisely because it impinged so much on everyday life.

Moving consumption on to the socialist agenda

Although socialist politics remained primarily focused on production rather than consumption, on working-class income rather than on expenditure, there were moments when these assumptions could be questioned. The final section of this chapter will examine two such moments – the ILP's Living Wage debate in the 1920s and the publication of Teresa Billington-Greig's book *The Consumer in Revolt* – and the extent to which they represented a gendered reading of the place of consumption within socialist politics.

After 1918 the ILP found itself in a new and difficult position as a political party. For the first time the Labour Party admitted individuals to membership and appeared to declare itself to be a socialist organisation with the adoption of Clause IV. In these circumstances what was to be distinctive about the ILP, particularly in relation to the Labour Party? David Howell has observed of the ILP in the 1920s, it 'was not a repository for settled positions and wisdoms. Rather its diverse personalities offered a kaleidoscope of styles and strategies; the Party was an arena in which issues were contested'.[121] Was this the opportunity for socialist women to reshape the socialist agenda?

Although the Communist Party attracted some of the socialist women who had been active before and throughout the war, the ILP remained the only significant socialist, as distinct from communist or labour, party in the 1920s. The ILP had always seen itself as being particularly sympathetic to women and women's issues, yet in the early 1920s there was a real concern that 'women are not taking the part they should in the life of the movement'.[122] At the time when the ILP had the opportunity to re-examine its purpose and role as a political organisation, women were significantly underrepresented in the decision-making fora of the party. They were also less visible in the party press – Brailsford's *New Leader* did not have a women's column and rarely included contributions from women. This was the context for women members when it came to shaping the debate about the role and policies of the ILP in the 1920s.

The Living Wage debate

For much of the 1920s the ILP took upon itself the role of think-tank for the wider Labour Party.[123] Its central proposal concerned the Living Wage and was formulated in the document *Socialism in Our Time* (1926), around which the party debated and propagandised as it sought to persuade the Labour Party of its merits. This was presented as a 'third way', as Gordon Brown has described it: 'a middle way between the views of Ramsay MacDonald and Lenin'.[124] Although originally formulated for the ILP by a four man committee, drawing upon J.A. Hobson's underconsumptionist theories, the greatest female influence on the Living Wage proposals came from a non-socialist woman, Eleanor Rathbone.[125] The Living Wage programme aimed at the redistribution of income and the expansion of mass purchasing power. It was enthusiastically adopted at the 1926 ILP Conference but was soundly defeated at the 1927 Labour Party Conference. What did socialist women make of this debate and to what extent was there a gender dimension to this re-evaluation of the socialist project? Was this a moment in which a politics of consumption could be developed?

Endowment of motherhood through child allowances, not in itself a new proposal, was the aspect of *Socialism in Our Time* which was directed at women and with which women ILPers particularly concerned themselves. For it was suggested that, in order to achieve a living wage for all, the family wage was too blunt an instrument as it could not discriminate between the different 'needs' of workers. Some men did not have any dependants to support, while other men supported larger families than the normative wife and three children, and, of course, women also worked to support dependants. It was therefore proposed that a minimum wage should be enforced in addition to a child allowance paid to the mother, thereby creating a living wage for all. In her review in *New Leader* of Rathbone's *The Disinherited Family* (1924), Helena Swanwick stressed that the question of a living wage 'affects not only the employer but the worker, the family, the consumer, the state as a whole and in all its parts'.[126] Yet as the discussion of the Living Wage and how it might be achieved rumbled on through the middle years of the 1920s, little attention was given to the consumer as such or to the balance between production and consumption within socialist politics. More attention was given in the socialist press to the detail of schemes of family allowances tried in other countries, particularly Australia,[127] than to the more feminist focus on the 'endowment of motherhood' as a means not only to give full status and recognition to the task of motherhood but also to achieve economic independence for women. It was not that 'the women's case' was not made, for example (from notes published for ILP speakers): 'Independence for women, and a real partnership in the home, can only be achieved when the unpaid work done in the home by wives, mothers and sisters is <u>recognised as work</u>. Family endowment would give women this recognition'.[128] But this was not central to the political debate within the ILP nor were the possible conservative consequences of such an argument explored. Nevertheless, Rathbone, despite not being a socialist, was invited to speak to the 1924 ILP Summer School, and the influence of her proposals runs through ILP discussions on how best to formulate a socialist policy for the times. References to the effect on women of a Living Wage, their status and independence are much more apparent in the early years of debate (1924 and 1925)[129] than later in the decade, when the principal focus moved from two groups who did not engage in paid labour – mothers and children – to another which also did not participate in the labour market – the unemployed. Like earlier socialists, the ILP of the 1920s found it hard to recognise that 'the unemployed' included women.[130] Thus the ILP's discussion of the Living Wage seemed to shift away from the possibility of a more woman-focused socialist policy.

How did ILP women view the Living Wage proposals? There was surprisingly little direct discussion within *New Leader*. Minnie Pallister commented that she wanted to see within her lifetime a separate income given to married women 'in respect of their work as housekeepers, or mothers'.[131] Helen Gault did not question the virtues of family allowances but did not think they should be available to all parents, only to the poorest. Her concern was that anything more would frustrate any chance of persuading the Labour Party to adopt the scheme.[132] Even when organised ILP women met with other women's organisations, the emphasis given to family allowances was as a means to alleviate poverty, particularly that experienced by children, rather than as a means to improve women's status or independence.[133]

What were the possibilities within the Living Wage debate of a politics of consumption? Tangential references were made to consumption. For example, when the ILPer Mrs Perriman spoke at the 1928 Labour Women's Conference in support of child allowances, she argued that they 'would serve the need for a redistribution of the national wealth, and at the same time be a real increase in the purchasing power of the working-class family'.[134] Her argument failed to persuade the conference, yet her view was very much in tune with Agnes Dollan's definition of socialism set out in 1923:

> Socialism is essentially concerned with the welfare of the home and the family. It is the friend of family life. Its main object is a decent home and worthy conditions of life for every family. As such it has a big appeal for women. Its successful advocacy and operation depends on women understanding and appreciating the need for Socialism. That means propaganda connecting Socialism with the home, family welfare, women in industry, peace, temperance, health, mothers' pensions, child welfare, and kindred subjects.[135]

It was possible to use this domesticised version of socialism as a way to challenge the socialist privileging of production over consumption. Thus Helena Swanwick, reflecting after attending the 1924 Labour Women's Conference, suggested:

> Whereas for so long, owing to the backwardness of the women's side, Labour conferences when dealing with economics, used to think chiefly in terms of wages and conditions of employment in 'gainful occupations', the balance is now being redressed and the administrator of the

family income is coming to her own, and the producer of human life is taking her place beside the producer of exchangeable commodities.[136]

For Swanwick this change was evidence of a modification of politics which the suffragists had foreseen, so that men were 'becoming sensitive to women and women's side of life work'. She thought this was apparent in all political parties but was particularly true of the Labour Party, 'whose sense of values more nearly approaches that of women'.[137] This rather optimistic assessment of the Labour Party was not shared by those women whose primary identification remained the ILP, as was apparent as the decade wore on. Nevertheless, Swanwick had revealed a sense of the changing balance between production and consumption within the politics of the Left and the way in which that might enable women's inclusion in the socialist project. But there was still a feeling that many women would agree with the women depicted in a story in *New Leader* for whom 'Production, Protection, and Capitalism are words that pass over our heads unheeded'.[138]

The consumer in revolt?

This chapter has been concerned to establish the extent to which socialist women in the period from the 1880s to the 1920s were able to reconfigure the agenda of socialism so that a politics based on consumption had an equal role to a politics centred on production. Although this was not an issue which was recognised by most socialists (men and women) of the period, there were certainly some who saw consumption as an important arena for making socialist politics. More specifically, some socialist women, like Margaretta Hicks, tried to develop a politics of consumption as a space in which women could access socialist ideas, while a few tried to imagine a socialism in which a politics of consumption was properly integrated.

It was Teresa Billington-Greig,[139] in her book *The Consumer in Revolt* (1912), who made the most concerted attempt in the period to challenge some of the ideas on the Left about consumption and its place on the political agenda. As Teresa Billington she had joined the ILP in 1903 and had been an organiser for the party in 1905, before becoming a WSPU organiser in 1906. Thereafter she was an energetic member of the Women's Freedom League from its inception until the end of 1910. By the time of *The Consumer in Revolt* she was not affiliated to any political organisation but her identity as a socialist woman is apparent throughout the book.

Her contention was that a damaging divorce existed between production and consumption at the level of theory as well as practice and that this was expressed through the labour movement on the one hand and the largely unorganised consumer on the other. This was damaging to progressive forces and had been engineered by capitalists in order to divide and rule. Although wage earners and consumers were often the same people, the collective interest between the two functions had been ignored. Thus:

> All the strength of the revolt of Labour, with its organised army of voters and its scouting party of intellectuals, has been turned to the satisfaction of the producer's demand for higher wages at whatever cost to the consuming public. Each complementary element of the economic partnership has tried to ignore the other element. Each has taken counsel alone, sought to benefit alone – and failed alone.[140]

Billington-Greig observed that the labour movement's attitude to consumers was that nothing needed to be done until after 'the present system has been remedied or destroyed', and then 'the consumers' problem' would be solved automatically.[141] In her analysis she distinguished socialists from the labour or trade union movement. She felt that, although in their theory socialists had stressed the relationship between production and consumption, 'in their practice and in the direction of their teaching the Socialists have been almost as completely obsessed by the workers' side of the economic problem as the Trade Unionists'. To make matters worse, there had been no similar body of 'organised consumers in revolt' to make balancing claims from the other side, and therefore socialists had concentrated on 'questions of wages and working conditions and their immediate effects' rather than on issues arising from consumption.[142] She concluded that for the Left generally 'the question of industry is one of settlement between the worker and the monopolist .... There is no duality; these two alone are conceived in a single fight; the consumer does not exist, except perhaps as a looker on.'[143] Just as Margaretta Hicks was beginning to argue at the same time, Billington-Greig observed of the industrial militancy of 1911–12 that the net result had been 'to take from the worker in his capacity of consumer all that he has been able to win in his capacity of rebellious worker'. Yet workers and consumers were unable to recognise their shared interests and saw each other as the problem rather than the system in which they were both located. She therefore proposed that in order to achieve the full expression of human needs there had to be a consumers' movement as well as a workers' movement, 'acting in concert along parallel lines, one on either side of the profiteer, ... [to] reduce him to impotence'.[144]

In *The Consumer in Revolt* Billington-Greig also addressed the gendering of economics. She claimed that '[t]here has been an economic divergence between the sexes almost from the dawn of history' and, in a similar way to Engels and Bebel, constructed a chronology of the dispossession of women from productive labour so that the archetypal worker came to be seen as male.[145] She even suggested the extent to which masculine pride was bound up with social understandings of productive labour. Within the dichotomous economic system described by Billington-Greig, the majority of consumers were female.[146] It was her contention that the domination of the world by the male producer was the foundation on which capitalism was built and that if consumers had had equivalent economic power, then this exploitative system might never have emerged. She concluded that 'the economic re-organisation of the world can only come when woman is active and free'.[147] This is the classic socialist argument with a strong feminist twist.

Although Brian Harrison has suggested that Billington-Greig's interest in consumerism was 'pioneering' and that she showed 'vision, independence, and imagination' in *The Consumer in Revolt*, he feels that the book's limitation was the lack of a 'route-map to guide her readers towards her destination'.[148] Yet Billington-Greig had some proposals to revolutionise what she saw as a flawed economic system. She was critical of both the labour and socialist movements of the period. For her, the only solution was the union of producers and consumers but, she argued, the limitations of the labour movement meant that little could be expected of them without an external spur to action – an organised consumers' movement. She argued that the existing cooperative societies were not yet such a movement because they did not take 'active educational and aggressive action in the fighting line of the movement of discontent'.[149] Although less critical of the socialist movement, in her eyes this remained a movement dominated by the needs of producers, although its focus on statist solutions provided some possibility for a reconfiguring of the agenda towards the 'one who needs and not the one who works'.[150] She also gave specific examples of attempts to build a tentative politics of consumption but concluded that as yet consumers' leagues were not strong enough to initiate independent action and had not yet been able to emancipate themselves from the producers' outlook on economics.[151] They had to be a counterbalance, rather than a subsidiary, to the workers' movement, using tactics such as 'white lists' and consumer boycotts as well as providing an opportunity to bring together the previously unorganised, such as sweated workers. Such a movement would 'awaken the average woman to her relation to the rest of the community, and to the vital matters affecting her which call for her presence in public affairs'. According to Billington-Greig, this was the way to mobilise the 'home-women'. As Hicks was also to argue, the strength of organised consumers working in an equal partnership with the workers' movement was that a 'boycott *plus* a strike is more than the strongest employer or the strongest combine would willingly face'. Billington-Greig also suggested the municipalisation of key services and the use of a form of contract-compliance such as fair wage clauses. Although presenting her ideas in a deliberately provocative fashion, hers was a passionate appeal which attempted to address the privileging of production over consumption in the labour and socialist movement. Using the kind of rhetoric familiar to socialists, she claimed:

> We do not live by bread alone, nor do we live alone for the making of bread. There must be free scope for the development of the spirit behind the consumers' revolt, and for its demand, not for the right to

work, but for the right to enjoy, with the necessary corollary of the reduction of work to its ultimate minimum.[152]

Yet, unlike the traditional socialist vision, here was a radical revisioning of the role of consumption in the politics of the Left. So why did it have so little effect on socialist men or women?

Undoubtedly Brian Harrison is right to describe Teresa Billington-Greig as a 'woman of ideas'.[153] Yet despite her vision she was never very successful at persuading others to revise their agendas once she became detached from any formal political organisation. One of the reasons for this seems to have been the critical stance she took to those she had to persuade. Harrison suggests that in her earlier book, *The Militant Suffrage Movement* (1911), she had unnecessarily narrowed her readership:[154] was this the problem with *The Consumer in Revolt*? The book was addressed to the Left and was reviewed in the socialist press. The reviewer in *Justice* welcomed the book as 'well worth perusal' without endorsing all the views expressed within it.[155] Under the heading 'A Timely Reminder', the emphasis on the consumer was seen positively, although the idea that socialists privileged production was denied. In contrast to Billington-Greig, it was argued that no consumers' league could change the mutual antagonism between producer and consumer which was a necessary condition of 'the class ownership of the means of production'. In sum, this was an encouraging review which prompted some reflection on the issue of consumption within *Justice*, but the reviewer's response also indicates how hard it was for socialists to reconsider their overall agenda and the pre-eminent role of production within it. Although neither *Labour Leader* nor *Forward* seems to have found space to review the work of this ex-ILPer, the *Daily Herald* did include a short review.[156] Here Billington-Greig was congratulated for producing a book 'full of suggestive thought'. The idea of the combination of a strike with a consumer boycott was seen as an innovative tactic, a 'flanking movement'. That Billington-Greig was critical of the socialist and trade union movements was acknowledged, although not defensively, and the idea of a consumers' league was seen as being beneficial to consumer and producer alike.

Although *The Consumer in Revolt* received some positive responses within the socialist press, none of the leading socialist women took the issues up immediately. This was partly because many of them were preoccupied with suffrage in 1912. This was also a time when the more discursive women's columns had been squeezed out of the socialist press and there was therefore less space for socialist women to reflect on the challenge that Billington-Greig made to the socialist project. What is clear is that, at much the same time as Teresa Billington-Greig was writing her book, Margaretta Hicks was coming to similar conclusions, although there is no evidence that Hicks had read *The Consumer in Revolt*. In comparing the two socialist women and their relative impact on creating a politics of consumption, it seems that Billington-Greig remained a 'woman of ideas', who from 1910 situated herself on the margins of both women's and socialist politics. In contrast, Hicks attempted to persuade a socialist party from the inside by putting her ideas into practice and propagandising both to unorganised women and to her own comrades. Unlike Billington-Greig, she did not let her criticisms of a masculinist socialism deafen her potential audience. She had also created the space within the BSP and its press to persist in her attempt to build a politics of consumption, whereas Billington-Greig remained isolated and lacked a strategy to translate her critique into a new politics.

So was consumption a fruitful area for socialist women to make a woman-focused politics and to reconfigure the socialist agenda? From the 1880s to the 1920s there were only a few moments when it was possible for socialists to conceive of a renegotiation of what constituted 'the political'. The crucial time for the creation of a socialist politics of consumption were the years immediately preceding the First World War – in terms of Billington-Greig's iconoclastic vision, Hick's practice and Pankhurst's proposal for a No Vote No Rent campaign. The rising cost of living provided the context for protests around consumption which could in turn become a *politics* of consumption and even a socialist politics of consumption. It was possible for socialist women to use consumption as a lever in a broader campaign because of the identification of women, particularly the unorganised 'home-women', with such everyday issues as the rising cost of food and rent. Here was a space which traditionally socialists had not recognised as having the potential for political action. The issue for socialist women was whether they were able to persuade themselves and their comrades that consumption was as necessary as production to socialism and the making of socialists.

Although the First World War saw international cost of living protests and brought food prices on to the mainstream agenda of various socialist groups, it also paradoxically saw the stifling of a tentative politics of consumption in Britain. Only the rent strikes of 1915 seemed to suggest renewed possibilities for such a politics. Yet in many ways these protests revealed a sexual division of politics, with the male arena of production rarely impinging on feminine consumption. Like other cost of living protests, these wartime rent strikes did little to shift the socialist agenda long-term. Similarly, the opportunity that the Living Wage debate presented in the 1920s to reorder socialist priorities was never translated into a reconceptualisation of the relationship between production and consumption within socialist politics. The more domesticated version of socialism which some ILP women espoused after the war seemed to suggest a potential for a politics of consumption, but this potential was dissipated by the focus on the welfare aspects of issues which could also be read as matters of consumption.

And yet all the examples in this chapter provide evidence that a range of socialist women were imagining a form of socialist politics which did not privilege production over consumption. Such imaginings created the possibility of a socialism which was intrinsically woman-focused and in which a socialist politics of consumption could play a central role. But at the end of the 1920s a socialist politics of consumption remained only a possibility, not yet a reality.

NOTES

1 Chapter 6 draws on K. Hunt, 'Negotiating the boundaries of the domestic: British socialist women and the politics of consumption', *Women's History Review*, 9, 2, 2000. This new and expanded version is published with the permission of Triangle Journals Ltd.
2 P. Thane, 'The women of the British Labour Party and feminism, 1906–45', in H. L. Smith (ed.), *British Feminism in the Twentieth Century*, Aldershot, Edward Elgar, 1990.
3 Manchester Women's History Group, 'Ideology in bricks and mortar. Women and housing in Manchester between the wars', *Women: Work, Culture and Community, North West Labour History*, 12, 1986–7.
4 The historiography of consumer protest is usually concerned with the achievement of consumer goals and not therefore with a politics of consumption, see M. van der Linden, 'Working-class consumer power', *International Labor and Working Class History*, 46, 1994. For a different approach to women and the politics of food, see M. Pugh, 'Women, food and politics, 1880–1930', *History Today*, 41, 1991.
5 See K. Hunt, 'Fractured universality: the language of British socialism before the First World War', in J. Belchem and N. Kirk (eds), *Languages of Labour*, Aldershot, Ashgate, 1997.
6 For a discussion of the historiography of food riots and cost of living protests in relation to a politics of consumption, see Hunt, 'Negotiating the boundaries of the domestic', pp. 391–3.
7 T. Kaplan, 'Female consciousness and collective action: the case of Barcelona, 1910–18', *Signs*, 7, 3, 1982, p. 564.
8 B. Davis, 'Food scarcity and the empowerment of the female consumer in World War I Berlin', in V. de Grazia and E. Furlough (eds), *The Sex of Things. Gender and Consumption in Historical Perspective*, Berkeley, University of California Press, 1996.
9 J. Smart, 'Feminists, food and the fair price: the cost of living demonstrations in Melbourne, August–September 1917', *Labour History*, 50, 1986, p. 131.
10 T. Kaplan, *Red City, Blue Period. Social Movements in Picasso's Barcelona*, Berkeley, University of California Press, 1992, p. 106. This is a reworking of her earlier article 'Female consciousness and collective action'.
11 Kaplan, 'Female consciousness and collective action', p. 566.
12 A. Clark, *The Struggle for the Breeches: Gender and the Making of the British Working Class*, Berkeley, University of California Press, 1995, p. 228; J. Vernon, *Politics and the People. A Study in English Political Culture*, Cambridge, Cambridge University Press, 1993, p. 378.
13 C. Midgley, *Women against Slavery. The British Campaigns, 1780–1870*, London, Routledge, 1992, p. 202.
14 M.L. Davies quoted in G. Scott, *Feminism and the Politics of Working Women. The Women's Co-operative Guild, 1880s to the Second World War*, London, UCL Press, 1998, p. 3.
15 M.L. Davies (ed.), *Life As We Have Known It*, London, Virago, 1977, p. xiii.
16 See C. Webb, *The Woman with the Basket: The History of the Women's Co-operative Guild*, Manchester, The Guild, 1927.
17 D. Frank, *Purchasing Power. Consumer Organizing, Gender and the Seattle Labor Movement, 1919–29*, New York, Cambridge University Press, 1994.
18 S. Levine, 'Workers' wives: gender, class and consumerism in the 1920s United States', *Gender and History*, 3, 1, 1991, p. 47.

19 D. Frank, 'Housewives, socialists, and the politics of food: the 1917 New York cost-of-living protests', *Feminist Studies*, 11, 2, 1985.
20 Ibid., p. 281.
21 *Justice*, 9 September 1893.
22 *Justice*, 23 September 1893.
23 *Justice*, 18 August 1894.
24 *Justice*, 16 June 1894.
25 Principally, the SDF's *Justice*, the ILP's *Labour Leader* and the *Clarion*.
26 *Justice*, 19 January 1901.
27 See P. Gurney, *Co-operative Culture and the Politics of Consumption, 1870–1930*, Manchester, Manchester University Press, 1996, particularly ch. 7.
28 *Justice*, 2 March 1901. See also the WLL's Trading Store set up in London in 1912 (*League Leaflet*, October 1912, February 1913).
29 *Justice*, 23 March 1901.
30 *Justice*, 16 February 1901.
31 See Hicks' earlier thoughts on the practical organisation of socialist women (*Clarion*, 23 February 1912).
32 *The Link*, July 1912, p. 4.
33 *The Link*, September 1912, p. 4.
34 *The Link*, October 1912, p. 4.
35 *Justice*, 26 October 1912.
36 *Clarion*, 1 November 1912.
37 *Justice*, 7 June 1913.
38 *Justice*, 9 November 1912.
39 *Justice*, 9 November 1912.
40 *Justice*, 22 November 1913.
41 *Justice*, 7 June 1913.
42 *Justice*, 21 June 1913.
43 *Justice*, 2 August 1913.
44 *Justice*, 6 December 1913.
45 *Daily Herald*, 9 March 1914.
46 *Justice*, 1 January 1914.
47 *The Link*, February 1913, p. 5.
48 *Clarion*, 20 June 1913.
49 *The Women's Dreadnought*, 3 October 1914.
50 *Justice*, 8 March, 29 March 1913.
51 *Justice*, 8 November 1913.
52 *Justice*, 13 December 1913. See also 9 July 1914.
53 *Justice*, 12 March 1914.
54 *Justice*, 6 August 1914; *Socialist Record*, October 1914.
55 *Justice*, 20 August 1914.
56 *Daily Herald*, 7 August, 25 August 1914.
57 *Socialist Record*, January 1915.
58 See R. Harrison, 'The War Emergency Workers' National Committee, 1914–20', in A. Briggs and J. Saville (eds), *Essays in Labour History, 1886–1923*, London, Macmillan, 1971; J.M. Winter, *Socialism and the Challenge of War. Ideas and Politics in Britain, 1912–18*, London, Routledge & Kegan Paul, 1974, ch. 7.
59 Winter, *Socialism and the Challenge of War*, pp. 199–202.
60 Ibid., p. 232.
61 *Justice*, 21 January 1915.
62 *Labour Leader*, 5 March 1914; *League Leaflet*, November 1912, p. 8.
63 Women's Labour League Executive Committee Minute Book, 25 January 1914, 20 February 1914, 27 March 1914, 22 April 1914.

64 B. Winslow, *Sylvia Pankhurst. Sexual Politics and Political Activism*, London, UCL Press, 1996, pp. 91–2.
65 *Justice*, 5 November 1914.
66 *Justice*, 3 December 1914.
67 *Justice*, 31 December 1914.
68 J. Bush, *Behind the Lines. East London Labour, 1914–19*, London, Merlin Press, 1984, p. 43.
69 *Justice*, 4 February 1915.
70 *Justice*, 20 May 1915.
71 *Justice*, 3 June 1915.
72 *Justice*, 18 November 1915, 2 November 1916.
73 For example, *The Call*, 6 July 1916.
74 *The Call*, 10 May 1917.
75 *The Call*, 17 May 1917.
76 *The Call*, 14 February 1918.
77 Sir W.H. Beveridge, *British Food Control*, London, Oxford University Press, 1928, p. 196.
78 B. Waites, *A Class Society at War. England, 1914–18*, Leamington Spa, Berg, 1987, p. 229.
79 For the Consumers' Council and its context see L.M. Barnett, *British Food Policy during the First World War*, London, Allen & Unwin, 1985.
80 Ibid., p. 154.
81 See, for example, *Herald*, 9 June 1917.
82 See the images in *Red Skirts on Clydeside: A Film about Women's Political Past*, Sheffield Film Co-op.
83 See D. Englander, *Landlord and Tenant in Urban Britain, 1838–1918*, Oxford, Clarendon Press, 1983; D. Englander (ed.), *The Diary of Fred Knee*, Coventry, Society for the Study of Labour History, 1977.
84 Englander, 'Introduction' to *Diary of Fred Knee*, p. 16. For an example of the ILP's positive response to the WNHC, see *Labour Leader*, 12 August 1915.
85 Englander, 'Introduction' to *Diary of Fred Knee*, p. 19.
86 *Clarion*, 30 April 1909.
87 D.B. Montefiore, *Some Words to Socialist Women*, London, Twentieth Century Press, 1908, p. 9.
88 *New Age*, 6 October 1904.
89 For example, *Labour Leader*, 5 May 1894.
90 *Labour Woman*, March 1914.
91 See A. Hughes and K. Hunt, 'A culture transformed? Women's lives in Wythenshawe in the 1930s', in A. Davies and S. Fielding (eds), *Workers' Worlds. Cultures and Communities in Manchester and Salford, 1880–1939*, Manchester, Manchester University Press, 1992.
92 See the experience of women in the Labour Party in Manchester in the 1930s, ibid., pp. 82–3. For gender tensions in inter-war local Labour politics which focused on the relative political importance of the consumption of local services, see M. Savage, 'Urban politics and the rise of the Labour Party, 1919–39', in L. Jamieson and H. Corr (eds), *State, Private Life and Political Change*, Basingstoke, Macmillan, 1990.
93 See discussion of women in the ILP in the 1920s in C. Collins, 'Women and Labour politics in Britain, 1893–1932', PhD, London School of Economics, 1991, ch. 5, esp. pp. 275–90.
94 E. Roberts, 'Women and the domestic economy, 1890–1970: the oral evidence', in M. Drake (ed.), *Time, Family and Community. Perspectives on Family and Community History*, Oxford, Blackwell, 1994, p. 130.

95 For example, when *Forward* called for a Rent Moratorium in August 1914, it urged: 'Get the nearest ILP branch to start a list of signatures of men who will unitedly agree to pay no rent for three months. Food first' (15 August 1914).
96 Englander, *Landlord and Tenant*, particularly ch. 7. See also J. Melling, *Rent Strikes. People's Struggle for Housing in West Scotland, 1890–1916*, Edinburgh, Polygon Books, 1983.
97 Englander, *Landlord and Tenant*, p. 125, see also pp. 124–6.
98 *Daily Herald*, 10 May 1912, 19 May 1913, quoted in Englander, *Landlord and Tenant*, pp. 142, 147.
99 *Women's Dreadnought*, 8 March 1914, quoted in Englander, *Landlord and Tenant*, p. 158. For the Leeds strike see ibid., pp. 155–61, and Q. Bradley, 'The Leeds Rent Strike of 1914' (http://www.qbradley.freeserve.co.uk/rentrick.htm).
100 Englander, *Landlord and Tenant*, pp. 205–6.
101 S. Damer, 'State, class and housing: Glasgow, 1885–1919', in J. Melling (ed.), *Housing, Social Policy and the State*, London, Croom Helm, 1980, p. 75.
102 H. Crawfurd, unpublished autobiography, quoted in H. Corr, 'Introduction' to Melling, *Rent Strikes*, p. viii.
103 N. Milton, *John Maclean*, London, Pluto Press, 1973, p. 91.
104 *Forward*, 16 February 1915.
105 *Forward*, 13 March 1915.
106 See, for example, *Forward*, 2 October 1915.
107 *Forward*, 27 November 1915.
108 *Forward*, 20 May 1916.
109 For example, *Labour Leader*, 21 October, 28 October 1915, 4 November 1915.
110 *Labour Leader*, 21 October 1915.
111 *Labour Leader*, 11 November 1915.
112 *Labour Leader*, 4 November, 18 November 1915.
113 W. Gallacher, *Revolt on the Clyde*, London, Lawrence & Wishart, 1936, pp. 52–5; T. Bell, *Pioneering Days*, London, Lawrence & Wishart, 1941.
114 *Herald*, 16 October 1915.
115 *Daily Herald*, 21 November 1913; Winslow, *Sylvia Pankhurst*, pp. 61–2. This aspect of Sylvia's politics is not mentioned in the recent M. Davis, *Sylvia Pankhurst. A Life in Radical Politics*, London, Pluto Press, 1999.
116 *Forward*, 3 January 1914.
117 *Forward*, 24 January 1914.
118 *Daily Herald*, 5 February, 25 February 1914.
119 *Daily Herald*, 19 February 1914.
120 E.S. Pankhurst, *The Suffragette Movement*, London, Virago, 1977, pp. 528–9.
121 D. Howell, 'Beyond the stereotypes: the Independent Labour Party, 1922–1932', *Scottish Labour History Society Journal*, 29, 1994, p. 22.
122 *New Leader*, 8 February 1924.
123 R.E. Dowse, *Left in the Centre. The Independent Labour Party, 1893–1940*, London, Longmans, 1966; Howell, 'Beyond the stereotypes'.
124 G. Brown, *Maxton*, Glasgow, Fontana, 1988, p. 21. See also Wertheimer's comment that this was a 'policy destined to seek salvation somewhere between Communism and Reformism' (E. Wertheimer, *Portrait of the Labour Party*, London, Putnam's & Sons, 1929, p. 17). For the Living Wage debate, see H.N. Brailsford, *Socialism for To-Day*, London, ILP, 1925; Dowse, *Left in the Centre*, ch. 11, pp. 98–9, 122–3; F.M. Leventhal, 'H.N. Brailsford and the *New Leader*', *Journal of Contemporary History*, 9, 1, 1974; F.M. Leventhal, *The Last Dissenter. H.N. Brailsford and His World*, Oxford, Clarendon, 1985, ch. 10.

125 For Rathbone, see J. Alberti, *Eleanor Rathbone*, London, Sage, 1996; S. Fleming, 'Eleanor Rathbone: spokeswoman for a movement', introduction to E. Rathbone, *The Disinherited Family*, Bristol, Falling Wall Press, 1986.
126 *New Leader*, 9 May 1924.
127 For example, G.C.T. Giles, 'Child Endowment (An Australian Plan)', *New Leader*, 2 May 1924.
128 ILP Information Committee, *Monthly Notes for Speakers*, 26, October 1925 (underlining in original text).
129 For example, Historicus, 'Families and Incomes. What is a Living Wage?', *New Leader*, 22 August 1924.
130 See Hunt, 'Fractured universality', pp. 72–4.
131 *New Leader*, 10 October 1924.
132 *New Leader*, 27 April 1928.
133 *New Leader*, 24 January 1930.
134 *New Leader*, 25 May 1928.
135 *New Leader*, 9 November 1923.
136 *New Leader*, 16 May 1924.
137 *New Leader*, 16 May 1924.
138 Marjorie Burford, 'The Women's Vote in Philip Street', *New Leader*, 7 November 1924.
139 For Teresa Billington-Greig see a profile in *Labour Leader*, 26 May 1905; B. Harrison, *Prudent Revolutionaries: Portraits of British Feminists between the Wars*, Oxford, Clarendon, 1987, ch. 2; and for a not entirely sympathetic pen portrait see Pankhurst, *The Suffragette Movement*, pp. 187–8.
140 T. Billington-Greig, *The Consumer in Revolt*, Stephen Swift, London, 1912, extracted in C. McPhee and A. FitzGerald (eds), *The Non-Violent Militant. Selected Writings of Teresa Billington-Greig*, London, Routledge & Kegan Paul, 1987, p. 253.
141 Ibid., p. 257.
142 Ibid., pp. 257–9.
143 Ibid., p. 260.
144 Ibid., pp. 261, 262.
145 Ibid., pp. 269, 270.
146 Ibid., pp. 272, 270.
147 Ibid., pp. 272–3.
148 Harrison, *Prudent Revolutionaries*, p. 60.
149 Billington-Greig, *The Consumer in Revolt*, in McPhee and FitzGerald (eds), *The Non-violent Militant*, pp. 276, 282.
150 Ibid., p. 283.
151 Ibid., p. 285.
152 Ibid., p. 294.
153 The title of the chapter on Billington-Greig in Harrison, *Prudent Revolutionaries*.
154 Ibid., p. 56.
155 *Justice*, 19 October 1912.
156 *Daily Herald*, 27 September 1912.

7

SOCIALIST WOMEN AND INTERNATIONALISM

Internationalism was an important part of the rhetoric of socialism and the women's movement.[1] This chapter is concerned with what internationalism meant to socialist women in particular, and how this translated into their politics. Although some attention has been given to reclaiming the history of the women's/suffrage internationals,[2] to add to the existing histories of the Socialist Internationals[3], there is little space in either literature for the specific experiences of socialist women. This might be because socialist women did not have an experience which was distinct from either, on the one hand, other socialists or, on the other hand, other suffragists. Yet the evidence suggests that to be a woman in the Socialist International usually meant marginality, whilst to raise socialist issues within the women's internationals was equally difficult. The focus here is therefore on the extent to which internationalism united British socialist women across their respective parties, both organisationally and rhetorically, and how this played out over time. In particular, the ways in which not only the First World War but also the Bolshevik Revolution challenged and reconfigured the meaning and organisational forms of internationalism for socialist women will be explored.

From the last quarter of the nineteenth century into the inter-war period, there were a number of transnational organisations in which British socialist women might become involved. On the one hand, the Second International (1889–1914) provided a means for representatives of socialist parties from across the world (principally from Europe) to meet and formulate guiding, if not binding, policy. From 1907 the congresses of the Second International were prefaced by international meetings of socialist women with their own supporting inter-congress organisation. After the war socialist internationalism was challenged by the formation of the communist Third International, which led for a time to two rival socialist international organisations (the 'Two-and-a-Half' International and the rump of the Second International) which in 1923 united to form the Labour and Socialist International (LSI).[4] The women's movement also sought to make links across national boundaries, eventually formalising these links in a number of transnational organisations: the International Council of Women (ICW), the International Woman Suffrage Alliance (IWSA) and the

Women's International League for Peace and Freedom (WILPF). In many ways the socialist and women's internationals were parallel universes, with no organisational links between them. Socialist women were, it seems, expected to choose between their socialism and their commitment to a woman-centred politics, yet individual socialist women can be found taking part in the deliberations of both the socialist and the women's internationals. Were these women exceptions and how does their experience enable us to understand what internationalism meant to socialist women?

One of the issues which was, and is, central to the aspiration of internationalism is the question of how to prevent conflict between nations. For many 'making war upon war' was crucial to their understanding of internationalism, and this was expressed in terms of campaigning for peace or, and this was not always the same, against militarism. Just as the term internationalism was often little interrogated and the tension between it and nationalism and/or patriotism too often ignored, so the differences between pacifism and anti-militarism and the implications of this for internationalism only really became apparent when tested by a world at war. Peace has usually been represented as a feminine, and often as a feminist, issue in opposition to the quintessentially masculine activity of war, with a particular focus on woman the mother who is called upon to sacrifice her sons. How did socialist women view this issue? Did socialist women make a specifically gendered argument in relation to peace and anti-militarism, or did even this depend on their party loyalties? Did the politics of peace force them to prioritise their socialism over their feminism or vice versa, or were socialist women divided amongst themselves over this issue?

In order to engage with these questions this chapter considers the meanings of internationalism available to socialist women. It then turns to the issues arising from British socialist women's involvement with internationalist organisations: the various socialist and communist internationals of the period as well as the women's and woman suffrage internationals. The particular issue of peace/anti-militarism will be highlighted, as it was central to internationalism and was often represented as being 'a woman's issue'. Finally, the extent to which a specifically socialist women's internationalism can be identified will be considered and thus what a focus on internationalism tells us about socialist women.

Interrogating internationalism

Despite the ubiquity of internationalism amongst socialists before the First World War, very little attention was given to defining the term itself. Certainly Ramsay MacDonald was not the only socialist who might be described, in Marquand's terms, as an 'instinctive internationalist'. MacDonald:

> spoke no foreign languages apart from a little French, he liked foreigners and got on well with them; and it is clear from his travel writings that he felt a sense of excitement and liberation when he went

abroad. Unlike many of his countrymen, he did not find it shocking or outrageous that foreigners should sometimes question Britain's motives or act in a way that did not conform to Britain's interests. At a deeper level still, he loathed violence and threats of violence.[5]

Amongst British male socialists, MacDonald was one of the more active participants in the Second International congresses and in the politics of internationalism. Does his rather vague version of internationalism, premised as much on delight in travel and 'foreigners' as on any explicit sense of international solidarity, tell us anything about the models of internationalism open to socialist women of the same period? Maybe it was this rather amorphous internationalism which the SDF Executive was criticising when it spoke in 1904 of an undifferentiated internationalism, a 'sort of gigantic steam roller', which was counterposed to its position of support for 'the old Liberal tradition of the rights of little people'.[6] Here there is some suggestion that the tension between nationalism and internationalism is an uncomfortable one in which there is no desire to obliterate the nationalist struggles of the colonised. Certainly, some socialists expressed internationalist sentiments which included unambiguous anti-imperialist views, although these were often presented in a highly rhetorical form.[7] Perhaps the individual most thoroughly identified with internationalism in pre-war British socialist politics was Keir Hardie. Although often represented as a sentimental commitment to international brotherhood, Hardie's internationalism, Kenneth Morgan maintains, 'was always hedged around by realism; it was never *merely* sentimental'. He saw the International as 'a kind of world-wide equivalent of the Labour Representation Committee at home, where different ideologies would be expressed, and reconciled gradually, through discussion, tolerance and pragmatic reform'.[8] His was an internationalism which centred on fraternity – was this therefore an internationalism which had space for socialist women or did some socialist women feel the need to create a more woman-focused version ?

Another possible influence on socialist women's conception of internationalism might be found in the women's/suffrage transnational organisations. Leila Rupp has shown how here too definitions of internationalism were never rigorous.[9] Attempting to balance the pull of national loyalties with the aspiration of internationalism, this early generation of women internationalists would have agreed with Carrie Chapman Catt's view that internationalism was 'a sentiment like love, or religion, or patriotism, which is to be experienced rather than defined in words'.[10] Rupp suggests that rather than ignoring their differences, particularly but not exclusively national differences, the women of the International Council of Women and International Woman Suffrage Alliance conceptualised internationalism 'as a stitched together quilt of existing differences rather than a wholly new piece of cloth. Unity came out of merging diversity.'[11] Yet, as will become apparent, some of these differences over suffrage, and especially between socialist women and the women's transnational organisations, became too profound to be accommodated even within the metaphor of a patchwork quilt. Historians of the Irish women's movement have noted how for Irish women this 'patchwork quilt of differences' did not give the nationalists amongst them sufficient recognition of the centrality of nationalism to their understanding of internationalism.[12] Nevertheless, Mineke Bosch has argued that the IWSA 'lent reality to the idea of an essential unity and equality of women by the use of a recurring set of gripping images around notions of difference - in fact by exaggerating differences and romanticizing them'. This was particularly apparent in the many national reports which were made to the congresses, where a delegate, often in national costume, emphasised the particularity of her national or even regional experience whilst 'at the same time asserting solidarity, equality, and unity of principle'.[13] For socialist women internationalists, it was their socialism, their participation in mixed-sex organisations and their adult suffragism which were to be differences too far for the transnational women's organisations. For British socialist women within the Second International the potential points of fracture for their internationalism were suffrage politics and party loyalty. It is an assessment of the relative importance of all these differences to British socialist women aspiring to a universalistic internationalism which forms the subject of this chapter.

British women and the Second International[14]

The histories of the Second International give very little space to women's participation and to the meaning of internationalism to socialist women. Amongst the variety of socialisms which existed in Britain before the First World War, all made some commitment to internationalism at the level of rhetoric, although the relationship between this and a sense of national identity, and even nationalism, was both awkward and largely unexplored. Internationalism certainly seems to have been an important aspect of the socialism of many British women. This could take in a range of different practices, from the rhetorical flourish; through travel and correspondence, networking with sisters and comrades from across the globe; sharing experiences and propagandising around the struggles and achievements of women and workers in other countries; to participation in formal international congresses and their supporting national organisations.

The most visible sign of a commitment to internationalism was attendance at an international congress. Indeed, in the early years of the Second International the only real opportunity for any socialist, whether man or woman, to formally express their internationalism was to be a delegate, speaker, translator or organiser at a congress. Women's participation rates were generally very low and the British delegations were no exception. On the one occasion when the International's congress was held within Britain – in London in 1896 – many British socialist women were able to attend for the first and last time.[15] But such low levels of participation were not unusual for socialist conferences generally.[16]

The usual reasons for women's under-representation – the cost, travel and disruption to domestic life – were amplified for International congresses.[17]

Although at national conferences many of the women who attended were accompanying their husbands, there is less evidence of this among the British delegations to the International. Female delegates were generally drawn from those who were virtually full-time political activists. Some of these women were mothers, but their political activism had already meant that they had had to make arrangements for childcare. As if to remind delegates of the practical problems faced by socialist mothers, Margaret MacDonald attended the 1910 congress when her pregnancy with her sixth child would have been evident to all.[18]

The limited number of British women attending International congresses was not an indication of socialist women's lack of interest in internationalism. In the SDF women may even have been more internationally minded than many of their socialist brothers, partly because they regarded the theory and practice of the German Social Democratic Party (SPD) on the Woman Question as a positive model. Some women SDFers played an important role in sustaining their party's internationalism through their journalism and through their friendship networks. Eleanor Marx was an important early figure, while later Dora Montefiore was to play a key role.[19] Montefiore was a friend of Clara Zetkin and Alexandra Kollontai. Together they were part of an international network of socialist women whose mutual friendship helped to reinforce a pre-existing commitment to internationalism.

ILP women also had international connections, although they do not seem to have been part of friendship networks in quite the same way as Montefiore. Margaret MacDonald was an assiduous attender of International congresses, although, according to her husband, 'most of the leading Socialist women of the Continent were against her'.[20] ILP women's experience of the International is largely explained by the difference in their conception of socialism compared with the Second International's Marxism. Their isolation within the International, particularly the Socialist Women's International, was compounded by the ILP's support for a limited women's franchise in opposition to the International's advocacy of adult suffrage. Moreover, although the different approaches of SDF and ILP women within the International must be set within the context of the politics of the divided parent British section, nevertheless, in such relatively confined circles, the personal relationships of the women concerned could colour their strategies. Certainly, in all their years of participation within the Socialist Women's International, there is little evidence that Margaret MacDonald and Dora Montefiore were able to put behind them the 'Belt Case' of 1899.[21] This case resulted from gossip by MacDonald about Montefiore's supposed improper relationship with George Belt, a married working-class man. The gossip led to Belt losing his job as an ILP organiser; to Montefiore being removed as Recording Secretary for the 1899 International Council of Women Congress; and, finally, to a libel action initiated by Belt against the MacDonalds. This was eventually settled out of court. Although the strain between MacDonald and Montefiore clearly did affect relationships between other socialist women, it would be wrong to see this as taking the form of a straightforward SDF/ILP divide or as itself being responsible for polarising the relationship between SDF and ILP women. Individuals such as Margaret Bondfield worked with both groups.[22]

What characterised the internationalism of British socialist women in the period of the Second International? For some women there was a clear commitment to internationalism, not only as a counter to nationalism, but as a means of linking the experiences of women across countries, in order to learn from and support one another. Dora Montefiore, for instance, was not only an active participant in the Second International and its women's movement but also attended the congresses of the large feminist international bodies, the ICW and the IWSA. Nor was she a complete maverick in this respect. Although Montefiore was not a typical British socialist woman, the concerns which prompted her links with other socialist and feminist women around the world were echoed in the experience of some of her less well-travelled socialist sisters. This kind of internationalism changed over time and, as women's positions on the suffrage polarised and socialist women's politics became more clearly differentiated from so-called 'bourgeois feminism', it became harder to make links between the two worlds. This is ironic in some respects, as the subject matter of the ICW and IWSA was often very close to that of the Socialist Women's International and its British section – social reform, particularly linked to the family, maternity, children and childcare were topics which brought women's interests together, as did anti-militarism. Yet women were divided by the politics of their parent organisations; socialist women were distinguished from non-socialists, and even SDF from ILP women. The desire to achieve international solidarity between women remained but differences on strategies and priorities became sharper. With no united socialist party, British socialist women were marked as much by their membership of particular socialist parties as they were by their gender.

British socialist women and the Socialist Women's International before 1914

Turning to the ways in which British women organised in relation to the Second International, it becomes apparent that there were areas of tension within their internationalist politics. This section explores the extent to which British socialist women were able to create an internationalist practice which could accommodate domestic differences. In particular, the focus is on the ways in which their participation was necessarily shaped by their membership of competing, and often brawling, political parties.

The first meeting of the Socialist Women's International was held immediately before the full International congress in Stuttgart in 1907. It was a largely female event controlled by women and provided the first formal opportunity for socialist women to meet within the setting of the International. Kathleen Kough of the SDF found this first congress 'a revelation and an inspiration'.[23] Many of the British socialist women who had previously attended International congresses now found they had an opportunity to speak and eagerly joined in the deliberations of the Women's Congress. The British delegation was particularly vocal in the suffrage debate because it was such a divided group. This division was apparent from the start of the congress, when the SDFer Dora Montefiore's right to take part in the meeting was challenged by other British women comrades. The ostensible grounds were that the Adult Suffrage Society, which she was representing, was not a socialist organisation. As the ILP objectors were supporters of limited women's suffrage, it seems more likely that they were trying to prevent the British case being made for adult suffrage. Their objections were overruled by Clara Zetkin and the conference voted to accept Montefiore.[24] Although this was all done 'in a perfectly friendly spirit',[25] according to the *Clarion*, it was at least an ironic gesture and probably explicit revenge by ILPers for the challenges made by the SDF within the International as a whole to the socialist credentials of the Labour Party.

Dora Montefiore was now able to participate in the suffrage debate, where she and Margaret MacDonald once again came into conflict. MacDonald accused Montefiore of preventing her from making the case for limited suffrage to the Women's Congress.[26] Despite the objections of some of the British delegation, the Women's Congress voted overwhelmingly in favour of adult suffrage. This debate showed a divided British women's delegation whose differences were carried over into the full congress's debate on suffrage. As we will see, suffrage was also a crucial and divisive issue for those British socialist women who participated in the women's internationals. At the second Socialist Women's Congress in 1910 suffrage was again an issue which caused bad feeling within the British delegation. This time MacDonald accused Montefiore of misrepresenting the limited suffrage case. In an exasperated report in *Labour Leader* she described some confusion over the calling of speakers from the British delegation:

> As both this year and three years ago, the WLL, ILP and Fabian women had already, for the sake of letting things go smoothly, put up quietly with much more of Mrs Montefiore than is justified by her influence or representative character in the British movement, and as Mrs Montefiore smilingly assured me, when I appealed to her to have the common courtesy to let one of us move our own League resolutions, that she would speak about them for us in the course of her speech, we felt it was time to make a public protest, and we walked out of the hall in a body.[27]

Here differences in party and suffrage politics were exacerbated by personal differences, as ILP and SDF women jostled to be the voice of British socialist women and to mould the Socialist Women's International to their views on the contentious issue of suffrage.

The first Socialist Women's Congress also called for the formation of an International Bureau for Socialist Women to maintain communication between national sections and to promote the implementation of the International's decisions. Just as the German SPD dominated the full International, so their large and successful women's organisation was the key to formalising the international network of socialist women. The meeting to set up Britain's own women's section of the International was called by SDF women. The Socialist Women's Bureau (British) included representatives from the SDF and its Women's Committee, Fabian Society, Clarion Scouts, Teachers' Association and the ASS. However the absence of women from the ILP and Women's Labour League meant that the group came to be seen as an SDF organisation to be marginalised by mainstream Labour and socialist women. For its part, the SDF sought to involve the ILP and to broaden the base of the Bureau but these overtures were largely unsuccessful.[28]

The initial object of the Socialist Women's Bureau (British) was to establish regular communication between the organised socialist women of all countries, and thereby to illustrate the virtues of internationalism. Unfortunately, communication within Britain was to be more problematic. The Bureau also began a comparative investigation of international social policy, including the provision of maternity pensions, and sponsored public meetings, such as the visit of Clara Zetkin and Alexandra Kollontai in 1909. Although the key issue of 'women and war' was discussed by the Bureau, it did not tackle the topic which had so divided the British women's delegation at Stuttgart: the suffrage. But then adult suffrage was an uncontentious position for most of those who chose to be involved in the Bureau. It seems that from 1907 to 1910 the Socialist Women's Bureau achieved at least as much as the equivalent men's organisation.[29] Yet part of the purpose of the national sections was to encourage socialist unity and to stop inter-party squabbling. Here success was much more limited and the Socialist Women's Bureau should be seen as an element in the jostling between the ILP and SDF for British leadership within the International.[30]

In 1910 the balance of forces changed. At the second Socialist Women's International Congress in Copenhagen the British delegation was again divided over suffrage. But the congress as a whole was somewhat overshadowed by the struggle between the Social Democratic Party (SDP), as the SDF had been re-christened in 1908, and the ILP. Moreover, the WLL was now determined to wrest the Bureau from the hands of the SDP. Consequently, after the Copenhagen congress, the League decided to call a fresh conference to form a British women's section. Effectively the ILP women seized the initiative and succeeded in establishing a new organisation – the Women's International Council of Socialist and Labour Organisations (British Section) – dominated by their own members.

Since the activities of the Women's International Council were not markedly different from those of the Bureau, it seems that ILP women were more interested in taking control for its own sake. The main thing was to marginalise the SDP. But factors outside the immediate control of SDP women ensured that the WLL was never seriously challenged within the Women's International Council. Maybe it did not seem to matter so much any more: with Margaret MacDonald dead and Dora Montefiore outside the British Socialist Party from the end of 1912 and travelling abroad, two of the main protagonists were no longer part of the picture. The SDP Women's Committee was dissolved at the beginning of 1912 as part of the move to establish the BSP. Although there were attempts to get the BSP to affiliate to the Women's International Council in late 1912, their membership was not accepted until mid-1914.[31] Moreover, the truncated and hastily arranged International congress at Basle in 1912 did not reawaken feelings of internationalism amongst British socialist women, despite its theme of peace. With the outbreak of the First World War, the Second International shattered as SPD deputies voted for war credits and the force of national allegiances splintered the fragile rhetoric of internationalism.

Thus British women contributed to the operation of the Second International and shared its aspirations but in a way which was constrained by the Second International's understanding of the Woman Question. Just as the constituent parties had an ambivalent relationship to the semi-autonomous organisation of socialist women within their national party structures, so the Second International itself allowed women space to organise but not the power to influence its deliberations. British women's organisation in relation to the International was further constrained by the combative relationship between their parent parties. By 1907, and the establishment of the Socialist Women's International, the relationship between British socialist women, formally and informally, was already marked by the differences in emphases of their socialism. In addition to this, they had their own personal and political divisions, particularly over the suffrage.

Socialist women and the women's internationals before 1914[32]

Despite the Second International's characterisation of autonomous women's organisations as 'bourgeois', many socialist women took part, sometimes critically and often ambivalently, in women's and women's suffrage organisations within Britain. In some cases this was translated into an activism which crossed national borders and which was fuelled by a commitment to a woman-focused internationalism.

The socialist press did not give systematic or even consistent coverage to the women's/women's suffrage internationals. Unsurprisingly, the fact that the 1899 International Council of Women was held in London meant both a greater involvement of British women, including socialist women, and also a greater interest from the press. The principal issue raised in the socialist press was the thorny one of 'sex versus class'. *Labour Leader* highlighted a contribution from the socialist Mrs Bridges Adams, who 'said that the emancipation of women was doomed to failure unless it ceased to be a sex movement and became part of the great effort on behalf of adult suffrage'.[33] This summed up what was to be the basis of the rather uncomfortable relationship that many socialist women had with the women's/suffrage internationals: the apparent privileging of gender over class and the priority given to limited women's suffrage rather than adult suffrage. Because of the latter it was easier for those ILPers who were limited suffragists rather than SDF adult suffragists to take part in the congresses of the International Woman Suffrage Alliance. Thus Isabella Ford of the ILP regularly attended IWSA congresses until her death in 1924, while the right of the SDFer Dora Montefiore to attend the same conferences was continually challenged.

In observing that 'the most troubling gap for those who longed for unity of women was the chasm that yawned between the bourgeois and socialist women's movements', Leila Rupp has suggested rather unfairly that the blame for this resides with socialist women.[34] Yet the women's internationals could be less than welcoming not only to the organisations of socialist women but also to individuals. Amongst British socialist women the experience of Dora Montefiore was the most extreme example.[35] Having been part of the organising committee for the ICW congress in 1899, Montefiore attended a series of IWSA congresses. Her right to participate was challenged because the only group who could officially represent Britain was the constitutionalist advocate of limited women's suffrage, the National Union of Women's Suffrage Societies. At the 1905 congress, Montefiore was a fraternal delegate from the Women's Social and Political Union, while at the 1909 congress she represented the Adult Suffrage Society. On both occasions her credentials to participate were challenged by other British delegates, revealing the extent of differences among socialist women and among suffragist women as well as between them. Although Montefiore persisted in trying to find a space for herself as an adult suffragist within the IWSA, the leadership sought to distance themselves from her.[36]

It was as a consequence of the 1909 IWSA congress – and Montefiore's treatment at it – that Clara Zetkin made explicit the attitude of organised socialist women to the IWSA. She made clear that Montefiore had only taken part in the congress 'with the definite object only of compelling the Alliance to give a decisive and clear declaration on the issue, "Women's or Ladies' Franchise", so that there could no longer remain any doubt as to its aim'. When Montefiore and the other representatives of the ASS found their right to participate in the congress challenged, they had walked out. Zetkin said that this revealed the IWSA as 'the buttress of the possessing class against equal political rights for the whole of the female sex .... In naked ugliness it now stands, as the embodiment of narrow class interests, and as the aspiration of propertied women for a political monopoly'.[37]

Yet other British socialist women did not experience the IWSA as either explicitly anti-socialist or as resistant to their particular combination of socialist, suffragist and internationalist politics. Although *The Times* reported of the IWSA in 1908: 'Socialist women are not supporting the congress',[38] Isabella Ford saw IWSA congresses rather differently. In 1909 she reported that 'the general drift of our movement is towards Socialism. Not always avowedly or consciously so by any means.'[39] Yet before we conclude that, unlike Dora Montefiore, Ford *was* able to juggle the socialist and women's internationals successfully, it is important to note that, although Ford attended international trade union congresses, she was not involved in the Socialist Women's International. In her internationalist practice she chose to put her energies into the IWSA, while domestically she prioritised her suffragism over her socialism in her day-to-day work, though never abandoning her ILP membership. Other socialist women still, like Ethel Snowden, could not even accept Ford's compromise. Snowden abandoned her ILP membership in 1909 in order to concentrate exclusively on the suffrage through the NUWSS. She was therefore not a formal member of a socialist party when she attended the IWSA congress in 1911.[40]

Fabian women were also to be found attending IWSA congresses. In 1909 they were fraternal delegates and reported that many of the congress participants were avowed socialists and that many were in favour of adult suffrage as the ultimate aim.[41] But maybe their reading of the IWSA arose from their location as moderate socialists and suffragists rather than from any shift in the intrinsic nature of the IWSA itself. Fabian women also attended the IWSA congress in 1913 in Budapest. Their version of socialism and suffragism did not seem to make the IWSA an unsympathetic arena, although they were hardly central to its deliberations. Nevertheless, Fabian women's politics seem to have been more acceptable: a version of socialism which did not stress class conflict and a suffragism which largely remained aligned with the NUWSS.

Clearly, then, in the years before the First World War British socialist women had different experiences of the relative inclusiveness of women's transnational organisations and different perceptions of the compatibility of women's internationalism with socialist internationalism.

Polarising socialist women: the 'Two-and-a-Half', Third, and Labour and Socialist Internationals

The outbreak of world war in 1914 not only destroyed the organisation of the Second International but, more importantly, undermined the faith of many in the power of internationalism. For others the failure of Second International member parties to abide by their collective commitment to a general strike to prevent the outbreak of war exposed the weaknesses of the International rather than the futility of internationalism itself. During the years of the war it was difficult to convene any international meeting, particularly one which included all the belligerents. However, the politics of internationalism were if anything more pressing than ever. Among other effects, this made the divide between labourism and socialism more complete, which was only to be further exacerbated by the responses of British socialists to the Bolshevik Revolution of 1917.

The British section of the Socialist Women's International continued to function during the war, communicating with other socialist women across national boundaries and across enemy lines. It helped to organise the International Conference of Socialist and Labour Women held at Berne in March 1915. Four of its members managed to attend the conference,[42] although the next month the British government prevented a larger group of women (including socialists) from travelling to the international women's peace congress in The Hague. In the war years Margaret Bondfield and Ethel Snowden were particularly associated with the internationalist work of socialist women, bringing to it their not uncomplicated ILP affiliation – Bondfield had earlier been an SDF member, while Snowden only rejoined the ILP during the war – as well as their support for a negotiated peace.

The war years saw a relaxation of sectarianism amongst the Left and a politics based on intersecting networks between and within the various groups of suffragists, of socialists and of peace activists/anti-militarists. In the immediate years after the war these allegiances were shuffled once again with a new factor on the international scene, the Russian Revolution, which had been so enthusiastically welcomed in 1917 by men and women across the British Left, from labourists to revolutionaries, at the Leeds Convention.[43] Socialist politics up to 1922/3 were remarkably fluid, as groups and individuals sought to place themselves in relation not only to the long-standing Labour Party but also to the potential and then actual Communist Party of Great Britain. In the early years after the war, when it was by no means clear which particular forms of communist, socialist and labour organisations would triumph, many sustained multiple affiliations which later would be proscribed and almost unimaginable. Once the Labour Party had finally voted against Communist Party affiliation and the CPGB was firmly a democratically centralised party under the jurisdiction of the Comintern, the spaces in which a socialist woman might make her politics had been significantly curtailed. Socialist women active in the pre-war and war years now found themselves irredeemably divided between those like Helen Crawfurd and Dora Montefiore who were now communist women and those who remained socialist women, particularly ILPers like Isabella Ford and Dorothy Jewson, whilst the negative pole of communism repelled other previously socialist women into a much closer identification with Labour. All of this had implications for which women were to be found in which of the Internationals of the Left during the 1920s.

For many socialists the war had demonstrated the bankruptcy of the Second International, yet there was some hesitancy over whether affiliation to the communist Third International, an altogether more disciplined organisation, was desirable. For a time, amongst ILPers in particular, there was a search for a 'third way'.[44] In 1920 the ILP voted to disaffiliate from the Second International while rejecting unconditional affiliation to the Third International. It was decided to explore further the terms under which the party might be admitted. In the same year the Labour Party decisively rejected the Third International and less emphatically voted not to disaffiliate from the Second International.[45] As a consequence, the Labour Party remained part of what was left of the Second International, while the ILP joined what was known as the 'Two-and-a-Half International'. Accounts of this International give little sense of the implications of what the initiative meant to socialist women and to women's internationalism.[46] Pamela Graves has suggested that Labour women took no part in the various debates on Communist Party affiliation held at the Labour Party annual conferences of the early 1920s and that by implication women were not interested in this issue.[47] Yet amongst socialist women the issue of which International to affiliate to and the relationship between socialist and communist politics does seem to have aroused passions.[48] Amongst those involved in these debates were Dora Montefiore, Sylvia Pankhurst, Helen Crawfurd and Ellen Wilkinson.

One of the women who most visibly sought her own journey through these lively times was Helen Crawfurd.[49] By 1918 she was a senior member in the Scottish Divisional Council of the ILP but was becoming increasingly disillusioned with the party's reformism. She thought the ILP should be joining with other left groups and the unaligned members of the wartime 'rebel networks' to form a new and radical Communist Party. Although some ILP women who managed to visit Russia, such as Ethel Snowden, were confirmed in their anti-communism,[50] Crawfurd's two-month stay strengthened her pro-Bolshevism.[51] She therefore argued for the ILP's affiliation to the Third International. When Crawfurd lost the argument, she joined the CP and severed her links with the ILP, while other socialist women, like Ellen Wilkinson, sustained a dual membership of both the ILP and the CP until finally forced to choose.

Socialist women continued to take part in the formal business of internationalism, but the uncertainty over the various Internationals to which socialist parties could affiliate delayed the re-establishment of a Socialist Women's International. When socialist women met together as part of the congress of the Labour and Socialist International (LSI, an amalgam of the rump of the Second International and the Two-and-a-Half International) in 1925, ILP women were represented by Margaret Bondfield, Dorothy Jewson and Helena Swanwick.[52] Later the same year socialist women met to discuss the revival of a Socialist Women's International and again ILP women – the only distinct group of British socialist women by this period – were part of the deliberations. In her report of the conference Minnie Pallister stressed how war was a woman's issue, hence the need for socialist women to meet from across the world. Forgetting an earlier tradition, she commented that 'now, for the first time, some tangible contact between the Socialist women of the world has been established in a permanent concrete form'.[53] Her comments were a little premature, as socialist women internationally encountered the same problems about the appropriateness of separate organisation and the relative power of a women's group in relation to the parent organisation as ILP women did domestically.

The following year there was considerable concern at the marginality of the women's organisation from the LSI as a whole. It was therefore decided to hold a meeting in December 1926 of socialist women representatives to endorse a constitution for submission to the International. One of the three British delegates was to be from the ILP. Dorothy Jewson's report of this conference suggested that the main issue for the women delegates was dealing with the interference of their male comrades. Structural and organisational matters took most of their time rather than any exploration of what internationalism now meant for socialist women as a specific group.[54] The relationship of ILP women to the LSI was hampered by the fact that from 1928 the party was no longer entitled to separate representation within the British delegation. The attendance of ILPers, and the pursuit of their resolutions, was now dependent on the Labour Party, to which the ILP was still a critical affiliate in the 1920s.[55] The distinct voice of British socialist women was never heard very loudly within the formal meetings of the LSI, but internationalism had not entirely atrophied.

As for those socialist women whose political journey took them into the Communist Party, internationalism remained a key part of their politics too. In the Third International of the 1920s internationalism was a central aspiration, although its meaning had become focused on the Comintern as an instrument of the only 'true' form of internationalism. Indeed, it has been argued that in Britain ordinary CPGB members were more aware of the international dimensions of the struggle for socialism, particularly in its anti-imperialist form, than their counterparts in any of the other organisations of the working class.[56] In its message to women the early party press, *The Communist*, emphasised international news about women, including reports of the International Communist Women's Conferences.[57] Helen Crawfurd was appointed the party's first women's organiser in 1922. Her prominence at this time suggests continuities with those interwoven strands of socialist and women's politics which Crawfurd had been part of before and during the war. Yet Sue Bruley has shown that, although a significant proportion of women foundation members of the CPGB had been politicised within the suffrage movement, as communist women they were expected to renounce completely all connections with 'diversionary' feminism.[58] Thus, although the CPGB sent delegates to the International Conferences of Communist Women, British women never played a prominent part and the party never put any real energy into this aspect of their internationalism. In the early days of the Communist Party British women were more likely to attend full Comintern congresses as technical workers or as translators rather than as delegates in their own right,[59] and only a handful of women members were able to visit Moscow.

For most the crucial contact in Moscow remained Clara Zetkin, who had been the fulcrum of the Socialist Women's International and who now brought her reputation and extensive networks to bear on the international organisation of communist women. She was in continual communication with leading British women communists in the early 1920s.[60] For some, like Dora Montefiore, this continued a friendship established many years before, while for others, such as Minnie Birch, who met Zetkin in Moscow in 1922 when attending the Fourth Congress as a technical worker, this was a new experience of the personal relationships which often cemented internationalism as a politics.[61] Indeed, maybe the pre-existing relationships, combined with the undoubted esteem that Zetkin herself was held in, strengthened the importance of internationalism to British communist women. For although internationalism was integral to the Comintern and was often read as merely loyalty to Moscow, the gender dynamic within this internationalism was less apparent. This was congruent with the domestic experience of communist women, as Bruley's study of the CPGB has shown. For the Party only gave fitful and ambiguous support to the organisation of women.[62] In particular, during the 1920s the distinction between cadre and supporter women in the party meant that in the sexual division of politics there was little space for a gendered understanding of internationalism. The exception to this continued to be the appeals to women not to 'let their sons die on behalf of capitalism'. Indeed in 1927 the International Women's Day celebrations centred on the necessity for 'the defeat of British imperialism'.[63]

Peace or anti-militarism? The issue for socialist women

Let us now turn to one area of internationalism in which women, including socialist women, were thought to have a special interest: the prevention of war. Although the work of Anne Wiltsher and particularly of Jill Liddington has retrieved the history of the pacifist strand within British feminism,[64] relatively little specific attention has been given to the ways in which socialist women responded to the question of how to prevent war. It has often been assumed that peace was a woman's issue and that pacifism was always the progressive position. It might therefore be thought that socialist women, whatever their other differences, might have united in their fight against the scourge of war. To what extent was this the case for British socialist women across the period from the 1880s to the 1920s and, in particular, how did the experience of being part of a nation at war affect the politics of peace for socialist women?

Peace was never a straightforward issue for British socialists.[65] Pacifist ideas could be found in the leading socialist organisations, although their association with liberalism meant that generally pacifism was more congenial to the politics of the ILP than to those of the SDF. Although there were areas of tension between pacifism and socialism, the aspiration to an ill-defined internationalism was something that many socialists shared with contemporary pacifists. What was to be divisive was when absolute pacifists came into conflict with those who saw the need for the use of force in specific circumstances, particularly in relation to the class struggle but also with regard to other forms of militancy, including suffrage militancy. This tension was to become most explicit during the First World War, particularly after the Russian Revolution. Here the distinction between campaigning for peace and being an anti-militarist became most apparent. As Joseph Clayton was to later characterise it: 'The bulk of ILP members were always anti-war .... In the British Socialist Party ... the majority were pacifist, aggressively pacifist.' Clayton went on to distinguish between the pacifists who believed that 'war was not the right way to settle international disputes, that the qualities produced by war did not tend to make good citizens and promote reasonableness in politics' and what he called the 'rebel' pacifists who 'had no particular objection to violence, if, and when, that violence was directed against "the capitalist system"'. He made it clear that no real agreement was possible between these two groups despite their joint opposition to war.[66] How did these tensions within the broader movement affect socialist women and the politics of peace?

Jill Liddington has characterised the women's peace movement in Britain by its 'episodic, cyclical history: women in their thousands became deeply involved for a few years, a few months, or a few weeks, then turned back to more immediate concerns'.[67] This sense that the priority given to peace as an issue waxed and waned is also apparent amongst socialist women – even those like Isabella Ford, who as a Quaker had deep-rooted pacifist convictions. A significant number of the women that Liddington includes in her study identified as socialist women. Yet it should not be assumed that the narratives of feminist pacifism and of socialist women's response to war are identical. The focus of this part of the chapter is thus to look at what peace meant to socialist women and how this affected their conception of internationalism.

Up until the years immediately preceding the outbreak of world war, socialist women do not seem to have been particularly preoccupied with peace as an issue.[68] Individuals such as Isabella Ford and Emmeline Pankhurst were active in the peace movement of the 1890s and were part of the protests against the Boer War.[69] But few of those who were to take an active role in opposing the First World War were involved in separate pacifist organisations before 1914, although, as Liddington has suggested, at certain moments the issue of how to prevent war, or the need to oppose a specific war, rapidly rose up the political agenda of socialist women. Helena Swanwick, who was to become an archetypal pacifist-feminist and to join the ILP during the war, remembered that, although she spoke on a 'Peace' platform at a suffrage meeting in 1908, she never joined a peace society, 'because I regarded peace not as a state you could work for in the abstract, but as the condition which could result from a just and fair conduct of national and international relations. And I felt that in working for the emancipation of women, I was contributing to the cause of peace.'[70] Many socialist women would have held a similar view, albeit that it was in working for socialism that they too were 'contributing to the cause of peace'. Nothing more needed to be done. Others saw 'Peace' as a distraction:

> 'Socialism is the hope of the workers', but the hope will never be attained if the workers are turned aside from their purpose by those whose object is to whittle away the socialist programme, and unnerve the arm of the proletariat by crying 'Peace! Peace!' when there is no peace.[71]

Thus, for whatever reason, peace was not a primary focus for the energies of socialist women in the early years of the twentieth century.

This attitude was changing in the years immediately preceding the war, with British and German rearmament proceeding apace and the Balkans becoming increasingly unstable. Within the Social Democratic Party Zelda Kahan was a vociferous opponent of rearmament and militarism in general, taking on her party leader, Hyndman, at party conferences and on the SDP/BSP executive from 1911 to 1913. This young woman (she was in her early thirties) clearly ruffled the feathers of the older male leadership, one of whom denounced her as 'Fraulein' Zelda Kahan, one of the 'comrades alien in blood and race' – an antisemitic as well as nationalist jibe. Although she and Hyndman shook hands at the 1913 conference, after a mild resolution opposing an increase in armaments was passed almost unanimously, Kahan nevertheless lost her seat on the executive that year at a conference from which many of the anti-militarists had stayed away.[72] Here was an example of a socialist woman taking a clear anti-militarist stance, against the mainstream, but it is interesting to note that she never made a gendered argument and certainly did not employ the essentialist views of a pacifist-feminist.

Collectively socialist women were also becoming concerned about increased militarism. Although the Socialist Women's Bureau (British) sent a resolution to the International Socialist Women's Congress in 1910, calling for international action by socialist women in the cause of peace,[73] generally peace was not seen by many on the Left, men and women, as being a 'women's issue' but was increasingly seen as a more urgent matter. The more general anxiety about the international situation was reflected in the decision in 1912 to call a meeting of the International at short notice to formulate responses to potential war. Clara Zetkin issued a manifesto for the congress in which she attempted to balance a gendered argument with a class analysis:

> This powerful meeting must show that in all countries Socialist women are united with the workers and the Socialist parties in waging war against war. The blood that is to drench the fields of battle is that of their sons, husbands and brothers. Women who have worked and wept refuse to give up their loved ones to be shamelessly and callously slaughtered through the frenzy of military and Imperialist factions.[74]

The one woman in the British delegation did not disagree with Zetkin's analysis but found herself disillusioned by the International's response. Dora Montefiore felt manipulated by the male leadership of the International and the British delegation and refused to vote for the International's manifesto on peace, which she saw as merely rhetorical, a 'lengthy climbdown, signifying nothing'.[75] Although this episode led to censure and ultimately to her resignation from the BSP, it also indicated the profound tension that now existed for socialists between anti-militarism and pacifism. While in Basle, Montefiore had spoken to a hastily convened meeting about her anti-militarist campaigning within the British Empire, particularly the fight against the compulsory military training of boys in Australia and New Zealand.[76] Subsequently she emphasised this aspect of her internationalism, always characterising it as anti-militarism rather than working for peace. In an open letter to Keir Hardie in 1913 she asked: 'Are you not yet convinced ... that unless women are organised and politically educated on the basis of the class struggle, they are just as much inclined as are men to fall on to the snare of capitalist militarism?'[77] For her, at this point, women could not be assumed to be naturally inclined to peace as an issue. Instead, preventing war involved a recognition of the nature of the capitalist system in its imperialist phase. The gendered argument became much more apparent amongst socialist women once the world war had begun.

Even amongst ILP women, whose organisation was thought to be more interested in peace,[78] there was little that delineated the work of women from that of men in the fight against war. Indeed some local studies suggest that at branch level the ILP gave no time to discuss international events, or to possible socialist responses, before the outbreak of war.[79] Nevertheless, during 1913 and early 1914 *Labour Woman* reported various discussions on possible campaigns against militarism.[80] For example, Ada Salter, in her presidential address to the 1914 Women's Labour League Conference, claimed that the League was 'avowedly Anti-Militarist'. She argued that the only guarantee against militarism was an international organisation of working men and women, organised with a common purpose and ideal.[81] In August 1914 the Socialist International proved that it was *not* such an organisation.

'Trying to stop a river with a handkerchief': socialist women and the First World War

Socialist women took part in the meetings across the country which protested against the outbreak of war, some in the women's meetings convened through suffragist organisations and others in meetings organised by their own parties. Most of the focus of historians, such as it is, has been on suffragists who took a stand against the war, who included some socialist women (e.g. Ethel Snowden, Isabella Ford, Helen Crawfurd) and some women whose wartime experience led them to Labour, and in some cases socialist, politics (e.g. Catherine Marshall, Helena Swanwick). Leila Rupp has suggested that at the international level opposition to war formed a fragile thread between socialist and non-socialist women.[82] This was to be most apparent when the International Congress of

Socialist Women, meeting in Berne in 1915, sent greetings to the international women's peace congress, which met in The Hague later the same year. Nationally, alliances were forged across previous divides, although it should be remembered that the women and men who actively opposed the war formed a small group even among socialists, let alone in the broader community. The vulnerability of anti-war activists to the attentions of the state and the crowd meant that in many cases sectarianism was put aside for the duration of the war.[83] Nevertheless, what did become apparent was that there were different understandings of what being a peace activist meant. The key issue was the degree to which force was thought to be a necessary tactic – absolute pacifism versus 'war against war'. These differences were the prelude to the formation of the Third International and the eventual theoretical and organisational gulf between socialism and communism.

For socialist women who had also been suffragettes at some point before the war, the argument for militant tactics had already been made and accepted. Although there were ironies in their position, ex-suffragettes were much less likely to be absolute pacifists, opposed to direct action. Indeed, many found it difficult to see how militants could become opponents of war. For example, her friends found it hard to understand the anti-war position of ILPer and former WSPU member Hannah Mitchell: '"What," they said,"you such a fighter and you won't fight for your country?"'[84]

While the predominantly male leadership of the ILP debated what actions were justified in the pursuit of peace, parties to the left of it such as the Socialist Labour Party saw what they thought was an opportunity to turn a capitalist war into a socialist revolution. Meanwhile, the British Socialist Party was split between the old guard who largely supported the war, and split away in 1916 to form the National Socialist Party, and an oppositional group who saw peace being achieved through the united action of socialist parties domestically and through international negotiation.[85] Women's voices were not heard in many of these debates yet at the rank-and-file level, and in local campaigning, it was often socialist women who were tenaciously maintaining an anti-war stand. The only female voice within the leaderships of the various socialist groupings was that of Sylvia Pankhurst of the East London Federation of Suffragettes/Worker's Suffrage Federation.[86] To what extent did socialist women who opposed the war make a gendered argument and was an anti-militarist rather than absolute pacifist position discernible?

Whatever their socialist affiliations, many women argued for an end to the war through a negotiated peace and in the meantime sought to alleviate the effect of the war on ordinary people. Some socialist women, such as Dora Montefiore and Mrs Cobden Sanderson, involved themselves in the various relief societies set up by the suffrage groups, such as the Women's Freedom League's Women's Suffrage National Aid Corps,[87] while Sylvia Pankhurst and the ELFS engaged in a range of public relief activities in London's East End.[88] Others who took an anti-war stand carried on with the propaganda work of meetings and journalism, although the spaces in which this was possible atrophied as meetings were broken up and even banned and the socialist press shrank due to wartime paper shortages. Certainly the overall impression of the socialist press during the war is predominantly a masculine one.

Wherever they made their case, socialist women who opposed the war made a range of arguments, including unequivocal pacifist feminism. Isabella Ford argued in 1915:

> Women have more to lose in this horrible business than some men have; for they often lose more than life itself when their men are killed; since they lose all that makes life worth living for, all that makes for happiness ... the destruction of the race is felt more bitterly and more deeply by those who through suffering and anguish have brought the race into the world.[89]

Here undoubtedly peace is a 'women's issue', but there is little that could be characterised as a specifically socialist argument. Catherine Marshall held similar views. She felt that women looked on war, 'as on all questions, from a different angle; their motherhood gave them a viewpoint all their own, and it gave them the right and the need to speak'.[90] These essentialist arguments seemed to be acceptable to male socialists, indeed many made a similar case.[91]

For others the appeal to women had to move beyond rhetoric, however heartfelt, to become part of a practical proposal to achieve a permanent peace. After the Hague Congress in 1915, Margaretta Hicks felt that although 'it is splendid to feel that we have still the bond of comradeship among all women', by itself this was not enough. She argued for a system of compulsory international arbitration and an international legislature. 'Merely to say we are in favour of stopping the war is like trying to stop a river with a handkerchief'.[92] Margaret Bondfield too wanted a vision of peace which was distinctive from the language of traditional pacifism. Appealing to women to act, she said: 'The peace they had in view was no flabby, emasculated thing – no drooping angel on a damp cloud – but something strong, real and robust'.[93] One way to ensure such robustness was underlined by Katharine Bruce Glasier in her rather optimistic claim that the two movements she identified with, the women's and the socialist movement, were acting together for peace and to defend the cause of women. She too emphasised that as mothers women knew the cost of war and therefore made her appeal 'to the motherheart of the women throughout the world'.[94] These were powerful ideas, which could override distinctions of class and which were favoured by both those who increasingly saw a class analysis of war as essential and those who continued to see war as principally a moral issue. There was no distinctive maternalist argument used exclusively by socialist women.

The tensions for socialist women between anti-militarism and pacifism became most apparent as the war wore on and were characteristic of the socialist movement as a whole. As one ILPer remembered: 'In England we failed to unite the anti-war struggle with the class struggle sufficiently, and with the result that we became isolated from the mass of the workers and too often tended to become bourgeois pacifists rather than working-class socialists'.[95] Yet there was one attempt to bring these elements together – the Women's Peace Crusade (WPC).[96] Of all the campaigns against the war, this was the one in which most socialist women took part and which, in some cases, transformed their politics.

The WPC was originally a response to the nature of the local branches of the Women's International League (WIL), which had been formed after the Hague Congress of 1915. Helen Crawfurd, one of the founders of the WPC, felt that WIL members 'were merely anti-war and not socialist'.[97] In contrast, the WPC was to be much more explicitly socialist and militant than the WIL – anti-militarist rather than pacifist.

The WPC was not a revolutionary body:[98] its demands were common among those who opposed the war but, building on their experience in the Glasgow rent strikes, WPC activists were innovative in that they took their campaign to working-class women within their communities. Beginning in Glasgow in 1916, and becoming a national phenomenon in 1917, the focus of the WPC remained the working-class woman in her neighbourhood. Through the pages of *Labour Leader* ILP women were mobilised in support of the WPC and the call for peace by negotiation.[99] By 1917 a language which referred more explicitly to countering imperialism and to the virtues of socialist internationalism became more apparent among socialist women who opposed the war. Helen Crawfurd now represented the war in terms of the profiteers who were robbing and plundering the people. Peace could only be secured 'if the peoples of the belligerent nations take their Imperialists in hand'. Her call was: 'Let us help to build anew the International, the only hope of a peace that shall be enduring.'[100] But the maternalist aspect of women's peace campaigning was also represented in the badge of the WPC, which sold in its thousands and which depicted the Angel of Peace protecting children.[101] Leading ILP women, such as Margaret Bondfield, Katharine Bruce Glasier and Ethel Snowden, now led the call for a women's peace campaign and were soon active in its cause.[102] Week by week *Labour Leader* reported new local WPCs and by November 1917 forty-eight active crusades were claimed with several more in the process of being formed. More than a quarter of a million free leaflets had been distributed and many thousands of badges and hundreds of banners sold in a few months. For a time the WPC swept up the energies of many leading socialist women, for example Charlotte Despard, who from the beginning of 1918 added her undivided energies to the WPC.[103]

The WPC galvanised many socialist women around a single-issue campaign in a short period of energetic and innovative woman-focused action, drawing on many of the experiences of suffragist/suffragette activists before the war. What it was unable to do in its short life was to cement together the rather different politics of peace which were becoming apparent amongst socialist women. What was increasingly dividing socialist women was the issue of the role of force in combating militarism as the experience of war became more protracted.

Facing up to the issue of force

When Isabella Ford argued for her anti-war position in 1915, she stressed that 'our whole raison d'être is the substitution of moral and spiritual force for physical force. If we do not urge this, we give the lie to all our former suffrage work … and we give away our opposition to the militant methods of the W.S. & P.U.'[104] Similarly, Katharine Bruce Glasier suggested that war was proof of the 'abstract theory that war involves the ultimate resting of all authority on force – an argument that, once allowed, must dispose for ever of women's claim to citizenship'.[105] These socialist women were clear that the use of forceful means would compromise the goal of a woman-friendly socialism as well as undermining their years of principled suffragism. Catherine Marshall underlined this 'pacifist' view with her contention that any vigorous argument could be classified as militarist and therefore reprehensible:

> I have heard socialists, who were ardent pacifists on international questions, talk like this of class warfare. I have heard suffragists talk like this of the struggle for sex equality. They were all talking pure militarism – they were all moved by the desire to dominate rather than co-operate, to vanquish and humiliate the enemy rather than to convert him to a friend.[106]

But other socialist women defined their anti-militarism rather differently. Like the Irish suffragist Hanna Sheehy-Skeffington, they were opposed to militarism when defined as an institutionalised response by authority to neutralise challenges to its power. They were not opposed to the weak using whatever power was at their disposal to win their battle.[107] As Skeffington argued, 'there are other pacifists (and I am one of them) who hold that while war must be ended if civilisation is to reign supreme, nevertheless there may still be times when armed aggression ought to be met with armed defence'.[108] For many it was the Russian Revolution which brought this issue into sharp focus.

The tension between pacifism and anti-militarism amongst socialist women and its effect on understandings of internationalism became most apparent at the end of the war. At the first meeting of the Women's International League for Peace and Freedom in Zurich in 1919 Britain was represented by a delegation with a significant number of socialist women, including Ford, Crawfurd, Despard and Snowden.[109] One area of contention was WILPF's attitude to the use of force. Helen Crawfurd told the congress of police violence against a workers' demonstration in Glasgow. She argued that because of this manifestation of force on the part of the authorities, it was difficult to counsel against force on the part of the people. Nevertheless, she said that she believed that

WILPF, which had advised against the use of force in the settlement of international disputes, could do no other than counsel against its use nationally.[110] Crawfurd was speaking in support of an amendment to a resolution which committed the League to supporting non-violence. The amendment sought to show solidarity with 'workers who are rising up everywhere to make an end of exploitation and to claim their world' whilst at the same time adhering to peaceful methods. It was therefore suggested, somewhat naively, that the privileged classes should give up their wealth without a struggle so that a 'cooperative system of production for human happiness' could be achieved with minimal bloodshed. Even Catherine Marshall and Helena Swanwick spoke in support of this amendment, the latter because she thought it would bring about a reconciliation between classes. But the congress decided it could not make this official policy as 'it would drive away many of our members who came from all classes of society and all races'.[111] Such an apparently socialist message was not thought to be compatible with the interests of an inclusive women's pacifist internationalism. What Swanwick observed of the British women's anti-war movement during the First World War might also be applied to the international movement. She identified three groups of women – feminist/suffragists, pacifists and socialists – and said of them: 'Those three strands of thought at first found it a little difficult to twist in with one another.'[112] Tensions were certainly apparent in the British delegation, with Ethel Snowden asking Ellen Wilkinson to tone down her speeches because of their 'revolutionary zeal'.[113]

The issue of force could not go away for socialist women opposed to militarism. As Jessie Stephen, a Women's Peace Crusade activist, argued at the 1920 ILP Conference:

> She had taken her stand during the war on pacifist platforms, and she was going to be consistent. If she was against armed force on behalf of the capitalist class she was against armed force to bring about the Socialist Republic, and if they brought about the Socialist Republic by armed force it meant that they would have to keep up that armed force …. She thought it was disgraceful that men and women, who belonged to a body like the ILP, which had upheld the anti-militarist standard during the war, should now suggest that the best way to attain their ends was to use armed force.[114]

This debate was as much about which International to affiliate to as it was about pacifism. The Russian Revolution meant that the issue of force remained a compelling one for all socialists in these years, but for those socialist women who were also pacifists it seems to have been a defining issue for their self-identification. Indeed, at the next WILPF congress, in Vienna in 1921, a resolution was passed, by just one vote, which condemned violent revolution even as an agent of social change.[115] As Sybil Oldfield has commented on the WILPF of the 1920s: 'these women had not resolved the problems of how oppression can be ended and justice established without recourse either to violence or to the threat of violence'.[116] For some socialist women who had fought against the war this now meant that their energies went elsewhere. In 1921 Helen Crawfurd explained her differences with pacifists:

> The real point of disagreement is this: My friends are Pacifists; *I am not, I have never been a Pacifist* .... *I love peace, but I love justice more.*
>
> My objection and opposition to the great European war was *that the men of all countries were being duped by their Capitalist exploiters.* When the workers cooperate internationally to overthrow *their* common enemy then ... I know what side of the barricades I am on. I want to save time by making my position absolutely clear – this and the question of revolution is the real difference in our viewpoint. I see revolution looming in the distance, and I was advocating the need for organisation to meet it.[117]

Yet, in writing her autobiography, she remembered a political life dedicated to ending war. For her, and other anti-militarists, it was possible to support revolutionary politics and to oppose war. Indeed, some believed it was the only effective way to achieve a truly peaceful world.

Peace as an issue for socialist women in the 1920s

In the 1920s anti-militarism continued to be a topic for party conferences and for the party presses. In the early years of the post-war period anti-militarism could draw together socialists and communists as well as pacifists, as in the 'Great Internationalist Anti-Militarist Demonstration' held in London in February 1922. Although there were no British women speakers at this meeting, leading socialist women such as Bondfield, Llewelyn Davies and Despard were involved in promoting the No More War demonstrations of that and subsequent years.[118]

The call for international disarmament became a crucial issue for the ILP. Their summer school in 1923 debated the matter, taking its lead from Helena Swanwick, who argued for world disarmament but was opposed to unilateralism. Even in the report of this meeting it is obvious that the divisions of the war continued, with ILP proponents of absolute disarmament arguing with those who believed that socialists might have to resort to force.[119] What is striking is that aside from Swanwick no other women seemed to have participated in the discussions, and the arguments about peace as a women's issue appear to have faded away among the new generation of ILP activists. The context had changed and even amongst pacifist-feminists in the 1920s the strand of feminism which linked maleness with violence was, according to Liddington, 'scarcely visible'.[120] Nevertheless, in some places a more woman-focused argument was still being made by ILP women. Thus Katharine Bruce Glasier persuaded the

Labour Party Women's Conference of 1927 to vote for universal disarmament by stressing the individual responsibility of every woman in the fight against imperialism and 'the need that bloodshed should be outlawed in our own minds'.[121] Internationalism was an increasing preoccupation of hers after the war, while in the earlier years of the decade Isabella Ford devoted nearly all her time to peace causes. She worked through the ILP, WIL and the Union of Democratic Control and, at her death in 1924, she was remembered as 'international through and through'.[122] Yet these were members of the older generation of socialist women radicalised before the dawn of the twentieth century. Were their concerns for peace and internationalism shared by the younger generation of socialist women activists?

One of the younger women was Minnie Pallister, who in the early 1920s saw militarism as a crucial issue for her politics and for her politicisation. In 1922 she argued strongly for the salience of internationalism to socialists: 'This is no time to be half-ashamed of our policy of International Socialism: it is time to preach it unceasingly .... The people have to choose, and choose quickly, between an international amalgamation of workers and the crushing of the workers by international combinations of big business interests.' Pallister also addressed the troubling issue of nationalism. She observed that: 'Pride of country is losing itself in an ever-increasing sense of internationalism. The perfectly legitimate love for the songs, customs, and scenery of one's native country is perilously akin to the narrow nationalism which is so easily exploited by the enemies of mankind.'[123] Her contribution is interesting both for her willingness to explicitly distance herself from nationalism and for her complete neglect of any gendered argument.

Ethel Snowden, from the generation between Glasier and Ford on the one hand and Pallister on the other, carried her peace activism into the early 1920s. At ILP conferences she regularly spoke on international issues and was particularly involved in the debate on whether to remain affiliated to the Second International. Snowden was also an advocate of complete disarmament. Although arguing with passion and giving a great deal of time to public speaking and campaigning for peace, increasingly Snowden's interests strayed from the political sphere and her voice was seldom heard there.

In the 1920s campaigning for peace was also an issue for the international women's organisations. The political affiliations of the fewer British women involved with these groups seemed to narrow in the 1920s, as socialist women found themselves to be less welcome while communist women were often banned. Ironically, this meant that many of the women who had been active in the women's anti-militarist campaign of the war were no longer welcome in international women's organisations campaigning for peace. Certainly, the large number of socialist, as opposed to Labour, women present in the British delegation to the 1919 WILPF congress was not to be repeated. Some of the British women who remained committed to the League and involved in its international organisation during the early 1920s, such as Annot Robinson, were long-time

ILPers.[124] But increasingly the politics of the Left became uncongenial. In effect, socialist women were squeezed internationally and domestically by, on the one hand, the need to distance themselves from communists and, on the other, the desire to distinguish themselves from Labour. This limited the spaces within which socialist women could pursue anti-militarist politics, particularly after the mid-1920s.

Nevertheless, some socialist women were still to be found arguing publicly for disarmament; thus Bondfield and Wilkinson were among the speakers who greeted the Peacemakers' Pilgrimage when it arrived in Hyde Park, London, in June 1926.[125] Locally socialist women like Selina Cooper were active in the organisation of the Pilgrimage as part of their continuing campaign for disarmament and international arbitration.[126] But others had different priorities at this time, given the worsening industrial situation of a General Strike and continuing Miners' Lockout. This was apparent in 1926, when the *New Leader* had various contributions from women on the effects of the industrial struggles but nothing on the Pilgrimage. The thorny issues around making a reality of the rhetoric around disarmament seemed to slip down the agenda of socialist women, at least in terms of the few spaces in which they could function as a collectivity, however heterogeneous. For those for whom this remained a defining issue, organisations such as the League of Nations Union, WILPF and even the overtly pacifist Women's Co-operative Guild claimed their allegiance.[127] Yet for most socialist women of the later 1920s the focus seems to have been more determinedly domestic, and the energies which had once been put into the 'war against war' for a time went elsewhere.

A socialist women's internationalism?

It can be argued that before the First World War a number of British socialists espoused and practised a woman-focused internationalism. What did this mean? One version of this internationalism is to be found in the manifesto for the new women's column, 'Our Women's Circle', in *Justice* , which sought 'to link up the endeavours of class-conscious working women in every country'.[128] One reader living in rural Scotland made clear her appreciation of this emphasis, welcoming the news of 'the organised fight of the working women in those lands against the forces of tyranny and reaction'. In saying: 'We recognise that we are one with them, and our hearts rejoice',[129] she made clear that internationalist aspirations could be sustained at a distance and without ever having to leave home. Here was a woman-focused politics which aspired to an inclusive but class-based internationalism. This position was typified by the view that:

> It is ... more than ever necessary that the working woman in England should learn solidarity with her working sisters in other lands, and should realise that it is not by alliances and compromises with the women of the master class that the hope of the workers will be realised,

but by conscious and practical fellowship with the workers of other lands.[130]

This contrasts with, for example, the President of the International Council of Women's understanding of internationalism, which was 'to provide a common centre for women workers of every race, faith, class and party, who are associating themselves together in the endeavour to leave the world better and more beautiful than they have found it'.[131] But it also contrasts with the emphases of ILP women, who tended to downplay the class solidarity element in their internationalism. Thus Margaret MacDonald and Mary Middleton, speaking for the Women's Labour League, reported that their members 'feel that international co-operation between women of similar sympathies is one of the most important parts of our work'. This meant that through 'correspondence, and by inviting visitors to this country to their meetings, they are able to keep in touch with the women of the British Colonies and all foreign countries'.[132] Here internationalism is seen in rather similar terms to the example cited earlier of Keir Hardie. It provided opportunities for practical networking rather than making what were seen as overly ideological claims.

It was not always felt by socialist women that a gendered version of internationalism was required, merely that women should be included within the broader vision. So when addressing an audience of women, in this case the 1914 WLL Conference, Katharine Bruce Glasier in her speech on war neither used a particularly gendered argument nor adopted a pacifist-feminist position. Instead she used a language of socialist internationalism which was similar to that employed by male comrades, but the difference was that it was employed by a woman speaking to women. She urged 'the people to use their political power to democratise foreign policy and replace our present system of armed peace by an alliance between all the workers of the world for the purpose of lifting the burdens of poverty'.[133] The context reveals that she did assume that the workers of the world included women, an assumption not always shared by other socialists. The rhetoric of socialism was often slippery in this respect, as it was in relation to other areas of 'difference'.

Yet despite the variety of emphases in socialist women's espousal of internationalism, it remains clear that the language of comradeship rather than that of sisterhood was the orthodoxy. Nevertheless, a number of the more enthusiastic internationalist socialist women claimed to be inspired by a sense of sisterhood, albeit undefined. For some it was possible to refuse the choice; thus Isabella Ford saw sisterhood as a complement to, rather than a replacement for, the comradeship of the sexes.[134] For others the optimistic claim to sisterhood became increasingly discordant with their experience of the international women's movement. Thus in 1904 Dora Montefiore greeted the ICW/IWSA congress as giving 'to women working all over the world in the cause of their sister women a feeling of solidarity and of sisterhood such as they never possessed before!'.[135] Later her language of sisterhood was replaced by a different emphasis; by 1909 she was arguing that 'in helping forward the development of women we are helping forward the development of the race'.[136] Indeed, what drew socialist women together was an assumption that internationalism meant the solidarity of the human race rather than the feminists' stress on the solidarity of a sex. Sustaining a woman-focused politics was crucial to many British socialist women but this did not need to be a separatist activity, hence the endorsement of a solidarity based on the human race as a whole rather than on one sex. This was the context for Dora Montefiore's comment that: 'In internationalism ... lies our hope for the future, for enlarged culture, for the spread of freethought, and for the realisation of the solidarity of the human race.'[137] It also explains the view taken by *Labour Leader* of the 1913 IWSA congress: 'It is an earnest of the day when not merely the sex but the Humanity of Woman shall be recognised.'[138] It was this desire to find a way to make a mixed-sex politics work for women socialists which explains some of the suspicion of activists in the single-sex IWSA towards socialist women. As Rupp has noted, IWSA critics of socialist women who participated in their organisation linked what they saw as 'aberrant' heterosexual relationships (usually with married socialist men) to the socialist women's political work with men and, she says, 'seemed to disapprove of both'.[139]

The other aspect of the internationalism of British socialist women before the First World War which deserves exploration is its relationship to imperialism. Antoinette Burton has revealed that: 'If suffrage was marked as an imperialized discourse in the early twentieth century, it remained, as it had been in the Victorian period, egalitarian and international in its rhetoric as well.'[140] These apparent contradictions might also be observed in relation to socialists of the same period. Nevertheless, some British socialist women did show an awareness of the issues: Isabella Ford felt, in relation to the 1909 IWSA congress, that 'the feeling of our common womanhood wiped out racial feeling as I have never before seen it wiped out'.[141] Dora Montefiore aspired to 'place fellowship above competitive imperialism' for by 1911 she was clear that 'International Socialism unites on the basis of THE CLASS STRUGGLE, NOT COLOR OR SEX STRUGGLE'.[142] But these were not the dominant views of socialists more generally or socialist women in particular. In Montefiore's case the evolution of her internationalism seems to have been directly affected by her unusual experience of extensive international travel and working with socialists and suffragists particularly in the United States and the White Dominions of the British Empire (specifically Australia and South Africa).[143]

What difference did the world war make to socialist women's internationalism? In many ways the rhetoric of internationalism remained unchanged despite the profound challenge that the war had posed. Ethel Snowden argued at the 1918 ILP Annual Conference that a meeting of the Socialist International should be convened so that representatives of Labour and Socialism could 'get together and look into one another's eyes, to understand, as they had never understood before, that only on the basis of International Socialism could a sound world be established, and this sad old world be lifted a little nearer to the stars of God'.[144] Here internationalism remains a heart-warming aspiration which the experience of the war had made even more essential to socialist politics. But the emphasis of that internationalism might now need to be somewhat different. Indeed, by 1917 a language which referred more explicitly to countering imperialism and to the virtues of socialist internationalism had became more apparent among socialist women. As Snowden herself observed that year, when asked about her decision to rejoin the ILP:

> the war has altered some of our views, and we have come to feel there are bigger things even than the women's suffrage questions involved in Internationalism. I think the ILP itself has come to appreciate the value of International Socialism as it never did before the war.[145]

Certainly, the failure of the Second International to sustain international solidarity meant that this aspect of socialist internationalism was underlined after the war. So Katharine Bruce Glasier said of the ILP in 1924: 'we were International Socialists from the first for we saw it was impossible for one country to gain by the hurt of another'.[146] Interestingly, neither Glasier nor Snowden made an argument which differentiated a particularly woman-focused internationalism, and the language they used was clearly marked by the politics of the pre-war ILP with its eschewal of the class struggle.

The language of internationalism employed by socialist women after the war was similar to that used before 1914. As Dorothy Jewson commented on attending a socialist international conference in 1926, what was most valuable was 'the rubbing shoulders together, the sympathy and better understanding, and the mutual desire for a real International, linking all nations in the Socialist faith'.[147] There remained something rather cosy about the glow that internationalism brought to those who experienced international gatherings. Yet the superficiality of this was revealed when the difficult issue was raised of the actual inclusiveness of this internationalism. This can be seen in the debate in 1927 on whether the ILP should affiliate to the League Against Imperialism, what Fenner Brockway (one of its advocates) termed 'The Coloured People's International'. Fear that it might represent a communist front overrode the opportunity that the League presented to broaden the scope of a largely Eurocentric socialist internationalism. To her credit, Jewson was one of the few who spoke up for the League.[148]

Amongst those socialist women who chose the Third International, the emphasis in their internationalism was somewhat different. As Helen Crawfurd remembered: 'The new International *unlike* the Second International welcomed the representatives of the exploited colonial workers, of whatever colour, race or creed.'[149] In a similar vein, Dora Montefiore recounted a meeting just after the war when she shared a platform with Sylvia Pankhurst on 'Class Struggle from the International Standpoint'. Montefiore claimed that there must be no 'conscious or unconscious understanding between Labour and Capital to exploit backward and coloured races, as these backward races would eventually be used by Capital to bring down the wages of white workers'.[150] Here we have an anti-racist internationalist sentiment being framed in a racist language, a not uncommon paradox apparent in the thinking of progressives of the period. From the evidence of her continual revisiting of the theme of how to create an inclusive internationalism, Dora Montefiore appears to have been wrestling, not always successfully, to frame a discourse and a practice which in interrogating internationalism resisted the dominant culture. As the fight against imperialism became an increasingly important part of the language of communist internationalism, so the appeal was increasingly to an international working class undifferentiated by gender, race or nationality. Yet, of course, the reality of these differences did not dissolve, as Dora Montefiore reminded the 1924 meeting of the Communist International in Moscow: 'when Marx said "workers of the world, unite" he did not mean to say "white workers of the world, unite"'.[151]

Looking at the Internationals of the 1920s (socialist and women's), it is clear that they were marked by the experience of the world war but also that they all looked with alarm at the growth of a new form of 'disciplined' internationalism – the Communist International. The gender dynamic within all of these Internationals was far less apparent in the 1920s than it had been before the war, and those British socialist women who had tried to develop a woman-focused internationalism were of less and less influence as the decade proceeded and as they became infirm, died or their commitment to socialism waned. The younger generation of women activists had accepted a more polarised socialist world, and many of them were much more ambivalent about the need to sustain a relationship between feminism and socialism.

If little time was spent across the whole period of the 1880s to the 1920s by British socialist women in discussing, either domestically or internationally, what they understood by internationalism, those that experienced international gatherings were convinced that they understood its meaning and importance. One of the British women delegates to the 1910 meeting of the Socialist Women's International commented:

> I hope never to miss an International Socialist Congress again. I am just realising what a big thing it is in which we have taken part. Whilst it is going on it sometimes seems weary and ineffective, but when one sees the delegates all gathered together like this one feels the enthusiasm and the immense meaning of it all.[152]

The 'immense meaning' of internationalism to socialist women up to the 1920s is hard to decipher. Could the aspiration of an inclusive internationalism override socialist women's other loyalties? In the organisational context of conferences and meetings, party could be an obstacle to harmonious relations but specific issues were equally divisive, particularly suffrage. Yet there was a strong desire to learn from the experience of women across the world and to feel part of something bigger than the nation state. The rhetoric of internationalism was an important way in which a divided movement (divided by party and by sex) could feel it was moving in the same direction. Solidarity with other national workers' and women's movements was sometimes easier than with other competing organisations within one's own country.

Just as building a distinct and coherent woman-focused socialism was more of an aspiration than a reality, so many of the Edwardian generation of socialist women took it for granted that internationalism was an essential part of their politics. But, like their male comrades, socialist women rarely explored the detail of what internationalism meant in terms of practical politics or reflected on the challenge that the aspiration of internationalism posed to socialism.

NOTES

1 Part of this chapter draws on K. Hunt, '"The immense meaning of it all". The challenges of internationalism for British socialist women before the First World War', *Socialist History*, 17, 2000.
2 E.F. Hurwitz, 'The international sisterhood', in R. Bridenthal and C. Koonz (eds), *Becoming Visible: Women in European History*, Boston, Houghton Mifflin, 1977; R.L. Sherrick, 'Toward universal sisterhood', *Women's Studies International Forum*, 5, 6, 1982; L.J. Rupp, 'Constructing internationalism: the case of transnational women's organizations, 1888–1945', *American Historical Review*, 99, 1994; A. Burton, *Burdens of History. British Feminists, Indian Women, and Imperial Culture, 1865–1915*, Chapel Hill, University of North Carolina Press, 1994, ch. 6; E.C. DuBois, 'Woman suffrage around the world: three phases of suffragist internationalism', in C. Daley and M. Nolan (eds), *Suffrage and Beyond. International Feminist Perspectives*, Auckland, Auckland University Press, 1994; L.J. Rupp, *Worlds of Women. The Making of an International Women's Movement*, Princeton, NJ, Princeton University Press, 1997; special issue on Feminisms and Internationalism, *Gender and History*, 10, 3, 1998.
3 G.D.H. Cole, *The Second International. 1889–1914*, London, Macmillan, 1956; J. Joll, *The Second International, 1889–1914*, London, Routledge, 1974.
4 See C. Collette, *The International Faith. Labour's Attitudes to European Socialism, 1918–39*, Aldershot, Ashgate, 1998.
5 D. Marquand, *Ramsay MacDonald*, London, Richard Cohen Books, 1997, pp. 164–5.
6 *Social Democrat*, April 1904, quoted in C. Tsuzuki, *H.M. Hyndman and British Socialism*, Oxford, Oxford University Press, 1961, p. 194.
7 See, for example, the discussion of Belfort Bax in B. Baker, *The Social Democratic Federation and the Boer War*, Our History, 59, 1974, pp. 4–5.
8 K. O. Morgan, *Keir Hardie. Radical and Socialist*, London, Weidenfeld & Nicolson, 1975, pp. 179, 180.
9 Rupp, *Worlds of Women*, p. 108.
10 Carrie Chapman Catt speaking to 1909 IWSA Congress, quoted in Rupp, *Worlds of Women*, p. 108.
11 Ibid., pp. 108–9.
12 M. Ward, 'Nationalism, pacifism, internationalism. Louie Bennett, Hanna Sheehy-Skeffington, and the problems of "defining feminism"', in A. Bradley and M. Valiulis (eds), *Gender and Sexuality in Modern Ireland*, Amherst, University of Massachusetts Press, 1997; L. Ryan, 'A question of loyalty: war, nation, and feminism in early twentieth-century Ireland', *Women's Studies International Forum*, 20, 1, 1997.

13 M. Bosch with A. Kloosterman (eds), *Politics and Friendship. Letters from the International Woman Suffrage Alliance, 1902–42*, Columbus, Ohio State University Press, 1990, p. 18.
14 For a more detailed discussion of British women and the Second International, see Hunt, ' "The immense meaning of it all" ', pp. 25–8.
15 *List of British and Foreign Delegates and Balance Sheet*, London, International Socialist Workers and Trades Union Congress, 1896.
16 See Appendix 2 in K. Hunt, *Equivocal Feminists. The Social Democratic Federation and the Woman Question, 1884–1911*, Cambridge, Cambridge University Press, 1996, p. 260.
17 See, for example, the discussion on the cheapest and quickest routes to Copenhagen for the International Congress in 1910 (*Labour Leader*, 10 June, 17 June 1910).
18 Sheila MacDonald was born three months after the International Socialist Women's Congress held in Copenhagen on 26 and 27 August 1910. For the MacDonalds' attitudes to childcare, see J. Cox (ed.), *A Singular Marriage. A Labour Love Story in Letters and Diaries. Ramsay and Margaret MacDonald*, London, Harrap, 1988, pp. 311–12.
19 See Y. Kapp, *Eleanor Marx: The Crowded Years, 1884–1898*, London, Lawrence & Wishart, 1976; and, for an exploration of Dora Montefiore's internationalism, see K. Hunt, 'Internationalism in practice: the politics of a British socialist and feminist before the First World War', paper to European Social Science History Conference, Amsterdam, March 1998.
20 J.R. MacDonald, *Margaret Ethel MacDonald*, London, Hodder & Stoughton, 4th edn, 1913, p. 226.
21 See C. Collette, 'Socialism and scandal: the sexual politics of the early labour movement', *History Workshop Journal*, 23, 1987.
22 See M. Bondfield, *A Life's Work*, London, Hutchinson, 1948.
23 *Justice*, 7 September 1907.
24 *Clarion*, 23 August 1907; D.B. Montefiore, *From a Victorian to a Modern*, London, Edward Archer, 1927, p. 120.
25 *Clarion*, 23 August 1907.
26 Ibid.
27 *Labour Leader*, 9 September 1910.
28 *Justice*, 9 November 1907; Women's Labour League Executive Committee Minute Book, National Museum of Labour History, 19 October 1910.
29 The British section of the Second International, the British National Committee, was in practice a men's organisation but for the one attendance by Ethel Bentham (British National Committee Minutes, 17 February 1911).
30 For the context, see D.J. Newton, *British Labour, European Socialism and the Struggle for Peace, 1889–1914*, Oxford, Clarendon Press, 1985.
31 *Socialist Record*, July 1914.
32 For a more detailed discussion of British socialist women and the women's internationals before 1914, see Hunt, ' "The immense meaning of it all" ', pp. 32–6.
33 *Labour Leader*, 8 July 1899.
34 Rupp, *Worlds of Women*, p. 34.
35 For Montefiore's experience of the women's internationals and her broader suffrage politics, see K. Hunt, 'Journeying through suffrage: the politics of Dora Montefiore', in C. Eustance, J. Ryan and L. Ugolini (eds), *A Suffrage Reader. Charting Directions in British Suffrage History*, London, Leicester University Press, 2000.
36 See A. Jacobs to R. Schwimmer, 16 December 1907, in Bosch with Kloosterman (eds), *Politics and Friendship*, p. 74. For a comparable experience, see the case of the Dutch socialist and suffragist Martina Kramers (ibid., pp. 126–9; Rupp, *Worlds of Women*, p. 95; and also L.J. Rupp, 'Sexuality and politics in the early twentieth century: the case of the international women's movement', *Feminist Studies*, 23, 3, 1997).

37 Extract from *Gleichheit*, 7 June 1909, translated in *Justice*, 3 July 1909.
38 *The Times*, 22 June 1908.
39 *Labour Leader*, 1 July 1909.
40 *Common Cause*, 25 May 1911.
41 *Fabian News*, June 1909.
42 The British delegates were Marion Phillips, Mary Longman, Ada Salter and Margaret Bondfield (*Labour Leader*, 8 April 1915).
43 S. White, 'Soviets in Britain: the Leeds Convention of 1917', *International Review of Social History*, 19, 1974; *Forward*, 9 June 1917; *Herald*, 9 June 1917; *Labour Leader*, 7 June 1917; *The Call*, 7 June 1917.
44 For the context to this debate and its effect on one stronghold of the ILP, see A. McKinlay, '"Doubtful wisdom and uncertain promise": strategy, ideology and organisation, 1918–1922', in A. McKinlay and R.J. Morris (eds), *The ILP on Clydeside, 1893–1932: From Foundation to Disintegration*, Manchester, Manchester University Press, 1991.
45 R. Miliband, *Parliamentary Socialism*, London, Merlin Press, 1972, p. 84.
46 Collette, *The International Faith*, ch. 2.
47 P. Graves, *Labour Women: Women in British Working-Class Politics, 1918–1939*, Cambridge, Cambridge University Press, 1994, p. 92.
48 For a discussion of these debates from the perspective of one of the key (male) ILPers, see G. Brown, *Maxton*, Glasgow, Fontana, 1988, pp. 104–7. See also Miliband, *Parliamentary Socialism*, pp. 82–92.
49 See H. Corr, 'Helen Crawfurd', in W. Knox (ed.), *Scottish Labour Leaders 1918–39*, Edinburgh, Mainstream, 1984; H. Crawfurd, 'Autobiography', unpublished typescript, National Museum of Labour History, CP/IND/MISC/10.
50 E. Snowden, *Through Bolshevik Russia*, London, Cassell, 1920. Helen Crawfurd reported the Soviet attitude to this book: 'The Bolsheviks considered that Mrs Snowden had the bourgeois outlook, and was rather a dilettante.' (*Forward*, 4 December 1920).
51 *Forward*, 4 December 1920. Crawfurd was one of the few British women to secure an interview with Lenin.
52 *New Leader*, 29 May 1925. For (predominantly Labour) women and the LSI in the 1920s, see Collette, *The International Faith*, pp. 155–8.
53 *New Leader*, 28 August 1925.
54 *New Leader*, 17 December 1926.
55 Collette, *The International Faith*, p. 63.
56 J. Callaghan, 'The Communists and the colonies: anti-imperialism between the wars', in G. Andrews, N. Fishman and K. Morgan (eds), *Opening the Books. Essays on the Social and Cultural History of British Communism*, London, Pluto Press, 1995, p. 13.
57 S. Bruley, *Feminism, Stalinism and the Women's Movement in Britain, 1920–1939*, New York, Garland, 1986, p. 67.
58 Ibid., p. 87.
59 For example, Doris Allison and Cedar Paul attended the Fourth Comintern Congress in 1922 as secretary and translator respectively (ibid., p. 73).
60 Ibid., p. 70.
61 For Montefiore's final visit to Zetkin, in Moscow in 1924, see Montefiore, *From a Victorian*, pp. 214–15. For Birch, see Bruley, *Feminism, Stalinism and the Women's Movement*, pp. 101–2. For another example of an international friendship, see Kollontai's letter to Montefiore published in *The Communist*, 21 October 1920.
62 Bruley, *Feminism, Stalinism and the Women's Movement*.
63 Ibid., p. 142.
64 A. Wiltsher, *Most Dangerous Women. Feminist Peace Campaigners of the Great War*, London, Pandora, 1985; J. Liddington, *The Long Road to Greenham: Feminism and Anti-Militarism*

in Britain since 1820, London, Virago, 1989. See also H. Brown, 'Pacifist feminism in Britain, 1870–1902: "The truest form of patriotism"', DPhil, University of York, 1999; S. Oldfield, *Spinsters of this Parish: The Life and Times of F.M. Mayor and Mary Sheepshanks*, London, Virago, 1984; J. Alberti, *Beyond Suffrage: Feminists in War and Peace, 1914–28*, Basingstoke, Macmillan, 1989.

65 J. Hinton, *Protests and Visions. Peace Politics in Twentieth Century Britain*, London, Hutchinson Radius, 1989.
66 J. Clayton, *The Rise and Decline of Socialism in Great Britain, 1884–1924*, London, Faber & Gwyer, 1926, p. 171.
67 Liddington, *The Long Road to Greenham*, p. 9.
68 R.J. Evans, *Comrades and Sisters. Feminism, Socialism and Pacifism in Europe, 1870–1945*, Brighton, Wheatsheaf, 1987, p. 124.
69 Brown, 'Pacifist feminism in Britain', pp. 66, 309, 346–7; J. Hannam, *Isabella Ford, 1855–1924*, Oxford, Blackwell, 1989, p. 84. At the Socialist International Congress in 1896, Mrs Pankhurst was elected to the committee to deal with the question of war (*Justice*, 28 July 1896).
70 H. Swanwick, *I Have Been Young*, London, Gollancz, 1935, p. 264.
71 *Justice*, 9 January 1909.
72 Tsuzuki, *H.M. Hyndman and British Socialism*, pp. 211–13.
73 *Reports of the Second International Conference of Socialist Women*, 1910, p. 27.
74 *Labour Leader*, 21 November 1912.
75 Montefiore, *From a Victorian*, p. 153.
76 Ibid., p. 154. This was also an issue for Charlotte Despard (*The Vote*, 20 June 1913).
77 *Daily Herald*, 27 June 1913.
78 See, for example, Marion Phillips in *Fabian News*, June 1913.
79 K.A. Rigby, 'Annot Robinson: socialist, suffragist, peacemaker. A biographical study', MA, Manchester Polytechnic, 1986, p. 71.
80 For example, *Labour Woman*, July, August 1913.
81 *Forward*, 31 January 1914.
82 Rupp, *Worlds of Women*, p. 35.
83 See, in particular, Sheila Rowbotham's account of the 'rebel networks' of war resisters (S. Rowbotham, *Friends of Alice Wheeldon*, London, Pluto, 1986). See also K. Weller, *'Don't be a Soldier!' The Radical Anti-War Movement in North London, 1914–18*, London, Journeyman, 1985.
84 H. Mitchell, *The Hard Way Up*, London, Virago, 1977, p. 185.
85 R. Challinor, *The Origins of British Bolshevism*, London, Croom Helm, 1977, pp. 126, 164–6.
86 See B. Winslow, *Sylvia Pankhurst. Sexual Politics and Political Activism*, London, UCL Press, 1996.
87 *The Vote*, 14 August 1914. For the activities of the WSNAC see *The Vote* and C. Eustance, '"Daring to be free": the evolution of women's political identities in the Women's Freedom League, 1907–30', DPhil, University of York, 1993, p. 276.
88 See Winslow, *Sylvia Pankhurst*, pp. 90–7; E.S. Pankhurst, *The Home Front*, London, Hutchinson, 1932.
89 *Leeds Weekly Citizen*, 12 March 1915.
90 *Labour Leader*, 4 March 1915.
91 See, for example, the ILPer Patrick Dollan's argument in *The Women's Dreadnought*, 10 June 1916, quoted in Wiltsher, *Most Dangerous Women*, p. 152.
92 *Justice*, 3 June 1915.
93 *Labour Leader*, 4 March 1915.
94 *Labour Leader*, 15 April 1915.
95 F. Brockway, 'Inside the Left', quoted in Rowbotham, *Friends of Alice Wheeldon*, p. 40.

96 J. Liddington, 'The Women's Peace Crusade: the history of a forgotten campaign', in D. Thompson (ed.), *Over Our Dead Bodies: Women against the Bomb*, London, Virago, 1983; Liddington, *The Long Road to Greenham*, ch. 6; J.J. Smyth, 'Rents, peace, votes: working-class women and political activity in the First World War', in E. Breitenbach and E. Gordon (eds), *Out of Bounds: Women in Scottish Society, 1800–1945*, Edinburgh, Edinburgh University Press, 1992.
 97 Crawfurd, 'Autobiography, p. 154.
 98 Smyth, 'Rents, peace, votes', p. 182.
 99 For example, *Labour Leader*, 21 June 1917.
100 *Forward*, 16 June 1917.
101 *Labour Leader*, 21 June 1917.
102 *Labour Leader*, 19 July 1917. Ethel Snowden recalled that she had addressed 133 public meetings for the WPC in less than a year (Wiltsher, *Most Dangerous Women*, p. 130).
103 *Labour Leader*, 15 November 1917; Wiltsher, *Most Dangerous Women*, p. 193. For Despard's anti-war politics see Eustance, ' "Daring to be free" ', pp. 258–9.
104 I.O. Ford, 'Attitudes to the War, 1915', Suffrage MSS, Manchester Central Library, M50/2/9/17.
105 *Labour Leader*, 15 April 1915.
106 C. Marshall, 'The future of women in politics', *Labour Year Book*, 1916, quoted in J. Vellacott, 'Feminist consciousness and the First World War', *History Workshop Journal*, 23, 1987, p. 89.
107 Ward, 'Nationalism, pacifism, internationalism', p. 64.
108 Ibid., pp. 67–8.
109 Of the twenty-five British delegates, sixteen cited Labour Party or ILP membership and three were involved with the WPC (*Report of International Congress of Women, Zurich*, Geneva, WILPF, 1919, p. 449).
110 Ibid., p. 127.
111 Ibid., pp. 127–8.
112 Ibid., p. 222.
113 Wiltsher, *Most Dangerous Women*, p. 205.
114 *ILP Annual Conference Report*, 1920, pp. 75–6. See also Ethel Snowden's speech, p. 74.
115 Liddington, *The Long Road to Greenham*, p. 139.
116 Oldfield, *Spinsters of this Parish*, p. 247.
117 *Forward*, 29 January 1921.
118 *Labour Leader*, 2 February, 16 March 1922; *New Leader*, 27 July 1923. For women's peace activities in the 1920s, see Liddington, *The Long Road to Greenham*, ch. 7.
119 *New Leader*, 14 September 1923.
120 Liddington, *The Long Road to Greenham*, p. 142.
121 *New Leader*, 20 May 1927.
122 *New Leader*, 25 July 1924.
123 *Labour Leader*, 31 August 1922.
124 For Robinson's peace work after the war see Rigby, 'Annot Robinson', ch. 8.
125 For the Peacemakers' Pilgrimage see Liddington, *The Long Road to Greenham*, pp. 144–6.
126 J. Liddington, *The Life and Times of a Respectable Rebel. Selina Cooper, 1864–1946*, London, Virago, 1984, p. 406.
127 For the Guild's peace activities in the 1920s, see G. Scott, *Feminism and the Politics of Working Women. The Women's Co-operative Guild, 1880s to the Second World War*, London, UCL Press, 1998, pp. 213–14; Collette, *The International Faith*, pp. 163–4.
128 *Justice*, 20 March 1909.
129 *Justice*, 1 May 1909.
130 *Justice*, 9 January 1909.

131 The Countess of Aberdeen (ed.), *The International Congress of Women 1899*, Vol. 1, London, T. Fisher Unwin, 1900, p. 48.
132 *Reports of the Second International Conference of Socialist Women*, 1910, p. 31.
133 *Labour Woman*, March 1913.
134 Hannam, *Isabella Ford*, p. 130.
135 *New Age*, 28 July 1904.
136 *Justice*, 20 March 1909.
137 *New Age*, 19 October 1905.
138 *Labour Leader*, 12 June 1913.
139 Rupp, 'Sexuality and politics', p. 594.
140 Burton, *Burdens of History*, p. 172.
141 *Labour Leader*, 2 July 1909.
142 Montefiore, *From a Victorian*, p. 192; *International Socialist* (Sydney), 30 December 1911 (capitalised in the original).
143 See Hunt, 'Internationalism in practice'.
144 *ILP Annual Conference Report*, 1918, p. 72.
145 *Labour Leader*, 1 March 1917.
146 *New Leader*, 25 April 1924.
147 *New Leader*, 17 December 1926.
148 *New Leader*, 26 August, 7 October 1927.
149 Crawfurd, 'Autobiography', p. 188.
150 Montefiore, *From a Victorian*, p. 202.
151 *Fifth Congress of the Communist International. Abridged report of meetings held at Moscow June 17th to July 8th, 1924*, London, CPGB, nd, p. 89, Communist Party of Australia Archive, Mitchell Library, Sydney, MLMSS 5021 ADD-ON 1936, Box 46. Nor was this only an issue which Montefiore was able to recognise as a communist, for she made a similar point when she experienced 'White Australia' in 1911 (*International Socialist* (Sydney), 30 December 1911).
152 *Labour Leader*, 16 September 1910.

CONCLUSION

This book has explored the complex ways in which socialist women negotiated between their loyalties to class, to party and to their sex and in so doing developed a distinctive political identity. Although the practice of socialist parties encouraged female socialists not to identify primarily, or even at all, as women in their political lives, there remained a significant group of socialist women which sought to develop a woman-focused socialist politics. The specific form that this took in Britain between the 1880s and the 1920s varied between individual women and over a range of issues, although for many it was suffrage politics which was decisive. The balance between those issues in which it was possible to foreground gender identity and those questions for which class or party loyalty was pre-eminent changed over time. Moreover, it was also subject to individual negotiation, as women wrestled with their personal priorities day to day and issue by issue.

When women decided to join the socialist movement, they entered organisations which were often new and prided themselves on their differences from the mainstream parties. In contrast to more established political parties there were no formal barriers to membership on the grounds of sex and women were able to participate at all levels of the movement. Socialist women from all parties soon found, however, that there was a gap between the rhetoric of equality and the practice of socialist organisations, while socialist theory was masculinist in its concerns and based on the interests of the male waged worker. Nonetheless, they challenged the view that 'women's emancipation' was marginal to the socialist project and could wait until after socialism had been achieved, and in so doing sought to reconfigure the meaning of socialism itself. They were inspired by socialism's promise of a new way of life, both in the present and in the future, to imagine the development of a different kind of politics – one which would address the interests of women as well as men; which would provide the possibility for women to develop their full potential as human beings; and which would enable women to work for socialism with men from a position of equality. Nonetheless, they debated with each other about how to theorise the precise relationship between socialism and the Woman Question and over what was meant by women's emancipation. They also recognised that in a mixed-sex politics which was premised on the rhetoric of equality of the sexes, but in a society in which men and women were in a very different social and economic position, urgent attention needed to be given to attracting women to socialist politics and ensuring that they played a full part. Again, however, socialist women differed about how this could best be done. In particular, they argued over the symbolic significance and practical benefits of women organising separately within socialist parties.

There were key moments which favoured women's attempts to develop a woman-focused socialism – in the pioneering days of the 1880s and 1890s, when men and women were excited by 'new life socialism', which appeared to offer the chance to redefine relationships between the sexes and reconsider accepted notions of masculinity and femininity; in the Edwardian era, when the suffrage movement brought the issue of women's engagement in politics to centre stage; in the immediate pre-war period, when some socialist women tried to develop a politics of consumption and to challenge the dominance of production as the focus for socialist politics; and in the 1920s, when the ILP, squeezed between the Labour Party and the Communist Party, sought to reposition itself. In all of these moments socialist women tried to make their voices heard – they argued with male colleagues at meetings and debated issues in their speeches and journalism as well as in letters to the press. They gained small victories, although overall it was difficult for them to revise socialist priorities in order to recognise the importance of gender as well as class. Nonetheless, we conclude that it is as important to examine the possibilities explored by socialist women – their dreams, their questions and their choices – as to measure their success purely in terms of changed policies, votes cast or the numbers of women elected. The latter are not unimportant; yet we would all understand more about political actors – of whatever period, place or affiliation – if we valued their evolving political imagination as highly as their pragmatic achievements. This is particularly the case for socialist women, as they struggled without any existing model to create a practice which not only remained socialist but also involved women as equal partners and began to challenge gender relations themselves.

The reality of socialist parties and individual socialists who marginalised women from the political agenda, and who steadfastly polarised class and gender identities, meant that socialist women consistently found their loyalties in tension. They often found themselves facing agonising choices over matters which were straightforward for fellow comrades, specifically socialist men and other female socialists who did not identify politically as women. By looking at the political journeys that individual socialist women made, the nature of these choices is revealed, as are the compromises that enabled socialist women to function politically. For some the difficult decision was eventually made to leave socialist politics behind to concentrate on campaigning for women's suffrage, while others slipped increasingly into labourism or felt that they had no other choice but to take their socialist convictions into the CP. Other choices were not so cataclysmic but were equally part of being a socialist woman: when to criticise the masculinism of their comrades and parties; when to make a gendered argument; when to emphasise difference and when to highlight commonality. These kinds of judgements and the range of responses to them are apparent in the three case studies presented here and are part of the continuing attempt by socialist women over this period to imagine a woman-focused socialism and to build their own political practice in the light of this. Individual socialist women negotiated this in slightly different ways to each other. Moreover, these choices could vary over time. The emphases within a political life could change over time and in response to the wider context. An individual might not be a socialist woman over her whole lifetime or might not be consistent in her juggling between loyalties to class, to gender and to party. An archetype 'socialist woman' does not explain very much unless she is seen as the aggregate of all those individual choices. For the socialist woman was a figure who was constantly in tension, albeit usually a creative tension, between her class and her gender politics.

By exploring three different areas of socialist women's practice – suffragism, a politics of consumption and internationalism – we have highlighted the creativity of many socialist women and their relative success in challenging the agenda of socialist parties and of the women's movement. The case studies have enabled us to explore in greater detail the main themes of the book, in particular the ways in which socialist women developed a political identity; the extent to which they could work together regardless of class and party and their efforts to create a woman-focused socialism. Women did try to work together as socialist women, and to make links with non-socialist women, as they took part in the suffrage campaign and in international organisations, and explored the possibilities of creating a politics out of everyday consumption. These issues, however, also reveal the fragility of links between women – whether between the 'bourgeois women's movement' and organised socialist women or between individual working-class and middle-class women. The case studies demonstrate that there was no straightforward link between party affiliation and positions taken on suffrage or on internationalism. Personal antipathies could inhibit cooperation, as in the case of Dora Montefiore and Margaret MacDonald in international organisations before the war, while loyalty to party did not prevent women within the ILP from taking very different positions on the suffrage. There were times at which the formation of competing organisations could exacerbate tensions and erect barriers between women, whilst at others they worked together beyond organisational boundaries.

In the Introduction we raised the question of whether the socialist and feminist politics of the period would look different if viewed through the perspective of socialist women. Socialist women themselves certainly thought this to be the case. Their attempts to highlight gender inequalities and oppression and to challenge prevailing definitions of socialism were made explicit as they campaigned for women's suffrage, developed their own version of internationalism and argued for a politics of consumption. We have argued that a focus on socialist women challenges conventional wisdoms about the suffrage movement, in particular those interpretations which label adult suffragists as anti-feminist or uninterested in women's enfranchisement. An examination of the arguments advanced by socialist women shows that it was not simply a question of whether or not to take an adult or a limited suffrage position. Socialist women were concerned to find ways to develop a tactical and theoretical position which would bring together their interests as socialists and as women. The second case study explored the attempt by a minority of socialist women to develop a politics around consumption. This was part of a broader concern to 'make socialists', in this case to reach ordinary women in their day-to-day lives. It was also an ambitious attempt, largely unsuccessful at the time, to revise the socialist agenda and to question the privileging of production over consumption in socialist politics. This way of looking at the socialist agenda or of situating consumption in relation to the politics of the period has not been a significant feature of the historiography to date. Finally, when it comes to the historiography of internationalism, socialist women are marginalised from discussions of socialist/labour internationalism without finding a place in the equivalent literature on women's internationalism. Yet by exploring the attempts by socialist women to find a space to develop a distinctive internationalism of their own, we arrive at a more nuanced understanding of the place of internationalism within socialist discourse and how this translated into a political practice for a range of socialist women. Taken together these three case studies raise important questions for historians of both the socialist and the women's movement.

It is our contention that socialist women cannot just be subsumed into mainstream narratives of the women's movement or of the socialist movement. As women who were socialists and yet who also recognised the importance of gender in their politics, the women discussed in this book *did* have a distinct perspective and shared many experiences. At the same time, we also argue that socialist women did not all hold the same views and that it is important to differentiate between them if we are to understand the richness of their ideas and their political practice.

Looking across the whole period, it is also clear that there were both continuities and discontinuities in the political experiences of socialist women. In the 1920s socialist women still faced the question of how to make socialism sensitive to gender inequalities and how to ensure that women played a full role in political life. On the other hand, the context had changed. The room for manoeuvre had been reduced as the political space shrank in which socialist women could make their politics. The influence of the trade union movement on the Labour Party created a formidable obstacle to women's ability to prioritise issues of particular relevance to their sex. In a world of mass unemployment, of fascism and eventually of war, class politics seemed to be able to override the more tentative woman-focused socialism which had been developing before the First World War and largely obliterate the memory of it. Women who had been influenced by the suffrage politics of the pre-war years, which emphasised the collective interests of women as a sex, reacted differently to politics in the inter-war years. Some, such as Margaret Bondfield and Ellen Wilkinson, sought careers within the Labour Party, which meant that they placed far less emphasis on gender questions. Others, including Helen Crawfurd and Dora Montefiore, chose the Communist Party as a focus for their politics. Yet there were others, in particular Dorothy Jewson, who retained a commitment to socialist politics viewed through the lens of gender and who continued to pursue an agenda which integrated a 'feminism' with socialism despite an increasingly difficult climate. How the socialist women of the 1930s and beyond struggled to sustain a woman-focused socialism remains a story yet to be told. It would add to what has been uncovered here – that socialist women are a distinct group determined to sustain a vision of the possibility of a socialism which is truly inclusive and where class does not always trump every other identity.

For those women engaged in labour and socialist politics today gender remains an area of considerable tension. The issues raised by this book are as relevant now as they were for women before the 1920s. Women still have to negotiate between competing loyalties, priorities and demands. Their political identity can only be understood if the complexities of their ideas and their shifting positions in relation to particular issues are recognised and understood through their own perspectives rather than through the eyes and priorities of others.

BIBLIOGRAPHY

Primary Sources

Archive collections

British National Committee Minutes (British Section of Second International), National Museum of Labour History.
Carpenter Collection, Sheffield Reference Library.
Communist Party of Australia Archive, Mitchell Library, Sydney.
Crawfurd, H., 'Autobiography', unpublished typescript, National Museum of Labour History.
Glasier Papers, Sidney Jones Library, Liverpool University.
Francis Johnson Collection of ILP Papers, British Library of Political and Economic Science, London School of Economics.
MacDonald Papers, Public Record Office.
Alf Mattison Diaries, Brotherton Library, Leeds University.
Pamphlets and leaflets of the SDF and BSP, Harvester Microfilm.
Suffrage MSS, Manchester Central Library.
Women's Labour League Executive Committee Minute Book, National Museum of Labour History.

Official papers

Bulletin of Monthly Correspondence of the IWSA.
Illustrated Report of the Proceedings of the Workers' Congress held in London July 1896, 1896.
ILP Annual Conference Reports.
ILP Information Committee, *Monthly Notes for Speakers*.
List of British and Foreign Delegates and Balance Sheet, London, International Socialist Workers and Trades Union Congress, 1896.
National Administrative Council Annual Reports.
National Union of Women Workers Annual Conference Reports.
People's Suffrage Federation First Annual Report, 1909–1910.
Report of International Congress of Women, Zurich, 1919.
Reports of the Second International Conference of Socialist Women, 1910.

BIBLIOGRAPHY

Newspapers

The Call
Christian Commonwealth
Clarion
Common Cause
Commonweal
The Communist
Daily Herald
Fabian News
Forward
Herald
International Socialist (Sydney)
Justice
Labour Leader
Labour Prophet
Labour Woman
League Leaflet
Leeds Weekly Citizen
The Link
New Age
New Leader
Northampton Pioneer
Our Corner
Social Democrat
Socialist Record
The Times
The Vote
Woman Worker
The Women's Dreadnought
Yorkshire Factory Times

Books and Articles

Aberdeen, The Countess of (ed.), *The International Congress of Women 1899*, London, T. Fisher Unwin, 1900.

Adult Suffrage Society, *To the Democracy*, leaflet 3, 1907.

Aveling, E.M. and E., 'The woman question', *Westminster Review*, January 1886.

Bebel, A., *Woman in the Past, Present and Future*, trans. H.B. Adams Walther, London, Modern Press, 1885.

Bell, T., *Pioneering Days*, London, Lawrence & Wishart, 1941.

Beveridge, Sir W.H., *British Food Control*, London, Oxford University Press, 1928.

Bondfield, M., *The Women's Suffrage Controversy*, ASS leaflet 1, nd (1905?).

Bondfield, M., *A Life's Work*, London, Hutchinson, 1948.

Brailsford, H.N., *Socialism for To-Day*, London, ILP, 1925.

Browne, W.F. Stella, 'One of our liberators: Dorothy Jewson', *Critic and Guide*, August 1925.

BIBLIOGRAPHY

Bryher, S., *An Account of the Labour and Socialist Movement in Bristol*, Bristol, Bristol Labour Weekly, 1929.
Clayton, J. (ed.), *Why I Joined the Independent Labour Party*, Leeds, Leeds ILP, c.1896.
Clayton, J., *The Rise and Decline of Socialism in Great Britain, 1884–1924*, London, Faber & Gwyer, 1926.
Davies, M.L. (ed.), *Life As We Have Known It*, London, Virago, 1977, 1st edn 1931.
Dawson, J., *Why Women Want Socialism*, London, ILP pamphlet, 4, 1909.
Engels, F., *The Origin of the Family, Private Property and the State*, London, Lawrence & Wishart, 1972.
Ford, I.O., *On the Threshold*, London, Edward Arnold, 1895.
Ford, I.O., *Women and Socialism*, London, ILP pamphlet, 1904; 2nd edn 1906.
Gallacher, W., *Revolt on the Clyde*, London, Lawrence & Wishart, 1936.
Gawthorpe, M., *Up Hill to Holloway*, Penobscot, Maine, Traversity Press, 1962.
Glasier, J.B., *Keir Hardie: The Man and His Message*, London, ILP, 1919.
Glasier, K.B., *Aimée Furniss, Scholar*, London, Clarion, 1896.
Glasier, K.B., *Socialism and the Home*, London, ILP, 1909.
Glasier, K.B., *Enid Stacy*, London, ILP, 1924.
MacDonald, J.R., *Margaret Ethel MacDonald*, London, Hodder & Stoughton, 4th edn, 1913.
Mitchell, H., *The Hard Way Up. The Autobiography of Hannah Mitchell, Suffragette and Rebel*, London, Virago, 1977.
Montefiore, D.B., *Some Words to Socialist Women*, London, Twentieth Century Press, 1908.
Montefiore, D.B., *The Position of Women in the Socialist Movement*, London, Twentieth Century Press, 1909.
Montefiore, D.B., *From a Victorian to a Modern*, London, Edward Archer, 1927.
Oxford, M. (ed.), *Myself When Young*, London, Muller, 1938.
Pallister, M., *The Orange-Box. Thoughts of a Socialist Propagandist*, London, Leonard Parsons, 1924.
Pallister, M., *Socialism for Women*, London, ILP, 1925.
Pankhurst, E.S., *The Suffragette Movement*, London, Virago, 1977, 1st edn 1931.
Pankhurst, E.S., *The Home Front*, London, Hutchinson, 1932.
Snowden, E., *The Woman Socialist*, London, George Allen, 1907.
Snowden, E., *Through Bolshevik Russia*, London, Cassell, 1920.
Snowden, Mrs P., *The Real Women's Party*, Glasgow, Reformers' Bookstall, 1920.
Stacy, E., 'A century of women's rights', in E. Carpenter (ed.), *Forecasts of the Coming Century*, Manchester, Labour Press, 1899.
Swanwick, H., *I Have Been Young*, London, Gollancz, 1935.
Varley, J., 'Yesterday and Today', *The Record*, March 1931.
Webb, C., *The Woman with the Basket: The History of the Women's Co-operative Guild*, Manchester, The Guild, 1927.
Wertheimer, E., *Portrait of the Labour Party*, London, Putnam's & Sons, 1929.
Wolstenholme Elmy, E., *Woman – The Communist*, London, ILP, 1904.
Woollcombe, J., 'Julia Varley: A lifelong campaigner', *The Gateway*, 3, 14, 1930.

BIBLIOGRAPHY

Secondary works

Books and articles

Akkerman, T. and Stuurman, S. (eds), *Perspectives on Feminist Thought in European History: From the Middle Ages to the Present*, London, Routledge, 1998.
Alberti, J., *Beyond Suffrage: Feminists in War and Peace, 1914–1928*, London, Macmillan, 1989.
Alberti, J., *Eleanor Rathbone*, London, Sage, 1996.
Alexander, S., 'Introduction' to M. Pember Reeves, *Round About a Pound a Week*, London, Virago, 1979.
Alexander, S., 'Fabian socialism and the "sex relation"', in S. Alexander, *Becoming a Woman and Other Essays in 19th and 20th Century Feminist History*, New York, New York University Press, 1995.
Alexander, S., 'The Fabian Women's Group, 1908–52', in S. Alexander, *Becoming a Woman and Other Essays in 19th and 20th Century Feminist History*, New York, New York University Press, 1995.
Anderson, B.S. and Zinsser, J.P., *A History of Their Own: Women in Europe from Prehistory to the Present*, Vol. II, Harmondsworth, Penguin, 1990.
Ardis, A., *New Women, New Novels: Feminism and Early Modernism*, New Brunswick, Rutgers University Press, 1990.
Baker, B., *The Social Democratic Federation and the Boer War*, *Our History*, 59, 1974.
Banks, O., *Faces of Feminism*, Oxford, Martin Robertson, 1981.
Banks, O., *The Biographical Dictionary of British Feminists, Vol. 1: 1800–1930*, Brighton, Wheatsheaf, 1985.
Barltrop, R., *Monument: The Story of the Socialist Party of Great Britain*, London, Pluto, 1975.
Barnett, L.M., *British Food Policy During the First World War*, London, Allen & Unwin, 1985.
Barrett, M., 'Marxist-feminism and the work of Karl Marx', in A. Phillips (ed.), *Feminism and Equality*, Oxford, Blackwell, 1987.
Barrow, L. and Bullock, I., *Democratic Ideas and the British Labour Movement, 1880–1914*, Cambridge, Cambridge University Press, 1996.
Beetham, M., *A Magazine of Her Own: Domesticity and Desire in the Women's Magazine, 1800–1914*, London, Routledge, 1996.
Belchem, J. and Kirk, N. (eds), *Languages of Labour*, Aldershot, Ashgate, 1997.
Bell, G., *Troublesome Business. The Labour Party and the Irish Question*, London, Pluto, 1982.
Bellamy, J. and Saville, J. (eds), *Dictionary of Labour Biography*, Vol. 2, London, Macmillan, 1974; Vol. 4, London, Macmillan, 1977; Vol. 6, London, Macmillan, 1982.
Bland, L., *Banishing the Beast. English Feminism and Sexual Morality, 1885–1914*, Harmondsworth, Penguin, 1995.
Bosch, M. with Kloosterman, A. (eds), *Politics and Friendship. Letters from the International Woman Suffrage Alliance, 1902–42*, Columbus, Ohio State University Press, 1990.
Boston, S., *Women Workers and the Trade Unions*, London, Davis Paynter, 1980.
Boxer, M.J. and Quataert, J.H. (eds), *Socialist Women: European Socialist Feminism in the Nineteenth and Early Twentieth Centuries*, New York, Elsevier, 1978.
Bradley, Q., 'The Leeds rent strike of 1914', http://www.qbradley.freeserve.co.uk/rentrick.htm

BIBLIOGRAPHY

Branson, N., *History of the Communist Party of Great Britain, 1927–1941*, London, Lawrence & Wishart, 1985.
Brivati, B. and Heffernan, R. (eds), *The Labour Party: A Centenary History*, Basingstoke, Macmillan, 2000.
Brown, G., *Maxton*, Glasgow, Fontana, 1988.
Bruley, S., *Feminism, Stalinism and the Women's Movement in Britain, 1920–1939*, New York, Garland, 1986.
Buhle, M.J., *Women and American Socialism, 1870–1920*, Urbana, University of Illinois Press, 1983.
Burgess, K., *The Challenge of Labour*, London, Croom Helm, 1980.
Burton, A., *Burdens of History. British Feminists, Indian Women, and Imperial Culture, 1865–1915*, Chapel Hill, University of North Carolina Press, 1994.
Bush, J., *Behind the Lines. East London Labour, 1914–19*, London, Merlin Press, 1984.
Caine, B., *Victorian Feminists*, Oxford, Oxford University Press, 1992.
Caine, B., 'Feminist biography and feminist history', *Women's History Review*, 3, 2, 1994.
Caine, B., *English Feminism, 1780–1980*, Oxford, Oxford University Press, 1997.
Callaghan, J., 'The Communists and the colonies: anti-imperialism between the wars', in G. Andrews, N. Fishman and K. Morgan (eds), *Opening the Books. Essays on the Social and Cultural History of British Communism*, London, Pluto Press, 1995.
Challinor, R., *The Origins of British Bolshevism*, London, Croom Helm, 1977.
Chew, D.N., *Ada Neild Chew: The Life and Writings of a Working Woman*, London, Virago, 1982.
Clark, A., *The Struggle for the Breeches: Gender and the Making of the British Working Class*, Berkeley, University of California Press, 1995.
Cole, G.D.H., *The Second International, 1889–1914*, London, Macmillan, 1956.
Collette, C., 'Socialism and scandal: the sexual politics of the early labour movement', *History Workshop Journal*, 23, 1987.
Collette, C., *For Labour and for Women: The Women's Labour League, 1906–18*, Manchester, Manchester University Press, 1989.
Collette, C., *The International Faith. Labour's Attitudes to European Socialism, 1918–39*, Aldershot, Ashgate, 1998.
Collette, C., 'Questions of gender: Labour and women', in B. Brivati and R. Heffernan (eds), *The Labour Party: A Centenary History*, Basingstoke, Macmillan, 2000.
Cott, N., 'On men's history and women's history', in H. Brod (ed.), *The Making of Masculinities. The New Men's Studies*, Boston, Allen & Unwin, 1987.
Coward, R., *Patriarchal Precedents: Sexuality and Social Relations*, London, Routledge & Kegan Paul, 1983.
Cowman, K., '"Giving them something to do": how the early ILP appealed to women', in M. Walsh (ed.), *Working Out Gender: Perspectives from Labour History*, Aldershot, Ashgate, 1999.
Cox, J. (ed.), *A Singular Marriage. A Labour Love Story in Letters and Diaries. Ramsay and Margaret MacDonald*, London, Harrap, 1988.
Cresswell, D'Arcy, *Margaret McMillan: A Memoir*, London, Hutchinson, 1948.
Crick, B., *George Orwell: A Life*, Harmondsworth, Penguin, 1982.
Crick, M., *The History of the Social Democratic Federation*, Halifax, Ryburn, 1994.
Cross, M., 'Flora Tristan's socialist propaganda in provincial France, 1843–1844', in B. Taithe and T. Thornton (eds), *Propaganda: Political Rhetoric and Identity, 1300–2000*, Stroud, Sutton, 1999.

Currell, M.E., *Political Women*, London, Croom Helm, 1974.
Damer, S., 'State, class and housing: Glasgow, 1885–1919', in J. Melling (ed.), *Housing, Social Policy and the State*, London, Croom Helm, 1980.
Davin, A., 'Imperialism and motherhood', *History Workshop Journal*, 5, 1978.
Davin, A., 'Feminism and labour history', in R. Samuel (ed.), *People's History and Socialist Theory*, London, Routledge & Kegan Paul, 1981.
Davis, B., 'Food scarcity and the empowerment of the female consumer in World War I Berlin', in V. de Grazia and E. Furlough (eds), *The Sex of Things. Gender and Consumption in Historical Perspective*, Berkeley, University of California Press, 1996.
Davis, M., *Sylvia Pankhurst. A Life in Radical Politics*, London, Pluto Press, 1999.
Davis, T., Durham, M., Hall, C., Langan, M. and Sutton, D., ' "The public face of feminism": early twentieth century writings on women's suffrage', in Centre for Contemporary Cultural Studies, *Making Histories: Studies in History Writing and Politics*, London, Hutchinson, 1982.
Dowse, R.E., *Left in the Centre: The Independent Labour Party, 1893–1940*, London, Longmans, 1966.
Draper, H. and Lipow, A.G., 'Marxist women versus bourgeois feminism', *Socialist Register*, London, Merlin Press, 1976.
DuBois, E.C., 'Woman suffrage and the Left: an international socialist-feminist perspective', *New Left Review*, 186, 1991.
DuBois, E.C., 'Woman suffrage around the world: three phases of suffragist internationalism', in C. Daley and M. Nolan (eds), *Suffrage and Beyond. International Feminist Perspectives*, Auckland, Auckland University Press, 1994.
Eisenstein, Z.R. (ed.), *Capitalist Patriarchy and the Case for Socialist Feminism*, New York, Monthly Review Press, 1979.
Englander, D. (ed.), *The Diary of Fred Knee*, Coventry, Society for the Study of Labour History, 1977.
Englander, D., *Landlord and Tenant in Urban Britain, 1838–1918*, Oxford, Clarendon Press, 1983.
Eustance, C., Ryan, J. and Ugolini, L. (eds), *A Suffrage Reader: Charting Directions in British Suffrage History*, London, Leicester University Press, 2000.
Evans, R.J., *Comrades and Sisters. Feminism, Socialism and Pacifism in Europe, 1870–1945*, Brighton, Wheatsheaf, 1987.
Fleming, S., 'Eleanor Rathbone: spokeswoman for a movement', introduction to E. Rathbone, *The Disinherited Family*, Bristol, Falling Wall Press, 1986.
Fleming, S. and Dallas, G., 'Jessie', *Spare Rib*, 32, February 1975.
Foote, G., *The Labour Party's Political Thought: A History*, Basingstoke, Macmillan, 1997.
Fox, P.A., 'Ethel Carnie Holdsworth's "revolt of the gentle": romance and the politics of resistance in working-class women's writing', in A. Ingram and D. Patai (eds), *Discovering Forgotten Radicals: British Women Writers, 1859–1939*, Chapel Hill, University of North Carolina Press, 1993.
Francis, M., 'Labour and gender', in D. Tanner, P. Thane and N. Tiratsoo (eds), *Labour's First Century*, Cambridge, Cambridge University Press, 2000.
Frank, D., 'Housewives, socialists and the politics of food: the 1917 New York cost-of-living protests', *Feminist Studies*, 11, 2, 1985.
Frank, D., *Purchasing Power. Consumer Organizing, Gender and the Seattle Labor Movement, 1919–29*, New York, Cambridge University Press, 1994.

BIBLIOGRAPHY

Gaffin, J. and Thoms, D., *Caring and Sharing: The Centenary History of the Cooperative Women's Guild*, Manchester, Manchester Cooperative Union, 1983.

Garner, L., *Stepping Stones to Women's Liberty: Feminist Ideas in the Women's Suffrage Movement, 1900–1918*, London, Heinemann, 1984.

Gordon, E., *Women and the Labour Movement in Scotland, 1850–1914*, Oxford, Clarendon Press, 1991.

Graves, P., *Labour Women: Women in British Working-Class Politics, 1918–1939*, Cambridge, Cambridge University Press, 1994.

Graves, P., 'An experiment in women-centered socialism: Labour women in Britain', in H. Gruber and P. Graves (eds), *Women and Socialism. Socialism and Women. Europe between the Two World Wars*, Oxford, Berghahn, 1998.

Grogan, S., *Flora Tristan: Life Stories*, London, Routledge, 1998.

Gruber, H. and Graves, P. (eds), *Women and Socialism. Socialism and Women. Europe between the Two World Wars*, Oxford, Berghahn, 1998.

Gurney, P., *Co-operative Culture and the Politics of Consumption, 1870–1930*, Manchester, Manchester University Press, 1996.

Hall, C., *White, Male and Middle Class: Explorations in Feminism and History*, Cambridge, Polity, 1992.

Hall, C., McClelland, K. and Rendall, J., *Defining the Victorian Nation: Class, Race, Gender and the Reform Act of 1867*, Cambridge, Cambridge University Press, 2000.

Hannam, J., ' "In the comradeship of the sexes lies the hope of progress and social regeneration": Women in the West Riding ILP, c.1890–1914', in J. Rendall (ed.), *Equal or Different. Women's Politics 1800–1914*, Oxford, Blackwell, 1987.

Hannam, J., *Isabella Ford, 1855–1924*, Oxford, Blackwell, 1989.

Hannam, J., 'Women and the ILP, 1890–1914', in D. James, T. Jowitt and K. Laybourn (eds), *The Centennial History of the Independent Labour Party*, Halifax, Ryburn, 1992.

Hannam, J., ' "I had not been to London": women's suffrage – a view from the regions', in J. Purvis and S.S. Holton (eds), *Votes for Women*, London, Routledge, 2000.

Hannam, J. and Hunt, K., 'Gendering the stories of socialism: an essay in historical criticism', in M. Walsh (ed.), *Working Out Gender: Perspectives from Labour History*, Aldershot, Ashgate, 1999.

Harrison, B., *Prudent Revolutionaries: Portraits of British Feminists between the Wars*, Oxford, Clarendon, 1987.

Harrison, R., 'The War Emergency Workers' National Committee, 1914–20', in A. Briggs and J. Saville (eds), *Essays in Labour History, 1886–1923*, London, Macmillan, 1971.

Hinton, J., *Labour and Socialism. A History of the British Labour Movement, 1867–1974*, Brighton, Wheatsheaf, 1983.

Hinton, J., *Protests and Visions. Peace Politics in Twentieth Century Britain*, London, Hutchinson Radius, 1989.

Hollis, P., *Jennie Lee: A Life*, Oxford, Oxford University Press, 1997.

Holton, S.S., *Feminism and Democracy: Women's Suffrage and Reform Politics in Britain, 1900–1918*, Cambridge, Cambridge University Press, 1986.

Holton, S.S., 'The suffragist and the "average" woman', *Women's History Review* 1, 1, 1992.

Holton, S.S., *Suffrage Days: Stories from the Women's Suffrage Movement*, London, Routledge, 1996.

Honeycutt, K., 'Clara Zetkin: A socialist approach to the problem of women's oppression', in J. Slaughter and R. Kern (eds), *European Women on the Left*, New York, Greenwood Press, 1981.

Hopkin, D., 'The socialist press in Britain, 1890–1910', in D. Boyce, J. Curran and P. Wingate (eds), *Newspaper History: From the 17th Century to the Present Day*, London, Constable, 1978.

Howell, D., *British Workers and the Independent Labour Party, 1888–1906*, Manchester, Manchester University Press, 1983.

Howell, D., 'Beyond the stereotypes: the Independent Labour Party, 1922–1932', *Scottish Labour History Society Journal*, 29, 1994.

Hughes, A. and Hunt, K., 'A culture transformed? Women's lives in Wythenshawe in the 1930s', in A. Davies and S. Fielding (eds), *Workers' Worlds. Cultures and Communities in Manchester and Salford, 1880–1939*, Manchester, Manchester University Press, 1992.

Hunt, K., *Equivocal Feminists. The Social Democratic Federation and the Woman Question, 1884–1911*, Cambridge, Cambridge University Press, 1996.

Hunt, K., 'Fractured universality: the language of British socialism before the First World War', in J. Belchem and N. Kirk (eds), *Languages of Labour*, Aldershot, Ashgate, 1997.

Hunt, K., '"The immense meaning of it all". The challenges of internationalism for British socialist women before the First World War', *Socialist History*, 17, 2000.

Hunt, K., 'Journeying through suffrage: the politics of Dora Montefiore', in C. Eustance, J. Ryan and L. Ugolini (eds), *A Suffrage Reader: Charting Directions in British Suffrage History*, London, Leicester University Press, 2000.

Hunt, K., 'Negotiating the boundaries of the domestic: British socialist women and the politics of consumption', *Women's History Review*, 9, 2, 2000.

Hunt, K. and Hannam, J., 'Propagandising as socialist women: the case of women's columns in British socialist newspapers, 1884–1914', in B. Taithe and T. Thornton (eds), *Propaganda: Political Rhetoric and Identity*, Stroud, Sutton, 1999.

Hurwitz, E.F., 'The international sisterhood', in R. Bridenthal and C. Koonz (eds), *Becoming Visible: Women in European History*, Boston, Houghton Mifflin, 1977.

Israel, K., 'Writing inside the kaleidoscope: re-presenting Victorian women public figures', *Gender and History*, 2, 1, 1990.

James, D., Jowitt, T. and Laybourn, K. (eds), *The Centennial History of the Independent Labour Party*, Halifax, Ryburn, 1992.

Joannou, M. and Purvis, J. (eds), *The Women's Suffrage Movement: New Feminist Perspectives*, Manchester, Manchester University Press, 1998.

John, A.V., *Elizabeth Robins: Staging a Life, 1862–1952*, London, Routledge, 1995.

John, A.V. and Eustance, C. (eds), *The Men's Share? Masculinities, Male Support and Women's Suffrage in Britain, 1890–1920*, London, Routledge, 1992.

Joll, J., *The Second International, 1889–1914*, London, Routledge, 1974.

Kaplan, T., 'Female consciousness and collective action: the case of Barcelona, 1910–18', *Signs*, 7, 3, 1982.

Kaplan, T., *Red City, Blue Period. Social Movements in Picasso's Barcelona*, Berkeley, University of California Press, 1992.

Kapp, Y., *Eleanor Marx: The Crowded Years, 1884–1898*, London, Lawrence & Wishart, 1976.

Kean, H., 'Searching for the past in present defeat: the construction of historical and political identity in British feminism in the 1920s and 1930s', *Women's History Review*, 3, 1, 1994.

BIBLIOGRAPHY

Kean, H., 'Suffrage autobiography: a study of Mary Richardson – suffragette, socialist and fascist', in C. Eustance, J. Ryan and L. Ugolini (eds), *A Suffrage Reader: Charting Directions in British Suffrage History*, London, Leicester University Press, 2000.

Kendall, W., *The Revolutionary Movement in Britain, 1900–21*, London, Weidenfeld & Nicolson, 1969.

Knox, W. (ed.), *Scottish Labour Leaders 1918–39*, Edinburgh, Mainstream, 1984.

Lake, M., 'Socialism and manhood: the case of William Lane', *Labour History*, 50, 1986.

Lake, M., 'Socialism and manhood: a reply to Bruce Scates', *Labour History*, 60, 1991.

Law, C., *Suffrage and Power: The Women's Movement, 1918–1928*, London, I.B. Tauris, 2000.

Laybourn, K., *The Rise of Socialism in Britain*, Stroud, Sutton, 1997.

Ledger, S., *The New Woman: Fiction and Feminism at the Fin de Siècle*, Manchester, Manchester University Press, 1997.

Leneman, L., *A Guid Cause: The Women's Suffrage Movement in Scotland*, Edinburgh, Mercat Press, 1995.

Leventhal, F.M., 'H.N. Brailsford and the *New Leader*', *Journal of Contemporary History*, 9, 1, 1974.

Leventhal, F.M., *The Last Dissenter. H.N. Brailsford and His World*, Oxford, Clarendon, 1985.

Levine, S., 'Workers' wives: gender, class and consumerism in the 1920s United States', *Gender and History*, 3, 1, 1991.

Levy, C., 'Education and self-education: staffing the early ILP', in C. Levy (ed.), *Socialism and the Intelligentsia, 1880–1914*, London, Routledge & Kegan Paul, 1987.

Liddington, J., 'The Women's Peace Crusade: the history of a forgotten campaign', in D. Thompson (ed.), *Over Our Dead Bodies: Women Against the Bomb*, London, Virago, 1983.

Liddington, J., *The Life and Times of a Respectable Rebel. Selina Cooper, 1864–1946*, London, Virago, 1984.

Liddington, J., *The Long Road to Greenham: Feminism and Anti-Militarism in Britain since 1820*, London, Virago, 1989.

Liddington, J. and Norris, J., *One Hand Tied Behind Us: The Rise of the Women's Suffrage Movement*, London, Virago, 1978.

Linklater, A., *An Unhusbanded Life*, London, Hutchinson, 1980.

Lowndes, G.A.N., *Margaret McMillan: The Children's Champion*, London, Museum Press, 1960.

MacCarthy, F., *William Morris: A Life for Our Time*, London, Faber & Faber, 1994.

Macintyre, S., *A Proletarian Science: Marxism in Britain, 1917–37*, Cambridge, Cambridge University Press, 1980.

McKinlay, A., '"Doubtful wisdom and uncertain promise": strategy, ideology and organisation, 1918–1922', in A. McKinlay and R.J. Morris (eds), *The ILP on Clydeside, 1893–1932: From Foundation to Disintegration*, Manchester, Manchester University Press, 1991.

Macnicol, J., *The Movement for Family Allowances, 1918–1945: A Study in Social Policy Development*, London, Heinemann, 1980.

McPhee, C. and Fitzgerald, A. (eds), *The Non-Violent Militant. Selected Writings of Teresa Billington-Greig*, London, Routledge & Kegan Paul, 1987.

Manchester Women's History Group, 'Ideology in bricks and mortar. Women and housing in Manchester between the wars', *Women: Work, Culture and Community, North West Labour History*, 12, 1986–7.

Mappen, E., *Helping Women at Work: The Women's Industrial Council, 1889–1914*, London, Hutchinson, 1985.

Marquand, D., *Ramsay MacDonald*, London, Richard Cohen Books, 1997.
Mayhall, L., 'Creating the "suffragette spirit": British feminism and the historical imagination', *Women's History Review*, 4, 3, 1995.
Melling, J., *Rent Strikes. People's Struggle for Housing in West Scotland, 1890–1916*, Edinburgh, Polygon Books, 1983.
Midgley, C., *Women Against Slavery. The British Campaigns, 1780–1870*, London, Routledge, 1992.
Miliband, R., *Parliamentary Socialism*, London, Merlin Press, 1972.
Milton, N., *John Maclean*, London, Pluto Press, 1973.
Morgan, D., *Suffragists and Liberals*, Oxford, Blackwell, 1975.
Morgan, K.O., *Keir Hardie. Radical and Socialist*, London, Weidenfeld & Nicolson, 1975.
Mulvihill, M., *Charlotte Despard: A Biography*, London, Pandora Press, 1989.
Neville, D., *To Make Their Mark: The Women's Suffrage Movement in the North East of England, 1900–1914*, Newcastle upon Tyne, History Workshop Trust/North East Labour History Society, 1997.
Newton, D.J., *British Labour, European Socialism and the Struggle for Peace, 1889–1914*, Oxford, Clarendon, 1985.
Newton, J.L., Ryan, M.P. and Walkowitz, J.R. (eds), *Sex and Class in Women's History*, London, Routledge & Kegan Paul, 1983.
Offen, K., 'Defining feminism: a comparative historical approach', *Signs*, 14, 1, 1988.
Oldfield, S., *Spinsters of this Parish: The Life and Times of F.M. Mayor and Mary Sheepshanks*, London, Virago, 1984.
Orloff, A.S., 'Reply: citizenship, policy and the political construction of gender interests', *International Labor and Working Class History*, 52, 1997.
Pateman, C., 'Feminist critiques of the public/private dichotomy', in A. Phillips (ed.), *Feminism and Equality*, Oxford, Blackwell, 1987.
Pedersen, S., *Family, Dependence, and the Origins of the Welfare State: Britain and France, 1914–1945*, Cambridge, Cambridge University Press, 1993.
Pelling, H., *Origins of the Labour Party*, Oxford, Oxford University Press, 1965.
Phillips, A., *Divided Loyalties: Dilemmas of Sex and Class*, London, Virago, 1987.
Pierson, S., *Marxism and the Origins of British Socialism*, Ithaca, Cornell University Press, 1973.
Porter, C., *Alexandra Kollontai*, London, Virago, 1980.
Pugh, M., 'Labour and women's suffrage', in K.D. Brown (ed.), *The First Labour Party, 1906–14*, London, Croom Helm, 1985.
Pugh, M., 'Women, food and politics, 1880–1930', *History Today*, 41, 1991.
Pugh, M., *The March of the Women: A Revisionist Analysis of the Campaign for Women's Suffrage, 1866–1914*, Oxford, Oxford University Press, 2000.
Purvis, J., 'Christabel Pankhurst and the Women's Social and Political Union', in M. Joannou and J. Purvis (eds), *The Women's Suffrage Movement: New Feminist Perspectives*, Manchester, Manchester University Press, 1998.
Quataert, J.H., 'Unequal partners in an uneasy alliance: women and the working class in Imperial Germany', in M.J. Boxer and J.H. Quataert (eds), *Socialist Women: European Socialist Feminism in the Nineteenth and Early Twentieth Centuries*, New York, Elsevier, 1978.
Quataert, J.H., *Reluctant Feminists in German Social Democracy, 1885–1917*, Princeton, NJ, Princeton University Press, 1979.
Riley, D., *'Am I That Name?' Feminism and the Category of 'Women' in History*, London, Macmillan, 1988.

Roberts, E., 'Women and the domestic economy, 1890–1970: the oral evidence', in M. Drake (ed.), *Time, Family and Community. Perspectives on Family and Community History*, Oxford, Blackwell, 1994.

Rose, S.O., 'Gender and labor history: the nineteeth century legacy', *International Review of Social History*, 38, 1993.

Rosen, A., *Rise Up Women! The Militant Campaign of the Women's Social and Political Union, 1903–1914*, London, Routledge & Kegan Paul, 1974.

Rowan, C., 'Women in the Labour Party, 1906–1920', *Feminist Review*, 12, 1982.

Rowan, C., '"Mothers vote Labour!" The state, the labour movement and working-class mothers, 1900–1918', in R. Brunt and C. Rowan (eds), *Feminism, Culture and Politics*, London, Lawrence & Wishart, 1982.

Rowbotham, S., *Women, Resistance and Revolution*, London, Allen Lane, 1972.

Rowbotham, S., *Friends of Alice Wheeldon*, London, Pluto, 1986.

Rowbotham, S., *Women in Movement: Feminism and Social Action*, London, Routledge, 1992.

Rowbotham, S., Segal, L. and Wainwright, H., *Beyond the Fragments: Feminism and the Making of Socialism*, London, Merlin, 1979.

Rowbotham, S. and Weeks, J., *Socialism and the New Life: The Personal and Sexual Politics of Edward Carpenter and Havelock Ellis*, London, Pluto, 1977.

Rubinstein, D., *Before the Suffragettes: Women's Emancipation in the 1890s*, Brighton, Harvester, 1986.

Rupp, L.J., 'Constructing internationalism: the case of transnational women's organizations, 1888–1945', *American Historical Review*, 99, 1994.

Rupp, L.J., 'Sexuality and politics in the early twentieth century: the case of the international women's movement', *Feminist Studies*, 23, 3, 1997.

Rupp, L.J., *Worlds of Women: The Making of an International Women's Movement*, Princeton, NJ, Princeton University Press, 1997.

Ryan, L., 'A question of loyalty: war, nation and feminism in early twentieth-century Ireland', *Women's Studies International Forum*, 20, 1, 1997.

Saraceno, C., 'Reply: citizenship is context specific', *International Labor and Working-Class History*, 52, 1997.

Sargent, L. (ed.), *Women and Revolution: The Unhappy Marriage of Marxism and Feminism: A Debate on Class and Patriarchy*, London, Pluto, 1981.

Savage, M., *The Dynamics of Working-Class Politics: The Labour Movement in Preston, 1880–1914*, Cambridge, Cambridge University Press, 1987.

Savage, M., 'Urban politics and the rise of the Labour Party, 1919–39', in L. Jamieson and H. Corr (eds), *State, Private Life and Political Change*, Basingstoke, Macmillan, 1990.

Savage, M. and Miles, A., *The Re-making of the British Working Class, 1840–1940*, London, Routledge, 1994.

Scates, B., 'Socialism, feminism and the case of William Lane', *Labour History*, 59, 1990.

Scott, G., *Feminism and the Politics of Working Women: The Women's Co-operative Guild, 1880s to the Second World War*, London, UCL Press, 1998.

Scott, J.W., *Gender and the Politics of History*, New York, Columbia University Press, 1988.

Scott, J.W., 'The imagination of Olympe de Gouges', in E.J. Yeo (ed.), *Mary Wollstonecraft and 200 Years of Feminisms*, London, Rivers Oram, 1997.

Sheffield Film Co-op, *Red Skirts on Clydeside: A Film about Women's Political Past*, Sheffield, Sheffield Film Co-op.

Sherrick, R.L., 'Toward universal sisterhood', *Women's Studies International Forum*, 5, 6, 1982.

Smart, J., 'Feminists, food and the fair price: the cost of living demonstrations in Melbourne, August–September 1917', *Labour History*, 50, 1986.

Smart, J., 'Jennie Baines: suffrage and an Australian connection', in J. Purvis and S.S. Holton (eds), *Votes for Women*, London, Routledge, 2000.

Smith, H.L., 'Sex vs. class: British feminists and the Labour movement, 1919–29', *Historian*, 47, 1984.

Smith, J., 'Taking the leadership of the labour movement: the ILP in Glasgow, 1906–1914', in A. McKinlay and R.J. Morris (eds), *The ILP on Clydeside, 1893–1932: From Foundation to Disintegration*, Manchester, Manchester University Press, 1991.

Smyth, J.J., 'Rents, peace, votes: working-class women and political activity in the First World War', in E. Breitenbach and E. Gordon (eds), *Out of Bounds: Women in Scottish Society, 1800–1945*, Edinburgh, Edinburgh University Press, 1992.

Sowerwine, C., *Sisters or Citizens? Women and Socialism in France since 1876*, Cambridge, Cambridge University Press, 1982.

Sowerwine, C., 'The socialist women's movement from 1850 to 1940', in R. Bridenthal, C. Koonz and S. Stuard (eds), *Becoming Visible: Women in European History*, Boston, Houghton Mifflin, 1987.

Stanley, L., *The Auto/Biographical I. The Theory and Practice of Feminist Auto/Biography*, Manchester, Manchester University Press, 1992.

Stanley, L. with Morley, A., *The Life and Death of Emily Wilding Davison*, London, Women's Press, 1988.

Steedman, C., *Childhood, Culture and Class in Britain: Margaret McMillan, 1860–1931*, London, Virago, 1990.

Tanner, D., Thane, P. and Tiratsoo, N. (eds), *Labour's First Century*, Cambridge, Cambridge University Press, 2000.

Taylor, A., *Annie Besant*, Oxford, Oxford University Press, 1992.

Taylor, B., *Eve and the New Jerusalem: Socialism and Feminism in the Nineteenth Century*, London, Virago, 1983.

Thane, P., 'The women of the British Labour Party and feminism, 1906–45', in H.L. Smith (ed.), *British Feminism in the Twentieth Century*, Aldershot, Edward Elgar, 1990.

Thompson, E.P., 'Homage to Tom Maguire', in A. Briggs and J. Saville (eds), *Essays in Labour History*, Vol. 1, London, Macmillan, 1967.

Thompson, E.P., *William Morris: Romantic to Revolutionary*, London, Merlin Press, 1977.

Thompson, L., *The Enthusiasts: A Biography of John and Katharine Bruce Glasier*, London, Victor Gollancz, 1971.

Thompson, P., *Socialists, Liberals and Labour. The Struggle for London 1885–1914*, London, Routledge & Kegan Paul, 1967.

Tsuzuki, C., *H.M. Hyndman and British Socialism*, Oxford, Oxford University Press, 1961.

Tuckett, A., 'Enid Stacy', *North West Labour History Society*, Bulletin 7, 1980–1.

Ugolini, L., ' "It is only justice to grant women's suffrage": Independent Labour Party men and women's suffrage, 1893–1905', in C. Eustance, J. Ryan and L. Ugolini (eds), *A Suffrage Reader: Charting Directions in British Suffrage History*, London, Leicester University Press, 2000.

van der Linden, M., 'Working-class consumer power', *International Labor and Working Class History*, 46, 1994.

Vellacott, J., 'Feminist consciousness and the First World War', *History Workshop Journal*, 23, 1987.

Vernon, B.D., *Ellen Wilkinson*, London, Croom Helm, 1982.

Vernon, J., *Politics and the People. A Study in English Political Culture*, Cambridge, Cambridge University Press, 1993.
Vicinus, M., *Independent Women: Work and Community for Single Women, 1850–1920*, London, Virago, 1985.
Vogel, L., *Marxism and the Oppression of Women*, London, Pluto, 1983.
Waites, B., *A Class Society at War. England, 1914–18*, Leamington Spa, Berg, 1987.
Walker, L., 'Party political women: a comparative study of Liberal women and the Primrose League, 1890–1914', in J. Rendall (ed.), *Equal or Different. Women's Politics 1800–1914*, Oxford, Blackwell, 1987.
Ward, M., 'Nationalism, pacifism and internationalism. Louie Bennett, Hanna Sheehy-Skeffington, and the problems of "defining feminism"', in A. Bradley and M. Valiulis (eds), *Gender and Sexuality in Modern Ireland*, Amherst, University of Massachusetts Press, 1997.
Waters, C., *British Socialists and the Politics of Popular Culture, 1884–1914*, Manchester, Manchester University Press, 1990.
Waters, C., 'New women and socialist-feminist fiction: the novels of Isabella Ford and Katharine Bruce Glasier', in A. Ingram and D. Patai (eds), *Discovering Forgotten Radicals: British Women Writers, 1859–1939*, Chapel Hill, University of North Carolina Press, 1993.
Weeks, J., *Sex, Politics and Society: The Regulation of Sexuality since 1800*, London, Longman, 1981.
Weller, K., *'Don't be a Soldier!' The Radical Anti-War Movement in North London, 1914–18*, London, Journeyman, 1985.
Wheedon, C., 'The limits of patriarchy: German feminist writers', in H. Forsas-Scott (ed.), *Textual Liberation: European Feminist Writing in the Twentieth Century*, London, Routledge, 1991.
White, S., 'Soviets in Britain: the Leeds Convention of 1917', *International Review of Social History*, 19, 1974.
Wiltsher, A., *Most Dangerous Women. Feminist Peace Campaigners of the Great War*, London, Pandora Press, 1985.
Winslow, B., *Sylvia Pankhurst. Sexual Politics and Political Activism*, London, UCL Press, 1996.
Winter, J.M., *Socialism and the Challenge of War. Ideas and Politics in Britain, 1912–18*, London, Routledge & Kegan Paul, 1974.
Woodhouse, T., *Nourishing the Liberty Tree: Liberals and Labour in Leeds, 1880–1914*, Keele, Keele University Press, 1996.
Yeo, E.J. (ed.), *Mary Wollstonecraft and 200 Years of Feminisms*, London, Rivers Oram, 1997.
Yeo, S., 'A new life: the religion of socialism in Britain, 1883–1896', *History Workshop Journal*, 4, 1977.

Unpublished theses

Balshaw, J.M., 'Suffrage, solidarity and strife: political partnerships and the women's movement, 1880–1930', PhD, University of Greenwich, 1999.
Beals, P., 'Fabian feminism, gender, politics and culture in London, 1880–1930', PhD, Rutgers University, 1989.
Brown, H., 'Pacifist feminism in Britain, 1870–1902: "The truest form of patriotism"', DPhil, University of York, 1999.

Collins, C., 'Women and Labour politics in Britain, 1893–1932', PhD, London School of Economics, 1991.
Eustance, C., ' "Daring to be free": the evolution of women's political identities in the Women's Freedom League, 1907–30', DPhil, University of York, 1993.
Graves, P., 'Women in British working-class politics, 1883–1939', PhD, University of Pittsburgh, 1989.
Holloway, G., 'A common cause? Class dynamics in the industrial women's movement, 1888–1918', PhD, University of Sussex, 1995.
Honeycutt, K., 'Clara Zetkin: a left-wing socialist and feminist in Wilhelmian Germany', PhD, Columbia University, 1975.
Hopkin, D., 'The newspapers of the Independent Labour Party, 1893–1906', PhD, University of Aberystwyth, 1981.
Lintell, H., 'Lily Bell: socialist and feminist, 1894–1898', MA, Bristol Polytechnic, 1990.
Lohman, J.S., 'Sex or class? English socialists and the woman question, 1884–1914', PhD, Syracuse University, 1979.
Reid, C.A.N., 'The origins and development of the Independent Labour Party in Manchester and Salford, 1880–1914', PhD, University of Hull, 1981.
Rigby, K.A., 'Annot Robinson: socialist, suffragist, peacemaker. A biographical study', MA, Manchester Polytechnic, 1986.
Ugolini, L., 'Independent Labour Party men and women's suffrage in Britain, 1893–1914', PhD, University of Greenwich, 1997.
Walker, L., 'The women's movement in England in the late nineteenth and early twentieth centuries', PhD, Manchester University, 1984.

Unpublished papers

Hunt, K., 'Making socialist woman: politicisation, gender and the Social Democratic Federation, 1884–1911', paper to Ninth Berkshire Conference on the History of Women, Vassar College, 1993.
Hunt, K., 'Internationalism in practice: the politics of a British socialist and feminist before the First World War', paper to European Social Science History Conference, Amsterdam, March 1998.
Thurlow, J.B., 'Julia Varley, 1871–1952', University of Sussex, 2000.

INDEX

adult suffrage 10, 12, 20, 23, 37, 48, 64, 106, 107, 108; *see also* limited women's suffrage
Adult Suffrage Society 110, 111, 112, 116, 118, 120, 123, 126, 175; socialist women as members of 1, 41, 42, 119, 127, 172
Aimée Furniss 83
Aked, Reverend C.F. 47
Alberti, Johanna 19
Alexander, Sally 76n55
Allan, Janie 113
Allison, Doris 198n59
Amalgamated Union of Clothing Operatives 46
Anderson, Bonnie 17
Anderson, William 100n20, 117, 123, 124, 130n26
Annakin, Ethel 35, 41, 47, 85; *see also* Snowden, Ethel
anti-imperialism 168, 179, 180, 190, 193–4
anti-militarism 125, 167, 171, 181, 182–3, 184, 185, 186; socialist women and 182–3, 187–91; versus pacifism 167, 182–3, 185–6, 187, 189
anti-slavery campaigns 136–7
anti-war campaigns 42, 43, 44, 138; opposition to First World War 183–91
Ashley, Sir William 147
Asquith, H.H. 122, 123, 125
autobiography 45, 48–9; reminiscences 48–9; suffrage activists 56n94
autonomy, women's 25, 32, 71, 89, 97, 174
Aveling, Edward 62–3, 100n20
Ayles, Bertha 39

Baines, Jennie 34, 39, 136
Baker, Jennie 118, 120, 130n28, n29,
133n136; adult suffrage 110, 111, 122, 132n104
Baker, John 130n28, n36
Banks, Olive 21, 48
Barbour, Mrs 151
Batten, Ellen 80
Bax, Ernest Belfort 21, 59, 65, 196n7
Beanland, Harriet 34
Bebel, August 17, 57, 58–9, 62–3, 75n8
Bell, Florence Harrison 31, 36
Bell, Lily 9, 10, 35, 61, 85, 100n7; male power 64–5; marriage and family, views of 62, 68; pseudonym of Isabella Bream Pearce, 9, 35, 75n25; sex versus class 63–4, 117–18; women's columns 90, 92, 102n65; women's emancipation 66, 83; women's suffrage 109, 112, 113, 114, 121
Bell, Tom 151
Belt, George 170–1
Bentham, Ethel 197n29
Besant, Annie 7, 36, 37–8, 67, 85; *The Link* 75n21
Billington-Greig, Teresa 10, 33, 39, 41, 71, 72–3, 76n46, 131n82; *The Consumer in Revolt*, 135, 156–9; consumption, politics of 156–61; suffrage 109, 121
biographical approaches 12, 25, 32–4, 52n7
Birch, Minnie 180, 198n61
birth control 37, 44, 74, 96, 128; as a political issue 60, 98
Blatchford, Robert 69
Boards of Guardians 5, 34, 37, 81, 82, 93; Battersea 47; Bradford 46; Poplar 34; St Pancras 82; Stockport 35
Boer War 181
Boggart Hole Clough 83, 85
Bolshevik Revolution 166, 177

221

INDEX

Bondfield, Margaret 7, 8, 31, 39, 56n97, 120, 122, 206; Adult Suffrage Society 110, 111; autobiography of 48; internationalism 177, 178, 198n42; peace 185, 186, 191; People's Suffrage Federation, 122; suffrage 119, 125, 127, 132n110
Borrett, Constance 128
Bosch, Mineke 169
bourgeois women's movement 17, 40, 62, 171, 174, 175, 205; *see also* women's movement
Boyce, Emma 42–3, 44
Bradford Trades Council 46
Brailsford, H.N. 153
Bream Pearce, Isabella 29n45, 31, 35, 46, 92; as Lily Bell, 9, 35, 75n25; women's suffrage 109; *see also* Bell, Lily
Bridges Adams, Mrs 175
Bristol Socialist Society 4, 7, 39, 50
British Socialist party 2–3, 6, 31, 43, 39, 82, 123, 126, 140, 144, 145, 160, 182; branches (East London) 126, (Salford) 81; consumption 142, 143; internationalism 174; pacifism 181; women organisers 39, 140; Women's Council 140–2, 144
Brockway, Fenner 113, 194
Brown, Gordon 153–4
Browne, Stella 104n106
Bruce Glasier, John 50, 68, 83, 100n20, 101n34, 102n39, 103n78
Bruce Glasier, Katharine 16, 22, 33, 36, 38, 39, 45, 47, 48, 52n12, 56n97, 66, 81,100n20, 102n34; class, definition of 64, 118–19; described as 84, 85, 87; disarmament, 189–90; economic assistance to families 71; internationalism and peace 185, 186, 187, 192, 194; journalism 61, 75n20; new political woman 83; novels 60–1, 83; personal life/marriage 68, 85; political journey of 1, 7, 49–51; separate women's organisation 90–1; socialism and feminism 50; women as a political group, 50, 51; women as wives and mothers 51, 185; women's nature, 70; women's suffrage 50–1, 114, 115; writing as Iona 51, 75n25; *see also* Conway, Katharine St John; Iona
Bruley, Sue 179, 180
Burton, Antoinette 193

Campbell, Paul 49
Carpenter, Edward 18, 39, 59, 68, 82
Catt, Carrie Chapman 168
Chartists 27n16, 46, 118, 120, 136
Chew, Ada Nield 35, 39, 41, 45–6, 124, 131n69; adult suffrage, 110, 111, 116; class versus sex 118; limited suffrage 119, 121; motherhood, marriage and family, views on 68–9, 70; women's suffrage 116–17
child care 34, 68, 71, 170, 171, 197n18
Child Care Committees 144
children's allowances 74, 154, 155
Christian Socialist 49
Christian World 38
Citizen Committees 143
citizens 50, 62, 66, 71, 73, 86, 120, 121, 181
citizenship 1, 11, 12, 72–4, 93, 117, 121, 127, 187
Clarion 4, 10, 58, 61, 88, 108, 141, 172; women's column in 90, 112; van 41, 67
Clash 84–5
class: analysis 185, 205; consciousness 88, 191; divisions 128; interests 175; issues 99; loyalties 11, 12, 36; oppression 57, 58–9, 62; relations 32; socialist women, background of 35–6, 37–40, 45, 90–1
class struggle/war 3, 5, 18, 21, 59, 60, 64, 67, 117, 134, 141, 142, 146, 150, 180, 183, 186, 193, 194
Clayton, Joseph 23, 181
Close, Agnes 40, 45–6
Clynes, J.R. 126
Coates Hansen, Marion 80, 116, 118
Cobden Sanderson, Mrs 36, 184
collective needs 66, 77n57
Collins, Clare 24–5, 41, 80
Comintern 8, 177, 179, 180, 198n59
Common Cause 116
Commonweal 62
The Communist 179
Communist Party 7, 8, 43, 44, 153, 179–80, 203; and ILP 6, 8, 44, 178; and Labour Party 177
communist women 8, 31, 44, 177, 178, 179–80, 190–1; internationalism of 194–5
comradeship 73, 82, 91, 118, 185, 192
Conciliation Bill 123
Connell, J. 87
conscientious objectors 47

INDEX

Conservative Party 2, 80, 81
The Consumer in Revolt 135, 156–9
Consumers' Council 147
consumption 21, 60, 204; impact of war 144–7; politics of 134–5, 136, 137–42, 146, 148, 150, 153, 154–61, 161n4, n6, 203, 205; trade unions and 137–8, 142, 143; as a woman's issue 139–40, 144; women as consumers 137, 139, 140, 141; *see also* production
Conway, Katharine St John 22, 33, 36, 38, 39; personal life and marriage 67–8; speaker 84, 101n34; *see also* Bruce Glasier, Katharine
Cooper, Selina 20, 35, 39, 41, 115, 119
co-operative commonwealth 59
cost of living 143, 144; protests 136, 138, 147, 160, 161n6
Crawfurd, Helen 31, 43–4, 113, 150, 151, 183, 186, 187–9, 198n50, 206; and Communist Party 177, 178, 179, 194
Crick, Martin 20
Cross, Mary 94
Currell, Melville 97

Daily Herald 123, 142, 150, 151, 159; leagues 143
Davies, Margaret Llewelyn 106, 120, 122–3, 124, 126, 137
Davis, Jenny 68
Dawson, Julia 61; adult suffrage 110, 112, 114, 116, 118; marriage and free love 62; pen name of Mrs D. Middleton Worrall 75n25; separate women's organisations 90–1; women as political activists 88; women's suffrage 108, 112, 121
De Gouges, Olympe 24
De Mattos, W.B. 67, 84
Dean, Elizabeth 81
democracy 10, 12, 46, 120–1, 125
democratic centralism 8, 177
democratic socialism 124
democratic suffragists 106, 107; franchise 123
Derbyshire, Ethel 34
Despard, Charlotte 36, 37, 71, 186, 187, 199n76; Adult Suffrage Society 110–11, 116; suffrage 125, 126
difference 79; and equality 79, 169, 192
disarmament 189–91
The Disinherited Family 154

Dollan, Agnes 43–4, 82, 155; Glasgow Women's Housing Association 150, 151; separate organisation for women 95–6
Dollan, Patrick 43, 103n95, 104n103, 126, 151, 199n91
domestic: labour 58; issues 90–1, 95, 141, 144, 148; politics of 147–9, 155–6, 160; sphere 134–5, 137

East London Federation of Suffragettes 42–3, 144, 145, 152, 184
economic independence 154; of socialist women 37–9; socialist women's attitude to 63, 65, 67, 70–2, 93, 128
endowment of motherhood 71, 93, 154
Engels, Frederick 17, 57, 58, 63, 75n8
equal: rights 44, 50, 62, 64, 67, 76n55, 81, 121, 175; position 72, 73, 83, 84–5, 89, 91
equality 2, 21, 79, 80, 100n2, n3; difference and 24–5, 79, 169, 192; economic 31, 60, 115; political 115, 120, 127; socialist rhetoric of 57, 60, 202–3; *see also* sex: equality
ethical socialism 3, 4, 59
ethnicity 11, 24

Fabian Society 2, 3, 37, 13n7, 37, 39, 71, 84; women 172, 176
Fabian Women's Group 4, 13n7, 28n29, 69, 71, 93, 143, 144
family: economic assistance 70–1; gender roles in 68–9; political issue, 60, 67, 171
family allowances 44, 70, 72, 73–4, 155; *see also* children's allowances; endowment of motherhood
family wage 68, 71, 154
'Famous Four' 22, 24, 33, 52n12
Fawcett, Millicent 109, 126
feminism 24, 33, 179, 180, 206; communism and 179; 'first 'wave' 10, 20, 32; histories of 24, 32, 48; ILP/SDF attitude to 21–2; socialism and 1–2, 9, 12, 17–20, 25, 33, 40, 58, 62, 105, 121, 204–6; strands of 11, 12, 25, 77n59, 172, 189
feminist: aspirations 72, 73, 121; history/historians 17, 20, 23, 24, 25; ideas 17, 92, 158; issues 48, 167; pacifism 181, 182, 185, 188, 189, 192;

politics 37, 47, 48; socialists as 80, 86, 127; type of 10, 14n33, 24
fiction 60–1
First World War 6, 7, 8, 22, 39, 41, 42–3, 47, 87, 140, 148, 169, 191, 193; cost of living protests 136, 160; internationalism 176–7; opposition to 143, 181, 183–91; rent strikes 147, 150; women's suffrage 124–6
food: politics of 146, 147
food riots 135–6, 147, 150, 161n6
Food Reform Association 144
force 180, 187–9
Ford, Isabella 20, 29n45, 36, 38, 40, 41, 75n20, 102n52, 132n125, 177; adult suffrage, view of 115–16, 132n115; conversion to socialism 45, 46, 48; integration of socialism and feminism 48, 64, 82, 124; International Woman Suffrage Alliance, involvement in 175, 176, 193; Leeds ILP 100n10; motherhood, views on 68–9; novels 60–1, 83; opposition to war 184, 187; pacifism of 181; peace 181, 183, 190; women's columns 93; women's suffrage 71–2, 109, 112, 115, 125; and Women's Social and Political Union 122
Ford, Jane 115
Forecasts of the Coming Century 66
Forward 20, 35, 43, 113, 118, 150, 151, 159; women's column in 113
Foster, Mary 40
Fox, Pamela 61
Francis, Martin 21
Frank, Dana 137, 138
free speech campaigns 2, 83, 86
friendship networks: international 170, 180

Gallacher, William 151
Gas Workers and General Labourers' Union 143
Gault, Helen 10, 31, 155, 86, 96, 98, 99
Gawthorpe, Mary 28n24, 31, 35, 41, 47, 121
gender: divisions 60, 68, 69, 79, 85, 128; identities 11, 41, 65, 87; inequalities 40, 44, 57, 99; issues 11, 21, 22, 13, 40, 43, 80, 146; loyalties 12, 36, 175, 203–5; perspective 12, 16, 18, 30n63, 31, 50, 57, 140, 195; politics 25, 35, 38, 45; relations 32, 61, 203; roles 5, 19, 32, 61, 68, 84, 99; socialist construction of 58
gendering of: consumption 140, 146, 147, 148, 153–4; economics 157–8; everyday life 134; housing/rent 147–9, 150; internationalism 180, 192; peace 167, 182, 183, 184; politics 9, 17, 22, 21, 24, 49, 57, 62–3, 82, 88, 99, 135, 146, 151
General Strike 191
Girls' Club Dinners 144
Gladstone, W.E. 46
Glasgow rent strikes 147, 150, 186
Glasgow Woman's Labour Party 35, 91–2, 101n31, 102n65
Glasgow Women's Housing Association 43, 150, 151
Glasgow Workers' Housing Association 151
Glasier, Lizzie 92, 103n78
Gleichheit (Equality) 89
Gordon, Eleanor 20
Gough, Mrs 152
Graves, Pamela 19, 37, 44, 97, 178
Gray, Mary 34, 36, 46–7, 108
Grogan, Susan 32
Groves, Florence 75n21
Gurney, Peter 139

Hall, Catherine 24
Hall, Stuart 11
Hammersmith Socialist Society 4
Hannam, June 22, 23
Hardie, Keir 3, 22; women's suffrage 22, 59, 113, 115; internationalism and peace 168, 192, 183
Harker, Elsie 102n66, 108, 119, 129n17
Harper, Mrs 92
Harrison, Brian 158, 159
Harrison, Royden 144
Henderson, Arthur 123
Hendin, Clara 35, 92, 110, 139–40
Hicks, Amie 33, 36, 37, 39, 40, 46, 83, 100n20; suffrage 108, 118
Hicks, Frances 36
Hicks, Margaretta 37, 39, 60, 82, 162n31; adult suffrage, 123; consumption, politics of 140–2, 147, 152, 156, 157–8, 159–60; cost of living campaign 143–4; food question 144–6; internationalism 185; *The Link* 75n21, 140; militancy, views on 119

INDEX

Hicks, William 37, 100n20
Hinton, James 21
historiography 11–12, 16, 51; biographical approaches 25, 32–4, 48, 51; gender and labour history 24, 25, 29n54, n56, 30n63; labour history 11, 12, 17, 18–19, 20–22; socialist history, new approaches 20, 22–3, 24–5; suffrage history 12, 19–20, 23
History of the Social Democratic Federation 20
Hobson, J.A. 154
Holdsworth, Ethel Carnie 61
Holton, Sandra 20, 32, 34, 106, 107, 123; *Feminism and Democracy* 107
Honeycutt, Karen 89
Hope, Mabel 121
Horrabin, Winifred 96, 98, 99, 102n54
housewives 149; political potential of 99, 136–8, 141–2, 143, 144, 146, 151, 160
housing: as rent 135; as welfare issue 135, 147, 150; as a woman's issue 149, 150
How Martyn, Edith 118
Howell, David 13n10, 22, 34, 153
human 202; race 193; rights 10, 65, 121; suffrage 42, 106, 115, 119, 125
humanist 10, 106
humanity 65, 123, 193
Hunt, Karen 23, 59
Hyndman, Henry Myers 21, 144, 147, 182

Independent Labour Party (ILP) 2, 5, 22–3, 61, 71, 88, 121, 130n36, 154, 163n95, 200n109; adult suffrage 108–9, 110–11, 112, 126; anti-militarism, 125, 181; Communist Party, attitude to 6, 8, 44, 177–8; Coming of Age conference 81; constructing its own history 16, 33, 55n76, 87, 124; cost of living 143; disarmament 189–90; feminism, attitude to 21–2; force 189; housing 150, 163n84; Labour Party, relationship with 126, 153, 179; League against Imperialism 194; limited franchise 106, 112–13, 126, 175; Living Wage campaign 72, 99, 126, 135, 153–5, 160; married couples in 82, 100–1n20; pacifism/peace 180, 183, 184, 188; SDF, relationship with 170–1, 172–4; Social Democratic Party, relationship with 173–4; sex versus class 117–18; sex equality, attitude to 21, 33, 46, 48, 60, 79–81, 93, 94, 95, 96, 100n3, 110; socialism of 3–4, 6, 39, 64, 155, 170; stereotype of 4, 5, 21–4, 29n38, 33–4; welfare 72–4; women as members of 1, 3, 7, 13n6, 31, 34–7, 39–44, 46–8, 53n26, 115, 136; women, recruitment of 86, 94–5, 127; women delegates to annual conferences 23, 81, 97, 100n13; women organisers 39, 47, 156; women's activities in 81–2, 128; women's attitude towards 79–80; women's branches of 91, 102n65; women's emancipation, attitudes to 59, 68, 74, 154, 155; women's influence in 153; women organising separately 90, 91–2, 93–9, 104n101; Women's Social and Political Union, attitude to 121, 122, 132n104; women's suffrage 22–3, 50–1, 60, 109, 112–13, 118, 123–4, 125–6, 132n105

Independent Labour Party branches 80; Ashton 81, 82; Bradford 110; Bristol 39; Glasgow; 20, 81, 95, 100n3, 102n62; Leeds 46, 47, 79, 100n10; Leicester 126; Limehouse 54n46; Liverpool 87; London 80, 81; London and Southern Counties Divisional Council 95; Manchester 41, 85, 100n10, 102n66, 110; Newcastle 39; North East Federation 82; Richmond 126; Scottish Divisional Council of 178; St Pancras 94; Stockton 110, 131n28; Wales 128; Wolverhampton 94; Woolwich 126, 130n72

Independent Labour Party women 22, 35, 98, 110; ILP, view of 79–80; international congresses, attendance at 170, 173–4, 176; internationalism 190, 192; Labour and Socialist International 179; Living Wage campaign 155–6; peace 181–3, 188; women's groups 25, 93–5, 114; women's suffrage, 115, 122, 124, 204

individual rights/individualism 66, 74, 77n57, 122

International Communist Women's Conferences 179

International Conference of Socialist and Labour Women (Berne 1915) 177

International Council of Women 166, 168, 171, 192; London Congress, (1899) 170, 174–5

INDEX

International Socialist Congress, Leeds 64
International Woman Suffrage Alliance 166, 168–9, 171, 175, 192; socialists, conflict with 175–6, 193
International Women's Day 180
international women's peace congress, The Hague (1915) 177, 184, 185
internationalism 187, 188, 190, 204, 205; gendering of 180, 192; impact of war 176–7, 193–4; meaning for socialist women 166–7, 168–9, 171, 176, 187, 192–6, 205; meaning for women's movement 168–9, 176; socialist definition of 167–8, 192; socialist internationals 171, 182–4, 194–5; woman-focused 167, 168, 174, 191, 194, 195–6; women's/suffrage internationals 171, 173–6, 192
Iona 61, 112; pen name of Katharine Bruce Glasier 50, 75n25
Ireland 7, 187
Irish women's movement 169

Jarvis (Scott), Rose 33, 34, 45, 92
Jewson, Dorothy 41, 44, 47, 73, 98, 127, 177, 206; internationalism 178, 194; women organising separately 95, 96
Johnston, Tom 113, 120
Joint Food Supply Committee 145
journalism 43; socialist women as journalists 35, 36, 38, 61, 81, 111, 170, 184
Justice 45, 58, 59, 61, 63, 64, 65, 67, 86, 141, 145, 159; suffrage 111–12; women's column in 90, 144, 146, 191

Kahan, Zelda 114, 182
Kaplan, Temma 136
Kenney, Annie 122
Kollontai, Alexandra 170, 198n61
Kough, Kathleen 42, 110, 113–14
Kramers, Martina 197n36

Labour and Socialist International 166, 178–9, 198n52
Labour Church 61, 88; Leeds 47
Labour Leader 16, 50, 58, 59–60, 61, 80, 81, 87, 127, 159, 172, 175, 193; cost of living 144; PSF 123; women's column in 90, 93, 109; Women's Peace Crusade 186; women's suffrage 112–13, 120, 124, 125

Labour Party 1, 6, 7, 8, 41, 72, 74, 97, 99, 104n106, 154, 156, 172, 109, 154; Communist Party, relationship with 177–8; history of 18–19, 21; ILP, relationship with 126, 153, 179; National Union of Women's Suffrage Societies, alliance with 20, 33, 82, 113, 116, 124, 132n121; People's Suffrage Federation 123; welfare issues 72, 98, 135, 163n92; women in 6, 17, 24–5, 36, 43, 44, 128, 163n92, 134–5, 130n28, 134–5, 198n52, 206; women MPs and councillors 43, 44, 48, 56n97; women voters, attitude to 86, 103n71, 127; women's sections in 36, 43, 94, 96, 97; women's suffrage 111, 115, 121, 125, 126
Labour Party Women's Conference 98, 99, 126, 190, 155
Labour Prophet 61
Labour Representation Committee 6, 115, 168
Labour Woman 183
Laird, Mary 150
Lancashire and Cheshire Textile and Other Workers' Labour Representation Committee 110, 115, 118
Lansbury, Dolly 122
Lansbury, George 150
Lanchester, Edith 62, 67, 75n30
Law, Cheryl 100n2, 127
Lawrence, Susan 56n97, 98, 125
Laybourn, Keith 23, 77n57
League Against Imperialism 194
League of Nations Union 191
Lee, H.W. 145
Leeds Convention (1917) 177
Leeds Tailoresses' Union 40, 46
Leeds Weekly Citizen 103n71
Leeds Women's Suffrage Society 109
Lenin, V.I. 154
Lerner, Gerda 25
Levine, Susan 137
Liberal Party 2, 3, 80, 81
Liddington, Jill 19, 20, 45, 106, 180, 181, 189
limited women's suffrage 9, 20, 21, 22, 25, 33, 42, 107, 112, 118–26, 128; versus adult suffrage 106, 108, 109–11, 114–17, 121, 123, 172–3, 175, 205
The Link (1888) 75n21
The Link (1911–12) 75n21, 82, 140

INDEX

Living Wage Campaign (ILP) 72, 99, 126, 135, 153–5, 160; socialist women and 154–5
London Kitchen Gardens 144
London Ropemakers' Union 40
London Trades Council 143
Longman, Mary 198n42
Lowrie, Barbara 79

Macarthur, Mary 42, 56n20, 110, 122, 125
MacDonald, James Ramsay 12, 67, 154; internationalism of 167–8
MacDonald, Margaret 39, 40, 68, 69, 71, 115, 170, 197n18; 'Belt case' 170–1; internationalism 172, 192, 204
McMillan, Margaret 22, 33, 36, 38, 45, 48, 56n97; biography of 20, 32; fiction 61; socialism and feminism, views on 48–9, 122
McMillan, Rachel 38
Maguire, Tom 100n10
making war on war 167, 184, 191
manhood suffrage 106, 107, 123, 124; Bill 113, 122
Mann, Jean 100n3
Mappen, Ellen 10
Marquand, David 167
marriage: free love 62, 67; new type of 67–8; paid work, and 67, 71; as political issue 60, 63, 81, 104n106
married women's work 67, 71, 95
Marshall, Catherine 125, 183, 185, 187, 188
Martyn, Caroline 22, 33, 36, 38, 75n20, 85; marriage, views on 62, 67; representation of 87
Marx, Eleanor 4, 33, 36, 39, 50, 100n20, 170; woman question 62–3
Marxism 5, 17, 21, 58, 59, 134
Mattison, Alf 84
Middleton Worrall, Mrs D. 75n25
Middleton, Mary 192
Midgley, Clare 136
militancy: suffrage 43–4, 50, 91, 93, 181, 184; socialist attitudes to suffrage militancy 113, 119–20, 187
The Militant Suffrage Movement 159
minimum wage 140–1, 154
Mitchell, Hannah 33, 35, 47, 67, 81, 82, 184; women organising separately 90, 96

mixed-sex politics 19, 20, 25, 51, 79, 80, 99, 169, 193, 203
Montefiore, Dora 10, 31, 33, 64, 92, 148, 174, 184; adult suffrage 109, 123; anti-militarism 183; 'Belt case' 170–1; communism 177; imperialism 194–5; internationalism 170, 192–3, 197n19, n35; international congresses, attendance at 171, 172, 175, 176, 204; political journey of 1–2, 41, 117; women's columns 61, 64; women's emancipation/woman question 65, 67, 69, 71; women's suffrage 109, 112, 126; Zetkin, relationship with 180, 198n61, 201n151, 206
Monthly Bulletin (ILP) 95
Morgan, Kenneth 168
Morris, William 2, 4, 39, 59, 68
motherhood 67–9, 81; endowment of 71
Muir, Mary 110, 114, 120, 133n136
municipal bodies 5, 19
Munitions Act 150

National Administrative Council (ILP) 36, 42, 44; women members of 97, 112, 122; women, recruitment of 94–5, 127
National Aid Corps 144
National Council for Adult Suffrage (1916) 125
National Federation of Women Workers 42
National Food Fund 144
National Socialist Party 184
National Women's Council (BSP) 140–2, 144; cost of living 143–4; food question 145–6, 147
National Union of Women Workers 40, 118
National Union of Women's Suffrage Societies 109, 125, 106, 107, 175; Labour Party, alliance with 20, 33, 82, 107, 113, 116, 124, 132n121; socialist women members of 10, 176; socialist women organisers 39, 116
National Workers' War Emergency Committee 144
nationalism: tension with internationalism 166–9, 190
negotiated peace 184, 186
New Leader 86, 95, 96, 102n54, 127, 153, 156, 191; Living Wage 154

INDEX

National Union of Railwaymen: Stratford branch 126
new life socialism 4–5, 16, 18, 27n17, 65, 203
new woman 83–5, 101n29
Newcastle Women's Association 36
No More War demonstration 189
Norris, Jill 19, 21, 45, 106
North of England Society for Women's Suffrage 116
Northern Voice 82
Northern Democrat 82

Oldacre, Annie 102n66
Oldfield, Sybil 188
On the Threshold 83
The Origin of the Family, Private Property and the State 17, 58
Owenite socialism 18

pacifism 167, 180–1, 184, 186, 187–9, 192; *see also* anti-militarism
Pallister, Minnie 39, 47, 94, 155; internationalism 178, 190; recruitment of women to ILP 95, 103n83, 128; socialism and women 72, 74
Pankhurst, Adela 136
Pankhurst, Christabel 122
Pankhurst, Emmeline 10, 31, 37, 40, 42, 86, 100n10, 181, 199n69; adult suffrage 109; Boggart Hole Clough 83, 85; description of 85; women's suffrage 112, 121
Pankhurst, Richard 37, 85
Pankhurst, Sylvia 20, 42, 71, 194; consumption, politics of 152; journalism 75n21, 113; rent strikes, 152, 160; women's suffrage 113, 125
party loyalties 12, 17, 18–19, 23, 25, 36, 39, 41, 49, 105, 128, 171, 202–5
Paul, Cedar 198n59
peace 124, 167, 184, 183, 192; campaigns of WW1 42, 43–4, 124, 186, 190–1, 200n118, n124; socialist women and 180, 181–7; woman's issue 180, 181, 182, 185, 189
Peacemakers' Pilgrimage (1926) 121, 200n125
People's Suffrage Federation 107, 122–4, 132n114
Perriman, Mrs 155

personal as politics 47, 51, 60, 65–66, 68, 81, 84–5, 123
Pettigrew, Agnes 119
Phillips, Marion 124, 125, 131n82, 198n42, 199n78
Phillips, Mary 113
Pilchard, Gladys 127–8
political equality campaign (ILP) 113
Printers, Warehousemen and Cutters' Trade Union, women's branch 144
Poor Law Guardians *see* Boards of Guardians
Poor Law, minority report of 70
production 60, 134, 138, 139, 146, 203; consumption, relationship with 146, 147, 150, 154, 155–6, 157–60, 205
propaganda: socialist 2, 5, 24, 40, 41, 61, 88–9, 111, 127–8, 135, 153, 155; women's contribution to 8, 17, 41, 60, 67, 184–5
propagandists: socialist women as 2, 7, 22, 33–5, 36, 37, 60, 66, 68, 82–6, 88–9, 99
prostitution 63, 67
public and private 134, 140, 149; challenge to separation of 61, 66, 136–7

Quataert, Jean 17, 62
Quelch, Harry 21, 59, 110–11

race 17, 24, 68, 69, 70, 194–5
radical liberal 45, 59
radical suffragists 106, 107
Railway Women's Guild 144
Rathbone, Eleanor 154
Rathcreedan, Lord 147
Red Clydeside 147, 150, 151
religion 16, 45, 47
rent 140, 163n95; gendered issue 148, 149, 151; No Vote No Rent strike 152, 160; strikes 145, 147, 148, 149–53, 160 (Glasgow) 43, 147, 150, 151; women's issue 149, 150, 151
Representation of the People Act (1918) 126
rights: and duties 66, 76n55; language of 120–1
The Rise of Socialism in Britain 23
Robinson, Annot 10, 70, 95, 1032n34, 124, 190, 200n124; women's political autonomy 98, 132n105
Rowan, Caroline 70
Rowbotham, Sheila 4, 18, 65

228

INDEX

Royden, Maude 125
Rupp, Leila 168, 175, 183, 193
Ruskin, John 59, 68
Russian Revolution 147, 177, 181, 187, 188

'Sage of the Northern Heights' 138–9
Salter, Ada 183, 198n42
Savage, Michael 29–30
School Boards 5; London 37; Hackney 54n46; Limehouse 54n46
Scotland 7, 20, 38, 49, 82, 95, 191
Scott, Gill 137
Scott, Joan 24, 32
Second International 5, 23, 35, 39, 101n20, 166, 168, 169, 171, 176, 177, 190, 194, 197n29; Congresses (London) 40, 169 (Stuttgart) 111, 112, 171–2; suffrage 111, 112, 170; woman question 58, 63, 174; women organising separately 89
Selbourne, Countess of 147
separate spheres 37, 68
sex: autonomy 68, 74, 89, 97; consciousness 37; disabilities 9; division (labour) 58, 138, (politics) 150, 160, 180; equality 2, 21, 47, 64, 79–81, 90, 94, 95, 96, 119, 121, 123, 187; oppression 9, 57, 58–9, 62, 70, 79; sex/class analogy 58; versus class 17–18, 20, 21, 22, 24, 25, 33, 41, 49, 58, 63, 64, 74, 105, 109, 117–20, 128, 175, 205–6; sex war 18, 64, 87, 187
sexuality 21, 60
Sheehy-Skeffington, Hanna 187
shopping 135, 137, 141, 142, 146–7
Simm, Lisbeth 39, 82, 148–9
sisterhood 192
slave woman 86
Smart, Judith 136
Smith, Harold 19
Snowden, Ethel 34, 35, 47, 41, 85, 93, 101n20, 132n105, 200n114; anti-communism 178, 198n50; ILP, membership of 176, 194; internationalism 176, 177, 187,193–4; marriage and motherhood, views on 68–9; men's attitude to, 84; peace 183, 186, 190, 200n102; women's emancipation 65, 71
Snowden, Philip 35, 101n20, 125–6
Social Democracy 61, 64, 92, 146

Social Democratic Federation (SDF) 2, 48, 54n46, 61, 78n88, 148; adult suffrage 23, 106, 108, 110–11, 112, 123, 175; branches (Kensal Town) 35 (Salford) 85; feminism, attitude to 21–2; ILP, relationship to 170–1, 172–4; internationalism 168, 170; Lanchester case 62; limited suffrage 108, 112; married couples in 100–1n20; pacifism, 180; propaganda, 88; People's Suffrage Federation, attitude to 123; sex versus class 117–18; socialism of 3, 6, 39, 59; Socialist Trading Store 139; stereotype of 4, 5, 21–2, 23, 29n38, 33–4; woman question 59, 64, 65, 67, 71, 74; women as members of 1, 3, 7, 31, 34–7, 39–43, 45–6, 48, 52n12, 102n66, 109, 114, 118, 121; women delegates to annual conferences 23, 81, 100n13; women's attitude to 80; women's separate organisation 90, 91–2, 93, 97; women's suffrage 109, 126; Workmen's National Housing Council 148; *see also* Women's Socialist Circles; Women's Education Committee
Social Democratic Party (British) 2, 121, 182; ILP, relationship with 173–4; women's committee 148, 174
Social Democratic Party (German) 5, 17, 63, 89, 97, 104n109, 170
Social Democrats 45, 114, 119, 140, 146
Social Democrat 111
social welfare 19, 42, 72–3, 93, 95, 127, 135, 155, 160, 171
socialism, British: characteristics of 2–7, 8, 205, 141, 189; consumption, politics of 134–6, 137, 138–40, 147, 148, 155, 158–61; housing and rent 147–9, 151; impact of war on 177; internationalism, meaning of 166–8, 169; local activism 4, 53n23; masculinist 9, 11, 20, 40, 61, 97, 151, 160, 202; pacifism 180–1, 187; peace 185; public and private 134–5; rhetoric of equality 60, 202–3; shopping 135, 138–40; socialist unity 6, 173; woman question 57, 58–9, 202; *see also* feminism and socialism
Socialism and the Home 68
Socialism for Women 72
Socialism in Our Time (1926) 153–4

socialist feminism/feminist 10, 12, 14n33, 17
socialist internationals 166, 167, 193–4, 195, 199n69
Socialist Labour Party 4, 43, 184
Socialist Leader 84
Socialist League 4
socialist newspapers/press 144, 151, 154, 159; opposition to war 184; trading 139; women's international organisations 174–5; women's suffrage 111–13
Socialist Party of America 97, 138
Socialist Party of Great Britain 4
Socialist Sunday Schools 4, 47, 103n78
socialist trading 139–40
socialist women 5, 7, 12, 47, 171; activities of 34–6, 81–2; autobiography and representation 45, 48–9, 55n77; biographical approaches to 32–4; class background of 35–6; class, use of 64–5, 118–19; communism, attitude to 177–8, 203; debating sex versus class 63–5, 117–18, 205–6; debating socialism and suffrage 105, 114–15, 205; definition of 7–9, 10–11, 31, 41, 51; economic independence of 37–9; male attitudes to 84–5; pioneering generation 37–40, 41; political, defining the 134, 147, 155–6, 158–61; political identity 2, 24–5, 49, 79, 121–2, 202, 206; political journeys of 43–4, 49–51, 203; politicisation of 44–9, 55n90, 141, 179; representation of 86–8, 102n50; socialism, view of 46, 47, 51; socialism and feminism, integration of 17, 33, 657, 105, 121, 128, 195, 206; suffrage generation 36–7; trade unionism 40, 46; woman question, theorising the 57, 60–74, 201–2; women's potential as political activists, attitudes to 86, 87–8, 128
Socialist Women's Bureau 35, 173, 182
Socialist Women's Circles *see* Women's Socialist Circles
Socialist Women's International 170, 171–4, 176, 177, 178, 179; Congresses (Berne, 1915) 183–4 (Copenhagen, 1910) 173, 182, 195, 197n18; peace 182–3; suffrage debates 172, 173; *see also* International Congress of Socialist Women

Somerville, Mrs 85
Speakers' Conference (1916) 125, 126
Sproson, Emma 94, 96
Stacy, Enid 22, 33, 36, 38, 39, 45, 49; description of 83–4, 87; journalism of 61, 75n20; personal life of 67–8; political journey of 7; women as political activists 86, 91; women's movement 40, 66; women's suffrage 108–9; women's emancipation, ideas about 65, 66
Steedman, Carolyn 32, 49, 61
Stephen, Jessie 42, 44, 188
Stockman, Margaret 123
Stocks, Mary 73
strikes: conversion of women to socialism 45, 48; Leeds Tailoresses' Strike 66, 48; London Dock Strike 49; women's role in 83
suffrage militancy *see* militancy
The Suffragette Movement 152
Swanwick, Helena 116, 125, 154, 155–6, 183, 189; internationalism 178, 187

Taylor, Barbara 18
Taylor, Kate 83, 92, 101n31
Taylor, Mary Alice 91
Thane, Pat 19, 134–5
Third International 8, 44, 166, 177–9, 184, 194
Thompson, Annie 54n46
Trades Union Congress 110
transnational organisations 166, 168, 176
Tristan, Flora 32, 55n77
Turner, Ben 48, 102n52
Two and a Half International 166, 178

Ugolini, Laura 22
Union of Democratic Control 190
universal suffrage 47, 106, 108, 111, 125

Varley, Julia 46
Vernon, Betty 47

Walker, Linda 97
war and women's nature 69, 173
Ward M. (Maud) M.A. 120, 132n110
Waters, Chris 16, 60
Watson, Edith 152
Weeks, Jeffrey 4, 21
Westminster Review 63
Wilkie, Annot 36; *see* Robinson, Annot

INDEX

Wilkinson, Ellen 41, 44, 47, 56n97, 84–5, 102n54, 191, 206; CP 178; women's suffrage 126, 127
Wilson, Lena 34
Wiltsher, Anne 180
Wishart, W.S. 131n72
wives of socialist men: political potential of 139–40, 146, 149, 151–2; politicisation of 88–91, 63; votes 119
Wolstenholme-Elmy, Elizabeth 67
woman-centred politics, developing a 7, 8, 14n25, 25, 49, 167
woman-focused politics/socialism, developing a 9, 11, 12, 14n25, 40, 42, 48, 51, 57, 73, 99, 105, 128, 134, 147, 160, 186, 191, 193, 203–5
Woman Question 23, 38, 41, 46, 47, 65, 93, 99, 134; debating the 57–60, 72, 74; socialist attitudes to 5, 20, 22, 24, 57, 62–3, 105, 112, 170, 201
Woman Under Socialism 17, 58
Woman Worker 69
womanhood suffrage 115
Woman's National Committee (US) 97
women organising separately 41, 47; ILP 72, 90, 91–2, 93–9, 100n3, 104n101, 178–9; SDF 90–1; Social Democratic Party, Germany 89, 97, 104n109; socialist women 89–100, 203; Women's Council, British Socialist Party 140–2; women's groups, effectiveness of 97–9
Women's Advisory Committee (ILP) 95
Women's Adult Schools 143
women's columns 35, 50, 64, 82, 89, 90–1, 93, 96, 99, 102n54, 159; Matrons and Maidens 61, 100n7; Our Women's Circle 61, 191; Our Women's Letter 61, 112
Women's Committee *see* Women's Education Committee
Women's Co-operative Guild 8, 18, 106, 119, 139, 140, 191, 200n127; consumption, politics of 137, 141, 142, 143; food 144; minimum wage 140–1; suffrage 115, 118
Women's Council *see* National Women's Council
Women's Dreadnought 75n21, 150
Women's Education Committee (SDF) 34, 35, 42, 43, 82, 92
women's emancipation 71–2, 181; meaning for socialist women 1, 9, 57, 60, 62–3, 65–6, 74, 127–8, 202–3; socialists and 59–60, 62, 93, 115
Women's Enfranchisement Bill 109, 110, 112, 115, 116, 118, 119, 120, 126, 130n36
Women's Freedom League 37, 122, 116, 127, 128, 156, 184
Women's Humanity League, Bradford 126
Women's Industrial Council 7, 8, 40, 143, 144
Women's International Council of Socialist and Labour Organisations, British section 173–4
Women's International League 43, 186, 190
Women's International League for Peace and Freedom 167, 188, 190–1; congresses (Zurich) 187–8
Women's Labour League 1, 8, 18, 41, 71, 94, 97, 123, 124, 172; anti-militarism 183; consumption, politics of 142–3, 144–5, 162n28; housing and rent 150–1; internationalism 173–4, 192; socialist women as members of 7, 48, 51, 98, 116; socialist women as organisers 39, 82
Women's Liberal Federation 45, 46, 97, 100n7
women's movement 34, 40, 44, 45, 51, 60, 65, 66, 67, 69, 71; socialist women's attitude to 40, 44, 62, 128; *see also* bourgeois women's movement
women's nature 58, 60, 69–70
Women's Peace Crusade 43, 186–7, 200n102, 200n109; Glasgow 186
Women's Protective and Provident League 83, 103n78
Women's Social and Political Union 17, 41, 92, 110, 120, 175, 187; socialist and labour groups, relationship with 112, 115, 121, 122, 132n104; socialist women as members 1, 10, 33, 35, 42–3, 82, 98, 109, 113, 117, 136, 184; socialist women as organisers 39, 156
Women's Socialist Circles 35, 41, 43, 92–3, 103n78; Bow and Bromley 34; Battersea 75; Northampton 92–3, 103n84
women's suffrage 12, 36–7, 41–2, 47, 50, 71, 109–28, 159, 194, 204; class basis of suffrage 118–19; class versus sex 117–18; First World War 124–6;

international organisations 170, 172, 175–6; language of democracy and rights 120–2; language of property 119–20; re-interpreting suffrage history 19–20, 106–8; socialism 105, 179, 203; socialist groups and 22–3; socialist press 111–13; socialist women and 41–2, 47, 106–29, 159, 174, 202, 203, 205
women's/suffrage internationals 166, 167, 168, 172, 174–6, 195; socialist women and 168–9, 171, 174–6, 190–1, 197n32
Women's Suffrage National Aid Corps 184
Women's Trade Union League 116
Woodhouse, Tom 20
Workers' Birth Control Group 44
Workers' Dreadnought 75n21
Workers' Socialist Federation 42, 43; *see also* East London Federation of Suffragettes
Workers' Suffrage Federation 42–3, 125; *see also* East London Federation of Suffragettes
Workmen's National Housing Council 148, 163n84

Yeo, Stephen 4, 16
Yorkshire Factory Times 48

Zeitz, Louise 97
Zetkin, Clara 17, 63, 76n50, 89, 170, 172, 175, 179–80, 182, 198n61
Zinsser, Judith 17